Concepts of Computational Intelligence using Machine Learning

Dr.J. Gladson Maria Britto

Dr.MD. Ashfaqul Hasan

Dr. Diana Moses

Published by

BONFRING®
Intellectual Integrity

Concepts of Computational Intelligence using Machine Learning

9 789392 537288 >

ISBN 978-93-92537-28-8

Authors

Dr.J. Gladson Maria Britto

Dr.MD. Ashfaqul Hasan

Dr. Diana Moses

Bonfring

309, 5th Street Extension, Gandhipuram,

Coimbatore-641 012, Tamil Nadu, India.

E-mail: info@bonfring.org

Website: www.bonfring.org

Preface

Over the past two decades, the field of *Machine Learning* has become one of the mainstays of information technology. Many successful machine learning applications have been developed, such as: machine vision (image processing) in the manufacturing industry for automation in assembly line, biometric recognition, handwriting recognition, medical diagnosis, speech recognition, text retrieval, natural language processing, and so on. Machine learning is so pervasive today that you probably use it several times a day, without knowing it. Examples of such "ubiquitous" or "invisible" usage include search engines, customer-adaptive web services, email managers (spam filters), computer network security, and so on. We are rethinking on everything we have been doing, with the aim of doing it differently using tools of machine learning for better success.

This book is for current and aspiring machine learning practitioners looking to implement solutions to real-world machine learning problems. This is an introductory book requiring no previous knowledge of machine learning or artificial intelligence (AI). We made a conscious effort not to focus too much on the math, but rather on the practical aspects of using machine learning algorithms. As mathematics (probability theory, in particular) is the foundation upon which machine learning is built, we won't go into the analysis of the algorithms in great detail.

There are many books on machine learning and AI. However, all of them are meant for graduate students or PhD students in computer science, and they're full of advanced mathematics. This is in stark contrast with how machine learning is being used, as a commodity tool in research and commercial applications. However, there are few resources out there that fully cover all the important aspects of implementing machine learning algorithm in practice, without requiring you to take advanced math courses. We hope this book will help people who want to apply machine learning without reading up on years' worth of calculus, linear algebra, and probability theory.

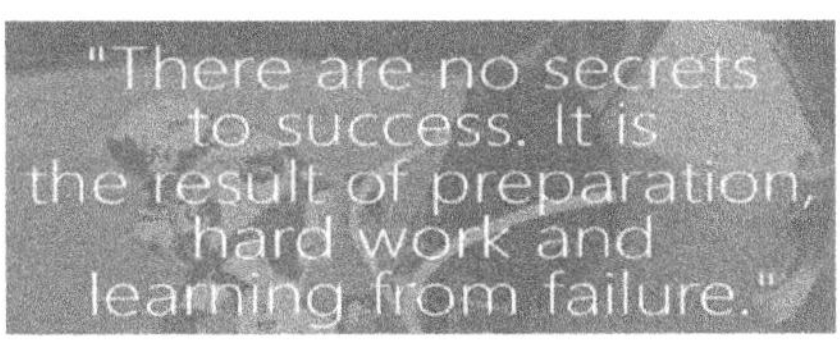

Acknowledgement

First and foremost, I thank, the Almighty God for endowing his immense blessing that helped me in each step of my progress towards the successful completion of this text book ***"Concepts of Computational Intelligence using Machine Learning"***.

I owe a warm debt of gratitude to my co-authors for their guidance, novel ideas, inspiration and brilliant discussions at every stage of this work. From my bottom of heart I thank him for made this as a good research work.

It is my privilege to thank the management and Dr.M. Sreedhar Reddy, Principal, MRCE and Dr.M. Ashok, Principal, MRIET for their constant support and cooperation to complete the text book.

I whole heartedly thank God almighty for giving me knowledge, wisdom and guidance in all aspects of my life. I express my profound thanks to the Management, The Director and The Principal of Methodist college of Engineering and Technology for their support in this initiative. Furthermore, I am grateful for the strength given by my family and friends always.

Most importantly, none of this would have been possible without the love and patience of our family. Words alone cannot describe the encouragement, affection and our parent, wife and children; I thank them for all the help, care and moral support provided throughout this work.

Dr.J. Gladson Maria Britto

Dr.MD. Ashfaqul Hasan

Dr. Diana Moses

Declaration

This text book is devoted to ***Almighty God*** for making it all possible, ***our family members** and* our ***Gurus*** for their loving, encouraging and everlasting support.

TABLE OF CONTENTS

CHAPTER 1

MACHINE LEARNING

1.1. Introduction

- A subset of artificial intelligence is machine learning, which refers to the concept that computer programs can automatically learn from and adapt to new data without being assisted by humans.
- Machine Learning, as the name says, is all about machines learning automatically without being explicitly programmed or learning without any direct human intervention. This machine learning process starts with feeding them good quality data and then training the machines by building various machine learning models using the data and different algorithms.
- The choice of algorithms depends on what type of data we have and what kind of task we are trying to automate.
- As for the formal definition of Machine Learning, we can say that a Machine Learning algorithm learns from experience E with respect to some type of task T and performance measure P, if its performance at tasks in T, as measured by P, improves with experience E.
- For example, If a Machine Learning algorithm is used to play chess. Then the experience E is playing many games of chess, the task T is playing chess with many players, and the performance measure P is the probability that the algorithm will win in the game of chess.

1.2. Artificial Intelligence

- **Intelligence:** The ability to learn and solve problems. To make computers intelligent so that they can act intelligently!
- Intelligence, as we know, is the ability to acquire and apply the **knowledge**. **Knowledge** is the information acquired through **experience**. Experience is the knowledge gained through **exposure (training)**. Summing the terms up, we get artificial intelligence as the "copy of something natural (i.e., human beings).

- **Intelligence** has been defined in many ways: the capacity for logic, understanding, self-awareness, learning, emotional knowledge, reasoning (the action of thinking about something in a logical, sensible way.), planning, creativity, critical thinking (the objective analysis and evaluation of an issue in order to form a judgment), and problem-solving.... Intelligence in computers or other machines is called artificial intelligence.

1.2.1. Why AI?

Today, the amount of data in the world is so humongous that humans fall short of **absorbing, interpreting, and making decisions of the entire data**, no, even part of the data. This complex decision-making requires beings that have higher cognitive skills (Cognitive skills are the core skills your brain uses to think, read, learn, remember, reason, and pay attention. Working together, they take incoming information and move it into the bank of knowledge you use every day at college, at work, and in life) than human beings. This is why we're trying to build machines better than us, in other words, AI. Another major characteristic that AI machines possess but we don't is **repetitive learning**. Humans are observed to find repetitive tasks highly boring. **Accuracy** is another factor in which we humans lack. Machines have extremely **high accuracy** in the tasks that they perform.

- **Artificial Intelligence (AI)** is wide-ranging branch of computer science concerned with building smart machines capable of performing tasks that typically require human intelligence. It is the endeavor to replicate or simulate human intelligence in machines.
- Artificial intelligence (AI) refers to the simulation of human intelligence in machines that are programmed to think like humans and mimic their actions. The term may also be applied to any machine that exhibits traits associated with a human mind such as learning and problem-solving.

The ideal characteristic of artificial intelligence is its ability to rationalize (justify) and take actions that have the best chance of achieving a specific goal.

1.2.2. Differences

- Artificial Intelligence and Machine Learning are correlated with each other, and yet they have some differences. Artificial Intelligence is an overarching concept that aims to create intelligence that mimics human-level intelligence.

- Artificial Intelligence is a general concept that deals with creating human-like critical thinking capability (the objective analysis and evaluation of an issue in order to form a judgment.) and reasoning skills for machines (is the ability to dynamically react to change and by doing this, reusing existing knowledge for new and unknown problems).
- On the other hand, Machine Learning is a subset or specific application of Artificial intelligence that aims to create machines that can learn autonomously from data.
- Machine Learning is specific, not general, which means it allows a machine to make predictions or take some decisions on a specific problem using data.

Deep learning is a branch of machine learning which is completely based on artificial neural networks, as neural network is going to mimic the human brain so deep learning is also a kind of mimic of human brain. In deep learning, we don't need to explicitly program everything.

Deep learning is a subset of machine learning in artificial intelligence that has networks capable of learning unsupervised from data that is unstructured or unlabeled. Also known as deep neural learning or deep neural network.

1.2.3. Uses

For example, when you are using a smart assistant, whether it's Google Assistant, Alexa, Siri, or Bixby, you more or less know that these assistants are based on AI. However, when we are using a feature such as the portrait mode effect while shooting a picture, we never consider that AI might be behind that too.

The YouTube rabbit hole wasting countless hours just watching the recommended videos. That recommended videos section has become so good at knowing my taste that it's scary. So, next time you are hitting play on a recommended video on YouTube or watching a recommended show on Netflix, or listening to a pre-created playlist on Spotify, or any other media and music streaming service for that matter, remember that AI is playing a big role in that.

The video game industry is probably one of the earliest adopters of AI. The integration started very small with the use of AI to generate random levels that people can play. However, that has increased to a level which goes far beyond what one can even imagine.

Do you know that whether you are using Google or Apple Maps for navigating, or calling an Uber, or booking a flight ticket, you are using AI? Both Google and Apple along with other navigation services use artificial intelligence to interpret hundreds of thousands of data point that they receive to give you real-time traffic data. When you are calling an Uber, both the pricing and the car that matches your ride request is decided by AI.

Did you know that the banking and finance industry heavily relies on artificial intelligence for things like customer service, fraud protection, investment, and more? A simple example is the automated emails that you receive from banks whenever you do an out of the ordinary transaction. Well, that's AI watching over your account and trying to warn you of any fraud.

AI is also being trained to look at large samples of fraud data and find a pattern so that you can be warned before it happens to you.

Smart Home Devices

- Many of the smart home devices that we buy use artificial intelligence to learn our behavior so that they can adjust the settings themselves to make the experience as frictionless as possible for us. Security and Surveillance.
- It is not possible for humans to keep monitoring multiple monitors with feeds from hundreds if not thousands of cameras at the same time, and hence, using AI makes perfect sense. With technologies like object recognition and facial recognition getting better and better every day, it won't be long when all the security camera feeds are being monitored by an AI and not a human.

Smart Speakers

- Not for nothing, many believe that smart speakers are all set for a big boom in technology. Aside from controlling smart home devices, they are also up to the task for several things like sending quick messages, setting reminders, checking the weather and getting the latest news.

Healthcare

- The use of artificial intelligence has given a new dimension to healthcare. With the introduction of AI-powered machines, it's become a bit easier to detect disease and diagnosis. Moreover, it's also playing a significant role in making the treatment and management processes more simplified.
- As a result, hospitals and healthcare centers are fast embracing AI-enabled technologies to facilitate everything from research to the detection of diseases.

Smart Email Apps

- If you still find your inbox cluttered (Jumped) with too many unwanted messages, chances are pretty high that you are still stuck with an old email app. Modern email apps like Spark make the most of AI to get rid of spam messages and also categorize emails so that you can quickly access the important ones.

- Smart phones use personal voice assistants like Siri, Alexa, Cortana, etc. These personal assistants are an example of ML-based speech recognition that uses Natural Language Processing to interact with the users and formulate a response accordingly.
- Machine Learning is also very important in healthcare diagnosis as it can be used to diagnose a variety of problems in the medical field. For example, Machine Learning is used in oncology to train algorithms that can identify cancerous tissue at the microscopic level at the same accuracy as trained physicians.
- Another famous application of Machine Learning is Google Maps. The Google Maps algorithm automatically picks the best route from one point to another by relying on the projections of different timeframes and keeping in mind various factors like traffic jams, roadblocks, etc.

1.2.4. Definition

Machine learning (ML) is the study of computer algorithms that improve automatically through experience and by the use of data. It is seen as a part of artificial intelligence.

Machine learning algorithms build a model based on sample data, known as "**training data**", in order **to make predictions or decisions** without being explicitly programmed to do so.

Machine learning algorithms are used in a wide variety of applications, such as email filtering and computer vision, where it is difficult or unfeasible to develop conventional algorithms to perform the needed tasks.

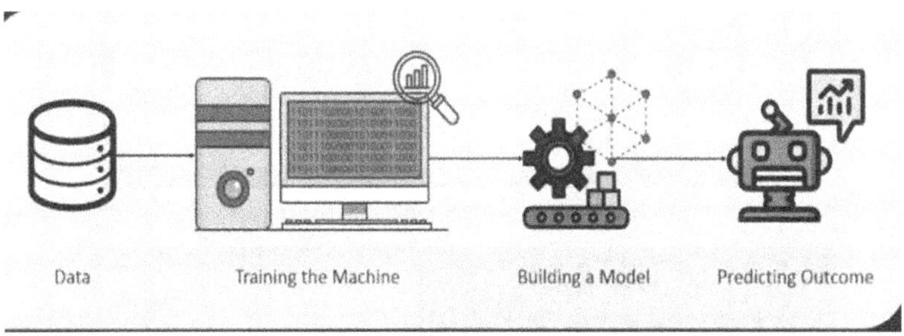

Fig. 1.1: ML Steps

A subset of machine learning is closely related to **computational statistics**, which focuses on making predictions using computers; but not all machine learning is statistical learning.

The study of mathematical optimization delivers methods, theory and application domains to the field of machine learning. **Data mining** is a related field of study, focusing on exploratory data analysis through unsupervised learning. In its application across business problems, machine learning is also referred to as **predictive analytics.**

1.2.5. Let's Understand what is ML Process

ML process involves building a predictive model that can be used to find a solution for a problem statement.

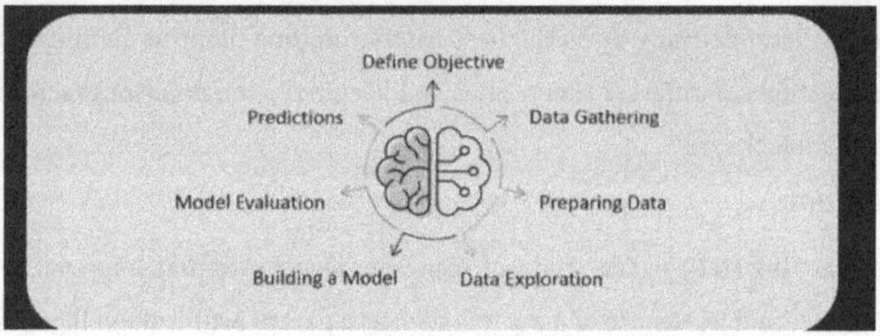

Fig. 1.2: ML Process

Suppose say we want to predict the possibility of rain by studying weather condition.

Second step is to gather data by collecting details about weather conditions, humidity level, temperature, pressure etc. from the web or manually.

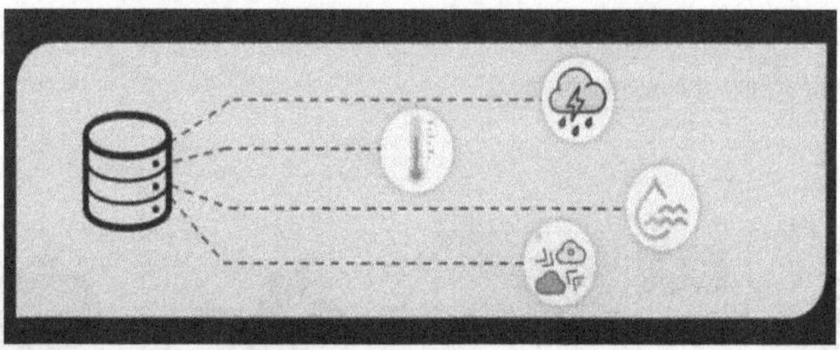

Fig. 1.3: Data Collection

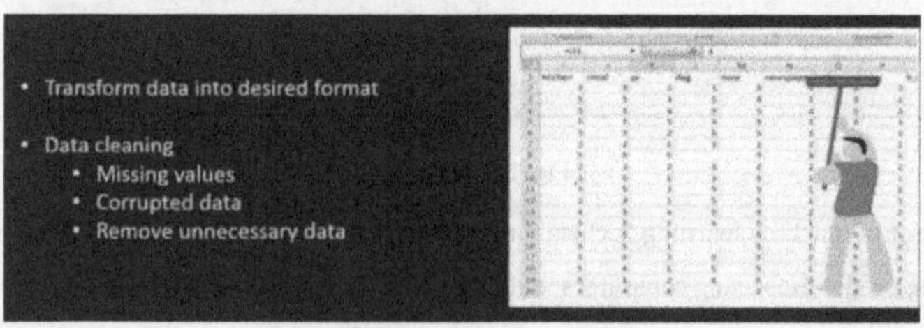

Fig. 1.4: Shows Data Cleaning

Third step is to Prepare Data by cleaning up the data.

Which involves getting rid of inconsistency in data and missing values or redundant variable.

Data Exploration (It is an approach similar to initial data analysis, whereby a data analyst uses **visual exploration** to understand **what is in a dataset and the characteristics of the data,** rather than through traditional data management systems.

- These characteristics can include size or amount of data, completeness of the data, correctness of the data, possible relationships amongst data elements or files/tables in the data.) also requires understanding the patterns (Pattern recognition is the process of recognizing regularities in data by a machine that uses machine learning algorithms. pattern recognition is the assignment of a label to a given input value) and trends in data. In this stage all the required insights are drawn and correlations between different variables is understood.

Correlation can understood as,

In predicting rainfall then we know that the possibilities will be higher if the temperature has fallen low. So it has to mapped.

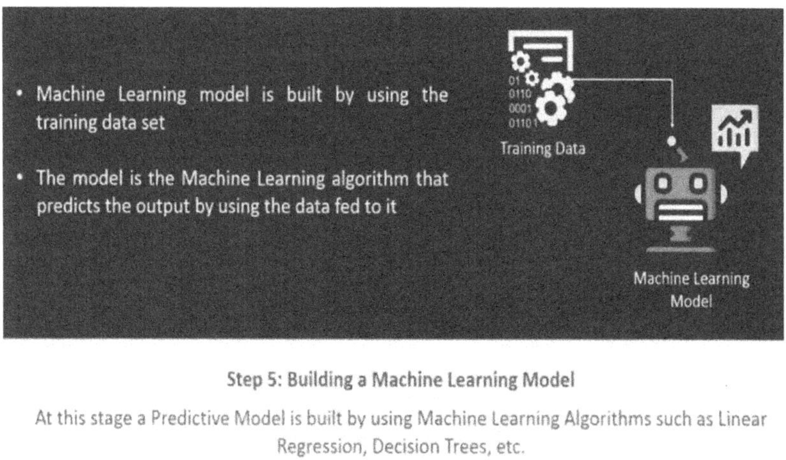

Fig. 1.5: Building a ML Model

Building a Machine Learning Model: A predictive model is built by using ML algorithms such as Linear Regression, Decision Trees etc.

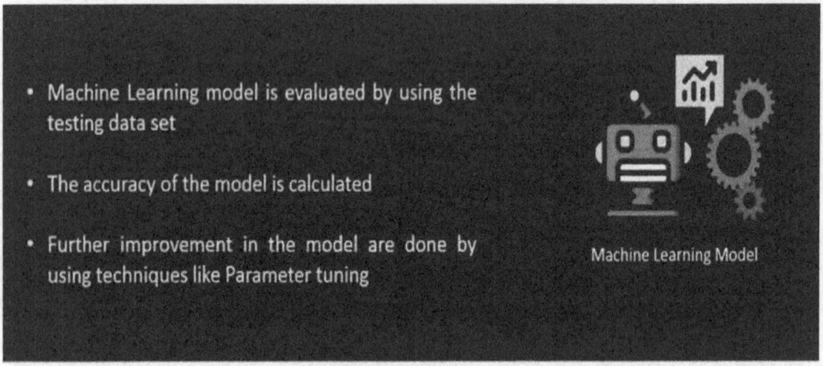

Step 6: Model Evaluation & Optimization

The efficiency of the model is evaluated and any further improvement in the model are implemented.

Fig. 1.6: Model Evaluation and Optimization

Model Evaluation and Optimization: The efficiency of the model is evaluated and any further improvement in the model are implemented.

Final is Predictions: The final outcome is predicted after performing parameter tuning and improving the accuracy of the model. In our case predicting the occurrence of rainfall in terms of **yes or no**. yes meaning it rains.

No meaning it will not.

1.2.6. Machine Learning Approaches/Types

Machine learning approaches are traditionally divided into three broad categories, depending on the nature of the "signal" or "feedback" available to the learning system:

Based on the methods and way of learning, machine learning is divided into mainly four types, which are:

- Supervised Machine Learning
- Unsupervised Machine Learning
- Semi-Supervised Machine Learning
- Reinforcement Learning

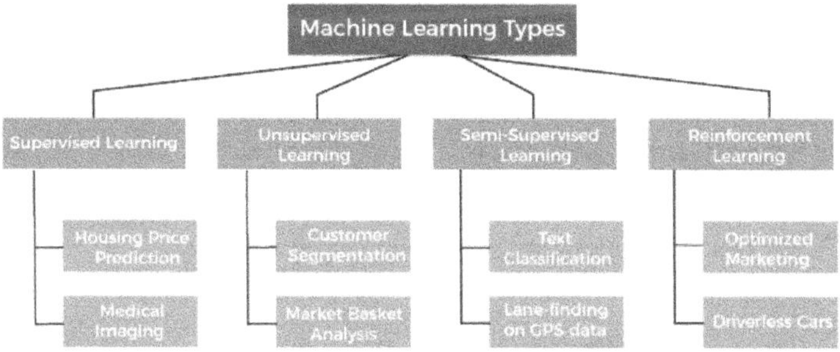

Fig. 1.7: ML Types

Supervised Learning

- As its name suggests, Supervised machine learning is based on supervision. It means in the supervised learning technique, we train the machines using the "labeled" dataset, and based on the training, the machine predicts the output. Here, the labeled data specifies that some of the inputs are already mapped to the output. More preciously, we can say; first, we train the machine with the input and corresponding output, and then we ask the machine to predict the output using the test dataset.
- Let's understand supervised learning with an example. Suppose we have an input dataset of cats and dog images. So, first, we will provide the training to the machine to understand the images, such as the **shape & size of the tail of cat and dog, Shape of eyes, colour, height (dogs are taller, cats are smaller), etc.** After completion of training, we input the picture of a cat and ask the machine to identify the object and predict the output. Now, the machine is well trained, so it will check all the features of the object, such as height, shape, color, eyes, ears, tail, etc., and find that it's a cat. So, it will put it in the Cat category. This is the process of how the machine identifies the objects in Supervised Learning.
- The computer is presented with example inputs and their desired outputs, given by a "teacher", and the goal is to learn a general rule that maps inputs to outputs.
  - Supervised Learning is the process of making an algorithm to learn to map an input to a particular output. This is achieved using the labelled datasets that you have collected. If the mapping is correct, the algorithm has successfully learned. Else, you make the necessary changes to the algorithm so that it can learn correctly. Supervised Learning algorithms can help make predictions for new unseen data that we obtain later in the future.

- This is similar to a teacher-student scenario. There is a teacher who guides the student to learn from books and other materials. The student is then tested and if correct, the student passes. Else, the teacher tunes the student and makes the student learn from the mistakes that he or she had made in the past. That is the basic principle of Supervised Learning.

Fig. 1.8: Supervised Learning

Ex: Suppose you have a niece who has just turned 2 years old and is learning to speak. She knows the words, Papa and Mumma, as her parents have taught her how she needs to call them. You want to teach her what a dog and a cat is. So what do you do? You either show her videos of dogs and cats or you bring a dog and a cat and show them to her in real-life so that she can understand how they are different.

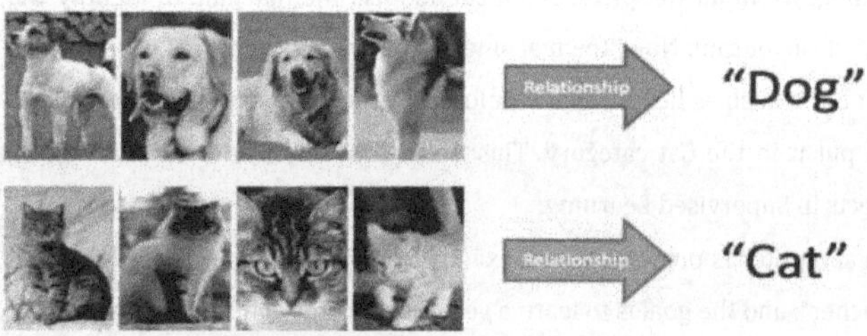

Fig. 1.9: Classification

- Now there are certain things you tell her so that she understands the differences between the 2 animals.
- Dogs and cats both have 4 legs and a tail.
- Dogs come in small to large sizes. Cats, on the other hand, are always small.

- Dogs have a long mouth while cats have smaller mouths.
- Dogs bark while cats meow.
- Different dogs have different ears while cats have almost the same kind of ears.
- Now you take your niece back home and show her pictures of different dogs and cats. If she is able to differentiate between the dog and cat, you have successfully taught her.

So what happened here? You were there to guide her to the goal of differentiating between a dog and a cat. You taught her every difference there is between a dog and a cat. You then tested her if she was able to learn. If she was able to learn, she called the dog as a dog and a cat as a cat. If not, you taught her more and were able to teach her.

- **You** acted as the **supervisor** and your niece acted as the **algorithm** that had to learn. You even knew what was a dog and what was a cat. Making sure that she was learning the correct thing. That is the principle that Supervised Learning follows.

Applications: Bioinformatics, Speech Recognition.

The main goal of the supervised learning technique is to map the input variable(x) with the output variable(y). Some real-world applications of supervised learning are **Risk Assessment, Fraud Detection, Spam filtering,** etc.

Categories of Supervised Machine Learning

Supervised machine learning can be classified into two types of problems, which are given below:

- Classification
- Regression

a) Classification

Classification algorithms are used to solve the classification problems in which the output variable is categorical, such as **"Yes" or No, Male or Female, Red or Blue, etc**. The classification algorithms predict the categories present in the dataset. Some real-world examples of classification algorithms are **Spam Detection, Email filtering, etc.**

Some popular classification algorithms are given below:

- Random Forest Algorithm
- Decision Tree Algorithm
- Logistic Regression Algorithm
- Support Vector Machine Algorithm

b) Regression

Regression algorithms are used to solve regression problems in which there is a linear relationship between input and output variables. These are used to predict continuous output variables, such as market trends, weather prediction, etc.

Some popular Regression algorithms are given below:

- Simple Linear Regression Algorithm
- Multivariate Regression Algorithm
- Decision Tree Algorithm
- Lasso Regression

Advantages

- Since supervised learning work with the labeled dataset so we can have an exact idea about the classes of objects.
- These algorithms are helpful in predicting the output on the basis of prior experience.

Disadvantages of Supervised Learning

Supervised Learning has a lot of challenges and disadvantages that you could face while working with these algorithms. Let's take a look at these.

- You could overfit your algorithm easily.
- Good examples need to be used to train the data.
- Computation time is very large for Supervised Learning.
- Unwanted data could reduce the accuracy.
- Pre-Processing of data is always a challenge.
- If the dataset is incorrect, you make your algorithm learn incorrectly which can bring losses.

Applications of Supervised Learning

Some common applications of Supervised Learning are given below:

- **Image Segmentation:** Supervised Learning algorithms are used in image segmentation. In this process, image classification is performed on different image data with pre-defined labels.
- **Medical Diagnosis:** Supervised algorithms are also used in the medical field for diagnosis purposes. It is done by using medical images and past labelled data with labels for disease conditions. With such a process, the machine can identify a disease for the new patients.

- **Fraud Detection** - Supervised Learning classification algorithms are used for identifying fraud transactions, fraud customers, etc. It is done by using historic data to identify the patterns that can lead to possible fraud.
- **Spam detection** - In spam detection & filtering, classification algorithms are used. These algorithms classify an email as spam or not spam. The spam emails are sent to the spam folder.
- **Speech Recognition** - Supervised learning algorithms are also used in speech recognition. The algorithm is trained with voice data, and various identifications can be done using the same, such as voice-activated passwords, voice commands, etc.

- ***Unsupervised Learning***
  - Unsupervised learning is different from the Supervised learning technique; as its name suggests, there is no need for supervision. It means, in unsupervised machine learning, the machine is trained using the unlabeled dataset, and the machine predicts the output without any supervision.
  - In unsupervised learning, the models are trained with the data that is neither classified nor labeled, and the model acts on that data without any supervision.
  - **The main aim of the unsupervised learning algorithm is to group or categories the unsorted dataset according to the similarities, patterns, and differences.** Machines are instructed to find the hidden patterns from the input dataset.
  - Let's take an example to understand it more preciously; suppose there is a basket of fruit images, and we input it into the machine learning model. The images are totally unknown to the model, and the task of the machine is to find the patterns and categories of the objects.
  - So, now the machine will discover its patterns and differences, such as colour difference, shape difference, and predict the output when it is tested with the test dataset.
  - No labels are given to the learning algorithm, leaving it on its own to find structure in its input.
  - Unsupervised learning can be a goal in itself (discovering hidden patterns in data) or a means towards an end (feature learning).
  - Unsupervised learning is the training of machine using information that is neither classified nor labeled and allowing the algorithm to act on that information without guidance.

- Here the task of machine is to group unsorted information according to similarities, patterns and differences without any prior training of data.
- Unlike supervised learning, no teacher is provided that means no training will be given to the machine. Therefore machine is restricted to find the hidden structure in unlabeled data by our-self.

For instance, suppose it is given an image having both dogs and cats which have not seen ever.

Fig. 1.10: Features of Dogs

- Thus the machine has no idea about the **features of dogs and cat** so we can't categorize it in dogs and cats. But it can categorize them according to their **similarities, patterns, and differences** i.e., we can easily categorize the above picture into two parts. **First** it first may contain all pics having dogs in it and **second part** may contain all pics having cats in it. Here you didn't learn anything before, means no training data or examples.
- It allows the model to work on its own to discover patterns and information that was previously undetected. It mainly deals with unlabelled (**Labeled** data is a group of samples that have been tagged with one or more labels e.g. like a name, a type, or a number) data.

Categories of Unsupervised Machine Learning

- Unsupervised Learning can be further classified into two types, which are given below:

1. Clustering
2. Association

1) Clustering

- The clustering technique is used when we want to find the inherent groups from the data. It is a way to group the objects into a cluster such that the objects with the most similarities remain in one group and have fewer or no similarities with the objects of other groups. An example of the clustering algorithm is grouping the customers by their purchasing behavior.
- Some of the popular clustering algorithms are given below:
    - **K-Means Clustering algorithm**
    - **Mean-shift algorithm**
    - **DBSCAN Algorithm**
    - **Principal Component Analysis**
    - **Independent Component Analysis**

2) Association

- Association rule learning is an unsupervised learning technique, which finds interesting relations among variables within a large dataset. The main aim of this learning algorithm is to find the dependency of one data item on another data item and map those variables accordingly so that it can generate maximum profit. This algorithm is mainly applied in **Market Basket analysis, Web usage mining, continuous production**, etc.
- Some popular algorithms of Association rule learning are **Apriori Algorithm, Eclat, FP-growth algorithm.**

Advantages

- These algorithms can be used for complicated tasks compared to the supervised ones because these algorithms work on the unlabeled dataset.
- Unsupervised algorithms are preferable for various tasks as getting the unlabeled dataset is easier as compared to the labelled dataset.

Disadvantages

- The output of an unsupervised algorithm can be less accurate as the dataset is not labelled, and algorithms are not trained with the exact output in prior.
- Working with Unsupervised learning is more difficult as it works with the unlabelled dataset that does not map with the output.

Applications of Unsupervised Learning

- **Network Analysis:** Unsupervised learning is used for identifying plagiarism and copyright in document network analysis of text data for scholarly articles.
- **Recommendation Systems:** Recommendation systems widely use unsupervised learning techniques for building recommendation applications for different web applications and e-commerce websites.
- **Anomaly Detection:** Anomaly detection is a popular application of unsupervised learning, which can identify unusual data points within the dataset. It is used to discover fraudulent transactions.
- **Singular Value Decomposition:** Singular Value Decomposition or SVD is used to extract particular information from the database. For example, extracting information of each user located at a particular location.

Supervised vs. Unsupervised Machine Learning

Parameters	**Supervised machine learning**	**Unsupervised machine learning**
Input Data	Algorithms are trained using labeled data.	Algorithms are used against data which is not labelled
Computational Complexity	Simpler method	Computationally complex
Accuracy	Highly accurate	Less accurate

Semi-Supervised Learning

Semi-Supervised learning is a type of Machine Learning algorithm that lies between Supervised and Unsupervised machine learning. It represents the intermediate ground between Supervised (With Labeled training data) and Unsupervised learning (with no labeled training data) algorithms and uses the combination of labeled and unlabeled datasets during the training period.

Although Semi-supervised learning is the middle ground between supervised and unsupervised learning and operates on the data that consists of a few labels, it mostly consists of unlabeled data. As labels are costly, but for corporate purposes, they may have few labels. It is completely different from supervised and unsupervised learning as they are based on the presence & absence of labels.

To overcome the drawbacks of supervised learning and unsupervised learning algorithms, the concept of Semi-supervised learning is introduced. The main aim of semi-supervised learning is to effectively use all the available data, rather than only labelled data like in supervised learning. Initially, similar data is clustered along with an unsupervised learning algorithm, and further, it helps to label the unlabeled data into labelled data. It is because labeled data is a comparatively more expensive acquisition than unlabeled data.

We can imagine these algorithms with an example. Supervised learning is where a student is under the supervision of an instructor at home and college. Further, if that student is self-analyzing the same concept without any help from the instructor, it comes under unsupervised learning. Under semi-supervised learning, the student has to revise himself after analyzing the same concept under the guidance of an instructor at college.

Advantages and Disadvantages of Semi-supervised Learning

Advantages

- It is simple and easy to understand the algorithm.
- It is highly efficient.
- It is used to solve drawbacks of Supervised and Unsupervised Learning algorithms.

Disadvantages

- Iterations results may not be stable.
- We cannot apply these algorithms to network-level data.
- Accuracy is low.
- **Reinforcement learning:** A computer program interacts with a dynamic environment in which it must perform a certain goal (such as driving a vehicle or playing a game against an opponent). As it navigates its problem space, the program is provided feedback that's analogous to rewards, which it tries to maximize.
    - Reinforcement learning is an area of Machine Learning. It is about taking suitable action to maximize reward in a particular situation. It is employed by various software and machines to find the best possible behavior or path it should take in a specific situation.
    - Reinforcement learning differs from the supervised learning in a way that in supervised learning the training data has the answer key with it so the model is trained with the correct answer itself whereas in reinforcement learning, there is no answer but the reinforcement agent decides what to do to perform the given task.

- In the absence of a training dataset, it is bound to learn from its experience.
- Example: The problem is as follows: We have an **agent and a reward,** with many hurdles in between. The agent is supposed to find the best possible path to reach the reward. The following problem explains the problem more easily.

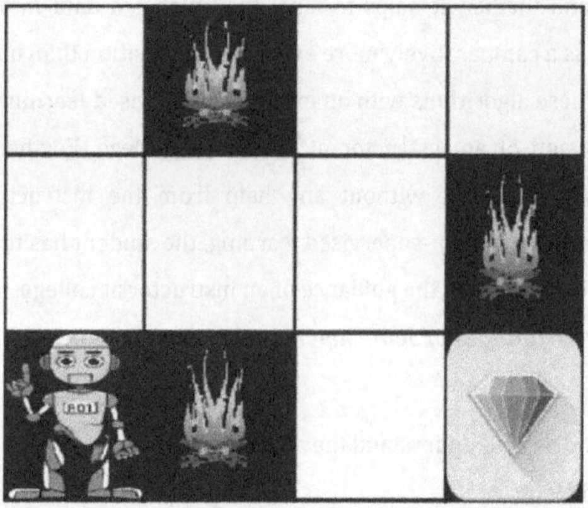

Fig. 1.11: Reinforcement Learning

The above image shows the **robot, diamond, and fire**. The goal of the robot is to get the reward that is the diamond and avoid the hurdles that are fire.

- The robot learns by trying all the possible paths and then choosing the path which gives him the reward with the least hurdles. Each right step will give the robot a reward and each wrong step will subtract the reward of the robot.
- The total reward will be calculated when it reaches the final reward that is the diamond.

Main points in Reinforcement learning:

- Input: The input should be an initial state from which the model will start.
- Output: There are many possible output as there are variety of solution to a particular problem.
- Training: The training is based upon the input, the model will return a state and the user will decide to reward or punish the model based on its output.
- The model keeps continues to learn.
- The best solution is decided based on the maximum reward.

Reinforcement Learning

- **Reinforcement learning works on a feedback-based process, in which an AI agent (A software component) automatically explore its surrounding by hitting & trail, taking action, learning from experiences, and improving its performance.** Agent gets rewarded for each good action and get punished for each bad action; hence the goal of reinforcement learning agent is to maximize the rewards.
- In reinforcement learning, there is no labeled data like supervised learning, and agents learn from their experiences only.
- The reinforcement learning process is similar to a human being; for example, a child learns various things by experiences in his day-to-day life. An example of reinforcement learning is to play a game, where the Game is the environment, moves of an agent at each step define states, and the goal of the agent is to get a high score. Agent receives feedback in terms of punishment and rewards.
- Due to its way of working, reinforcement learning is employed in different fields such as **Game theory, Operation Research, Information theory, multi-agent systems.**

A reinforcement learning problem can be formalized using **Markov Decision Process (MDP).** In MDP, the agent constantly interacts with the environment and performs actions; at each action, the environment responds and generates a new state.

Categories of Reinforcement Learning

Reinforcement learning is categorized mainly into two types of methods/algorithms:

- **Positive Reinforcement Learning:** Positive reinforcement learning specifies increasing the tendency that the required behaviour would occur again by adding something. It enhances the strength of the behaviour of the agent and positively impacts it.
- **Negative Reinforcement Learning:** Negative reinforcement learning works exactly opposite to the positive RL. It increases the tendency that the specific behaviour would occur again by avoiding the negative condition.

Real-world Use cases of Reinforcement Learning

- **Video Games:**

  RL algorithms are much popular in gaming applications. It is used to gain super-human performance. Some popular games that use RL algorithms are **AlphaGO** and **AlphaGO Zero**.

- **Resource Management:**

  The "Resource Management with Deep Reinforcement Learning" paper showed that how to use RL in computer to automatically learn and schedule resources to wait for different jobs in order to minimize average job slowdown.

- **Robotics:**

  RL is widely being used in Robotics applications. Robots are used in the industrial and manufacturing area, and these robots are made more powerful with reinforcement learning. There are different industries that have their vision of building intelligent robots using AI and Machine learning technology.

- **Text Mining**

  Text-mining, one of the great applications of NLP, is now being implemented with the help of Reinforcement Learning by Sales force company.

Advantages and Disadvantages of Reinforcement Learning

Advantages

- It helps in solving complex real-world problems which are difficult to be solved by general techniques.
- The learning model of RL is similar to the learning of human beings; hence most accurate results can be found.
- Helps in achieving long term results.

Disadvantage

- RL algorithms are not preferred for simple problems.
- RL algorithms require huge data and computations.
- Too much reinforcement learning can lead to an overload of states which can weaken the results.

Difference between Reinforcement learning and Supervised Learning

• Reinforcement learning	• Supervised learning
• Reinforcement learning is all about making decisions sequentially. In simple words we can say that the output depends on the **state of the current input and the next input depends on the output of the previous input**	• In Supervised learning the decision is made on **the initial input or the input given at the start**
• In Reinforcement learning **decision is dependent**, So we give labels to sequences of dependent decisions	• Supervised learning the **decisions are independent** of each other so labels are given to each decision.
• Example: Chess game	• Example: Object recognition

Important Terms

DATA: It can be any unprocessed fact, value, text, sound or picture that is not being interpreted and analyzed. Data is the most important part of all Data Analytics, Machine Learning, Artificial Intelligence. Without data, we can't train any model and all modern research and automation will go vain. Big Enterprises are spending lots of money just to gather as much certain data as possible.

Example: Why did Facebook acquire WhatsApp by paying a huge price of $19 billion?

The answer is very simple and logical – it is to have access to the users' information that Facebook may not have but WhatsApp will have. This information of their users is of paramount importance to Facebook as it will facilitate the task of improvement in their services.

INFORMATION: Data that has been interpreted and manipulated and has now some meaningful inference for the users.

KNOWLEDGE: Combination of inferred information, experiences, learning and insights. Results in awareness or concept building for an individual or organization.

How we split data in Machine Learning?

- Training Data: The part of data we use to train our model. This is the data which your model actually sees (both input and output) and learn from.
- Validation Data: The part of data which is used to do a frequent evaluation of model, fit on training dataset along with improving involved hyper parameters (initially set parameters before the model begins learning). This data plays it's part when the model is actually training.
- Testing Data: Once our model is completely trained, testing data provides the unbiased (Balanced) evaluation. When we feed in the inputs of Testing data, our model will predict some values (without seeing actual output). After prediction, we evaluate our model by comparing it with actual output present in the testing data. This is how we evaluate and see how much our model has learned from the experiences feed in as training data, set at the time of training.

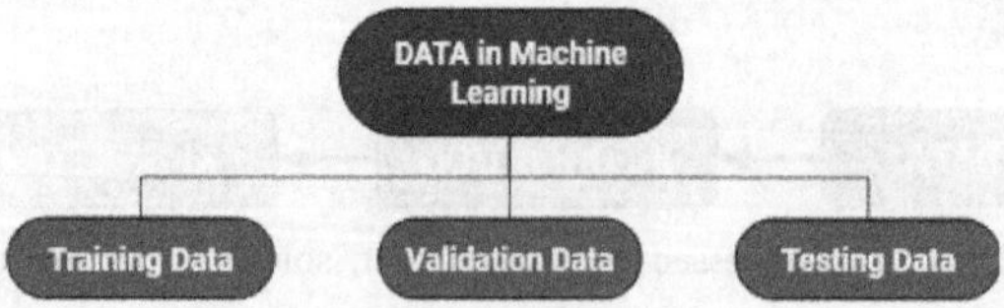

Fig. 1. 12: Shows Data in ML

Consider an example: There's a Shopping Mart Owner who conducted a survey for which he has a long list of questions and answers that he had asked from the customers, this list of questions and answers is **DATA**. Now every time when he want to infer anything and can't just go through each and every question of thousands of customers to find something relevant as it would be time-consuming and not helpful. In order to reduce this overhead and time wastage and to make work easier, data is manipulated through software, calculations, graphs etc. As per own convenience, this inference from manipulated data is **Information**. So, Data is must for Information. Now **Knowledge** has its role in differentiating between two individuals having same information. Knowledge is actually not a technical content but is linked to human thought process.

Properties of Data

1. Volume: Scale of Data. With growing world population and technology at exposure, huge data is being generated each and every millisecond.
2. Variety: Different forms of data – healthcare, images, videos, audio clippings.
3. Velocity: Rate of data streaming and generation.
4. Value: Meaningfulness of data in terms of information which researchers can infer from it.
5. Veracity: Certainty and correctness in data we are working on.

Some Facts about Data

- As compared to 2005, 300 times i.e. 40 Zettabytes of data will be generated by 2020.
- By 2011, healthcare sector has a data of 161 Billion Gigabytes.
- 400 Million tweets are sent by about 200 million active users per day.
- Each month, more than 4 Billion hours of video streaming is done by the users.
- 30 Billion different types of contents are shared every month by the user.
- It is reported that about 27% of data is inaccurate and so 1 in 3 business idealists or leaders don't trust the information on which they are making decisions.

The above-mentioned facts are just a glimpse of the actually existing huge data statistics. When we talk in terms of real world scenario, the size of data currently present and is getting generated each and every moment is beyond our mental horizons to imagine.

1.2.7. What is the difference between Artificial Intelligence and Machine Learning?

Artificial Intelligence and Machine Learning are correlated with each other, and yet they have some differences. Artificial Intelligence is an overarching concept that aims to create intelligence that mimics human-level intelligence. Artificial Intelligence is a general concept that deals with creating human-like critical thinking capability and reasoning skills for machines. On the other hand, Machine Learning is a subset or specific application of Artificial intelligence that aims to create machines that can learn autonomously from data. Machine Learning is specific, not general, which means it allows a machine to make predictions or take some decisions on a specific problem using data.

1.2.8. Well Posed Learning Problems

Well Posed Learning Problem – A computer program is said to learn from Experience E in context to some task T and some performance measure P, if its performance on T, as was measured by P, upgrades with experience E.

Any **problem can be segregated as well-posed learning problem if it has three traits:**

- **Task**
- **Performance Measure**
- **Experience**

Certain **examples** that efficiently defines the well-posed learning problem are:

1. **To better filter emails as spam or not**
    - Task – Classifying emails as spam or not.
    - Performance Measure – The fraction of emails accurately classified as spam or not spam.
    - Experience – Observing you label emails as spam or not spam.
2. **A Checkers Learning Problem**
    - Task – Playing checkers game.
    - Performance Measure – Percent of games won against opposer.
    - Experience – Playing implementation games against itself.

3. **Handwriting Recognition Problem**
   - Task – Acknowledging handwritten words within portrayal (a representation of someone).
   - Performance Measure – percent of words accurately classified.
   - Experience – a directory of handwritten words with given classifications.
4. **Fruit Prediction Problem**
   - Task – Forecasting different fruits for recognition.
   - Performance Measure – Able to predict maximum variety of fruits.
   - Experience – Training machine with the largest datasets of fruits images.
5. **Face Recognition Problem**
   - Task – Predicting different types of faces.
   - Performance Measure – Able to predict maximum types of faces.
   - Experience – Training machine with maximum amount of datasets of different face images.
6. **Automatic Translation of Documents**
   - Task – Translating one type of language used in a document to other language.
   - Performance Measure – Able to convert one language to other efficiently.
   - Experience – Training machine with a large dataset of different types of languages.

1.2.9. Design a Learning System in Machine Learning

- "Machine Learning enables a Machine to Automatically learn from Data, Improve performance from an Experience and predict things without explicitly programmed."
- In Simple Words, When we fed the Training Data to Machine Learning Algorithm, this **algorithm will produce a mathematical model** and with the help of the mathematical model, the machine will make a prediction and take a decision without being explicitly programmed. Also, during training data, the more machine will work with it the more it will get experience and the more it will get experience the more efficient result is produced.
- According to Arthur Samuel **"Machine Learning enables a Machine to Automatically learn from Data, Improve performance from an Experience and predict things without explicitly programmed."**

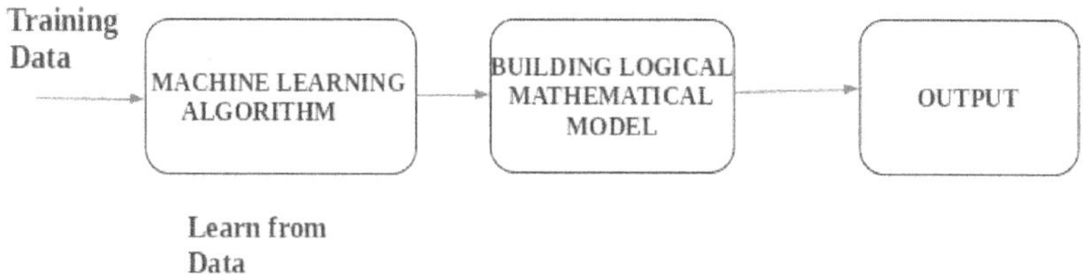

Fig. 1.13: Shows Process of ML

Example: In Driverless Car, the training data is fed to Algorithm like how to Drive Car in Highway, Busy and Narrow Street with factors like speed limit, parking, stop at signal etc. After that, a Logical and Mathematical model is created on the basis of that and after that, the car will work according to the logical model. Also, the more data the data is fed the more efficient output is produced.

Designing a Learning System in Machine Learning

According to Tom Mitchell, **"A computer program is said to be learning from experience (E), with respect to some task (T). Thus, the performance measure (P) is the performance at task T, which is measured by P, and it improves with experience E."**

Example: In Spam E-Mail-detection.

- **Task, T:** To classify mails into Spam or Not Spam.
- **Performance measure, P:** Total percent of mails being correctly classified as being "Spam" or "Not Spam".
- **Experience, E:** Set of Mails with label "Spam".

Steps for Designing Learning System are:

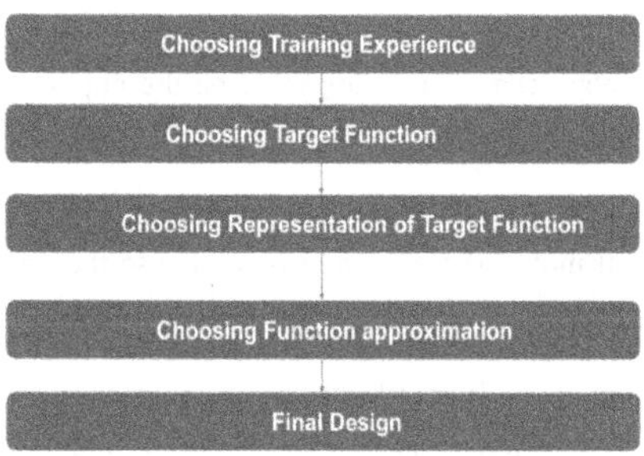

Fig. 1.14: Steps for Designing Learning System

Step 1) Choosing the Training Experience: The very important and first task is to **choose the training data or training experience** which will be fed to the Machine Learning Algorithm. It is important to note that the data or experience that we fed to the algorithm must have a significant impact on the Success or Failure of the Model. So Training data or experience should be chosen wisely.

Below are the attributes which will impact on Success and Failure of Data:

- The training experience will be able to provide direct or indirect feedback regarding choices.
- For example: While Playing chess the training data will provide feedback to itself like instead of this move if this is chosen the chances of success increases.
- Second important attribute is the degree to which the learner will control the sequences of training examples. For example: when training data is fed to the machine then at that time accuracy is very less but when it gains experience while playing again and again with itself or opponent the machine algorithm will get feedback and control the chess game accordingly.
- Third important attribute is how it will represent the distribution of examples over which performance will be measured.
- For example, a Machine learning algorithm will get experience while going through a number of different cases and different examples. Thus, Machine Learning Algorithm will get more and more experience by passing through more and more examples and hence its performance will increase.

Step 2- Choosing target function: The next important step is choosing the target function. It means according to the knowledge fed to the algorithm the machine learning will choose NextMove function which will describe what type of legal moves should be taken.

- For example: While playing chess with the opponent, when opponent will play then the machine learning algorithm will decide what be the number of possible legal moves taken in order to get success.

Step 3- Choosing Representation for Target function: When the machine algorithm will know all the possible legal moves the next step is to choose the optimized move using any representation.

- I.e. using linear Equations, Hierarchical Graph Representation, Tabular form etc. The NextMove function will move the Target move like out of these move which will provide more success rate.

- For Example: while playing chess machine have 4 possible moves, so the machine will choose that optimized move which will provide success to it.

Step 4- Choosing Function Approximation Algorithm: An optimized move cannot be chosen just with the training data. **The training data had to go through with set of example and through these examples the training data will approximates which steps are chosen and after that machine will provide feedback on it.**

- For Example: When a training data of Playing chess is fed to algorithm so at that time it is not machine algorithm will fail or get success and again from that failure or success it will measure while next move what step should be chosen and what is its success rate.

Step 5- Final Design: The final design is created at last when system goes from number of examples, failures and success, correct and incorrect decision and what will be the next step etc.

- Example: DeepBlue is an intelligent computer which is ML-based won chess game against the chess expert Garry Kasparov, and it became the first computer which had beaten a human chess expert.

1.2.10. Perspectives and Issues in Machine Learning

The Historical Perspectives of Machine Learning are the current concepts of machine learning that culminate (conclude) from two significant perspectives which are **perspective of Statisticians** and **perspective of Computer Scientists**.

The Perspective of Statisticians

- The Statisticians' perspective is related to the study, understanding, and interpretation of data. The field of data analysis has its origins in mathematics, more specifically, statistics.
- Probability is a concept of statistics in which an understanding of how likely an occurrence can happen, is studied. The models based on probability were devised in statistics to model the world around us.
- The following two simple examples will allow you to understand the statistics and probability.
- **Example#1:** In a particular exam, the collection of data on how many questions were answered correctly by the students who attempted the exams. And bar graphs could be plotted to understand and predict how many students may pass the exams if another set of students go through the same exam.

Example#2: The statisticians analyzed several books and recorded the number of times a word occurred (word frequency) in a body of text and attempted to create a model that explained which word was the most widely used or least used in the English language for instance.

Statisticians did the study of data to understand and make predictions of the world around us.

The Perspective of Computer Scientists

During the 1950s, computer experts started to realize that the hardcoding (A hardcode is a part of a computer program which cannot be altered in any way except by changing the source code of the program itself.

This means that if the software has already been compiled and made into an executable, the hardcoded portion of the program stays constant no matter what is done to the software. This is usually done for certain fixed parameters and values that should always be constant, like Pi or the speed of light.

The process of creating a hardcode is known as hardcoding of every decision that a computer is programmed to make in a never-ending if and else statements are causing the computer systems to become very inefficient.

- Computer scientists foresaw that it would be better, that computer could look at data and recognize patterns and make the best decisions. This idea of identifying patterns in data and making decisions is the basic idea behind Machine Learning (ML).
- To avoid hard coding, the programming rules to make decisions as mentioned before, the rules of distribution from statistics got into play. But, using the distributions of statistics as generators of data created huge discrepancies between the data generated by statistical models, the data generated in the real world.
- In other words, both types of data did not reveal the same results.

Despite that, machine learning continued to evolve with extremely flexible models based more and more on data and lesser on human coded if and else statements.

- These ML models have proven to be better than previously crafted modeling techniques. The current ML models became so accurate in correlating themselves with the real world that predictions have become a key output after sufficient data input.

These ML models help us better understand cancer tumors better than medical doctors and can beat the champions in the game of "Go."

1.2.11. Top Challenges

There's no doubt that Artificial Intelligence is very popular with it being a hot topic in tech circles!

1. Limited Knowledge

- Artificial Intelligence may be a buzzword in tech circles but there are very few people who understand what it is. Many myths are floating about Artificial Intelligence such as only big companies like Google, Facebook, etc. have AI capabilities or even that AI can become smarter than humans and end the world!
- This lack of knowledge about how Artificial Intelligence is practically implemented in the day to day operations of companies means that it is very difficult for smaller and mid-level companies to use it successfully. Another factor that leads to limited knowledge of AI is that there are very few AI experts that can apply AI solutions to real-life business problems. Most of the smaller companies struggle to find good AI talent that can form theirs in house AI team.
- However, a solution to this is that these companies can outsource their Artificial Intelligence and Data Science team.

2. Black Box Problem

- Artificial Intelligence algorithms are like block boxes, which means humans know what the prediction generated by the algorithm is but they don't know how it arrived at that prediction. This means that people have no means of understanding the inner working of AI algorithms.
- This makes them slightly unreliable. There is no way to understand how AI algorithms arrive at their predictions. An approach that aims to solve this problem is **Local interpretable model-agnostic explanations or LIME.** This means that the AI algorithm will also provide the pieces of data that led to its eventual (final) prediction. So if humans are provided the rationale (basic) behind why an algorithm made a particular prediction, it eliminates the black box problem and also makes the algorithm more trustworthy in general.

3. High Computing Power

- Artificial Intelligence is becoming more and more popular but it takes up a lot of computing power to train the AI. As deep learning algorithms become more and more complex, it becomes even more difficult to arrange the number of cores and GPUs they require to work efficiently. This is the reason that Artificial Intelligence is still underused in some fields like asteroid tracking, healthcare deployment, even though it could contribute a lot of value.
- Another factor is that Artificial Intelligence algorithms require a supercomputer's computing power at complex levels of computing. There are only a few supercomputers in the world and they are expensive, so this limits the types of algorithms that can be implemented and also reduces the companies that can try high-level AI to those that have high levels of resources.
- The integration of Cloud Computing and parallel processing systems have made it easier to work with artificial intelligence but it is still a power that few can afford to utilize fully.

4. Artificial Intelligence Bias

- Artificial Intelligence Bias is also a challenge for companies to fully integrate AI into their business practices. AI bias can unconsciously enter into the Artificial Intelligence Systems that are developed by human beings as they are inherently biased.
- The bias may also creep into the systems because of the flawed data that is generated by human beings.
- For example, Amazon recently found out that their Machine Learning based recruiting algorithm was biased against women. This algorithm was based on the number of resumes submitted over the past 10 years and the candidates hired. And since most of the candidates were men, so the algorithm also favored men over women. Well, the only way to handle this is that AI researchers manually try to remove the bias while developing and training the AI systems and selecting the data.

5. Data Scarcity (Lack)

- Artificial Intelligence algorithms learn from the data already available. Therefore, the better the data they are provided, the better the final algorithm will be.
- However, this requires a lot of data that may sometimes not even be available. The only method to resolve this is to understand the available data and the data that is missing.

When the AI experts know the data that is missing, they may be able to obtain it if it is data that is publicly available or even buy it from third parties data vendors.

- However, some data is difficult or even illegal to obtain. In that case, some AI algorithms use synthetic data which is artificially created from scratch while simulating the real data. This method is using synthetic data is a good option when there is data scarcity and there is not enough data available to train the AI model.

6. Situation-specific Learning

- Artificial Intelligence algorithms can be trained for a particular situation but they cannot transfer their learning from one situation to another. For example, humans can use their experiences in a situation to help them in other situations as well. But this is not possible for AI algorithms as they are trained on data for only one specified task.
- However, what if AI could transfer their learning in one situation to another related situation instead of developing a new AI model from scratch? This can be done using transfer learning wherein an AI model is trained on data in a particular situation but it can transfer its learning to another similar situation without starting from scratch. This means that an AI model developed for a particular task can then be used as a starting point for another AI model for a related task.
- The most important thing to remember is that these challenges cannot just be handled in a short time. So companies must familiarise themselves with Artificial Intelligence and understand the process to create AI solutions. Then they must create an AI strategy for its implementation into their work culture. After the strategy is created, it is much easier to just follow it and handle the challenges as they arise.

1.2.12. Concept Learning and the General to Specific Ordering

Concepts in Machine Learning can be thought of as a **Boolean-valued** function defined over a large set of training data.

In terms of machine learning, the concept learning can be formulated as **"Problem of searching through a predefined space of potential hypotheses for the hypothesis that best fits the training examples"-Tom Michell**.

Notations

To this task we have following notations:

1. Ø (Represents a hypothesis which rejects all.)
2. < ? , ? , ? , ? > (Accepts all)
3. <true, false, ? , ? > (Accepts some)

The hypothesis Ø will reject all the data samples. The hypothesis <? , ? , ? , ? > will accept all the data samples. The '?' notation indicates that the values of this specific feature do not affect the result.

Introduction

Find-S algorithm is a basic concept learning algorithm in machine learning. Find-S algorithm finds the most specific hypothesis that fits all the positive examples. We have to note here that the algorithm considers only those positive training example. Find-S algorithm starts with the most specific hypothesis and generalizes this hypothesis each time it fails to classify an observed positive training data. Hence, Find-S algorithm moves from the most specific hypothesis to the most general hypothesis.

Important Representation:

1. ? indicates that any value is acceptable for the attribute.
2. Specify a single required value (e.g., Cold) for the attribute.
3. ϕ indicates that no value is acceptable.
4. **The most general hypothesis is represented by: {?, ?, ?, ?, ?, ?}**
5. **The most specific hypothesis is represented by: {ϕ, ϕ, ϕ, ϕ, ϕ, ϕ}**

Steps Involved In Find-S:

1. Start with the most specific hypothesis. h = {ϕ, ϕ, ϕ, ϕ, ϕ, ϕ}
2. Take the next example and if it is negative, then no changes occur to the hypothesis.
3. If the example is positive and we find that our initial hypothesis is too specific then we update our current hypothesis to general condition.
4. Keep repeating the above steps till all the training examples are complete.
5. After we have completed all the training examples we will have the final hypothesis when can used to classify the new examples.

Example:

Consider the following data set having the data about which particular seeds are poisonous.

EXAMPLE	COLOR	TOUGHNESS	FUNGUS	APPEARANCE	POISONOUS
1.	GREEN	HARD	NO	WRINKELD	YES
2.	GREEN	HARD	YES	SMOOTH	NO
3.	BROWN	SOFT	NO	WRINKLED	NO
4.	ORANGE	HARD	NO	WRINKLED	YES
5.	GREEN	SOFT	YES	SMOOTH	YES
6.	GREEN	HARD	YES	WRINKLED	YES
7.	ORANGE	HARD	NO	WRINKLED	YES

ATTRIBUTES ON WHICH THE CONCEPT DEPENDS ON   CONCEPT

Fig. 1.15: Data Set

First we consider the hypothesis to be more specific hypothesis. Hence, our hypothesis would be:

h = {ϕ, ϕ, ϕ, ϕ, ϕ, ϕ}

Consider example 1:

The data in example 1 is {GREEN, HARD, NO, WRINKLED}. We see that our initial hypothesis is more specific and we have to generalize it for this example. Hence, the hypothesis becomes:

h = {GREEN, HARD, NO, WRINKLED}

Consider example 2:

Here we see that this example has a negative outcome. Hence we neglect this example and our hypothesis remains the same.

h = {GREEN, HARD, NO, WRINKLED}

Consider example 3:

Here we see that this example has a negative outcome. Hence we neglect this example and our hypothesis remains the same.

h = {GREEN, HARD, NO, WRINKLED}

Consider example 4:

The data present in example 4 is {ORANGE, HARD, NO, WRINKLED}. We compare every single attribute with the initial data and if any mismatch is found we replace that particular attribute with general case ("? "). After doing the process the hypothesis becomes:

h = {?, HARD, NO, WRINKLED}

Consider example 5:

The data present in example 5 is {GREEN, SOFT, YES, SMOOTH}. We compare every single attribute with the initial data and if any mismatch is found we replace that particular attribute with general case ("? "). After doing the process the hypothesis becomes:

h = {?, ?, ?, ?}

Since we have reached a point where all the attributes in our hypothesis have the general condition, the example 6 and example 7 would result in the same hypothesizes with all general attributes.

h = {?, ?, ?, ?}

Hence, for the given data the final hypothesis would be:

Final Hypothesis: h = {?, ?, ?, ?}

Algorithm

1. Initialize h to the most specific hypothesis in H

2. For each positive training instance x

   For each attribute constraint a, in h

   If the constraint a, is satisfied by x

   Then do nothing

   Else replace a, in h by the next more general constraint that is satisfied by x

3. Output hypothesis h

General-to-specific Ordering

For instance, general-to-**specific ordering**. Any instance classified positive by will be classified positive by, therefore is more general than. Let and be Boolean-valued functions **defined** over X. Then is more-general-than-or-equal-to if and only if. More-general-than and more-**specific**-than are also useful.

In the last post, we said that all concept learning problems share 1 thing in common regarding their structure, and it is the fact that we can order the hypotheses from the most specific one to the most general one. This will enable the machine learning algorithm to explore the hypothesis space exhaustively, without having to enumerate through each and every hypothesis in this space, which is absolutely impossible when you have an infinitely large hypothesis space. Now, we will talk about the general-to-specific ordering and show you how we can use this to define a sense of order among our hypotheses in a hypothesis space in any concept learning problem.

As a reminder, take a look at our old example regarding Joe wanting to play golf on a specific day or not. Remember that we would like to learn the concept of Play about Joe.

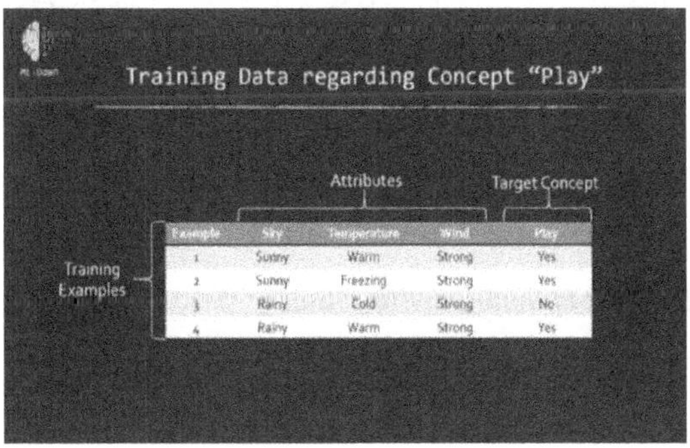

Fig. 1.16: Shows Concepts

Now, consider the following 2 hypotheses:

h_1 = <Rainy, Warm, Strong>

h_2 = <Rainy, ?, Strong>

The question is which instances and how many of them are classified positive by each one of these hypotheses (i.e., satisfy these hypotheses). For h1, only example number 4 is satisfactory, while for h2, both example 3 and 4 are satisfactory and classified as positive. Why is that? What is the difference between these 2 hypotheses? The answer lies into the strictness of the constraints that are imposed by each one of these hypotheses. As you can see, h1 imposes more constraints compared to h2! Naturally, h2 is able to classify more examples as positive than h1! Actually, in this example, we can claim the following:

"If an example could satisfy h_1, it will FOR SURE satisfy h_2, but NOT the other way around"

This is because h2 is more general than h1. This has been demonstrated below: h2 encompasses more possibilities than h1. If we have an instance with the values: **<Rainy, Freezing, Strong>**, h2 will classify it as positive but h1 will not be satisfied by it. But when h1 classifies an instance as positive, say, <Rainy, Warm, Strong>, then it is certain that h2 will also classify it as positive.

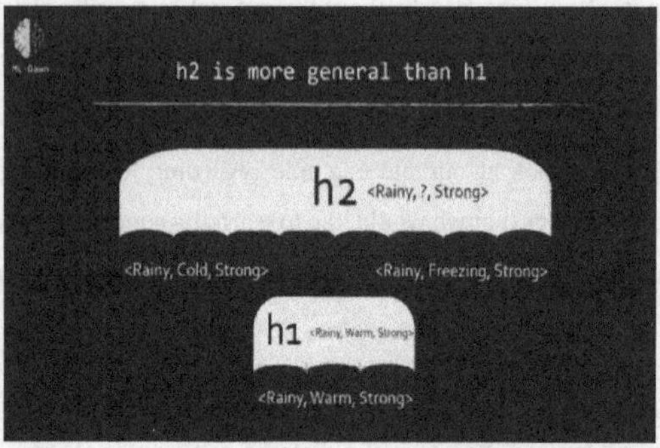

Fig. 1.17: Hypothesis

1.2.13. ML – Candidate Elimination Algorithm

The candidate elimination algorithm incrementally builds the version space given a hypothesis space H and a set E of examples. The examples are added one by one; each example possibly shrinks the version space by removing the hypotheses that are inconsistent with the example. The candidate elimination algorithm does this by updating the general and specific boundary for each new example.

- You can consider this as an extended form of Find-S algorithm.
- Consider both positive and negative examples.
- Actually, positive examples are used here as Find-S algorithm (Basically they are generalizing from the specification).
- While the negative example is specified from generalize form.

Terms Used:

- **Concept learning:** Concept learning is basically learning task of the machine (Learn by Train data).
- **General Hypothesis:** Not Specifying features to learn the machine.
- **G = {'?', '?','?','?'...}:** Number of attributes.
- **Specific Hypothesis:** Specifying features to learn machine (Specific feature).

- **S= {'pi','pi','pi'...}:** Number of pi depends on number of attributes.
- **Version Space:** It is intermediate of general hypothesis and Specific hypothesis. It not only just written one hypothesis but a set of all possible hypothesis based on training data-set.

Algorithm:

Step1: Load Data set

Step2: Initialize General Hypothesis and Specific Hypothesis.

Step3: For each training example

Step4: If example is positive example

if attribute_value == hypothesis_value:

Do nothing

else:

replace attribute value with '?' (Basically generalizing it)

Step5: If example is Negative example

Make generalize hypothesis more specific.

Example:

Consider the dataset given below:

Sky	Temperature	Humid	Wind	Water	Forest	Output
sunny	warm	normal	strong	warm	same	yes
sunny	warm	high	strong	warm	same	yes
rainy	cold	high	strong	warm	change	no
sunny	warm	high	strong	cool	change	yes

Algorithmic Steps:

Initially :G =[[?, ?, ?, ?, ?, ?], [?, ?, ?, ?, ?, ?], [?, ?, ?, ?, ?, ?],

[?, ?, ?, ?, ?, ?], [?, ?, ?, ?, ?, ?], [?, ?, ?, ?, ?, ?]]

S = [Null, Null, Null, Null, Null, Null]

For instance 1 :<'sunny','warm','normal','strong','warm ','same'> and positive output.

G1 = G

S1 = ['sunny','warm','normal','strong','warm ','same']

For instance 2 :<'sunny','warm','high','strong','warm ','same'> and positive output.

G2 = G

S2 = ['sunny','warm',?,'strong','warm ','same']

For instance 3 :<'rainy','cold','high','strong','warm ','change'> and negative output.

G3 = [['sunny', ?, ?, ?, ?, ?], [?, 'warm', ?, ?, ?, ?], [?, ?, ?, ?, ?, ?], [?, ?, ?, ?, ?, ?], [?, ?, ?, ?, ?, ?], [?, ?, ?, ?, ?, 'same']]

S3 = S2

For instance 4 :<'sunny','warm','high','strong','cool','change'> and positive output.

G4 = G3

S4 = ['sunny','warm',?,'strong', ?, ?]

At last, by synchronizing the G4 and S4 algorithm produce the output.

Output:

G = [['sunny', ?, ?, ?, ?, ?], [?, 'warm', ?, ?, ?, ?]]

S = ['sunny','warm',?,'strong', ?, ?]

1.2.14. A Concept Learning Task

A machine is said to be learning from **past Experiences** (data feed in) with respect to some class of **Tasks**, if it's **Performance** in a given Task improves with the Experience. For example, assume that a machine has to predict whether a customer will buy a specific product lets say "Antivirus" this year or not. The machine will do it by looking at the **previous knowledge/past experiences** i.e. the data of products that the customer had bought every year and if he buys Antivirus every year, then there is a high probability that the customer is going to buy an antivirus this year as well. This is how machine learning works at the basic conceptual level.

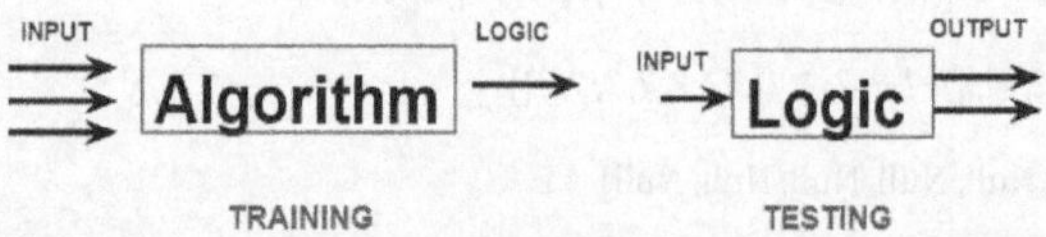

Concept Learning as Search

Searching Algorithms are designed to check for an element or retrieve an element from any data structure where it is stored. Based on the type of search operation, these algorithms are generally classified into two categories:

1. **Sequential Search:** In this, the list or array is traversed sequentially and every element is checked. For example: Linear Search.

2. **Interval Search:** These algorithms are specifically designed for searching in sorted data-structures. These type of searching algorithms are much more efficient than Linear Search as they repeatedly target the center of the search structure and divide the search space in half. For Example: Binary Search.

Linear Search to Find the Element "20" in a Given List of Numbers

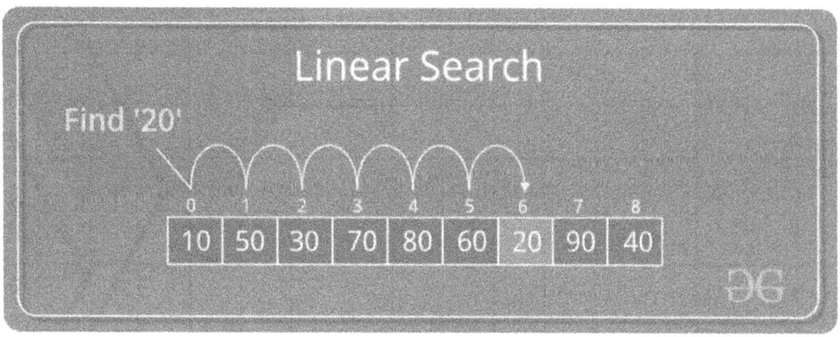

Fig. 1.18: Linear Search

1.2.15. Well-posed Learning Problems-design a Learning System in Machine Learning

Machine Learning enables a Machine to Automatically learn from Data, Improve performance from an Experience and predict things without explicitly programmed."

In Simple Words, When we fed the Training Data to Machine Learning Algorithm, this algorithm will produce a mathematical model and with the help of the mathematical model, the machine will make a prediction and take a decision without being explicitly programmed. Also, during training data, the more machine will work with it the more it will get experience and the more it will get experience the more efficient result is produced.

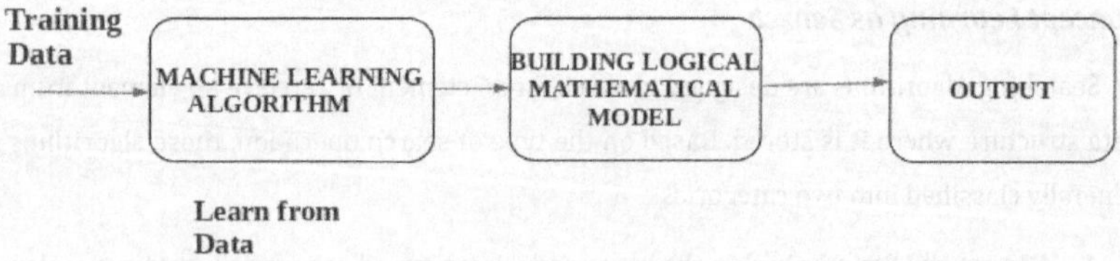

Fig. 1.19: ML Steps / Process

Example: In Driverless Car, the training data is fed to Algorithm like how to Drive Car in Highway, Busy and Narrow Street with factors like speed limit, parking, stop at signal etc. After that, a Logical and Mathematical model is created on the basis of that and after that, the car will work according to the logical model. Also, the more data the data is fed the more efficient output is produced.

Examples

1. To better filter emails as spam or not Task – Classifying emails as spam or not.

   Performance Measure – The fraction of emails accurately classified as spam or not spam.

   Experience – Observing you label emails as spam or not spam.

2. A checkers learning problem

   Task – Playing checkers game.

   Performance Measure – Percent of games won against opposer.

   Experience – Playing implementation games against itself.

3. Handwriting Recognition Problem

   Task – Acknowledging handwritten words within portrayal.

   Performance Measure – Percent of words accurately classified.

   Experience – A directory of handwritten words with given classifications.

4. A Robot Driving Problem

   Task – Driving on public four-lane highways using sight scanners.

   Performance Measure – Average distance progressed before a fallacy.

   Experience – Order of images and steering instructions noted down while observing a human driver.

1.2.16. Perspectives and Issues in Machine Learning

Perspective on ML is that it involves searching a very large space of possible hypothesis to determine one that best fits the observed data and any prior knowledge held by the learner.

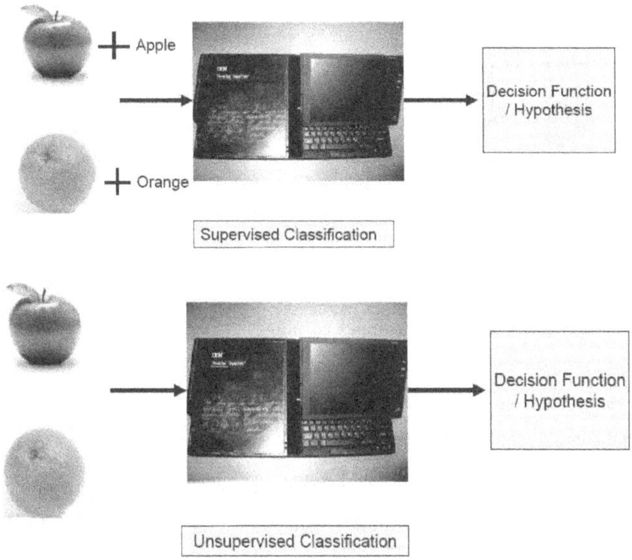

Fig. 1.20: Example for Unsupervised Classification

Issues in ML

1. Understanding Which Processes Need Automation

It's becoming increasingly difficult to separate fact from fiction in terms of Machine Learning today. Before you decide on which AI platform to use, you need to evaluate which problems you're seeking to solve. The easiest processes to automate are the ones that are done manually every day with no variable output. Complicated processes require further inspection before automation. While Machine Learning can definitely help automate some processes, not all automation problems need Machine Learning.

The easiest processes to automate are the ones that are done manually every day with no variable output. Complicated processes require further inspection before automation. While Machine Learning can definitely help automate some processes, not all automation problems need Machine Learning.

Fig. 1.21: Quality Data Plays

2. Lack of Quality Data

The number one problem facing Machine Learning is the lack of good data. While enhancing algorithms often consumes most of the time of developers in AI, data quality is essential for the algorithms to function as intended. Noisy data, dirty data, and incomplete data are the quintessential enemies of ideal Machine Learning.

The solution to this conundrum (challenge) is to take the time to evaluate and scope data with meticulous data governance, data integration, and data exploration until you get clear data. You should do this before you start.

3. Inadequate Infrastructure

Machine Learning requires vast amounts of data churning capabilities. Legacy systems often can't handle the workload and buckle under pressure. You should check if your infrastructure can handle Machine Learning. If it can't, you should look to upgrade, complete with hardware acceleration and flexible storage.

4. Implementation

Organizations often have analytics engines working with them by the time they choose to upgrade to Machine Learning. Integrating newer Machine Learning methodologies into existing methodologies is a complicated task.

Maintaining proper interpretation and documentation goes a long way to easing implementation. Partnering with an implementation partner can make the implementation of services like anomaly detection, predictive analysis, and ensemble modeling much easier.

5. Lack of Skilled Resources

Deep analytics and Machine Learning in their current forms are still new technologies. Thus, there is a shortage of skilled employees available to manage and develop analytical content for Machine Learning. Data scientists often need a combination of domain experience as well as in- depth knowledge of science, technology, and mathematics.

Recruitment will require you to pay large salaries as these employees are often in high-demand and know their worth. You can also approach your vendor for staffing help as many managed service providers keep a list of skilled data scientists to deploy anytime.

CHAPTER 2

CONCEPT LEARNING AND THE GENERAL TO SPECIFIC ORDERING

2.1. Concept Learning and the General to Specific Ordering

- Concepts in Machine Learning can be thought of as a **Boolean-valued** function defined over a large set of training data.

A Concept Learning Task

A machine is said to be learning from **past Experiences** (data feed in) with respect to some class of **Tasks**, if it's **Performance** in a given Task improves with the Experience. For example, assume that a machine has to predict whether a customer will buy a specific product lets say "Antivirus" this year or not. The machine will do it by looking at the **previous knowledge/past experiences** i.e. the data of products that the customer had bought every year and if he buys Antivirus every year, then there is a high probability that the customer is going to buy an antivirus this year as well. This is how machine learning works at the basic conceptual level.

E.G:

Taking a very simple example, one possible target concept may be to *Find the day when my friend Ramesh enjoys his favorite sport.* We have some attributes/features of the day like, **Sky**, **Air, Temperature**, **Humidity**, **Wind**, **Water**, **Forecast** and based on this we have a target Concept named **EnjoySport**.

We have the following training example available:

Example	**Sky**	**AirTemp**	**Humidity**	**Wind**	**Water**	**Forecast**	**EnjoySport**
1	Sunny	Warm	Normal	Strong	Warm	Same	Yes
2	Sunny	Warm	High	Strong	Warm	Same	Yes
3	Rainy	Cold	High	Strong	Warm	Change	No
4	Sunny	Warm	High	Strong	Cool	Change	Yes

Let's Design the problem formally with **TPE** (Task, Performance, Experience):

Problem: Leaning the day when Ramesh enjoys the sport.

Task T: Learn to predict the value of **EnjoySport** for an arbitrary day, based on the values of the attributes of the day.

Performance measure P: Total percent of days (EnjoySport) correctly predicted.

Training experience E: A set of days with given labels (EnjoySport: Yes/No).

Let us take a very simple hypothesis representation which consists of a **conjunction** of constraints in the instance attributes. We get a hypothesis h_i with the help of example i for our training set as below:

hi(x) := <x1, x2, x3, x4, x5, x6>

Where x1, x2, x3, x4, x5 and x6 are the values of **Sky**, **AirTemp**, **Humidity**, **Wind**, **Water** and **Forecast**.

Hence h1 will look like (the first row of the table above):

h1(x=1): <Sunny, Warm, Normal, Strong, Warm, Same > *Note: x=1 represents a positive hypothesis / Positive example.*

We want to find the most suitable hypothesis which can represent the concept. For example, Ramesh enjoys his favorite sport only on **cold days** with **high humidity** (This seems independent of the values of the other attributes present in the training examples).

h(x=1) = <?, Cold, High, ?, ?, ?>

Here? indicates that any value of the attribute is acceptable.

<u>**Note:**</u> The most generic hypothesis will be <?, ?, ?, ?, ?, ?> where every day is a positive example and the most specific hypothesis will be <?,?,?,?,?,?> where no day is a positive example.

We will discuss the two most popular approaches to find a suitable hypothesis, they are:

1. Find-S Algorithm
2. List-Then-Eliminate Algorithm

The most suitable way to find a good hypothesis will be to start with both the directions, by taking the most general and the most specific boundaries. This approach is called a **CANDIDATE-ELIMINATION** Learning Algorithm.

In terms of machine learning, the concept learning can be formulated as **"Problem of searching through a predefined space of potential hypotheses for the hypothesis that best fits the training examples"**.

Notations Used

To this task we have following notations:

1. Ø (Represents a hypothesis which rejects all.)
2. < ? , ? , ? , ? > (Accepts all)
3. <true, false, ? , ? > (Accepts some)

The hypothesis Ø will reject all the data samples. The hypothesis <? , ? , ? , ?> will accept all the data samples. The '?' notation indicates that the values of this specific feature do not affect the result.

Find-S Algorithm - Introduction

Find-S algorithm is a basic concept learning algorithm in machine learning. Find-S algorithm finds the most specific hypothesis that fits all the positive examples. We have to note here that the algorithm considers only those positive training example. Find-S algorithm starts with the most specific hypothesis and generalizes this hypothesis each time it fails to classify an observed positive training data. Hence, Find-S algorithm moves from the most specific hypothesis to the most general hypothesis.

Important Representation

1. ? indicates that any value is acceptable for the attribute.
2. specify a single required value (e.g., Cold) for the attribute.
3. ϕ indicates that no value is acceptable.
4. **The most general hypothesis is represented by: {?, ?, ?, ?, ?, ?}**
5. **The most specific hypothesis is represented by: {ϕ, ϕ, ϕ, ϕ, ϕ, ϕ}**

Steps Involved in Find-S

1. Start with the most specific hypothesis.
   h = {ϕ, ϕ, ϕ, ϕ, ϕ, ϕ}
2. Take the next example and if it is negative, then no changes occur to the hypothesis.
3. If the example is positive and we find that our initial hypothesis is too specific then we update our current hypothesis to general condition.
4. Keep repeating the above steps till all the training examples are complete.
5. After we have completed all the training examples we will have the final hypothesis when can used to classify the new examples.

Example

Consider the following data set having the data about which particular seeds are poisonous.

EXAMPLE	COLOR	TOUGHNESS	FUNGUS	APPEARANCE	POISONOUS
1.	GREEN	HARD	NO	WRINKELD	YES
2.	GREEN	HARD	YES	SMOOTH	NO
3.	BROWN	SOFT	NO	WRINKLED	NO
4.	ORANGE	HARD	NO	WRINKLED	YES
5.	GREEN	SOFT	YES	SMOOTH	YES
6.	GREEN	HARD	YES	WRINKLED	YES
7.	ORANGE	HARD	NO	WRINKLED	YES

ATTRIBUTES ON WHICH THE CONCEPT DEPENDS ON **CONCEPT**

First we consider the hypothesis to be more specific hypothesis. Hence, our hypothesis would be:

h = {ϕ, ϕ, ϕ, ϕ, ϕ, ϕ}

Example 1:

The data in example 1 is {GREEN, HARD, NO, WRINKLED}. We see that our initial hypothesis is more specific and we have to generalize it for this example. Hence, the hypothesis becomes:

h = {GREEN, HARD, NO, WRINKLED}

Consider example 2:

Here we see that this example has a negative outcome. Hence we neglect this example and our hypothesis remains the same.

h = {GREEN, HARD, NO, WRINKLED}

Consider example 3:

Here we see that this example has a negative outcome. Hence we neglect this example and our hypothesis remains the same.

h = {GREEN, HARD, NO, WRINKLED}

Consider example 4:

The data present in example 4 is {ORANGE, HARD, NO, WRINKLED}. We compare every single attribute with the initial data and if any mismatch is found we replace that particular attribute with general case ("?"). After doing the process the hypothesis becomes:

h = {?, HARD, NO, WRINKLED}

Consider example 5:

The data present in example 5 is {GREEN, SOFT, YES, SMOOTH}. We compare every single attribute with the initial data and if any mismatch is found we replace that particular attribute with general case ("?"). After doing the process the hypothesis becomes:

h = {?, ?, ?, ?}

Since we have reached a point where all the attributes in our hypothesis have the general condition, the example 6 and example 7 would result in the same hypothesizes with all general attributes.

h = {?, ?, ?, ?}

Hence, for the given data the final hypothesis would be:

Final Hypothesis: h = {?,?,?,?}

Flow Chart

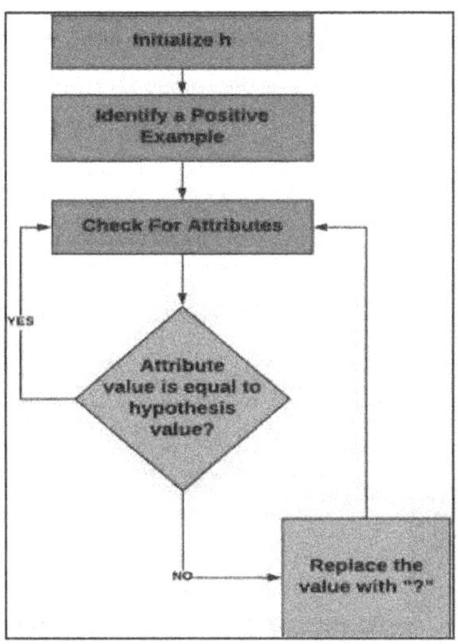

Fig. 2.1: Find 'S' Flowchart

Algorithm

1. Initialize h to the most specific hypothesis in H
2. For each positive training instance x

   For each attribute constraint a, in h

      If the constraint a, is satisfied by x

      Then do nothing

      Else replace a, in h by the next more general constraint that is satisfied by x
3. Output hypothesis h

2.2. General-to-specific Ordering

For instance, general-to-**specific ordering**. Any instance classified positive by will be classified positive by, therefore is more general than. Let and be Boolean-valued functions **defined** over X. Then is more-general-than-or-equal-to if and only if. More-general-than and more-**specific**-than are also useful.

In the last post, we said that all concept learning problems share 1 thing in common regarding their structure, and it is the fact that we can order the hypotheses from the most specific one to the most general one. This will enable the machine learning algorithm to explore the hypothesis space exhaustively, without having to enumerate through each and every hypothesis in this space, which is absolutely impossible when you have an infinitely large hypothesis space. Now, we will talk about the general-to-specific ordering and show you how we can use this to define a sense of order among our hypotheses in a hypothesis space in *any* concept learning problem.

As a reminder, take a look at our old example regarding Joe wanting to play golf on a specific day or not. Remember that we would like to learn the concept of Play about Joe.

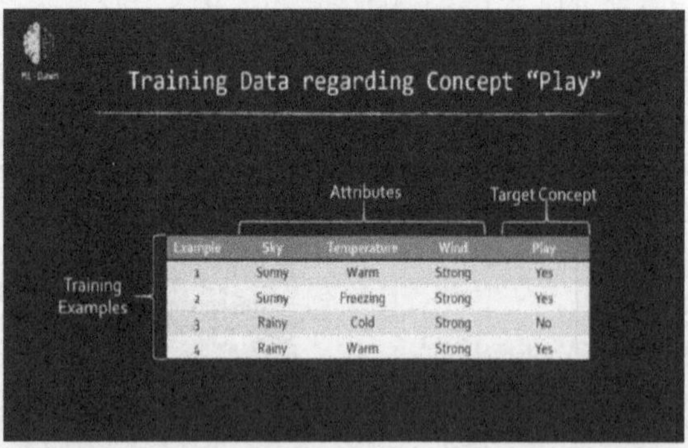

Example	Sky	Temperature	Wind	Play
1	Sunny	Warm	Strong	Yes
2	Sunny	Freezing	Strong	Yes
3	Rainy	Cold	Strong	No
4	Rainy	Warm	Strong	Yes

Now, consider the following 2 hypotheses:

h_1 = <Rainy, Warm, Strong>

h_2 = <Rainy, ?, Strong>

The question is which instances and how many of them are classified positive by each one of these hypotheses (i.e., satisfy these hypotheses). For h1, only example number 4 is satisfactory, while for h2, both example 3 and 4 are satisfactory and classified as positive. Why is that? What is the difference between these 2 hypotheses? The answer lies into the strictness of the constraints that are imposed by each one of these hypotheses. As you can see, h1 imposes more constraints compared to h2! Naturally, h2 is able to classify more examples as positive than h1! Actually, in this example, we can claim the following:

"If an example could satisfy h_1, it will FOR SURE satisfy h_2, but NOT the other way around"

This is because h2 is more general than h1. This has been demonstrated below: h2 encompasses more possibilities than h1. If we have an instance with the values: <Rainy, Freezing, Strong>, h2 will classify it as positive but h1 will not be satisfied by it. But when h1 classifies an instance as positive, say, **<Rainy, Warm, Strong>**, then it is certain that h2 will also classify it as positive.

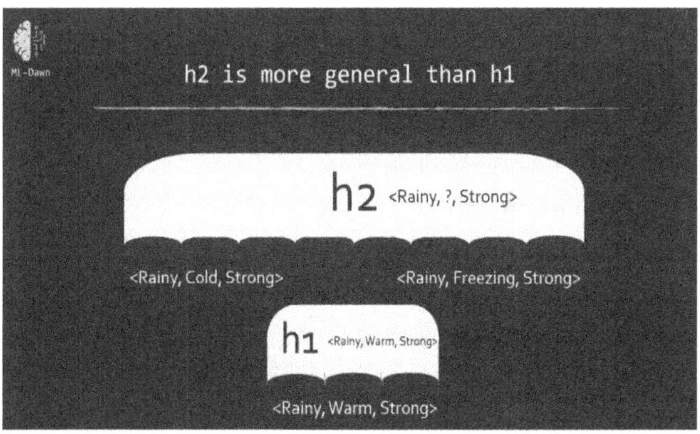

Fig. 2.2: General Hypothesis

2.3. FIND S Algorithm – Maximally Specific Hypothesis

FIND S Algorithm is used to find the Maximally Specific Hypothesis. Using the Find-S algorithm gives a single maximally specific hypothesis for the given set of training examples.

Solved Example 2

Example	*Sky*	*AirTemp*	*Humidity*	*Wind*	*Water*	*Forecast*	*EnjoySport*
1	Sunny	Warm	Normal	Strong	Warm	Same	Yes
2	Sunny	Warm	High	Strong	Warm	Same	Yes
3	Rainy	Cold	High	Strong	Warm	Change	No
4	Sunny	Warm	High	Strong	Cool	Change	Yes

1. Initialize *h* to the most specific hypothesis in *H*

h0 = <Ø, Ø, Ø, Ø, Ø, Ø>

Step – 1 of Find-S Algorithm

Step 2 of Find-S Algorithm First iteration

h0 = (ø, ø, ø, ø, ø, ø, ø)

X1 = <Sunny, Warm, Normal, Strong, Warm, Same>

h1 = <Sunny, Warm, Normal, Strong, Warm, Same>

Step 2 of Find-S Algorithm Second iteration

h1 = <Sunny, Warm, Normal, Strong, Warm, Same>

X2 = <Sunny, Warm, High, Strong, Warm, Same>

h2 = <Sunny, Warm, ?, Strong, Warm, Same>

Step 2 of Find-S Algorithm Third iteration

h2 = <Sunny, Warm, ?, Strong, Warm, Same>

X3 = <Rainy, Cold, High, Strong, Warm, Change> – No

X3 is Negative example Hence ignored

h3 = <Sunny, Warm, ?, Strong, Warm, Same>

Step 2 of Find-S Algorithm Fourth iteration

h3 = <Sunny, Warm, ?, Strong, Warm, Same>

X4 = <Sunny, Warm, High, Strong, Cool, Change>

h4 = <Sunny, Warm, ?, Strong, ?, ?>

Step 3

The final maximally specific hypothesis is **<Sunny, Warm, ?, Strong, ?, ?>**

Example - 2

example	*citations*	*size*	*inLibrary*	*price*	*editions*	*buy*
1	some	small	no	affordable	many	no
2	many	big	no	expensive	one	yes
3	some	big	always	expensive	few	no
4	many	medium	no	expensive	many	yes
5	many	small	no	affordable	many	yes

1. How many concepts are possible for this instance space?

   Solution: 2 * 3 * 2 * 2 * 3 = 72

2. How many hypotheses can be expressed by the hypothesis language?

   Solution: 4 * 5 * 4 * 4 * 5 = 1600

   Semantically Distinct Hypothesis = (3 * 4 * 3 * 3 * 4) + 1 = 433

3. Apply the FIND-S algorithm by hand on the given training set. Consider the examples in the specified order and write down your hypothesis each time after observing an example.

Step 1:

h0 = (ø, ø, ø, ø, ø)

Step 2:

X1 = (some, small, no, expensive, many) – No

Negative Example Hence Ignore

h1 = (ø, ø, ø, ø, ø)

X2 = (many, big, no, expensive, one) – Yes

h2 = (many, big, no, expensive, one)

X3 = (some, big, always, expensive, few) – No

Negative example hence Ignore

h3 = (many, big, no, expensive, one)

X4 = (many, medium, no, expensive, many) – Yes

h4 = (many, ?, no, expensive, ?)

X5 = (many, small, no, affordable, many) – Yes

h5 = (many, ?, no, ?, ?)

Step 3:

Final Maximally Specific Hypothesis is: h5 = (many, ?, no, ?, ?)

Example 3:

Sky	Temperature	Humid	Wind	Water	Forest	Output
sunny	warm	normal	strong	warm	same	yes
sunny	warm	high	strong	warm	same	yes
rainy	cold	high	strong	warm	change	no
sunny	warm	high	strong	cool	change	yes

Steps:

Initially: G = [[?, ?, ?, ?, ?, ?], [?, ?, ?, ?, ?, ?], [?, ?, ?, ?, ?, ?],

[?, ?, ?, ?, ?, ?], [?, ?, ?, ?, ?, ?], [?, ?, ?, ?, ?, ?]]

S = [Null, Null, Null, Null, Null, Null]

For instance 1: <'sunny','warm','normal','strong','warm ','same'> and positive output.

G1 = G

S1 = ['sunny','warm','normal','strong','warm ','same']

For instance 2: <'sunny','warm','high','strong','warm ','same'> and positive output.

G2 = G

S2 = ['sunny','warm',?,'strong','warm ','same']

For instance 3: <'rainy','cold','high','strong','warm ','change'> and negative output.

G3 = [['sunny', ?, ?, ?, ?, ?], [?, 'warm', ?, ?, ?, ?], [?, ?, ?, ?, ?, ?], [?, ?, ?, ?, ?, ?], [?, ?, ?, ?, ?, ?], [?, ?, ?, ?, ?, 'same']]

S3 = S2

For instance 4 : <'sunny','warm','high','strong','cool','change'> and positive output.

G4 = G3

S4 = ['sunny','warm',?,'strong', ?, ?]

At last, by synchronizing the G4 and S4 algorithm produce the output.

Final Maximally Specific Hypothesis is

G = [['sunny', ?, ?, ?, ?, ?], [?, 'warm', ?, ?, ?, ?]]

S = ['sunny','warm',?,'strong', ?, ?]

Example with another Detailed Explanation

Finding A Maximally Specific Hypothesis

FIND-S: Step-1

Example	*Sky*	*AirTemp*	*Humidity*	*Wind*	*Water*	*Forecast*	*EnjoySport*
1	Sunny	Warm	Normal	Strong	Warm	Same	Yes
2	Sunny	Warm	High	Strong	Warm	Same	Yes
3	Rainy	Cold	High	Strong	Warm	Change	No
4	Sunny	Warm	High	Strong	Cool	Change	Yes

Solution

Step 1: Initialize to most specific hypothesis in H

0=< Ø Ø Ø Ø Ø Ø >

FIND-S: Step-2

Example	*Sky*	*AirTemp*	*Humidity*	*Wind*	*Water*	*Forecast*	*EnjoySport*
1	Sunny	Warm	Normal	Strong	Warm	Same	Yes
2	Sunny	Warm	High	Strong	Warm	Same	Yes
3	Rainy	Cold	High	Strong	Warm	Change	No
4	Sunny	Warm	High	Strong	Cool	Change	Yes
ai	a1	a2	a3	a4	a5	a6	

For each positive training instance in X

for each attribute constraint ai in h

If the constraint ai is satisfied by X

then do nothing

else

replace ai in h by the next more general constraint that is satisfied by x

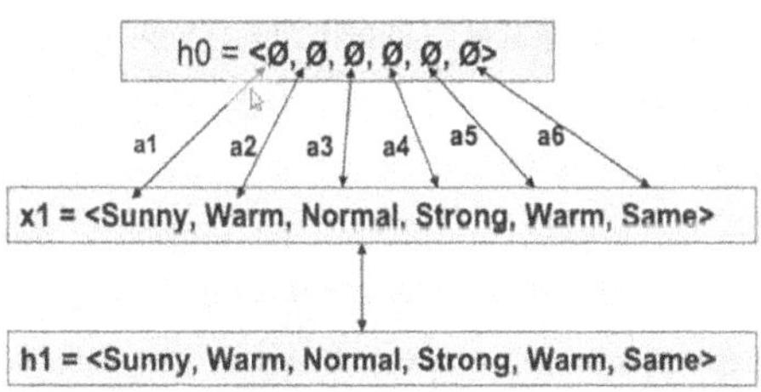

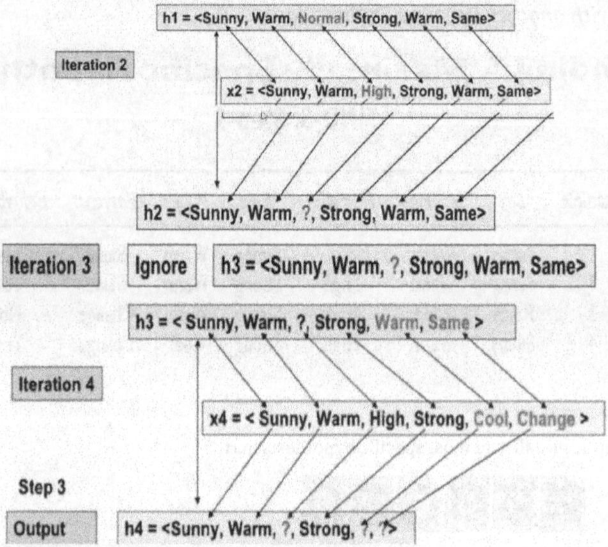

2.4. Version Space

- It is intermediate of general hypothesis and Specific hypothesis. It not only just written one hypothesis but a set of all possible hypothesis based on training data-set.
- The set of concepts consistent with a set of. training examples is called a **version space** (for that set of examples).
- **Version space** method involves identifying all concepts consistent with a set of training examples.
- A **version space** is a hierarchical representation of knowledge that enables you to keep track of all the useful information supplied by a sequence of **learning** examples without remembering any of the examples.
- The **candidate elimination algorithm** incrementally builds the version space given a hypothesis space H and a set E of examples. The examples are added one by one; each example possibly shrinks the version space by removing the hypotheses that are inconsistent with the example.
- A hypothesis "h" is consistent with a set of training examples D of target concept c if and only if h(x) = c(x) for each training example in D.
- The version space VS with respect to hypothesis space H and training examples D is the subset of hypothesis from H consistent with all training examples in D.

- The hypothesis space used by a machine learning system is the set of all hypotheses that might possibly be returned by it. It is typically defined by a Hypothesis Language, possibly in conjunction with a Language Bias.

2.5. ML - Candidate Elimination Algorithm

The candidate elimination algorithm incrementally builds the version space given a hypothesis space H and a set E of examples. The examples are added one by one; each example possibly shrinks the version space by removing the hypotheses that are inconsistent with the example. The candidate elimination algorithm does this by updating the general and specific boundary for each new example.

- You can consider this as an extended form of Find-S algorithm.
- Consider both positive and negative examples.
- Actually, positive examples are used here as Find-S algorithm (Basically they are generalizing from the specification).
- While the negative example is specified from generalize form.

Terms Used

Concept learning: Concept learning is basically learning task of the machine (Learn by Train data).

General Hypothesis: Not Specifying features to learn the machine.

G = {'?', '?','?','?'...}: Number of attributes.

Specific Hypothesis: Specifying features to learn machine (Specific feature).

S= {'pi','pi','pi'...}: Number of pi depends on number of attributes.

Version Space: It is intermediate of general hypothesis and Specific hypothesis. It not only just written one hypothesis but a set of all possible hypothesis based on training data-set.

Algorithm

- Load Data set.
- Initialize G to the set of maximally general hypotheses in H.
- Initialize S to the set of maximally specific hypotheses in H.
- For each training example d.
    - If d is a positive example.
    - Remove from G any hypothesis that does not include.

- For each hypothesis s in S that does not include d, remove s from S.
- Add to S all minimal generalizations h of s such that h includes d.
  - Some member of G is more general than h.
    - Remove from S any hypothesis that is more general than another hypothesis in S.
- For each training example d.
  - If d is a negative example.
  - Remove from S any hypothesis that does not include.
  - For each hypothesis g in G that does not included.
  - Remove g from G.
- Add to G all minimal generalizations h of g such that,
  - h does not included.
  - Some member of S is more specific than h.
- Remove from G any hypothesis that is less general than another hypothesis in G.
- If G or S, ever becomes empty, data not consistent (with H).

Example 1:

Consider the dataset given below:

Sky	Temperature	Humid	Wind	Water	Forest	Output
sunny	warm	normal	strong	warm	same	yes
sunny	warm	high	strong	warm	same	yes
rainy	cold	high	strong	warm	change	no
sunny	warm	high	strong	cool	change	yes

Algorithmic steps:

Initially: G =[[?, ?, ?, ?, ?, ?], [?, ?, ?, ?, ?, ?], [?, ?, ?, ?, ?, ?], [?, ?, ?, ?, ?, ?], [?, ?, ?, ?, ?, ?], [?, ?, ?, ?, ?, ?]]

S = [Null, Null, Null, Null, Null, Null]

For instance 1: <'sunny','warm','normal','strong','warm ','same'> and positive output.

G1 = G

S1 = ['sunny','warm','normal','strong','warm ','same']

For instance 2: <'sunny','warm','high','strong','warm ','same'> and positive output.

G2 = G

S2 = ['sunny','warm',?,'strong','warm ','same']

For instance 3: <'rainy','cold','high','strong','warm ','change'> and negative output.

G3 = [['sunny', ?, ?, ?, ?, ?], [?, 'warm', ?, ?, ?, ?], [?, ?, ?, ?, ?, ?], [?, ?, ?, ?, ?, ?], [?, ?, ?, ?, ?, ?], [?, ?, ?, ?, ?, 'same']]

S3 = S2

For instance 4: <'sunny','warm','high','strong','cool','change'> and positive output.

G4 = G3

S4 = ['sunny','warm',?,'strong', ?, ?]

At last, by synchronizing the G4 and S4 algorithm produce the output.

Output:

G = [['sunny', ?, ?, ?, ?, ?], [?, 'warm', ?, ?, ?, ?]]

S = ['sunny','warm',?,'strong', ?, ?]

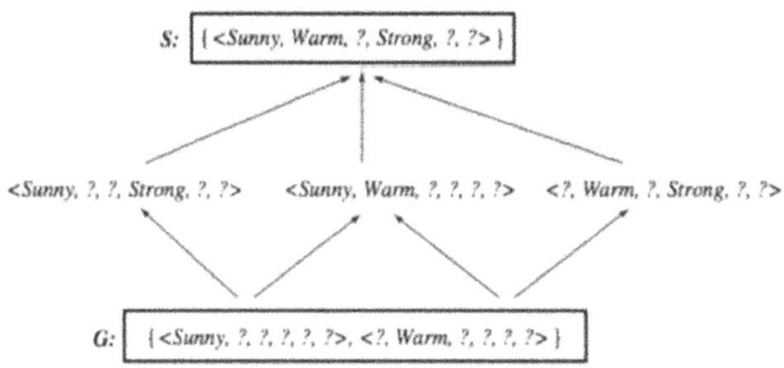

Example 2:

Example	Citations	Size	In Library	Price	Editions	Buy
1	Some	Small	No	Affordable	One	No
2	Many	Big	No	Expensive	Many	Yes
3	Many	Medium	No	Expensive	Few	Yes
4	Many	Small	No	Affordable	Many	Yes

Solution

S0: (0, 0, 0, 0, 0) Most Specific Boundary

G0: (?, ?, ?, ?, ?) Most Generic Boundary

The first example is negative, the hypothesis at the specific boundary is consistent, hence we retain it, and the hypothesis at the generic boundary is inconsistent hence we write all consistent hypotheses by removing one "?" at a time.

S1: (0, 0, 0, 0, 0)

G1: (Many,?,?,?, ?) (?, Big,?,?,?) (?,Medium,?,?,?) (?,?,?,Exp,?) (?,?,?,?,One) (?,?,?,?,Few)

The second example is positive, the hypothesis at the specific boundary is inconsistent, hence we extend the specific boundary, and the consistent hypothesis at the generic boundary is retained and inconsistent hypotheses are removed from the generic boundary.

S2: (Many, Big, No, Exp, Many)

G2: (Many,?,?,?, ?) (?, Big,?,?,?) (?,?,?,Exp,?) (?,?,?,?,Many)

The third example is positive, the hypothesis at the specific boundary is inconsistent, hence we extend the specific boundary, and the consistent hypothesis at the generic boundary is retained and inconsistent hypotheses are removed from the generic boundary.

S3: (Many, ?, No, Exp, ?)

G3: (Many,?,?,?,?) (?,?,?,exp,?)

The fourth example is positive, the hypothesis at the specific boundary is inconsistent, hence we extend the specific boundary, and the consistent hypothesis at the generic boundary is retained and inconsistent hypotheses are removed from the generic boundary.

S4: (Many, ?, No, ?, ?)

G4: (Many,?,?,?,?)

Learned Version Space by Candidate Elimination Algorithm for given data set is:
(Many, ?, No, ?, ?) (Many, ?, ?, ?, ?)

Candidate Elimination Algorithm Concept

- Using Version Space.
- Consider both positive and negative result.
- For positive example: tend to generalize specific hypothesis.
- For Negative example: tend to make general hypothesis more specific.

Example 3:

Find the maximally general hypothesis and maximally specific hypothesis for the training examples given in the table using the candidate elimination algorithm.

Training Example:

Sky	Temp	Humidity	wind	water	Forecast	sport
Sunny	warm	Normal	Strong	warm	same	Yes
Sunny	warm	High	Strong	warm	same	Yes
Rainy	cold	High	Strong	warm	change	No
Sunny	warm	High	Strong	cool	change	Yes

Step 1:

Initialize G & S as most General and specific hypothesis.

G ={'?', '?','?','?', '?','?'}

S = {'φ','φ','φ','φ','φ','φ'}

Step 2:

for each +ve example: make a specific hypothesis more general.

s = {'φ','φ','φ','φ','φ','φ'}

Take the most specific hypothesis as your 1st positive instance.

h={'sunny', 'warm','Normal', 'Strong', 'warm', 'same'}

General hypothesis will remain same: **G ={'?', '?','?','?', '?','?'}**

Step 3:

Compare with another positive instance for each attribute.

if (attribute value = hypothesis value) do nothing.

else

replace the hypothesis value with more general constraint '?'.

Since instance 2 is also positive so we will compare with it. In instance 2 attribute humidity is changing so we will generalize that attribute.

S={'sunny', 'warm','?', 'Strong', 'warm', 'same'}

General hypothesis will remain same: **G ={'?', '?','?','?', '?','?'}**

Step 4:

Instance 3 is negative so for each -ve example make general hypothesis more specific.

We will make the general hypothesis more specific by comparing all the attributes of the negative instance with the positive instance if attribute found different to create a dedicated set for the attribute.

G ={<'sunny', '?','?','?', '?','?'> , <'?', 'warm','?','?', '?','?'> , <'?', '?','Normal','?', '?','?'> , < '?', '?','?','?', '?','same'>}

Specific hypothesis will be same: **S={'sunny', 'warm','?', 'Strong', 'warm', 'same'}**

Step 5:

Instance 4 is positive so repeat step 3:

S={'sunny', 'warm','?', 'Strong', '?', '?'}

Discard the general hypothesis set which is contradicting with a resultant specific hypothesis here humidity and forecast attribute is contradicting.

G ={<'sunny', '?','?','?', '?','?'> , <'?', 'warm','?','?', '?','?'> }

:. Maximally specific and general hypothesis are:

S={'sunny', 'warm','?', 'Strong', '?', '?'}

G ={<'sunny', '?','?','?', '?','?'> , <'?', 'warm','?','?', '?','?'> }

Diagram

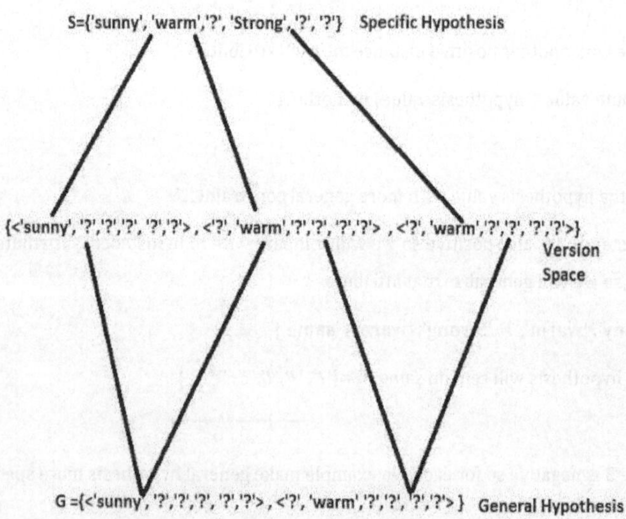

2.6. Remarks on Version Spaces

The version space learned by the CANDIDATE-ELIMINATION algorithm will converge toward the hypothesis that correctly describes the target concept, provided.

1. There are no errors in the training examples.
2. There is some hypothesis in H that correctly describes the target concept.

In fact, as new training examples are observed, the version space can be monitored to determine the remaining ambiguity regarding the true concept and to determine when sufficient training examples have been observed to unambiguously identify the target concept.

3. The target concept is exactly learned when the S and G boundary sets converge to a single, identical, hypothesis.

A version space description consists of two complementary trees:

1. One that contains nodes connected to overly general models.
2. One that contains nodes connected to overly specific models.

2.7. Remarks on Candidate-Elimination Algorithm

Version space learned by Candidate-Elimination algorithm will converge towards correct hypothesis provided: - no errors in training examples - there is a hypothesis in H that describes target concept in such cases algorithm may converge to empty version space.

Version space learned by Candidate-Elimination algorithm will converge towards correct hypothesis provided: - no errors in training examples - there is a hypothesis in H that describes target concept in such cases algorithm may converge to empty version space.

- If algorithm can request next training example (e.g. from teacher) can increase speed of convergence by requesting examples that split the version space.

E.g. T5: Sunny, Warm, Normal, Light, Warm, Samei satisfies 3 hypotheses in previous example.

* If T5 positive, S generalised, 3 hypotheses eliminated.

* If T5 negative, G specialised, 3 hypotheses eliminated - Optimal query strategy is to request examples that exactly split version space - converge in $\lceil \log 2|VS| \rceil$ steps.

However, this is not always possible.

When using (i.e. not training) a classifier that has not completely converged, new examples may be,

1. Classed as positive by all $h \in VS$.

2. Classed as negative by all h ∈ VS.

3. Classed as positive by some, and negative by other, h ∈ V S.

Cases 1 and 2 are unproblematic. In case 3. may want to consider proportion of positive vs. negative classifications (but then a priori probabilities of hypotheses are relevant).

2.8. Inductive Bias

Version space learned by Candidate-Elimination algorithm will converge towards correct hypothesis provided:

- no errors in training examples.
- there is a hypothesis in H that describes target concept.

Example

Consider the training data.

Example:

Example	Sky	Temp	Humid	Wind	Water	Forecast	EnjoySport
1	Sunny	Warm	Normal	Strong	Warm	Same	Yes
2	Cloudy	Warm	Normal	Strong	Warm	Same	Yes
3	Rainy	Warm	Normal	Strong	Warm	Same	No

No hypotheses consistent with 3 examples. Most specific hypothesis consistent with Ex 1 and 2 and representable in H: h.

?, Warm, Normal, Strong, Warm, Same

But this is inconsistent with Ex 3

Need more expressive hypothesis representation language.

E.g. allow disjunctive or negative attribute values:

Sky = Sunny ∨ Cloudy

sky != Rainy

CHAPTER 3

DECISION TREE LEARNING

3.1. Decision Tree Learning

- Decision tree algorithm falls under the category of supervised learning. They can be used to solve both regression and classification problems.
- Decision tree uses the tree representation to solve the problem in which each leaf node corresponds to a class label and attributes are represented on the internal node of the tree.
- We can represent any Boolean function on discrete attributes using the decision tree.

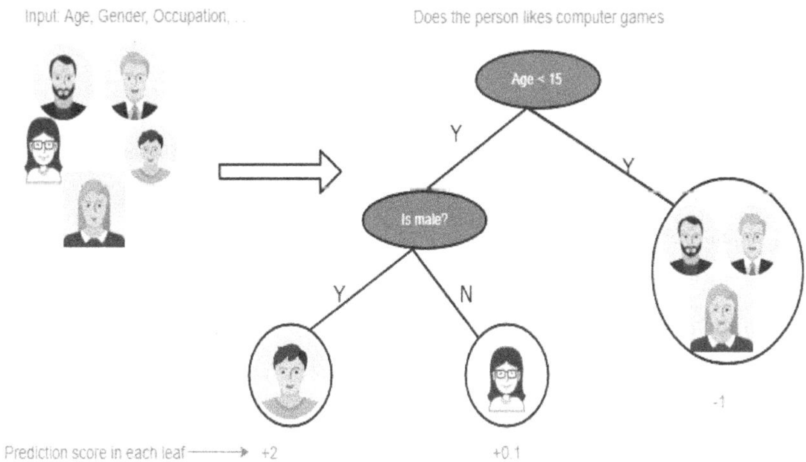

Fig. 3.1: Decision Tree with its Attributes

Some Assumptions that we made while Using Decision Tree

- At the beginning, we consider the whole training set as the root.
- Feature values are preferred to be categorical. If the values are continuous then they are discretized prior to building the model.
- On the basis of attribute values records are distributed recursively.
- We use statistical methods for ordering attributes as root or the internal node.

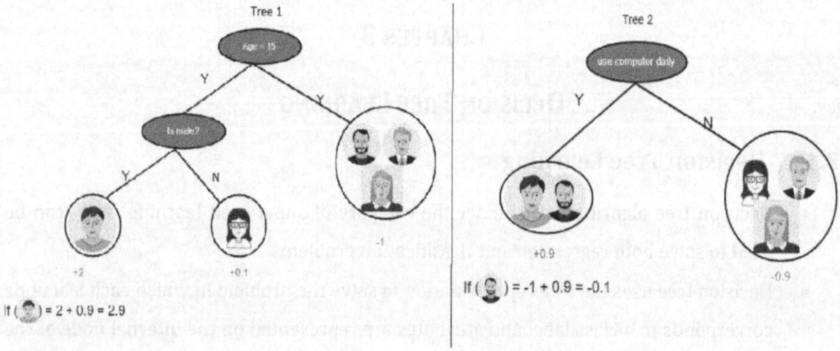

Fig. 3.2: Decision Tree

The above image that Decision Tree works on the Sum of Product form which is also known as Disjunctive Normal Form. In the above image, we are predicting the use of computer in the daily life of the people.

In Decision Tree the major challenge is to identification of the s: attribute for the root node in each level. This process is known as attribute selection. We have two popular attribute selection measure

1. Information Gain
2. Gini Index

Information Gain

When we use a node in a decision tree to partition the training instances into smaller subsets the entropy changes. Information gain is a measure of this change in entropy. Definition: Suppose S is a set of instances, A is an attribute, Sv is

1. the subset of S with A = v, and Values (A) is the set of all possible values of A, then

$$Gain(S, A) = Entropy(S) - \sum_{v \epsilon Values(A)} \frac{|S_v|}{|S|} . Entropy(S_v)$$

Entropy

Entropy is the measure of uncertainty of a random variable, it characterizes the impurity of an arbitrary collection of examples. The higher the entropy more the information content. Definition: Suppose S is a set of instances, A is an attribute, Sv is the subset of S with A = v, and Values (A) is the set of all possible values of A, then,

$$Gain(S, A) = Entropy(S) - \sum_{v \epsilon Values(A)} \frac{|S_v|}{|S|} . Entropy(S_v)$$

Example:

For the set X = {a,a,a,b,b,b,b,b}

Total instances: 8

Instances of b: 5

Instances of a: 3

$$Entropy H(X) = - \left[\left(\frac{3}{8}\right) log_2 \frac{3}{8} + \left(\frac{5}{8}\right) log_2 \frac{5}{8} \right]$$

=-[0.375 * (-1.415) + 0.625 * (-0.678)]

=-(-0.53-0.424)

= 0.954

3.2. Building Decision Tree Using Information Gain

The essentials:

- Start with all training instances associated with the root node.
- Use info gain to choose which attribute to label each node with.
- Note: No root-to-leaf path should contain the same discrete attribute twice.
- Recursively construct each subtree on the subset of training instances that would be classified down that path in the tree.

The border cases:

- If all positive or all negative training instances remain, label that node "yes" or "no" accordingly.
- If no attributes remain, label with a majority vote of training instances left at that node.
- If no instances remain, label with a majority vote of the parent's training instances.

Example:

Now, lets draw a Decision Tree for the following data using Information gain.

Training Set: 3 Features and 2 Classes

X	Y	Z	C
1	1	1	I
1	1	0	I
0	0	1	II
1	0	0	II

Here, we have 3 features and 2 output classes.

To build a decision tree using Information gain. We will take each of the feature and calculate the information for each feature in the Fig. Split on 'Y'.

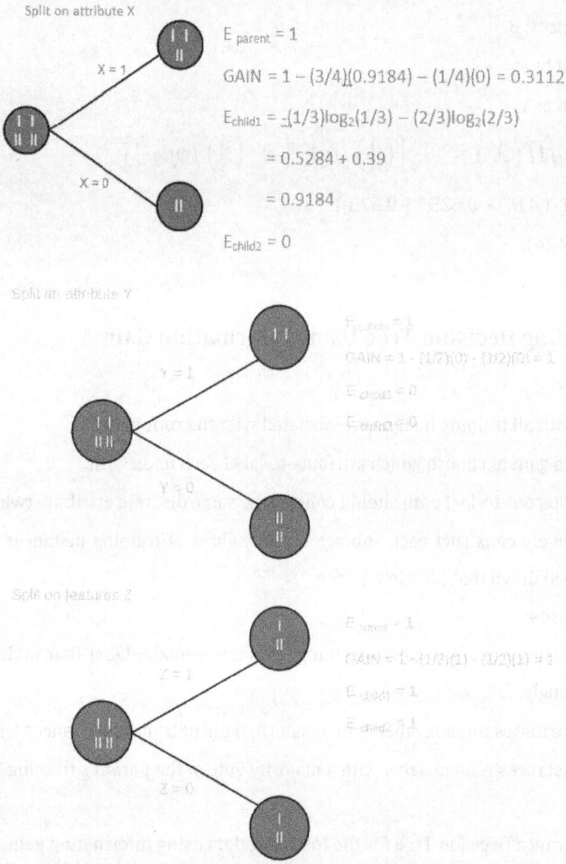

Fig. 3.3: To Build a Decision Tree Using Information Gain

From the above images we can see that the information gain is maximum when we make a split on feature Y. So, for the root node best suited feature is feature Y. Now we can see that while splitting the dataset by feature Y, the child contains pure subset of the target variable. So we don't need to further split the dataset.

The final tree for the above dataset would be in the following Fig.

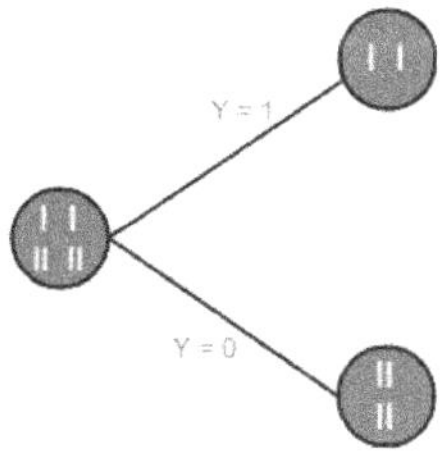

Gini Index

- Gini Index is a metric to measure how often a randomly chosen element would be incorrectly identified.
- It means an attribute with lower Gini index should be preferred.
- Sklearn supports "Gini" criteria for Gini Index and by default, it takes "gini" value.

The Formula for the calculation of the Gini Index is given below.

$$GiniIndex = 1 - \sum_j p_j^2$$

Example:

Lets consider the dataset in the diagram below and draw a decision tree using gini index.

Index	A	B	C	D	E
1	4.8	3.4	1.9	0.2	positive
2	5	3	1.6	1.2	positive
3	5	3.4	1.6	0.2	positive
4	5.2	3.5	1.5	0.2	positive
5	5.2	3.4	1.4	0.2	positive
6	4.7	3.2	1.6	0.2	positive
7	4.8	3.1	1.6	0.2	positive
8	5.4	3.4	1.5	0.4	positive
9	7	3.2	4.7	1.4	negative
10	6.4	3.2	4.7	1.5	negative
11	6.9	3.1	4.9	1.5	negative
12	5.5	2.3	4	1.3	negative
13	6.5	2.8	4.6	1.5	negative
14	5.7	2.8	4.5	1.3	negative
15	6.3	3.3	4.7	1.6	negative
16	4.9	2.4	3.3	1	negative

In the dataset above there are 5 attributes from which attribute E is the predicting feature which contains 2 (Positive & Negative) classes. We have an equal proportion for both the classes.

In Gini Index, we have to choose some random values to categorize each attribute. These values for this dataset are:

A	B	C	D
>= 5	>= 3.0	>= 4.2	>= 1.4
< 5	< 3.0	< 4.2	< 1.4

Calculating Gini Index for Var A:

Value >= 5: 12

Attribute A >= 5 & class = positive: $\frac{5}{12}$

Attribute A >= 5 & class = negative: $\frac{7}{12}$

Gini(5, 7) = 1 - $\left[\left(\frac{5}{12}\right)^2 + \left(\frac{7}{12}\right)^2\right] = 0.4860$

Value < 5: 4

Attribute A < 5 & class = positive: $\frac{3}{4}$

Attribute A < 5 & class = negative: $\frac{1}{4}$

Gini(3, 1) = 1 - $\left[\left(\frac{3}{4}\right)^2 + \left(\frac{1}{4}\right)^2\right] = 0.375$

By adding weight and sum each of the gini indices:

$$gini(Target, A) = \left(\frac{12}{16}\right) * (0.486) + \left(\frac{4}{16}\right) * (0.375) = 0.45825$$

Calculating Gini Index for Var B:

Value >= 3: 12

Attribute B >= 3 & class = positive: $\frac{8}{12}$

Attribute B >= 5 & class = negative: $\frac{4}{12}$

Gini(5, 7) = 1 - $\left[\left(\frac{8}{12}\right)^2 + \left(\frac{4}{12}\right)^2\right] = 0.4460$

Value < 3: 4

Attribute A < 3 & class = positive: $\frac{0}{4}$

Attribute A < 3 & class = negative: $\frac{4}{4}$

Gini(3, 1) = 1 - $\left[\left(\frac{0}{4}\right)^2 + \left(\frac{4}{4}\right)^2\right] = 1$

By adding weight and sum each of the gini indices:

$$gini(Target, B) = \left(\frac{12}{16}\right) * (0.446) + \left(\frac{0}{16}\right) * (0) = 0.3345$$

Using the same approach we can calculate the Gini index for C and D attributes.

	Positive	Negative
For A|>= 5.0	5	7
|<5	3	1

Ginin Index of A = 0.45825

	Positive	Negative
For B|>= 3.0	8	4
|< 3.0	0	4

Gini Index of B= 0.3345

	Positive	Negative
For C|>= 4.2	0	6
|< 4.2	8	2

Gini Index of C= 0.2

	Positive	Negative
For D|>= 1.4	0	5
|< 1.4	8	3

Gini Index of D = 0.273. The following Fig. shows the decision tree diagram.

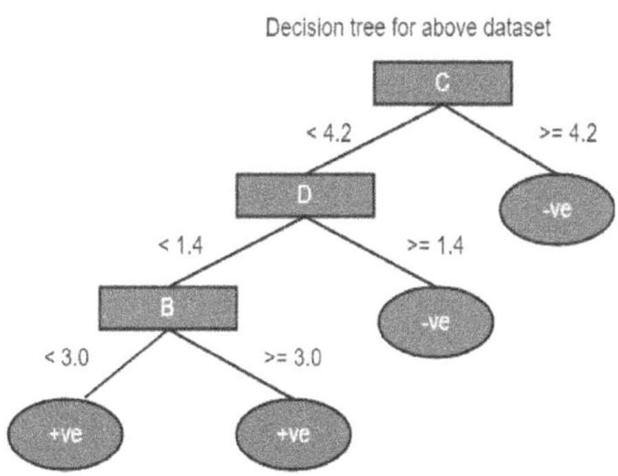

Fig. 3.4: Decision Tree Diagram

3.3. Types of Decision Tree Algorithms Are

1. **Iterative Dichotomiser 3 (ID3):** This algorithm uses Information Gain to decide which attribute is to be used classify the current subset of the data. For each level of the tree, information gain is calculated for the remaining data recursively.

2. **C4.5:** This algorithm is the successor of the ID3 algorithm. This algorithm uses either Information gain or Gain ratio to decide upon the classifying attribute. It is a direct improvement from the ID3 algorithm as it can handle both continuous and missing attribute values.
3. **Classification and Regression Tree (CART):** It is a dynamic learning algorithm which can produce a regression tree as well as a classification tree depending upon the dependent variable.

3.4. Decision Tree Representation

Decision Tree

Decision tree is the most powerful and popular tool for classification and prediction. A Decision tree is a flowchart like tree structure, where each internal node denotes a test on an attribute, each branch represents an outcome of the test, and each leaf node (terminal node) holds a class label. The following Fig. represents decision Tree diagram.

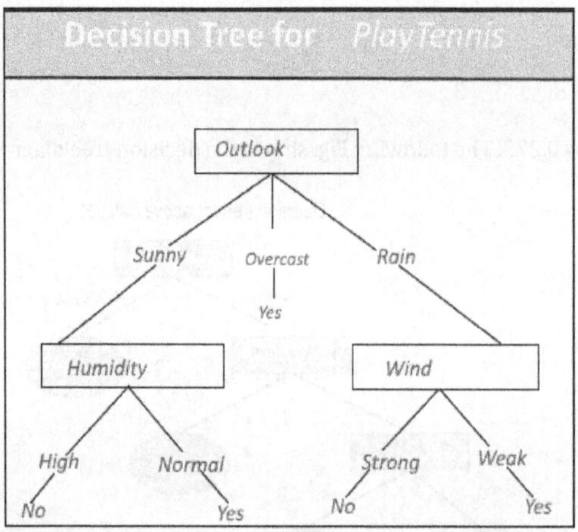

Fig. 3.5: A Decision Tree for the Concept Play Tennis

Construction of Decision Tree

A tree can be *"learned"* by splitting the source set into subsets based on an attribute value test. This process is repeated on each derived subset in a recursive manner called *recursive partitioning*. The recursion is completed when the subset at a node all has the same value of the target variable, or when splitting no longer adds value to the predictions. The construction of decision tree classifier does not require any domain knowledge or parameter setting, and therefore is appropriate for exploratory knowledge discovery. Decision trees can handle high dimensional data. In general decision tree classifier has good accuracy. Decision tree induction is a typical inductive approach to learn knowledge on classification.

Decision Tree Representation Explanation

Decision trees classify instances by sorting them down the tree from the root to some leaf node, which provides the classification of the instance. An instance is classified by starting at the root node of the tree, testing the attribute specified by this node, then moving down the tree branch corresponding to the value of the attribute as shown in the above figure. This process is then repeated for the sub tree rooted at the new node.

The decision tree in above figure classifies a particular morning according to whether it is suitable for playing tennis and returning the classification associated with the particular leaf. (in this case Yes or No).

For example, the instance

(Outlook = Rain, Temperature = Hot, Humidity = High, Wind = Strong)

Would be sorted down the leftmost branch of this decision tree and would therefore be classified as a negative instance.

In other words we can say that decision tree represent a disjunction of conjunctions of constraints on the attribute values of instances.

Outlook = Sunny ^ Humidity = Normal) v (Outlook = Overcast) v (Outlook = Rain ^ Wind = Weak)

Strengths and Weakness of Decision Tree Approach

The strengths of decision tree methods are:

Decision trees are able to generate understandable rules.

- Decision trees perform classification without requiring much computation.
- Decision trees are able to handle both continuous and categorical variables.
- Decision trees provide a clear indication of which fields are most important for prediction or classification.

The Weaknesses of Decision Tree Methods

Decision trees are less appropriate for estimation tasks where the goal is to predict the value of a continuous attribute.

- Decision trees are prone to errors in classification problems with many class and relatively small number of training examples.
- Decision tree can be computationally expensive to train. The process of growing a decision tree is computationally expensive. At each node, each candidate splitting field must be sorted before its best split can be found. In some algorithms, combinations of fields are used and a search must be made for optimal combining weights. Pruning algorithms can also be expensive since many candidate sub-trees must be formed and compared.

3.5. Decision Tree

It is a tool that has applications spanning several different areas. Decision trees can be used for classification as well as regression problems. The name itself suggests that it uses a flowchart like a tree structure to show the predictions that result from a series of feature-based splits. It starts with a root node and ends with a decision made by leaves.

Terminologies

Root Nodes – It is the node present at the beginning of a decision tree from this node the population starts dividing according to various features.

Decision Nodes – The nodes we get after splitting the root nodes are called Decision Node.

Leaf Nodes – The nodes where further splitting is not possible are called leaf nodes or terminal nodes.

Sub-tree – Just like a small portion of a graph is called sub-graph similarly a sub-section of this decision tree is called sub-tree.

Pruning – Is nothing but cutting down some nodes to stop overfitting. The fig. shows splitting.

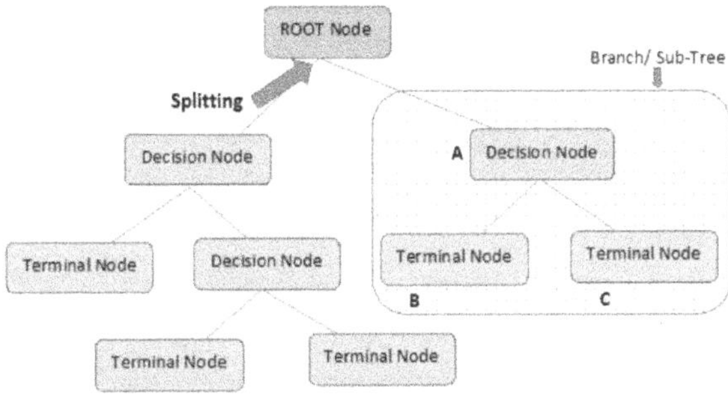

Fig. 3.6: Shows Splitting from Root Node

Example 1:

Day	Weather	Temperature	Humidity	Wind	Play?
1	Sunny	Hot	High	Weak	No
2	Cloudy	Hot	High	Weak	Yes
3	Sunny	Mild	Normal	Strong	Yes
4	Cloudy	Mild	High	Strong	Yes
5	Rainy	Mild	High	Strong	No
6	Rainy	Cool	Normal	Strong	No
7	Rainy	Mild	High	Weak	Yes
8	Sunny	Hot	High	Strong	No
9	Cloudy	Hot	Normal	Weak	Yes
10	Rainy	Mild	High	Strong	No

Decision trees are upside down which means the root is at the top and then this root is split into various several nodes. Decision trees are nothing but a bunch of if-else statements in layman terms. It checks if the condition is true and if it is then it goes to the next node attached to that decision.

In the below diagram the tree will first ask what is the weather? Is it sunny, cloudy, or rainy? If yes then it will go to the next feature which is humidity and wind. It will again check if there is a strong wind or weak, if it's a weak wind and it's rainy then the person may go and play. The Fig. Shows.

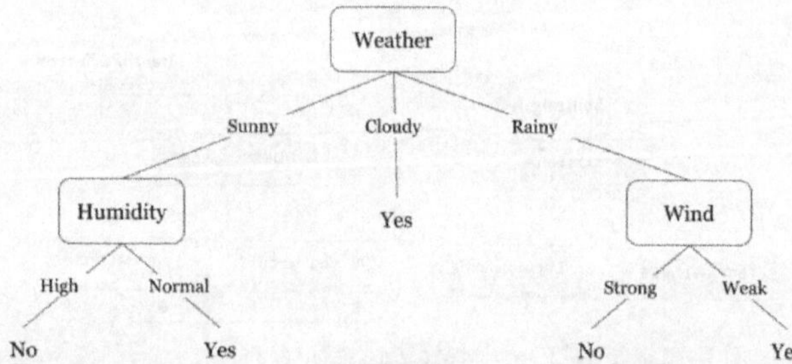

Fig. 3.7: Shows Whether We Can Play or not Depends up on the Condition

If the *weather is cloudy* then we must go to play.

The goal of machine learning is to decrease uncertainty or disorders from the dataset and for this, we use decision trees.

3.5.1. Entropy

- Entropy is nothing but the uncertainty in our dataset or measure of disorder. Let me explain this with the an example.
- Suppose you have a group of friends who decides which movie they can watch together on Sunday. There are 2 choices for movies, one is ***"Lucy"*** and the second is ***"Titanic"*** and now everyone has to tell their choice. After everyone gives their answer we see that *"Lucy" gets 4 votes* and *"Titanic" gets 5 votes*. Which movie do we watch now? Isn't it hard to choose 1 movie now because the votes for both the movies are somewhat equal.
- This is exactly what we call disorderness, there is an equal number of votes for both the movies, and we can't really decide which movie we should watch. It would have been much easier if the votes for "Lucy" were 8 and for "Titanic" it was 2. Here we could easily say that the majority of votes are for "Lucy" hence everyone will be watching this movie.
- In a decision tree, the output is mostly "yes" or "no"

The formula for Entropy is shown below:

$$E(S) = -p_{(+)}\log p_{(+)} - p_{(-)}\log p_{(-)}$$

Here p_+ is the probability of positive class.

P $_-$ is the probability of negative class

S - is the subset of the training example

Entropy basically measures the **impurity of a node**. Impurity is the degree of randomness; it tells how random our data is. A **pure sub-split** means that either you should be getting "yes", or you should be getting "no".

Suppose a *feature* has 8 "yes" and 4 "no" initially, after the first split the left node *gets 5 'yes' and 2 'no'* whereas right node *gets 3 'yes' and 2 'no'.*

here the split is not pure, why? Because we can still see some negative classes in both the nodes. In order to make a decision tree, we need to calculate the impurity of each split, and when the purity is 100%, we make it as a leaf node.

To check the impurity of feature 2 and feature 3 we will take the help for Entropy formula.

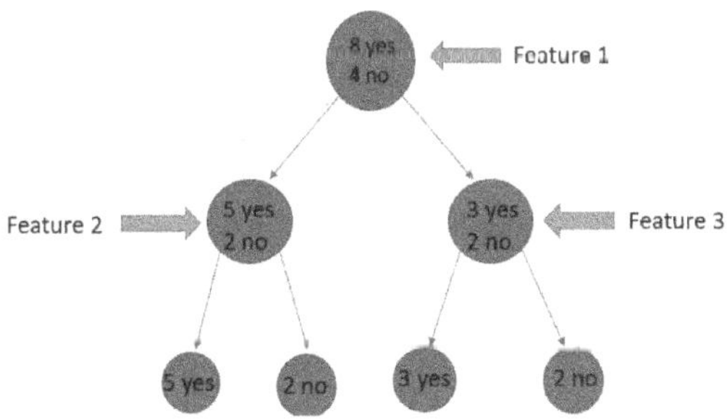

Fig. 3.8: Shows Features Classification

$$\Rightarrow -\left(\frac{5}{7}\right)log_2\left(\frac{5}{7}\right) - \left(\frac{2}{7}\right)log_2\left(\frac{2}{7}\right)$$

$$\Rightarrow -(0.71 * -0.49) - (0.28 * -1.83)$$

$$\Rightarrow -(-0.34) - (-0.51)$$

$$\Rightarrow 0.34 + 0.51$$

$$\Rightarrow 0.85$$

FOR FEATURE 3,

$$\Rightarrow -\left(\frac{3}{5}\right)log_2\left(\frac{3}{5}\right) - \left(\frac{2}{5}\right)log_2\left(\frac{2}{5}\right)$$

$$\Rightarrow -(0.6 * -0.73) - (0.4 * -1.32)$$

$$\Rightarrow -(-0.438) - (-0.528)$$

$$\Rightarrow 0.438 + 0.528$$

$$\Rightarrow 0.966$$

We can clearly see from the tree itself that left node has low entropy or more purity than right node since left node has a greater number of "yes" and it is easy to decide here.

Always remember that the higher the Entropy, the lower will be the purity and the higher will be the impurity the goal of machine learning is to decrease the uncertainty or impurity in the dataset, here by using the entropy we are getting the impurity of a particular node, we don't know if the parent entropy or the entropy of a particular node has decreased or not.

3.5.2. Information Gain

Information gain measures the reduction of uncertainty given some feature and it is also a deciding factor for which attribute should be selected as a decision node or root node.

$$Information\ Gain = E(Y) - E(Y|X)$$

It is just entropy of the full dataset – entropy of the dataset given some feature.

To understand this better let's consider an example:

Suppose our entire population has a total of 30 instances. The dataset is to predict whether the person will go to the gym or not. Let's say 16 people go to the gym and 14 people don't.

Now we have two features to predict whether he/she will go to the gym or not.

Feature 1 is **"Energy"** which takes two values *"high" and "low"*

Feature 2 is **"Motivation"** which takes 3 values *"No motivation", "Neutral" and "Highly motivated".*

Let's see how our decision tree will be made using these 2 features. We'll use information gain to decide which feature should be the root node and which feature should be placed after the split.

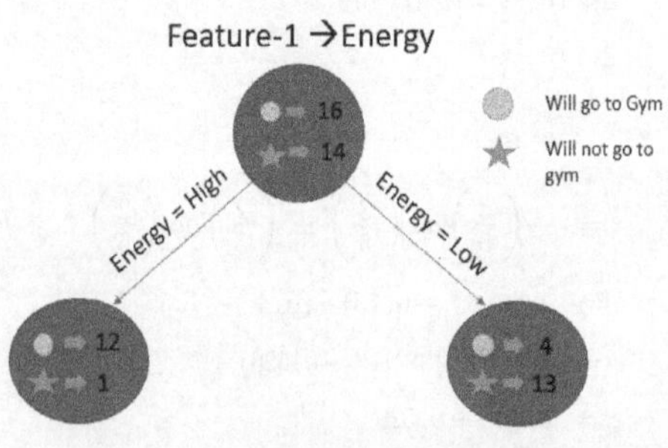

Fig. 3.9: Decision Tree based on Feature 1

$$E(Parent) = -\left(\frac{16}{30}\right)\log_2\left(\frac{16}{30}\right) - \left(\frac{14}{30}\right)\log_2\left(\frac{14}{30}\right) \approx 0.99$$

$$E(Parent|Energy = \text{"high"}) = -\left(\frac{12}{13}\right)\log_2\left(\frac{12}{13}\right) - \left(\frac{1}{13}\right)\log_2\left(\frac{1}{13}\right) \approx 0.39$$

$$E(Parent|Energy = \text{"low"}) = -\left(\frac{4}{17}\right)\log_2\left(\frac{4}{17}\right) - \left(\frac{13}{17}\right)\log_2\left(\frac{13}{17}\right) \approx 0.79$$

To see the weighted average of entropy of each node we will do as follows:

$$E(Parent|Energy) = \frac{13}{30} * 0.39 + \frac{17}{30} * 0.79 = 0.62$$

Now we have the value of E(Parent) and E(Parent|Energy), information gain will be:

$$\begin{aligned} Information\ Gain &= E(parent) - E(parent|energy) \\ &= 0.99 - 0.62 \\ &= 0.37 \end{aligned}$$

Our parent entropy was near 0.99 and after looking at this value of information gain, we can say that the entropy of the dataset will decrease by 0.37 if we make "Energy" as our root node.

Similarly, we will do this with the other feature "Motivation" and calculate its information gain.

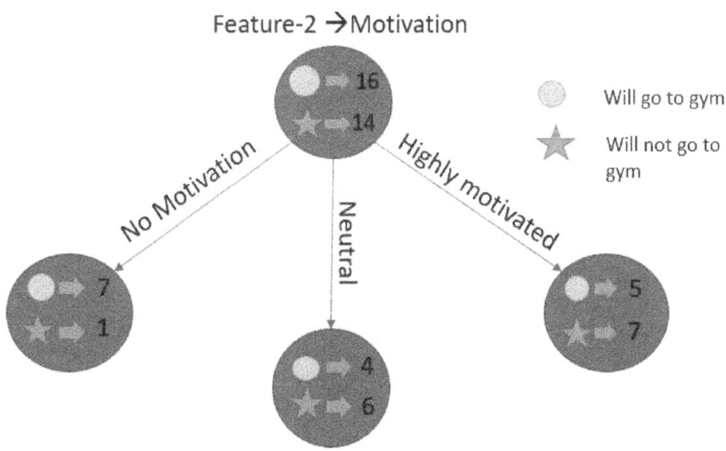

Fig. 3.10: Decision Tree based on Feature

Let's calculate the entropy here:

$$E(Parent) = 0.99$$

$$E\left(Parent|Motivation = "No\ motivation"\right) = -\left(\frac{7}{8}\right)log_2\left(\frac{7}{8}\right) - \frac{1}{8}\log_2\left(\frac{1}{8}\right) = 0.54$$

$$E(Parent|Motivation = "Neutral") = -\left(\frac{4}{10}\right)log_2\left(\frac{4}{10}\right) - \left(\frac{6}{10}\right)\log_2\left(\frac{6}{10}\right) = 0.97$$

$$E(Parent|Motivation = "Highly\ motivated") = -\left(\frac{5}{12}\right)log_2\left(\frac{5}{12}\right) - \left(\frac{7}{12}\right)\log_2\left(\frac{7}{12}\right) = 0.98$$

To see the weighted average of entropy of each node we will do as follows:

$$E(Parent|Motivation) = \frac{8}{30} * 0.54 + \frac{10}{30} * 0.97 + \frac{12}{30} * 0.98 = 0.86$$

Now we have the value of E(Parent) and E(Parent|Motivation), information gain will be:

$$Information\ Gain = E(Parent) - E(Parent|Motivation)$$
$$= 0.99 - 0.86$$
$$= 0.13$$

We now see that the "Energy" feature gives more reduction which is 0.37 than the "Motivation" feature. Hence we will select the feature which has the highest information gain and then split the node based on that feature.

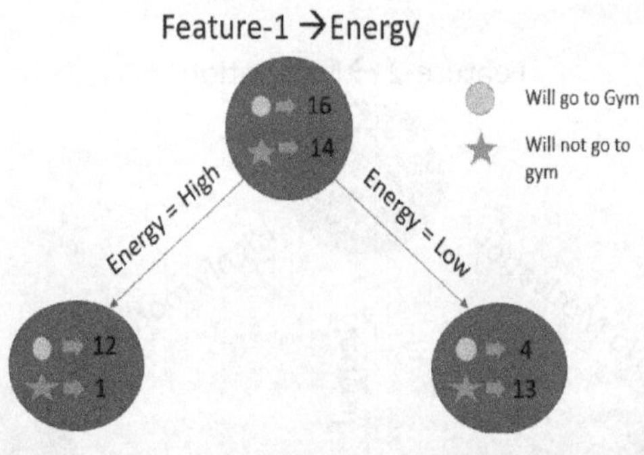

Fig. 3.11: Decision Tree based on Feature 1 with Binary Classification

In this example "Energy" will be our root node and we'll do the same for sub-nodes. Here we can see that when the energy is "high" the entropy is low and hence we can say a person will definitely go to the gym if he has high energy, but what if the energy is low? We will again split the node based on the new feature which is "Motivation".

Usually, real-world datasets have a large number of features, which will result in a large number of splits, which in turn gives a huge tree. Such trees take time to build and can lead to overfitting. That means the tree will give very good accuracy on the training dataset but will give bad accuracy in test data.

There are many ways to tackle this problem through hyperparameter tuning. We can set the maximum depth of our decision tree using the ***max_depth*** parameter. The more the value of ***max_depth***, the more complex your tree will be. The training error will off-course decrease if we increase the ***max_depth*** value but when our test data comes into the picture, we will get a very bad accuracy. Hence you need a value that will not overfit as well as underfit our data and for this, you can use GridSearchCV.

Another way is to set the minimum number of samples for each spilt. It is denoted by ***min_samples_split***. Here we specify the minimum number of samples required to do a spilt. For example, we can use a minimum of 10 samples to reach a decision. That means if a node has less than 10 samples then using this parameter, we can stop the further splitting of this node and make it a leaf node.

There are more hyper parameters such as:

min_samples_leaf – represents the minimum number of samples required to be in the leaf node. The more you increase the number, the more is the possibility of overfitting.

max_features – it helps us decide what number of features to consider when looking for the best split.

Pruning

It is another method that can help us avoid overfitting. It helps in improving the performance of the tree by cutting the nodes or sub-nodes which are not significant. It removes the branches which have very low importance.

There are mainly 2 ways for pruning:

i. **Pre-pruning** – we can stop growing the tree earlier, which means we can prune/remove/cut a node if it has low importance **while growing** the tree.

ii. **Post-pruning** – once our **tree is built to its depth**, we can start pruning the nodes based on their significance.

3.6. Decision Tree Classification Algorithm

- Decision Tree is a Supervised learning technique that can be used for both classification and Regression problems, but mostly it is preferred for solving Classification problems. It is a tree-structured classifier, where internal nodes represent the features of a dataset, branches represent the decision rules and each leaf node represents the outcome.
- In a Decision tree, there are two nodes, which are the Decision Node and Leaf Node. Decision nodes are used to make any decision and have multiple branches, whereas Leaf nodes are the output of those decisions and do not contain any further branches.
- The decisions or the test are performed on the basis of features of the given dataset.
- *It is a graphical representation for getting all the possible solutions to a problem/decision based on given conditions.*
- It is called a decision tree because, similar to a tree, it starts with the root node, which expands on further branches and constructs a tree-like structure.
- In order to build a tree, we use the CART algorithm, which stands for Classification and Regression Tree algorithm.
- A decision tree simply asks a question, and based on the answer (Yes/No), it further split the tree into subtrees.
- Below diagram explains the general structure of a decision tree:

A decision tree can contain categorical data (YES/NO) as well as numeric data.

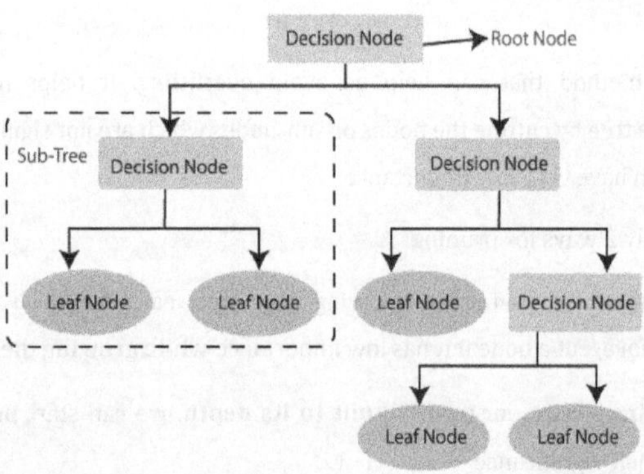

Fig. 3.12: Shows Decision Tree can Contain Categorical Data

Why use Decision Trees?

There are various algorithms in Machine learning, so choosing the best algorithm for the given dataset and problem is the main point to remember while creating a machine learning model. Below are the two reasons for using the Decision tree:

- Decision Trees usually mimic human thinking ability while making a decision, so it is easy to understand.
- The logic behind the decision tree can be easily understood because it shows a tree-like structure.

Decision Tree Terminologies

- **Root Node:** Root node is from where the decision tree starts. It represents the entire dataset, which further gets divided into two or more homogeneous sets.
- **Leaf Node:** Leaf nodes are the final output node, and the tree cannot be segregated further after getting a leaf node.
- **Splitting:** Splitting is the process of dividing the decision node/root node into sub-nodes according to the given conditions.
- **Branch/Sub Tree:** A tree formed by splitting the tree.
- **Pruning:** Pruning is the process of removing the unwanted branches from the tree.
- **Parent/Child node:** The root node of the tree is called the parent node, and other nodes are called the child nodes.

How does the Decision Tree Algorithm Work?

In a decision tree, for predicting the class of the given dataset, the algorithm starts from the root node of the tree. This algorithm compares the values of root attribute with the record (real dataset) attribute and, based on the comparison, follows the branch and jumps to the next node.

For the next node, the algorithm again compares the attribute value with the other sub-nodes and move further. It continues the process until it reaches the leaf node of the tree. The complete process can be better understood using the below algorithm:

1. It begins with the original set S as the root node.
2. On each iteration of the algorithm, it iterates through the very unused attribute of the set S and calculates **Entropy(H)** and **Information gain(IG)** of this attribute.
3. It then selects the attribute which has the smallest Entropy or Largest Information gain.

4. The set S is then split by the selected attribute to produce a subset of the data.
5. The algorithm continues to recur on each subset, considering only attributes never selected before.

Example: Suppose there is a candidate who has a job offer and wants to decide whether he should accept the offer or Not. So, to solve this problem, the decision tree starts with the root node (Salary attribute by ASM). The root node splits further into the next decision node (distance from the office) and one leaf node based on the corresponding labels. The next decision node further gets split into one decision node (Cab facility) and one leaf node. Finally, the decision node splits into two leaf nodes (Accepted offers and Declined offer). Consider the below diagram:

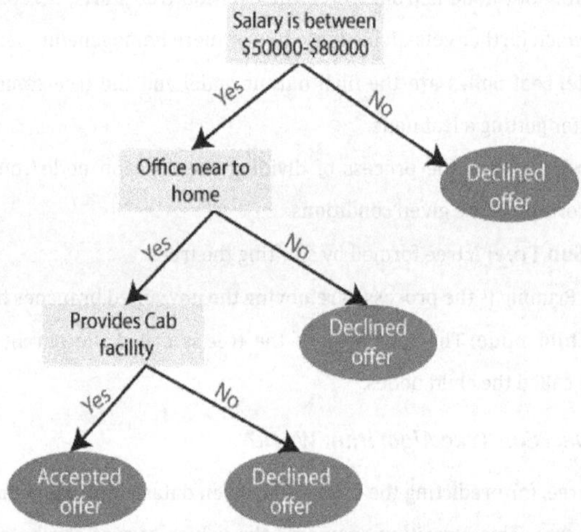

Fig. 3.13: Shows Decision Tree Example (Salary Parameter)

Attribute Selection Measures

While implementing a Decision tree, the main issue arises that how to select the best attribute for the root node and for sub-nodes. So, to solve such problems there is a technique which is called as **Attribute selection measure or ASM.** By this measurement, we can easily select the best attribute for the nodes of the tree. There are two popular techniques for ASM, which are:

- **Information Gain**
- **Gini Index**

1. Information Gain:

- Information gain is the measurement of changes in entropy after the segmentation of a dataset based on an attribute.
- It calculates how much information a feature provides us about a class.
- According to the value of information gain, we split the node and build the decision tree.
- A decision tree algorithm always tries to maximize the value of information gain, and a node/attribute having the highest information gain is split first. It can be calculated using the below formula:

1. Information Gain= Entropy(S) - [(Weighted Avg) *Entropy (each feature)

Entropy: Entropy is a metric to measure the impurity in a given attribute. It specifies randomness in data. Entropy can be calculated as:

Entropy(s)= -P(yes)log2 P(yes)- P(no) log2 P(no)

Where,

- **S= Total number of samples**
- **P(yes)= probability of yes**
- **P(no)= probability of no**

2. Gini Index:

   - Gini index is a measure of impurity or purity used while creating a decision tree in the CART (Classification and Regression Tree) algorithm.
   - An attribute with the low Gini index should be preferred as compared to the high Gini index.
   - It only creates binary splits, and the CART algorithm uses the Gini index to create binary splits.
   - Gini index can be calculated using the below formula:

$$\text{Gini Index} = 1 - \sum_j P_j^2$$

Pruning: Getting an Optimal Decision tree.

Pruning is a process of deleting the unnecessary nodes from a tree in order to get the optimal decision tree.

A too-large tree increases the risk of overfitting, and a small tree may not capture all the important features of the dataset. Therefore, a technique that decreases the size of the learning tree without reducing accuracy is known as Pruning. There are mainly two types of tree **pruning** technology used:

- **Cost Complexity Pruning**
- **Reduced Error Pruning**

Advantages of the Decision Tree

- It is simple to understand as it follows the same process which a human follow while making any decision in real-life.
- It can be very useful for solving decision-related problems.
- It helps to think about all the possible outcomes for a problem.
- There is less requirement of data cleaning compared to other algorithms.

Disadvantages of the Decision Tree

- The decision tree contains lots of layers, which makes it complex.
- It may have an overfitting issue, which can be resolved using the **Random Forest algorithm.**
- For more class labels, the computational complexity of the decision tree may increase.

3.7. Hypothesis Space Search in Decision Tree Learning

In most supervised machine learning algorithm, our main goal is to find out a possible hypothesis from the hypothesis space that could possibly map out the inputs to the proper outputs.

The following figure shows the common method to find out the possible hypothesis from the Hypothesis space:

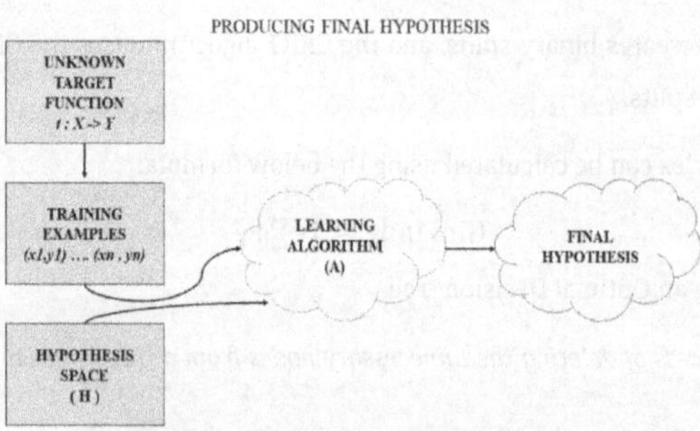

Fig. 3.14: Producing Final Hypothesis

Hypothesis Space (H)

Hypothesis space is the set of all the possible legal hypothesis. This is the set from which the machine learning algorithm would determine the best possible (only one) which would best describe the target function or the outputs.

Hypothesis (h)

A hypothesis is a function that best describes the target in supervised machine learning. The hypothesis that an algorithm would come up depends upon the data and also depends upon the restrictions and bias that we have imposed on the data. To better understand the Hypothesis Space and Hypothesis consider the following coordinate that shows the distribution of some data:

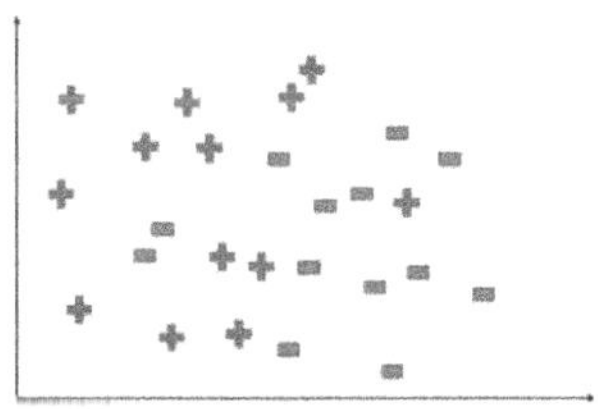

Fig. 3.15: Distribution of Data

Say suppose we have test data for which we have to determine the outputs or results. The test data is as shown below:

We can predict the outcomes by dividing the coordinate as shown below:

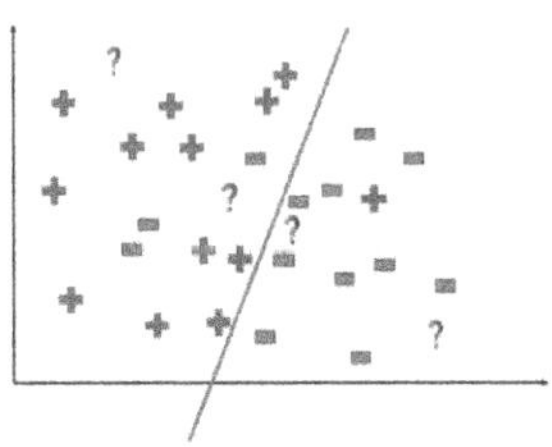

So the test data would yield the following result:

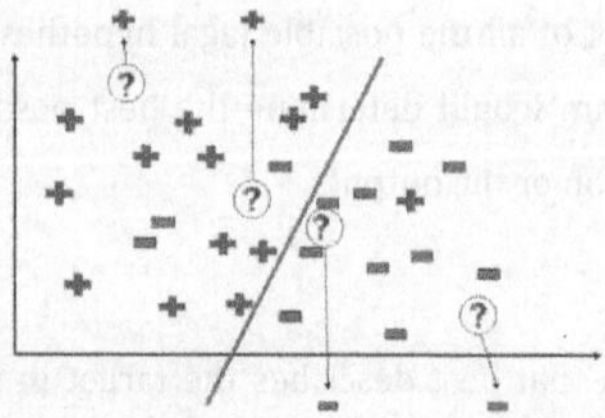

Fig. 3.16: Shows Classification Before / After

But note here that we could have divided the coordinate plane as:

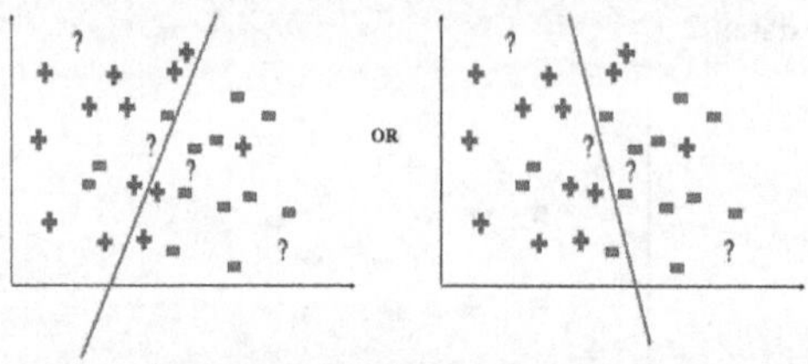

Fig. 3.17: Divided the Coordinate Plane

The way in which the coordinate would be divided depends on the data, algorithm and constraints.

- All these legal possible ways in which we can divide the coordinate plane to predict the outcome of the test data composes of the Hypothesis Space.
- Each individual possible way is known as the hypothesis.

Hence, in this example the hypothesis space would be like:

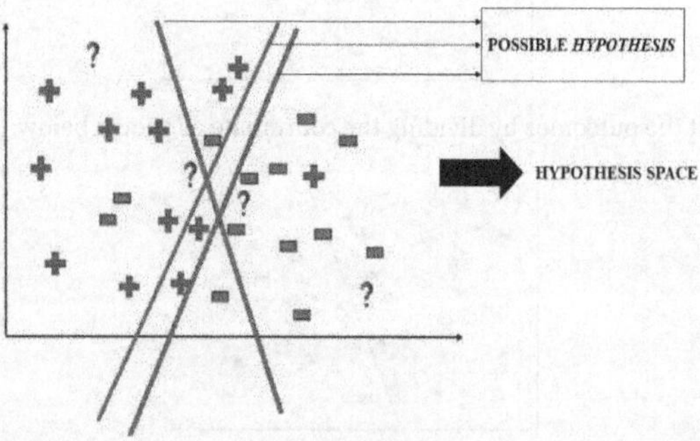

Fig. 3.18: Possible Hypothesis

3.8. Best Hypothesis Search

The idea behind the current best hypothesis search is to maintain a single hypothesis and to adjust it as a new example arise in order to maintain consistency.

The hypothesis space **H** is a set of hypothesis that learning algorithm is designed to entertain. The learning algorithm believes that one hypothesis is correct, that is, it believes the sentence:

$h_1 \vee h_2 \vee h_3 \vee \ldots \vee h_n$

Hypothesis that are not consistent with the example can be ruled out.

There are two possible ways to be inconsistent with an example:

1. False negative: In this hypothesis, the example should be negative but in fact it is positive.
2. False positive: In this type of hypothesis, the example should be positive but in fact it is negative.

if the example is consistent with the hypothesis then do not change it. If the example is false negative then, generalize the hypothesis and if the example is false positive then specialize the hypothesis.

```
function CURRENT-BEST-LEARNING (examples) return a hypothesis
H<- any hypothesis consistent with the first example in examples
for each remaining example in examples do
if e is a false positive for H then
H<- choose a specialization of H is consistent with examples
else if e is a false negative for H then
H<- choose a generalization of H is consistent with examples
if no consistent specialization/generalization can be found
then fail
return H
```

The current best hypothesis learning algorithm searches for a consistent hypothesis and backtracks the algorithm when no solution is found.

Notice that each time, we consider generalizing or specializing the hypothesis, we must check for consistency with other examples, because an arbitrary increase or decrease in the extension might include or exclude previously seen negative or positive examples.

Generalization and specialization are defined as operations that change the extension of hypothesis.

The current best hypothesis algorithm and its variants have been used in many learning systems.

Disadvantages

Checking all the previous instances over again for each modification is very expensive.

The search process may involve a great deal of backtracking. Hypothesis space can be a doubly exponentially large place.

The more general than and "more specific than" relations between hypothesis provide logical structure on hypothesis space that makes efficient search possible.

3.9. Inductive Learning Algorithm

Inductive Learning Algorithm (ILA) is an iterative and inductive machine learning algorithm which is used for generating a set of a classification rule, which produces rules of the form "IF-THEN", for a set of examples, producing rules at each iteration and appending to the set of rules.

Basic Idea

There are basically two methods for knowledge extraction firstly from domain experts and then with machine learning.

For a very large amount of data, the domain experts are not very useful and reliable. So we move towards the machine learning approach for this work.

To use machine learning One method is to replicate the experts logic in the form of algorithms but this work is very tedious, time taking and expensive.

So we move towards the inductive algorithms which itself generate the strategy for performing a task and need not instruct separately at each step.

Need of ILA in Presence of other Machine Learning Algorithms

The ILA is a new algorithm which was needed even when other reinforcement learnings like ID3 and AQ were available.

- The need was due to the pitfalls which were present in the previous algorithms, one of the major pitfalls was lack of generalization of rules.

- The ID3 and AQ used the decision tree production method which was too specific which were difficult to analyse and was very slow to perform for basic short classification problems.
- The decision tree-based algorithm was unable to work for a new problem if some attributes are missing.
- The ILA uses the method of production of a general set of rules instead of decision trees, which overcome the above problems.

3.10. The Inductive Learning Algorithm (ILA)

General requirements at start of the algorithm:

1. List the examples in the form of a table 'T' where each row corresponds to an example and each column contains an attribute value.
2. Create a set of m training examples, each example composed of k attributes and a class attribute with n possible decisions.
3. Create a rule set, R, having the initial value false.
4. Initially all rows in the table are unmarked.

Steps in the algorithm:

Step 1:

Divide the table 'T' containing m examples into n sub-tables (t1, t2,.....tn). One table for each possible value of the class attribute. (repeat steps 2-8 for each sub-table).

Step 2:

Initialize the attribute combination count 'j' = 1.

Step 3:

For the sub-table on which work is going on, divide the attribute list into distinct combinations, each combination with 'j' distinct attributes.

Step 4:

For each combination of attributes, count the number of occurrences of attribute values that appear under the same combination of attributes in unmarked rows of the sub-table under consideration, and at the same time, not appears under the same combination of attributes of other sub-tables. Call the first combination with the maximum number of occurrences the max-combination 'MAX'.

Step 5:

If 'MAX' = = null, increase 'j' by 1 and go to Step 3.

Step 6:

Mark all rows of the sub-table where working, in which the values of 'MAX' appear, as classified.

Step 7:

Add a rule (IF attribute = "XYZ" –> THEN decision is YES/ NO) to R whose left-hand side will have attribute names of the 'MAX' with their values separated by AND, and its right-hand side contains the decision attribute value associated with the sub-table.

Step 8:

If all rows are marked as classified, then move on to process another sub-table and go to Step 2. else, go to Step 4. If no sub-tables are available, exit with the set of rules obtained till then.

An Example Showing the Use of ILA

Suppose an example set having attributes Place type, weather, location, decision and seven examples, our task is to generate a set of rules that under what condition what is the decision.

Example 1:

Example no.	Place type	weather	location	decision
I)	hilly	winter	kullu	Yes
II)	mountain	windy	Mumbai	No
III)	mountain	windy	Shimla	Yes
IV)	beach	windy	Mumbai	No
V)	beach	warm	goa	Yes
VI)	beach	windy	goa	No
VII)	beach	warm	Shimla	Yes

Step 1

Subset 1

S. no	place type	weather	location	decision
1	hilly	winter	kullu	Yes
2	mountain	windy	Shimla	Yes
3	beach	warm	goa	Yes
4	beach	warm	Shimla	Yes

Subset 2

s.no	place type	weather	location	decision
5	mountain	windy	Mumbai	No
6	beach	windy	Mumbai	No
7	beach	windy	goa	No

Step (2-8) at iteration 1

Row 3 & 4 column weather is selected and row 3 & 4 are marked.

The rule is added to R IF weather is warm then a decision is yes.

At iteration 2

Row 1 column place type is selected and row 1 is marked.

The rule is added to R IF place type is hilly then the decision is yes.

At iteration 3

Row 2 column location is selected and row 2 is marked.

The rule is added to R IF location is Shimla then the decision is yes.

At iteration 4

Row 5&6 column location is selected and row 5&6 are marked.

The rule is added to R IF location is Mumbai then a decision is no.

At iteration 5

Row 7 column place type & the weather is selected and row 7 is marked.

Rule is added to R IF place type is beach AND weather is windy then the decision is no.

Finally we get the rule set:-

Rule Set

- **Rule 1:** IF the weather is warm THEN the decision is yes.
- **Rule 2:** IF place type is hilly THEN the decision is yes.
- **Rule 3:** IF location is Shimla THEN the decision is yes.
- **Rule 4:** IF location is Mumbai THEN the decision is no.
- **Rule 5:** IF place type is beach AND the weather is windy THEN the decision is no.

3.11. Decision Tree Induction

Decision Tree is a supervised learning method used in data mining for classification and regression methods. It is a tree that helps us in decision-making purposes. The decision tree creates classification or regression models as a tree structure. It separates a data set into smaller subsets, and at the same time, the decision tree is steadily developed. The final tree is a tree with the decision nodes and leaf nodes. A decision node has at least two branches. The leaf nodes show a classification or decision. We can't accomplish more split on leaf nodes-The uppermost decision node in a tree that relates to the best predictor called the root node. Decision trees can deal with both categorical and numerical data.

Key Factors

Entropy

Entropy refers to a common way to measure impurity. In the decision tree, it measures the randomness or impurity in data sets.

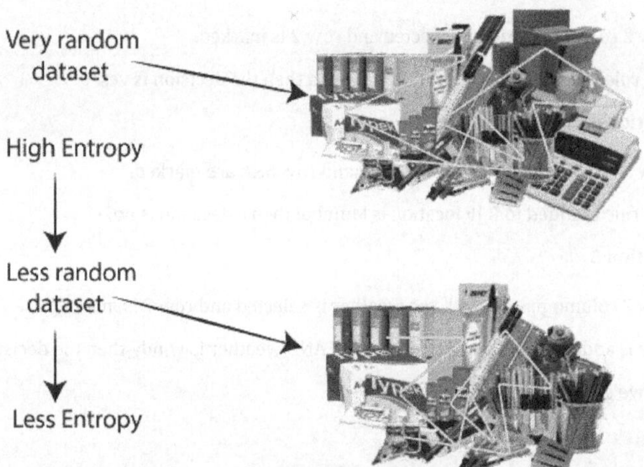

Fig. 3.19: Shows Impurity in Data Sets

Information Gain

Information Gain refers to the decline in entropy after the dataset is split. It is also called **Entropy Reduction**. Building a decision tree is all about discovering attributes that return the highest data gain.

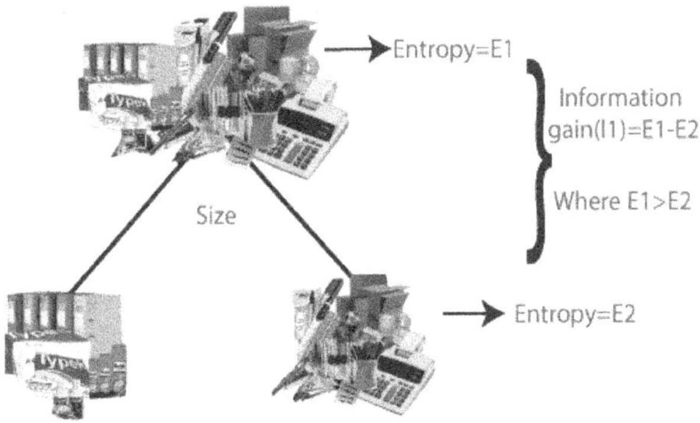

Fig. 3.20: Shows Decision Trees-Entropy

In short, a decision tree is just like a flow chart diagram with the terminal nodes showing decisions. Starting with the dataset, we can measure the entropy to find a way to segment the set until the data belongs to the same class.

Why are decision trees useful?

It enables us to analyze the possible consequences of a decision thoroughly.

It provides us a framework to measure the values of outcomes and the probability of accomplishing them.

It helps us to make the best decisions based on existing data and best speculations.

In other words, we can say that a decision tree is a hierarchical tree structure that can be used to split an extensive collection of records into smaller sets of the class by implementing a sequence of simple decision rules. A decision tree model comprises a set of rules for portioning a huge heterogeneous population into smaller, more homogeneous, or mutually exclusive classes. The attributes of the classes can be any variables from nominal, ordinal, binary, and quantitative values, in contrast, the classes must be a qualitative type, such as categorical or ordinal or binary. In brief, the given data of attributes together with its class, a decision tree creates a set of rules that can be used to identify the class.

One rule is implemented after another, resulting in a hierarchy of segments within a segment. The hierarchy is known as the **tree**, and each segment is called a **node**. With each progressive division, the members from the subsequent sets become more and more similar to each other. Hence, the algorithm used to build a decision tree is referred to as recursive partitioning. The algorithm is known as **CART** (Classification and Regression Trees).

Consider the given example of a factory where,

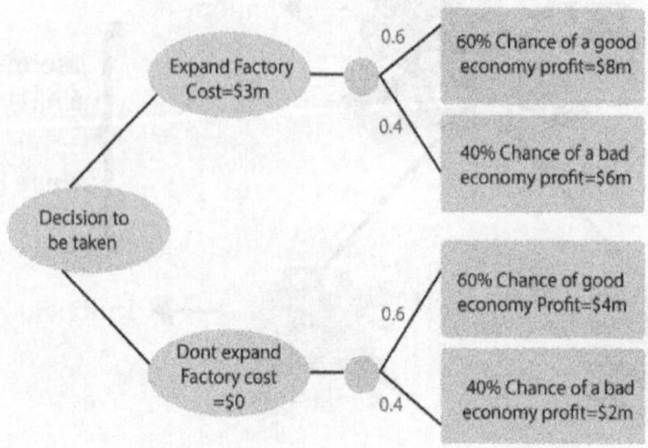

Fig. 3.21: Shows Decision Tree Example Profit Rate

Expanding factor costs $3 million, the probability of a good economy is 0.6 (60%), which leads to $8 million profit, and the probability of a bad economy is 0.4 (40%), which leads to $6 million profit.

Not expanding factor with 0$ cost, the probability of a good economy is 0.6(60%), which leads to $4 million profit, and the probability of a bad economy is 0.4, which leads to $2 million profit.

The management teams need to take a data-driven decision to expand or not based on the given data.

Net Expand = (0.6 *8 + 0.4*6) - 3 = $4.2M

Net Not Expand = (0.6*4 + 0.4*2) - 0 = $3M

$4.2M > $3M, therefore the factory should be expanded.

Decision tree Algorithm

The decision tree algorithm may appear long, but it is quite simply the basis algorithm techniques is as follows:

The **algorithm** is based on three parameters: **D, attribute_list, and Attribute_selection_method.**

Generally, we refer to **D** as a **data partition.**

Initially, **D** is the entire set of **training tuples** and their related **class levels** (input training data).

The parameter **attribute_list** is a set of **attributes** defining the tuples.

Attribute_selection_method specifies a **heuristic process** for choosing the attribute that "best" discriminates the given tuples according to **class.**

Attribute_selection_method process applies an **attribute selection measure**.

Advantages of Using Decision Trees

- A decision tree does not need scaling of information.
- Missing values in data also do not influence the process of building a choice tree to any considerable extent.
- A decision tree model is automatic and simple to explain to the technical team as well as stakeholders.
- Compared to other algorithms, decision trees need less exertion for data preparation during pre-processing.
- A decision tree does not require a standardization of data.

3.12. Issues in Decision Tree Learning

1. Avoiding Overfitting the Data

When we are designing a machine learning model, a model is said to be a good machine learning model, if it generalizes any new input data from the problem domain in a proper way. This helps us to make predictions in the future data, that data model has never seen. Now, suppose we want to check how well our machine learning model learns and generalizes to the new data.

A machine learning algorithm is said to be overfitted, when we train it with a lot of data. When a model gets trained with so much of data, it starts learning from the noise and inaccurate data entries in our data set. Then the model does not categorize the data correctly, because of too much of details and noise. The causes of overfitting are the non-parametric and non-linear methods.

2. Incorporating Continuous-Valued Attributes

Our initial definition of ID3 is restricted to attributes that take on a discrete set of values.

1. The target attribute whose value is predicted by learned tree must be discrete valued.
2. The attributes tested in the decision nodes of the tree must also be discrete valued.

This second restriction can easily be removed so that continuous-valued decision attributes can be incorporated into the learned tree. For an attribute A that is continuous-valued, the algorithm can dynamically create a new Boolean attribute A, that is true if $A < c$ and false otherwise. The only question is how to select the best value for the threshold c.

3. Alternative Measures for Selecting Attributes

There is a natural bias in the information gain measure that favors attributes with many values over those with few values.

- As an extreme example, consider the attribute Date, which has a very large number of possible values. What is wrong with the attribute Date? Simply put, it has so many possible values that it is bound to separate the training examples into very small subsets. Because of this, it will have a very high information gain relative to the training examples.
- However, having very high information gain, its a very poor predictor of the target function over unseen instances.

Alternate Measure-1

One alternative measure that has been used successfully is the gain ratio (Quinlan 1986). The gain ratio measure penalizes attributes such as Date by incorporating a term, called split information that is sensitive to how broadly and uniformly the attribute splits the data:

- Entropy (S), Attribute (I), Avg. Information
- Gain vale

4. Handling Missing Attribute Values

In certain cases, the available data may be missing values for some attributes. For example, in a medical domain in which we wish to predict patient outcome based on various laboratory tests, it may be that the Blood-Test-Result is available only for a subset of the patients. In such cases, it is common to estimate the missing attribute value based on other examples for which this attribute has a known value.

Method-1

One strategy for dealing with the missing attribute value is to assign it the value that is most common among training examples at node n. Alternatively, we might assign it the most common value among examples at node n that have the classification c(x). The elaborated training example using this estimated value for A(x) can then be used directly by the existing decision tree learning algorithm.

5. Handling Attributes with Differing Costs

In some learning tasks the instance attributes may have associated costs. For example, in learning to classify medical diseases we might describe patients in terms of attributes such as Temperature, BiopsyResult, Pulse, BloodTestResults, etc. These attributes vary significantly in their costs, both in terms of monetary cost and cost to patient comfort.

In such tasks, we would prefer decision trees that use low-cost attributes where possible, relying on high-cost attributes only when needed to produce reliable classifications.

ID3 can be modified to consider attribute costs by introducing a cost term into the attribute selection measure. For example, we might divide the Gain by the cost of the attribute, so that lower-cost attributes would be preferred. While such cost-sensitive measures do not guarantee finding an optimal cost-sensitive decision tree, they do bias the search in favour of low-cost attributes.

CHAPTER 4

ARTIFICIAL NEURAL NETWORK (ANN)

4.1. Artificial Neural Network

The term "Artificial neural network" refers to a biologically inspired sub-field of artificial intelligence modeled after the brain. An Artificial neural network is usually a computational network based on biological neural networks that construct the structure of the human brain. Similar to a human brain has neurons interconnected to each other, artificial neural networks also have neurons that are linked to each other in various layers of the networks. These neurons are known as nodes.

Artificial neural network tutorial covers all the aspects related to the artificial neural network. In this tutorial, we will discuss ANNs, Adaptive resonance theory, Kohonen self-organizing map, Building blocks, unsupervised learning, Genetic algorithm, etc.

What is Artificial Neural Network?

The term "**Artificial Neural Network**" is derived from Biological neural networks that develop the structure of a human brain. Similar to the human brain that has neurons interconnected to one another, artificial neural networks also have neurons that are interconnected to one another in various layers of the networks. These neurons are known as nodes.

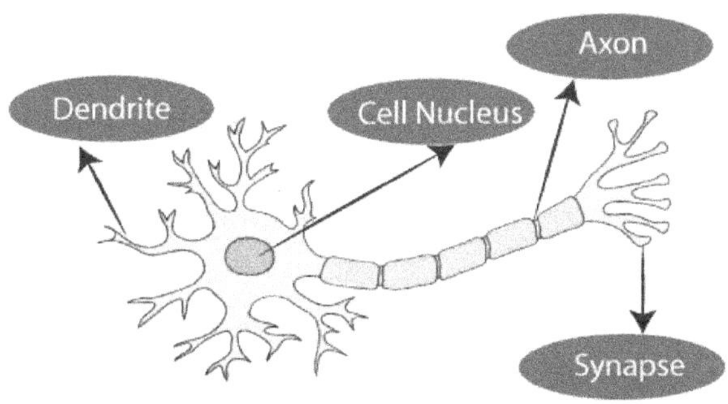

Fig. 4.1: The Typical Diagram of Biological Neural Network

The given figure illustrates the typical diagram of Biological Neural Network.

The typical Artificial Neural Network looks something like the given figure.

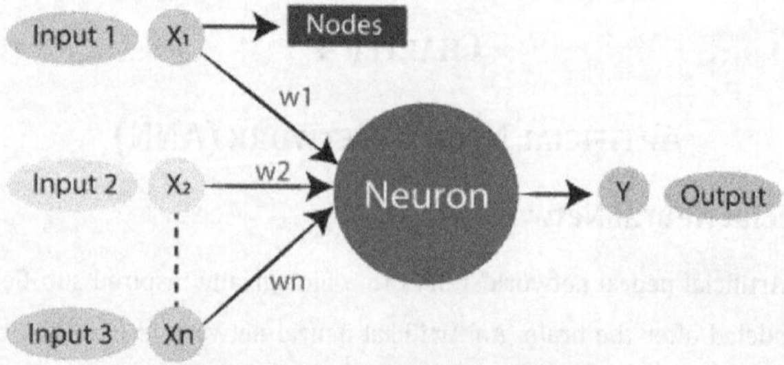

Fig. 4.2: Biological Neural Network Represent

Dendrites from Biological Neural Network represent inputs in Artificial Neural Networks, cell nucleus represents Nodes, synapse represents Weights, and Axon represents Output.

Relationship between Biological neural network and artificial neural network:

Biological Neural Network	Artificial Neural Network
Dendrites	Inputs
Cell nucleus	Nodes
Synapse	Weights
Axon	Output

An **Artificial Neural Network** in the field of **Artificial intelligence** where it attempts to mimic the network of neurons makes up a human brain so that computers will have an option to understand things and make decisions in a human-like manner. The artificial neural network is designed by programming computers to behave simply like interconnected brain cells.

There are around 1000 billion neurons in the human brain. Each neuron has an association point somewhere in the range of 1,000 and 100,000. In the human brain, data is stored in such a manner as to be distributed, and we can extract more than one piece of this data when necessary from our memory parallelly. We can say that the human brain is made up of incredibly amazing parallel processors.

We can understand the artificial neural network with an example, consider an example of a digital logic gate that takes an input and gives an output. "OR" gate, which takes two inputs. If one or both the inputs are "On," then we get "On" in output. If both the inputs are "Off," then we get "Off" in output. Here the output depends upon input. Our brain does not perform the same task. The outputs to inputs relationship keep changing because of the neurons in our brain, which are "learning."

4.2. The Architecture of an Artificial Neural Network

To understand the concept of the architecture of an artificial neural network, we have to understand what a neural network consists of. In order to define a neural network that consists of a large number of artificial neurons, which are termed units arranged in a sequence of layers. Lets us look at various types of layers available in an artificial neural network.

Fig. Artificial Neural Network primarily consists of three layers:

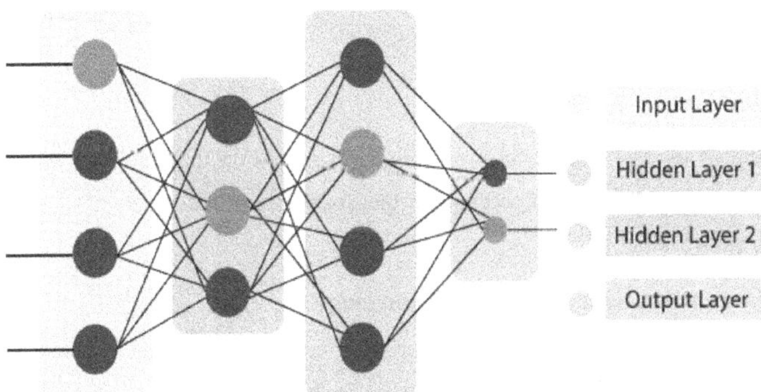

Fig. 4.3: ANN Layers

Input Layer

As the name suggests, it accepts inputs in several different formats provided by the programmer.

Hidden Layer

The hidden layer presents in-between input and output layers. It performs all the calculations to find hidden features and patterns.

Output Layer

The input goes through a series of transformations using the hidden layer, which finally results in output that is conveyed using this layer.

The artificial neural network takes input and computes the weighted sum of the inputs and includes a bias. This computation is represented in the form of a transfer function.

$$\sum_{i=1}^{n} Wi * Xi + b$$

It determines weighted total is passed as an input to an activation function to produce the output. Activation functions choose whether a node should fire or not. Only those who are fired make it to the output layer. There are distinctive activation functions available that can be applied upon the sort of task we are performing.

Advantages of Artificial Neural Network (ANN)

Parallel Processing Capability

Artificial neural networks have a numerical value that can perform more than one task simultaneously.

Storing Data on the Entire Network

Data that is used in traditional programming is stored on the whole network, not on a database. The disappearance of a couple of pieces of data in one place doesn't prevent the network from working.

Capability to Work with Incomplete Knowledge

After ANN training, the information may produce output even with inadequate data. The loss of performance here relies upon the significance of missing data.

Having a Memory Distribution

For ANN is to be able to adapt, it is important to determine the examples and to encourage the network according to the desired output by demonstrating these examples to the network. The succession of the network is directly proportional to the chosen instances, and if the event can't appear to the network in all its aspects, it can produce false output.

Having Fault Tolerance

Extortion of one or more cells of ANN does not prohibit it from generating output, and this feature makes the network fault-tolerance.

Disadvantages of Artificial Neural Network

Assurance of Proper Network Structure

There is no particular guideline for determining the structure of artificial neural networks. The appropriate network structure is accomplished through experience, trial, and error.

Unrecognized behavior of the Network

It is the most significant issue of ANN. When ANN produces a testing solution, it does not provide insight concerning why and how. It decreases trust in the network.

Hardware Dependence

Artificial neural networks need processors with parallel processing power, as per their structure. Therefore, the realization of the equipment is dependent.

Difficulty of Showing the Issue to the Network

ANNs can work with numerical data. Problems must be converted into numerical values before being introduced to ANN. The presentation mechanism to be resolved here will directly impact the performance of the network. It relies on the user's abilities.

The Duration of the Network is Unknown

The network is reduced to a specific value of the error, and this value does not give us optimum results.

4.3. How do Artificial Neural Networks Work?

Artificial Neural Network can be best represented as a weighted directed graph, where the artificial neurons form the nodes. The association between the neurons outputs and neuron inputs can be viewed as the directed edges with weights. The Artificial Neural Network receives the input signal from the external source in the form of a pattern and image in the form of a vector. These inputs are then mathematically assigned by the notations x(n) for every n number of inputs. The fig. shows the inputs/outputs.

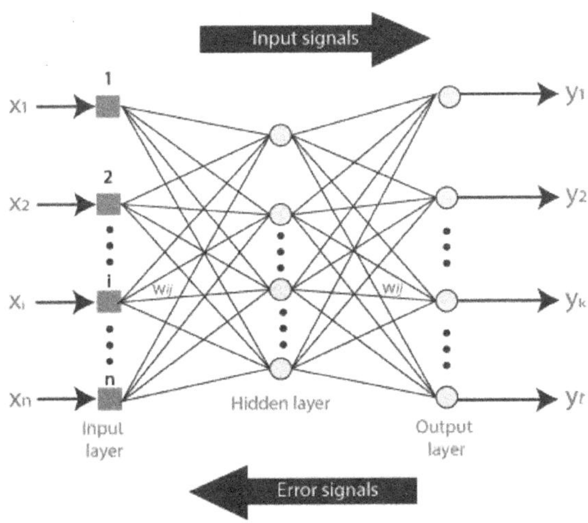

Fig. 4.4: Inputs/Outputs in ANN

Afterward, each of the input is multiplied by its corresponding weights (these weights are the details utilized by the artificial neural networks to solve a specific problem). In general terms, these weights normally represent the strength of the interconnection between neurons inside the artificial neural network. All the weighted inputs are summarized inside the computing unit.

If the weighted sum is equal to zero, then bias is added to make the output non-zero or something else to scale up to the system's response. Bias has the same input, and weight equals to 1. Here the total of weighted inputs can be in the range of 0 to positive infinity. Here, to keep the response in the limits of the desired value, a certain maximum value is benchmarked, and the total of weighted inputs is passed through the activation function.

The activation function refers to the set of transfer functions used to achieve the desired output. There is a different kind of the activation function, but primarily either linear or non-linear sets of functions. Some of the commonly used sets of activation functions are the Binary, linear, and Tan hyperbolic sigmoidal activation functions. Let us take a look at each of them in details:

Binary

In binary activation function, the output is either a one or a 0. Here, to accomplish this, there is a threshold value set up. If the net weighted input of neurons is more than 1, then the final output of the activation function is returned as one or else the output is returned as 0.

Sigmoidal Hyperbolic

The Sigmoidal Hyperbola function is generally seen as an "**S**" shaped curve. Here the tan hyperbolic function is used to approximate output from the actual net input. The function is defined as:

F(x) = (1/1 + exp(-????x))

Where ???? is considered the Steepness parameter.

4.4. Types of Artificial Neural Network

There are various types of Artificial Neural Networks (ANN) depending upon the human brain neuron and network functions, an artificial neural network similarly performs tasks. The majority of the artificial neural networks will have some similarities with a more complex biological partner and are very effective at their expected tasks. For example, segmentation or classification.

Feedback ANN

In this type of ANN, the output returns into the network to accomplish the best-evolved results internally. As per the **University of Massachusetts**, Lowell Centre for Atmospheric Research. The feedback networks feed information back into itself and are well suited to solve optimization issues. The Internal system error corrections utilize feedback ANNs.

Feed-Forward ANN

A feed-forward network is a basic neural network comprising of an input layer, an output layer, and at least one layer of a neuron. Through assessment of its output by reviewing its input, the intensity of the network can be noticed based on group behavior of the associated neurons, and the output is decided. The primary advantage of this network is that it figures out how to evaluate and recognize input patterns.

4.5. Neural Networks Representation

Neural networks are artificial systems that were inspired by biological neural networks. These systems learn to perform tasks by being exposed to various datasets and examples without any task-specific rules. The idea is that the system generates identifying characteristics from the data they have been passed without being programmed with a pre-programmed understanding of these datasets.

Neural networks are based on computational models for threshold logic. Threshold logic is a combination of algorithms and mathematics. Neural networks are based either on the study of the brain or on the application of neural networks to artificial intelligence. The work has led to improvements in finite automata theory.

Components of a typical neural network involve neurons, connections, weights, biases, propagation function, and a learning rule. Neurons will receive an input $p_j(t)$ from predecessor neurons that have an activation $a_j(t)$, threshold, an activation function f, and an output function f_{out}. Connections consist of connections, weights and biases which rules how neuron 'I' transfers output to neuron 'J'. Propagation computes the input and outputs the output and sums the predecessor neurons function with the weight. The learning rule modifies the weights and thresholds of the variables in the network.

4.6. Types of Neural Networks

There are *seven* types of neural networks that can be used.

- The first is a multilayer perceptron which has three or more layers and uses a nonlinear activation function.

- The second is the convolution neural network that uses a variation of the multilayer perceptrons.
- The third is the recursive neural network that uses weights to make structured predictions.
- The fourth is a recurrent neural network that makes connections between the neurons in a directed cycle. The long short-term memory neural network uses the recurrent neural network architecture and does not use activation function.
- The final two are sequence to sequence modules which uses two recurrent networks and shallow neural networks which produces a vector space from an amount of text. These neural networks are applications of the basic neural network demonstrated below.

For the example, the neural network will work with three vectors: a vector of attributes X, a vector of classes Y, and a vector of weights W. The code will use 100 iterations to fit the attributes to the classes. The predictions are generated, weighed, and then outputted after iterating through the vector of weights W. The neural network handles backpropagation.

What are Artificial Neural Networks?

Artificial Neural Networks contain artificial neurons which are called **units**. These units are arranged in a series of layers that together constitute the whole Artificial Neural Networks in a system. A layer can have only a dozen units or millions of units as this depends on the complexity of the system. Commonly, Artificial Neural Network has an input layer, output layer as well as hidden layers. The input layer receives data from the outside world which the neural network needs to analyze or learn about. Then this data passes through one or multiple hidden layers that transform the input into data that is valuable for the output layer. Finally, the output layer provides an output in the form of a response of the Artificial Neural Networks to input data provided.

In the majority of neural networks, units are interconnected from one layer to another. Each of these connections has weights that determine the influence of one unit on another unit. As the data transfers from one unit to another, the neural network learns more and more about the data which eventually results in an output from the output layer.

How do Artificial Neural Networks Learn?

Artificial neural networks are trained using a training set. For example, suppose you want to teach an ANN to recognize a cat. Then it is shown thousands of different images of cats so that the network can learn to identify a cat. Once the neural network has been trained enough using images of cats, then you need to check if it can identify cat images correctly. This is done by making the ANN classify the images it is provided by deciding whether they are cat images or not. The output obtained by the ANN is corroborated by a human-provided description of whether the image is a cat image or not. If the ANN identifies incorrectly then back-propagation is used to adjust whatever it has learned during training. Back-propagation is done by fine-tuning the weights of the connections in ANN units based on the error rate obtained. This process continues until the artificial neural network can correctly recognize a cat in an image with minimal possible error rates.

Characteristics of Artificial Neural Network

- It is neurally implemented mathematical model.
- It contains huge number of interconnected processing elements called neurons to do all operations.
- Information stored in the neurons are basically the weighted linkage of neurons.
- The input signals arrive at the processing elements through connections and connecting weights.
- It has the ability to learn, recall and generalize from the given data by suitable assignment and adjustment of weights.
- The collective behavior of the neurons describes its computational power, and no single neuron carries specific information.

How Simple Neuron Works?

Let there are two neurons **X** and **Y** which is transmitting signal to another neuron **Z**. Then, **X** and **Y** are input neurons for transmitting signals and **Z** is output neuron for receiving signal. The input neurons are connected to the output neuron, over a interconnection links (**A** and **B**) as shown in figure.

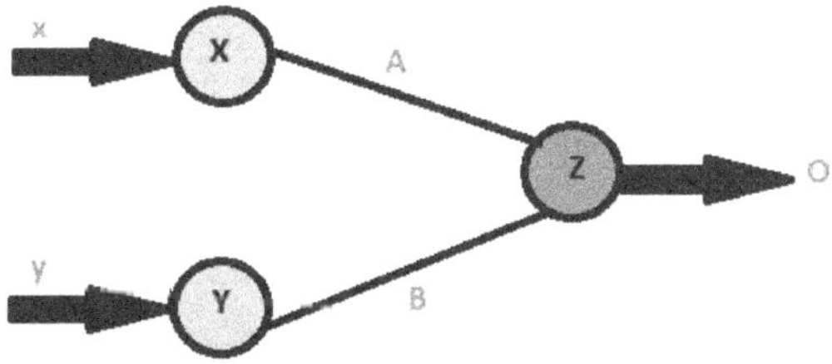

Architecture of a Simple Artificial Neuron Net

Fig. 4.5: Neuron Architecture of a Simple ANN

For above neuron architecture, the net input has to be calculated in the way.

$$I = xA + yB$$

Where x and y are the activations of the input neurons X and Y. The output z of the output neuron Z can be obtained by applying activations over the net input.

$$O = f(I)$$

Output = Function (net input calculated)

The function to be applied over the net input is called activation function. There are various activation function possible for this.

What are the Types of Artificial Neural Networks?

1. Feed forward Neural Network

The feed forward neural network is one of the most basic artificial neural networks. In this ANN, the data or the input provided travels in a single direction. It enters into the ANN through the input layer and exits through the output layer while hidden layers may or may not exist. So the feed forward neural network has a front propagated wave only and usually does not have backpropagation.

2. Recurrent Neural Network

The Recurrent Neural Network saves the output of a layer and feeds this output back to the input to better predict the outcome of the layer. The first layer in the RNN is quite similar to the feed-forward neural network and the recurrent neural network starts once the output of the first layer is computed. After this layer, each unit will remember some information from the previous step so that it can act as a memory cell in performing computations.

3. Convolutional Neural Network

A Convolutional neural network has some similarities to the feed-forward neural network, where the connections between units have weights that determine the influence of one unit on another unit. But a CNN has one or more than one convolutional layers that use a convolution operation on the input and then pass the result obtained in the form of output to the next layer. CNN has applications in speech and image processing which is particularly useful in computer vision.

4. Modular Neural Network

A Modular Neural Network contains a collection of different neural networks that work independently towards obtaining the output with no interaction between them. Each of the different neural networks performs a different sub-task by obtaining unique inputs compared to other networks. The advantage of this modular neural network is that it breaks down a large and complex computational process into smaller components, thus decreasing its complexity while still obtaining the required output.

5. Radial Basis Function Neural Network

Radial basis functions are those functions that consider the distance of a point concerning the center. RBF functions have two layers. In the first layer, the input is mapped into all the Radial basis functions in the hidden layer and then the output layer computes the output in the next step. Radial basis function nets are normally used to model the data that represents any underlying trend or function.

4.7. Applications of Artificial Neural Networks

1. Social Media

Artificial Neural Networks are used heavily in Social Media. For example, let's take the **'People you may know'** feature on Facebook that suggests you people that you might know in real life so that you can send them friend requests. Well, this magical effect is achieved by using Artificial Neural Networks that analyze your profile, your interests, your current friends, and also their friends and various other factors to calculate the people you might potentially know. Another common application of Machine Learning in social media is **facial recognition.** This is done by finding around 100 reference points on the person's face and then matching them with those already available in the database using convolutional neural networks.

2. Marketing and Sales

When you log onto E-commerce sites like Amazon and Flipkart, they will recommend your products to buy based on your previous browsing history. Similarly, suppose you love Pasta, then Zomato, Swiggy, etc. will show you restaurant recommendations based on your tastes and previous order history. This is true across all new-age marketing segments like Book sites, Movie services, Hospitality sites, etc. and it is done by implementing **personalized marketing**. This uses Artificial Neural Networks to identify the customer likes, dislikes, previous shopping history, etc. and then tailor the marketing campaigns accordingly.

3. Healthcare

Artificial Neural Networks are used in Oncology to train algorithms that can identify cancerous tissue at the microscopic level at the same accuracy as trained physicians. Various rare diseases may manifest in physical characteristics and can be identified in their premature stages by using **Facial Analysis** on the patient photos. So the full-scale implementation of Artificial Neural Networks in the healthcare environment can only enhance the diagnostic abilities of medical experts and ultimately lead to the overall improvement in the quality of medical care all over the world.

4. Personal Assistants

I am sure you all have heard of Siri, Alexa, Cortana, etc. and also heard them based on the phones you have!!! These are personal assistants and an example of speech recognition that uses **Natural Language Processing** to interact with the users and formulate a response accordingly. Natural Language Processing uses artificial neural networks that are made to handle many tasks of these personal assistants such as managing the language syntax, semantics, correct speech, the conversation that is going on, etc.

- Every new technology need assistance from the previous one i.e. data from previous ones and these data are analyzed so that every pros and cons should be studied correctly. All of these things are possible only through the help of neural network.
- Neural network is suitable for the research on *Animal behavior, predator/prey relationships and population cycles.*
- It would be easier to do *proper valuation* of property, buildings, automobiles, machinery etc. with the help of neural network.
- Neural Network can be used in betting on horse races, sporting events, and most importantly in stock market.
- It can be used to predict the correct judgment for any crime by using a large data of crime details as input and the resulting sentences as output.
- By analyzing data and determining which of the data has any fault (files diverging from peers) called as *Data mining, cleaning and validation* can be achieved through neural network.
- Neural Network can be used to predict targets with the help of echo patterns we get from sonar, radar, seismic and magnetic instruments.

- It can be used efficiently in *Employee hiring* so that any company can hire the right employee depending upon the skills the employee has and what should be its productivity in future.
- It has a large application in *Medical Research*.
- It can be used to for *Fraud Detection* regarding credit cards, insurance or taxes by analyzing the past records.

Appropriate Problems – for ANN

Most appropriate for problems where

- Instances have many attribute-value pairs
- Target function output may be discrete-valued, real-valued, or a vector of several real- or discrete-valued attributes
- Training examples may contain errors
- Long training times are acceptable
- Fast evaluation of the learned target function may be required
- The ability for humans to understand the learned target function is not Important

4.8. Perceptron

- In Machine Learning and Artificial Intelligence, Perceptron is the most commonly used term for all folks. It is the primary step to learn Machine Learning and Deep Learning technologies, which consists of a set of weights, input values or scores, and a threshold. ***Perceptron is a building block of an Artificial Neural Network***. Initially, in the mid of 19th century, **Mr. Frank Rosenblatt** invented the Perceptron for performing certain calculations to detect input data capabilities or business intelligence. Perceptron is a linear Machine Learning algorithm used for supervised learning for various binary classifiers. This algorithm enables neurons to learn elements and processes them one by one during preparation. In this tutorial, "Perceptron in Machine Learning," we will discuss in-depth knowledge of Perceptron and its basic functions in brief. Let's start with the basic introduction of Perceptron.

What is the Perceptron model in Machine Learning?

Perceptron is Machine Learning algorithm for supervised learning of various binary classification tasks. Further, ***Perceptron is also understood as an Artificial Neuron or neural network unit that helps to detect certain input data computations in business intelligence***.

Perceptron model is also treated as one of the best and simplest types of Artificial Neural networks. However, it is a supervised learning algorithm of binary classifiers. Hence, we can consider it as a single-layer neural network with four main parameters, i.e., **input values, weights and Bias, net sum, and an activation function.**

What is Binary Classifier in Machine Learning?

In Machine Learning, binary classifiers are defined as the function that helps in deciding whether input data can be represented as vectors of numbers and belongs to some specific class.

Binary classifiers can be considered as linear classifiers. In simple words, we can understand it as a ***classification algorithm that can predict linear predictor function in terms of weight and feature vectors.***

Basic Components of Perceptron

Mr. Frank Rosenblatt invented the perceptron model as a binary classifier which contains three main components. These are as follows in the diagram:

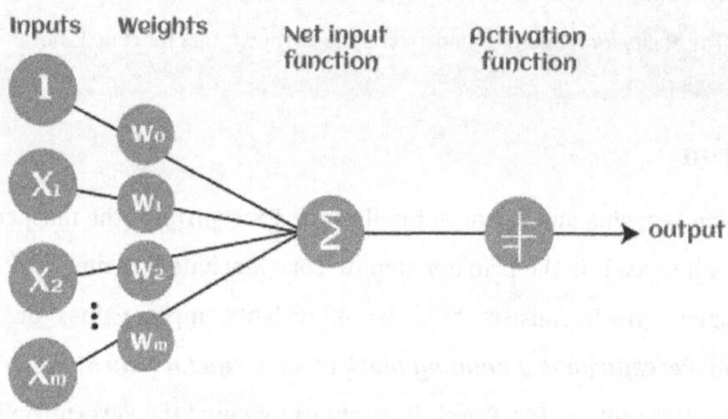

Fig. 4.6: Parts of Perceptron

- **Perceptron consists of four different mathematical parts**
    - ***First is*** input value or one input layer
    - ***Second,*** the net sum
    - ***Third,*** weight and bias
    - ***Fourth,*** Activation function

Input Nodes or Input Layer

This is the primary component of Perceptron which accepts the initial data into the system for further processing. Each input node contains a real numerical value.

Wight and Bias

Weight parameter represents the strength of the connection between units. This is another most important parameter of Perceptron components. Weight is directly proportional to the strength of the associated input neuron in deciding the output. Further, Bias can be considered as the line of intercept in a linear equation.

Activation Function

These are the final and important components that help to determine whether the neuron will fire or not. Activation Function can be considered primarily as a step function.

Types of Activation functions were represented in the below Fig.

- Sign function
- Step function, and
- Sigmoid function

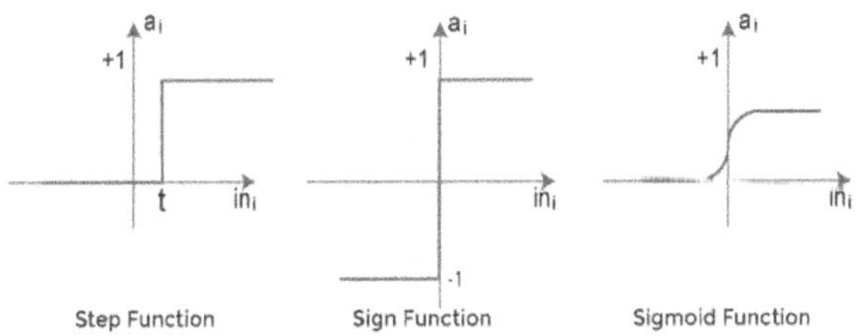

Fig. 4.7: Different Activation Functions

The data scientist uses the activation function to take a subjective decision based on various problem statements and forms the desired outputs. Activation function may differ (e.g., Sign, Step, and Sigmoid) in perceptron models by checking whether the learning process is slow or has vanishing or exploding gradients.

How does Perceptron Work?

In Machine Learning, Perceptron is considered as a single-layer neural network that consists of four main parameters named input values (Input nodes), weights and Bias, net sum, and an activation function. The perceptron model begins with the multiplication of all input values and their weights, then adds these values together to create the weighted sum. Then this weighted sum is applied to the activation function 'f' to obtain the desired output. This activation function is also known as the **step function** and is represented by **'f'**.

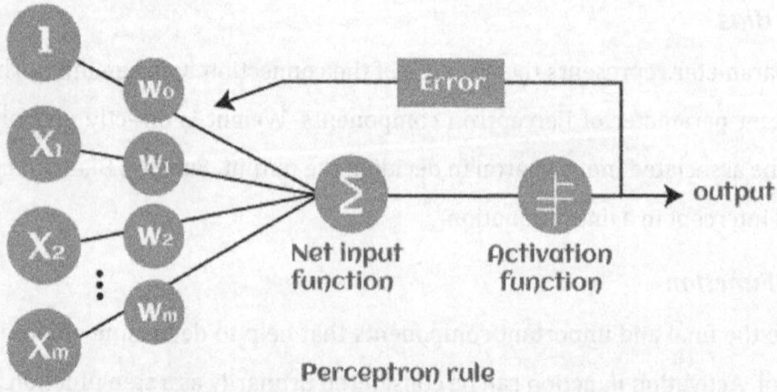

Fig. 4.8: Perceptron Rule

This step function or Activation function plays a vital role in ensuring that output is mapped between required values (0,1) or (-1,1). It is important to note that the weight of input is indicative of the strength of a node. Similarly, an input's bias value gives the ability to shift the activation function curve up or down.

Perceptron model works in two important steps as follows:

Step-1

In the first step first, multiply all input values with corresponding weight values and then add them to determine the weighted sum. Mathematically, we can calculate the weighted sum as follows:

$$\sum wi*xi = x1*w1 + x2*w2 + \ldots wn*xn$$

Add a special term called **bias 'b'** to this weighted sum to improve the model's performance.

$$\sum wi*xi + b$$

Step-2

In the second step, an activation function is applied with the above-mentioned weighted sum, which gives us output either in binary form or a continuous value as follows:

$$Y = f(\sum wi*xi + b)$$

4.9. Types of Perceptron Models

Based on the layers, Perceptron models are divided into two types. These are as follows:

1. Single-layer Perceptron Model
2. Multi-layer Perceptron model

Single Layer Perceptron Model

This is one of the easiest Artificial neural networks (ANN) types. A single-layered perceptron model consists feed-forward network and also includes a threshold transfer function inside the model. The main objective of the single-layer perceptron model is to analyze the linearly separable objects with binary outcomes.

In a single layer perceptron model, its algorithms do not contain recorded data, so it begins with inconstantly allocated input for weight parameters. Further, it sums up all inputs (weight). After adding all inputs, if the total sum of all inputs is more than a pre-determined value, the model gets activated and shows the output value as +1.

If the outcome is same as pre-determined or threshold value, then the performance of this model is stated as satisfied, and weight demand does not change. However, this model consists of a few discrepancies triggered when multiple weight inputs values are fed into the model. Hence, to find desired output and minimize errors, some changes should be necessary for the weights input.

"Single-layer perceptron can learn only linearly separable patterns."

Multi-Layered Perceptron Model

Like a single-layer perceptron model, a multi-layer perceptron model also has the same model structure but has a greater number of hidden layers.

The multi-layer perceptron model is also known as the Backpropagation algorithm, which executes in two stages as follows:

- **Forward Stage:** Activation functions start from the input layer in the forward stage and terminate on the output layer.
- **Backward Stage:** In the backward stage, weight and bias values are modified as per the model's requirement. In this stage, the error between actual output and demanded originated backward on the output layer and ended on the input layer.

Hence, a multi-layered perceptron model has considered as multiple artificial neural networks having various layers in which activation function does not remain linear, similar to a single layer perceptron model. Instead of linear, activation function can be executed as sigmoid, TanH, ReLU, etc., for deployment.

A multi-layer perceptron model has greater processing power and can process linear and non-linear patterns. Further, it can also implement logic gates such as AND, OR, XOR, NAND, NOT, XNOR, NOR.

Advantages of Multi-Layer Perceptron:

- A multi-layered perceptron model can be used to solve complex non-linear problems.
- It works well with both small and large input data.
- It helps us to obtain quick predictions after the training.
- It helps to obtain the same accuracy ratio with large as well as small data.

Disadvantages of Multi-Layer Perceptron:

- In Multi-layer perceptron, computations are difficult and time-consuming.
- In multi-layer Perceptron, it is difficult to predict how much the dependent variable affects each independent variable.
- The model functioning depends on the quality of the training.

4.10. Perceptron Function

Perceptron function "f(x)" can be achieved as output by multiplying the input 'x' with the learned weight coefficient 'w'.

Mathematically, we can express it as follows:

f(x)=1; if w.x+b>0

otherwise, f(x)=0

- 'w' represents real-valued weights vector.
- 'b' represents the bias.
- 'x' represents a vector of input x values.

Characteristics of Perceptron

The perceptron model has the following characteristics.

1. Perceptron is a machine learning algorithm for supervised learning of binary classifiers.
2. In Perceptron, the weight coefficient is automatically learned.
3. Initially, weights are multiplied with input features, and the decision is made whether the neuron is fired or not.
4. The activation function applies a step rule to check whether the weight function is greater than zero.
5. The linear decision boundary is drawn, enabling the distinction between the two linearly separable classes +1 and -1.
6. If the added sum of all input values is more than the threshold value, it must have an output signal; otherwise, no output will be shown.

4.11. Limitations of Perceptron Model

A perceptron model has limitations as follows:

- The output of a perceptron can only be a binary number (0 or 1) due to the hard limit transfer function.
- Perceptron can only be used to classify the linearly separable sets of input vectors. If input vectors are non-linear, it is not easy to classify them properly.

Future of Perceptron

The future of the Perceptron model is much bright and significant as it helps to interpret data by building intuitive patterns and applying them in the future. Machine learning is a rapidly growing technology of Artificial Intelligence that is continuously evolving and in the developing phase; hence the future of perceptron technology will continue to support and facilitate analytical behavior in machines that will, in turn, add to the efficiency of computers.

The perceptron model is continuously becoming more advanced and working efficiently on complex problems with the help of artificial neurons.

4.12. Multi-Layer Feed Forward Networks

Consider the following network in the below figure.

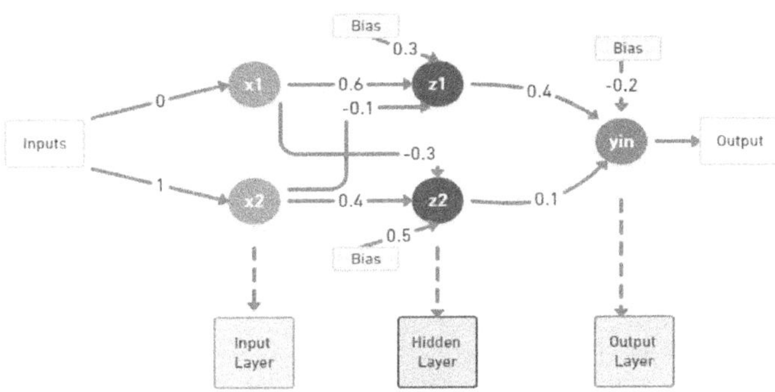

Fig. 4.9: Multi-Layer Feed Forward Networks

Backpropagation Network (BPN)

The network in the above figure is a simple multi-layer feed-forward network or backpropagation network. It contains three layers, the input layer with two neurons x_1 and x_2, the hidden layer with two neurons z_1 and z_2 and the output layer with one neuron y_{in}.

Now let's write down the weights and bias vectors for each neuron.

Note: The weights are taken randomly.

Input layer: i/p – $[x_1\ x_2] = [0\ 1]$

Here since it is the input layer only the input values are present.

Hidden layer: $z_1 - [v_{11}\ v_{21}\ v_{01}] = [0.6\ -0.1\ 03]$

Here v_{11} refers to the weight of first input x_1 on z_1, v_{21} refers to the weight of second input x_2 on z_1 and v_{01} refers to the bias value on z_1.

$z_2 - [v_{12}\ v_{22}\ v_{02}] = [-0.3\ 0.4\ 0.5]$

Here v_{12} refers to the weight of first input x_1 on z_2, v_{22} refers to the weight of second input x_2 on z_2 and v_{02} refers to the bias value on z_2.

Output layer: $y_{in} - [w_{11}\ w_{21}\ w_{01}] = [0.4\ 0.1\ -0.2]$

Here w_{11} refers to the weight of first neuron z_1 in a hidden layer on y_{in}, w_{21} refers to the weight of second neuron z_2 in a hidden layer on y_{in} and w_{01} refers to the bias value on y_{in}. Let's consider three variables, k which refers to the neurons in the output layer, 'j' which refers to the neurons in the hidden layer and 'i' which refers to the neurons in the input layer.

Therefore,

k = 1

j = 1, 2(meaning first neuron and second neuron in hidden layer)

i = 1, 2(meaning first and second neuron in the input layer)

Below are some conditions to be followed in BPNs.

Conditions/Constraints

1. In BPN, the activation function used should be differentiable.
2. The input for bias is always 1.

To proceed with the problem, let:

Target value, t = 1

Learning rate, $\alpha = 0.25$

Activation function = Binary sigmoid function

Binary sigmoid function, $f(x) = (1+e^{-x})^{-1}$ (1)

And, $f'(x) = f(x)[1-f(x)]$ (2)

There are three steps to solve the problem:

1. Computing the output, y.
2. Backpropagation of errors, i.e., between output and hidden layer, hidden and input layer.
3. Updating weights.

Step 1:

The value y is calculated by finding y_{in} and applying the activation function.

y_{in} is calculated as:

$$y_{in} = w_{01} + z_1{*}w_{11} + z_2{*}w_{21} \quad (3)$$

Here, z_1 and z_2 are the values from hidden layer, calculated by finding z_{in1}, z_{in2} and applying activation function to them.

z_{in1} and z_{in2} are calculated as:

$$z_{in1} = v_{01} + x_1{*}v_{11} + x_2{*}v_{21} \quad (4)$$

$$z_{in2} = v_{02} + x_1{*}v_{12} + x_2{*}v_{22} \quad (5)$$

From (4)

$z_{in1} = 0.3 + 0{*}0.6 + 1{*}(-0.1)$

$z_{in1} = 0.2$

$z_1 = f(z_{in1}) = (1+e^{-0.2})^{-1}$ From (1)

$\mathbf{z_1 = 0.5498}$

From (5)

$z_{in2} = 0.5 + 0{*}(-0.3) + 1{*}0.4$

$z_{in2} = 0.9$

$z_2 = f(z_{in2}) = (1+e^{-0.9})^{-1}$ From (1)

$\mathbf{z_2 = 0.7109}$

From (3)

$y_{in} = (-0.2) + 0.5498{*}0.4 + 0.7109{*}0.1$

$y_{in} = 0.0910$

$y = f(y_{in}) = (1+e^{-0.0910})^{-1}$ From (1)

$\mathbf{y = 0.5227}$

Here, y is not equal to the target 't', which is 1. And we proceed to calculate the errors and then update weights from them in order to achieve the target value.

Step 2:

(a) Calculating the Error between Output and Hidden Layer

Error between output and hidden layer is represented as δ_k, where k represents the neurons in output layer as mentioned above. The error is calculated as:

$$\delta_k = (t_k - y_k) * f'(y_{ink}) \qquad (6)$$

Where, $f'(y_{ink}) = f(y_{ink})[1 - f(y_{ink})]$ From (2)

Since k = 1 (Assumed above),

$$\delta = (t - y)\, f'(y_{in}) \qquad (7)$$

Where, $f'(y_{in}) = f(y_{in})[1 - f(y_{in})]$

$f'(y_{in}) = 0.5227[1 - 0.5227]$

$f'(y_{in}) = 0.2495$

Therefore,

$\delta = (1 - 0.5227) * 0.2495$ From (7)

δ = 0.1191, is the error

Note: (Target – Output) i.e., (t – y) is the error in the output not in the layer. Error in a layer is contributed by different factors like weights and bias.

(b) Calculating the Error between Hidden and Input Layer

Error between hidden and input layer is represented as δ_j, where j represents the number of neurons in the hidden layer as mentioned above. The error is calculated as:

$$\delta_j = \delta_{inj} * f'(z_{inj}) \qquad (8)$$

where,

$$\delta_{inj} = \sum_{k=1 \text{ to } n} (\delta_k * w_{jk}) \qquad (9)$$

$$f'(z_{inj}) = f(z_{inj})[1 - f(z_{inj})] \qquad (10)$$

Since k = 1(Assumed above) eq. (9) becomes:

$$\delta_{inj} = \delta * w_{j1} \qquad (11)$$

As j = 1, 2, we will have one error values for each neuron and total of 2 errors values.

$$\delta_1 = \delta_{in1} * f'(z_{in1}) \qquad (12), \text{ From (8)}$$

$\delta_{in1} = \delta * w_{11}$ From (11)

$\delta_{in1} = 0.1191 * 0.4$ From weights vectors

$\delta_{in1} = 0.04764$

$f'(z_{in1}) = f(z_{in1})[1 - f(z_{in1})]$

$f'(z_{in1}) = 0.5498[1 - 0.5498]$ As $f(z_{in1}) = z_1$

$f'(z_{in1}) = 0.2475$

Substituting in (12)

$\boldsymbol{\delta_1 = 0.04674 * 0.2475 = 0.0118}$

$$\delta_2 = \delta_{in2} * f'(z_{in2}) \qquad (13), \text{From } (8)$$

$\delta_{in2} = \delta * w_{21}$ From (11)

$\delta_{in2} = 0.1191 * 0.1$ From weights vectors

$\delta_{in2} = 0.0119$

$f'(z_{in2}) = f(z_{in2})[1 - f(z_{in2})]$

$f'(z_{in2}) = 0.7109[1 - 0.7109]$ As $f(z_{in2}) = z_2$

$f'(z_{in2}) = 0.2055$

Substituting in (13)

$\boldsymbol{\delta_2 = 0.0119 * 0.2055 = 0.00245}$

The errors have been calculated, the weights have to be updated using these error values.

Step 3:

The formula for updating weights for output layer is:

$$w_{jk}(new) = w_{jk}(old) + \Delta w_{jk} \qquad (14)$$

$$\text{where, } \Delta w_{jk} = \alpha * \delta_k * z_j \qquad (15)$$

Since k = 1, (15) becomes:

$$\Delta w_{jk} = \alpha * \delta * z_i \qquad (16)$$

The formula for updating weights for hidden layer is:

$$v_{ij}(new) = v_{ij}(old) + \Delta v_{ij} \qquad (17)$$

$$\text{where, } \Delta v_i = \alpha * \delta_j * x_i \qquad (18)$$

From (14) and (16)

$w_{11}(new) = w_{11}(old) + \Delta w_{11} = 0.4 + \alpha * \delta * z_1 = 0.4 + 0.25 * 0.1191 * 0.5498 = 0.4164$

$w_{21}(new) = w_{21}(old) + \Delta w_{21} = 0.1 + \alpha * \delta * z_2 = 0.1 + 0.25 * 0.1191 * 0.7109 = 0.12117$

$w_{01}(new) = w_{01}(old) + \Delta w_{01} = (-0.2) + \alpha * \delta * bias = (-0.2) + 0.25 * 0.1191 * 1 = -0.1709$, kindly note the 1 taken here is input considered for bias as per the conditions.

These are the updated weights of the output layer.

From (17) and (18)

$v_{11}(new) = v_{11}(old) + \Delta v_{11} = 0.6 + \alpha * \delta_1 * x_1 = 0.6 + 0.25 * 0.0118 * 0 = 0.6$

$v_{21}(new) = v_{21}(old) + \Delta v_{21} = (-0.1) + \alpha * \delta_1 * x_2 = (-0.1) + 0.25 * 0.0118 * 1 = 0.00295$

$v_{01}(new) = v_{01}(old) + \Delta v_{01} = 0.3 + \alpha * \delta_1 * bias = 0.3 + 0.25 * 0.0118 * 1 = 0.00295$, kindly note the 1 taken here is input considered for bias as per the conditions.

$v_{12}(new) = v_{12}(old) + \Delta v_{12} = (-0.3) + \alpha * \delta_2 * x_1 = (-0.3) + 0.25 * 0.00245 * 0 = -0.3$

$v_{22}(new) = v_{22}(old) + \Delta v_{22} = 0.4 + \alpha * \delta_2 * x_2 = 0.4 + 0.25 * 0.00245 * 1 = 0.400612$

$v_{02}(new) = v_{02}(old) + \Delta v_{02} = 0.5 + \alpha * \delta_2 * bias = 0.5 + 0.25 * 0.00245 * 1 = 0.500612$, kindly note the 1 taken here is input considered for bias as per the conditions.

These are all the updated weights of the hidden layer.

These three steps are repeated until the output 'y' is equal to the target 't'.

This is how the BPNs work. The backpropagation in BPN refers to that the error in the present layer is used to update weights between the present and previous layer by backpropagating the error values.

4.13. Back-propagation Algorithm

Backpropagation is the essence of neural network training. It is the method of fine-tuning the weights of a neural network based on the error rate obtained in the previous epoch (i.e., iteration). Proper tuning of the weights allows you to reduce error rates and make the model reliable by increasing its generalization.

Backpropagation in neural network is a short form for "backward propagation of errors." It is a standard method of training artificial neural networks. This method helps calculate the gradient of a loss function with respect to all the weights in the network.

How Backpropagation Algorithm Works

The Backpropagation algorithm in neural network computes the gradient of the loss function for a single weight by the chain rule. It efficiently computes one layer at a time, unlike a native direct computation. It computes the gradient, but it does not define how the gradient is used. It generalizes the computation in the delta rule. The fig. Shows Backpropagation algorithm.

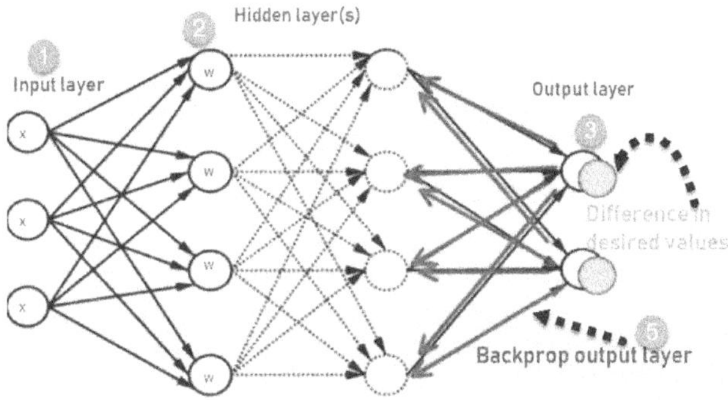

Fig. 4.10: Backpropagation Algorithm (Working)

How Backpropagation Algorithm Works.

1. Inputs X, arrive through the preconnected path.
2. Input is modeled using real weights W. The weights are usually randomly selected.
3. Calculate the output for every neuron from the input layer, to the hidden layers, to the output layer.
4. Calculate the error in the outputs.

$$Error_B = \text{Actual Output} - \text{Desired Output}$$

5. Travel back from the output layer to the hidden layer to adjust the weights such that the error is decreased.

Keep repeating the process until the desired output is achieved.

Why we Need Backpropagation?

Most prominent advantages of Backpropagation are:

- Backpropagation is fast, simple and easy to program.
- It has no parameters to tune apart from the numbers of input.
- It is a flexible method as it does not require prior knowledge about the network.
- It is a standard method that generally works well.
- It does not need any special mention of the features of the function to be learned.

What is a Feed Forward Network?

A feed forward neural network is an artificial neural network where the nodes never form a cycle. This kind of neural network has an input layer, hidden layers, and an output layer. It is the first and simplest type of artificial neural network.

4.14. Types of Backpropagation Networks

Two Types of Backpropagation Networks are:

- Static Back-propagation
- Recurrent Backpropagation

Static Back-propagation

It is one kind of backpropagation network which produces a mapping of a static input for static output. It is useful to solve static classification issues like optical character recognition.

Recurrent Backpropagation

Recurrent Backpropagation in data mining is fed forward until a fixed value is achieved. After that, the error is computed and propagated backward.

The main difference between both of these methods is: that the mapping is rapid in static back-propagation while it is nonstatic in recurrent backpropagation.

Backpropagation Key Points

- Simplifies the network structure by elements weighted links that have the least effect on the trained network.
- You need to study a group of input and activation values to develop the relationship between the input and hidden unit layers.
- It helps to assess the impact that a given input variable has on a network output. The knowledge gained from this analysis should be represented in rules.
- Backpropagation is especially useful for deep neural networks working on error-prone projects, such as image or speech recognition.
- Backpropagation takes advantage of the chain and power rules allows backpropagation to function with any number of outputs.

Disadvantages of Using Backpropagation

- The actual performance of backpropagation on a specific problem is dependent on the input data.
- Backpropagation algorithm in data mining can be quite sensitive to noisy data.
- You need to use the matrix-based approach for backpropagation instead of mini-batch.

4.15. Backpropagation Algorithm

- **Backpropagation** is one of the important concepts of a neural network. Our task is to classify our data best. For this, we have to update the weights of parameter and bias, but how can we do that in a deep neural network? In the linear regression model, we use gradient descent to optimize the parameter. Similarly here we also use gradient descent algorithm using Backpropagation.
- For a single training example, **Backpropagation** algorithm calculates the gradient of the **error function**. Backpropagation can be written as a function of the neural network. Backpropagation algorithms are a set of methods used to efficiently train artificial neural networks following a gradient descent approach which exploits the chain rule.
- The main features of Backpropagation are the iterative, recursive and efficient method through which it calculates the updated weight to improve the network until it is not able to perform the task for which it is being trained. Derivatives of the activation function to be known at network design time is required to Backpropagation.
- Now, how error function is used in Backpropagation and how Backpropagation works? Let start with an example and do it mathematically to understand how exactly updates the weight using Backpropagation.

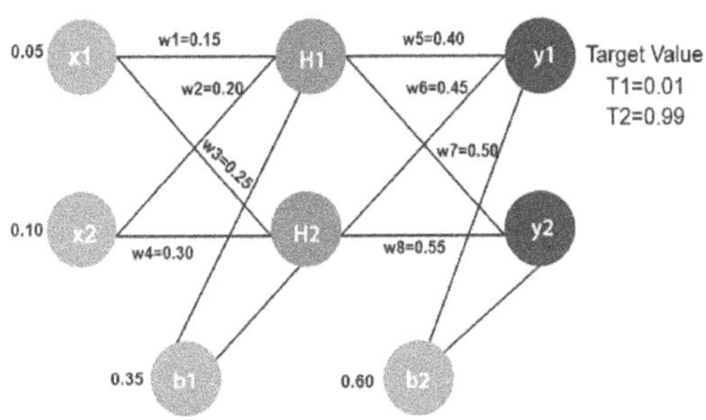

Fig. 4.11: Example for Backpropagation

Input values

X1=0.05

X2=0.10

Initial weight

W1=0.15 w5=0.40

W2=0.20 w6=0.45

W3=0.25   w7=0.50

W4=0.30   w8=0.55

Bias Values

b1=0.35 b2=0.60

Target Values

T1=0.01

T2=0.99

Now, we first calculate the values of H1 and H2 by a forward pass.

Forward Pass

To find the value of H1 we first multiply the input value from the weights as,

$H1=x1\times w_1+x2\times w_2+b1$

$H1=0.05\times 0.15+0.10\times 0.20+0.35$

$\mathbf{H1=0.3775}$

To calculate the final result of H1, we performed the sigmoid function as,

$$H1_{final} = \frac{1}{1+\frac{1}{e^{H1}}}$$

$$H1_{final} = \frac{1}{1+\frac{1}{e^{0.3775}}}$$

$$\mathbf{H1_{final} = 0.593269992}$$

We will calculate the value of H2 in the same way as H1.

$H2=x1\times w_3+x2\times w_4+b1$

$H2=0.05\times 0.25+0.10\times 0.30+0.35$

$\mathbf{H2=0.3925}$

To calculate the final result of H1, we performed the sigmoid function as,

$$H2_{final} = \frac{1}{1+\frac{1}{e^{H2}}}$$

$$H2_{final} = \frac{1}{1+\frac{1}{e^{0.3925}}}$$

$$\mathbf{H2_{final} = 0.596884378}$$

Now, we calculate the values of y1 and y2 in the same way as we calculate the H1 and H2.

To find the value of y1, we first multiply the input value i.e., the outcome of H1 and H2 from the weights as,

$y1=H1\times w_5+H2\times w_6+b2$

$y1=0.593269992\times 0.40+0.596884378\times 0.45+0.60$

$\mathbf{y1=1.10590597}$

To calculate the final result of y1 we performed the sigmoid function as,

$$y1_{final}=\frac{1}{1+\frac{1}{e^{y1}}}$$

$$y1_{final}=\frac{1}{1+\frac{1}{e^{1.10590597}}}$$

$$\mathbf{y1_{final}=0.75136507}$$

We will calculate the value of y2 in the same way as y1.

$y2=H1\times w_7+H2\times w_8+b2$

$y2=0.593269992\times 0.50+0.596884378\times 0.55+0.60$

$\mathbf{y2=1.2249214}$

To calculate the final result of H1, we performed the sigmoid function as,

$$y2_{final}=\frac{1}{1+\frac{1}{e^{y2}}}$$

$$y2_{final}=\frac{1}{1+\frac{1}{e^{1.2249214}}}$$

$$\mathbf{y2_{final}=0.772928465}$$

Our target values are 0.01 and 0.99. Our y1 and y2 value is not matched with our target values T1 and T2.

Now, we will find the **total error**, which is simply the difference between the outputs from the target outputs. The total error is calculated as,

$$E_{total}=\sum\frac{1}{2}(\text{target}-\text{output})^2$$

So, the total error is,

$$= \frac{1}{2}(t1 - y1_{final})^2 + \frac{1}{2}(T2 - y2_{final})^2$$

$$= \frac{1}{2}(0.01 - 0.75136507)^2 + \frac{1}{2}(0.99 - 0.772928465)^2$$

$$= 0.274811084 + 0.0235600257$$

$$E_{total} = \mathbf{0.29837111}$$

Now, we will backpropagate this error to update the weights using a backward pass.

Backward Pass at the Output Layer

To update the weight, we calculate the error correspond to each weight with the help of a total error. The error on weight w is calculated by differentiating total error with respect to w.

$$Error_w = \frac{\partial E_{total}}{\partial w}$$

We perform backward process so first consider the last weight w5 as,

$$Error_{w5} = \frac{\partial E_{total}}{\partial w5}$$

$$E_{total} = \frac{1}{2}(T1 - y1_{final})^2 + \frac{1}{2}(T2 - y2_{final})^2$$

From equation two, it is clear that we cannot partially differentiate it with respect to w5 because there is no any w5. We split equation one into multiple terms so that we can easily differentiate it with respect to w5 as,

$$\frac{\partial E_{total}}{\partial w5} = \frac{\partial E_{total}}{\partial y1_{final}} \times \frac{\partial y1\_final}{\partial y1} \times \frac{\partial y1}{\partial w5}$$

Now, we calculate each term one by one to differentiate E_{total} with respect to w5 as,

$$\frac{\partial E_{total}}{\partial y1_{final}} = \frac{\partial(\frac{1}{2}(T1 - y1_{final})^2 + \frac{1}{2}(T2 - y2_{final})^2)}{\partial y1_{final}}$$

$$= 2 \times \frac{1}{2} \times (T1 - y1_{final})^{2-1} \times (-1) + 0$$

$$= -(T1 - y1_{final})$$

$$= -(0.01 - 0.75136507)$$

$$\frac{\partial E_{total}}{\partial y1_{final}} = 0.74136507$$

$$y1_{final} = \frac{1}{1 + e^{-y1}}$$

$$\frac{\partial y1_{final}}{\partial y1} = \frac{\partial(\frac{1}{1 + e^{-y1}})}{\partial y1}$$

$$= \frac{e^{-y1}}{(1 + e^{-y1})^2}$$

$$= e^{-y1} \times (y1_{final})^2$$

$$y1_{final} = \frac{1}{1 + e^{-y1}}$$

$$e^{-y1} = \frac{1 - y1_{final}}{y1_{final}}$$

Putting the value of e^{-y} in equation.

$$= \frac{1 - y1_{final}}{y1_{final}} \times (y1_{final})^2$$

$$= y1_{final} \times (1 - y1_{final})$$

$$= 0.75136507 \times (1 - 0.75136507)$$

$$\frac{\partial y1_{final}}{\partial y1} = 0.186815602$$

$$y1 = H1_{final} \times w5 + H2_{final} \times w6 + b2$$

$$\frac{\partial y1}{\partial w5} = \frac{\partial(H1_{final} \times w5 + H2_{final} \times w6 + b2)}{\partial w5}$$

$$= H1_{final}$$

$$\frac{\partial y1}{\partial w5} = 0.596884378$$

So, we put the values of $\frac{\partial E_{total}}{\partial y1_{final}}$, $\frac{\partial y1_{final}}{\partial y1}$, and $\frac{\partial y1}{\partial w5}$ in equation to find the final result.

$$\frac{\partial E_{total}}{\partial w5} = \frac{\partial E_{total}}{\partial y1_{final}} \times \frac{\partial y1_{final}}{\partial y1} \times \frac{\partial y1}{\partial w5}$$

$$= 0.74136507 \times 0.186815602 \times 0.593269992$$

$$\mathbf{Error_{w5}} = \frac{\partial \mathbf{E_{total}}}{\partial \mathbf{w5}} = \mathbf{0.0821670407}$$

Now, we will calculate the updated weight $w5_{new}$ with the help of the following formula.

$$w5_{new} = w5 - \eta \times \frac{\partial E_{total}}{\partial w5} \text{ Here, } \eta = \text{learning rate} = 0.5$$

$$= 0.4 - 0.5 \times 0.0821670407$$

$$\mathbf{w5_{new} = 0.35891648}$$

In the same way, we calculate $w6_{new}$, $w7_{new}$, and $w8_{new}$ and this will give us the following values.

$w5_{new}$=0.35891648

$w6_{new}$=408666186

$w7_{new}$=0.511301270

$w8_{new}$=0.561370121

Backward Pass at Hidden Layer

Now, we will backpropagate to our hidden layer and update the weight w1, w2, w3, and w4 as we have done with w5, w6, w7, and w8 weights.

We will calculate the error at w1 as,

$$\text{Error}_{w1} = \frac{\partial E_{total}}{\partial w1}$$

$$E_{total} = \frac{1}{2}(T1 - y1_{final})^2 + \frac{1}{2}(T2 - y2_{final})^2$$

From equation, it is clear that we cannot partially differentiate it with respect to w1 because there is no any w1. We split equation into multiple terms so that we can easily differentiate it with respect to w1 as,

$$\frac{\partial E_{total}}{\partial w1} = \frac{\partial E_{total}}{\partial H1_{final}} \times \frac{\partial H1\_final}{\partial H1} \times \frac{\partial H1}{\partial w1}$$

Now, we calculate each term one by one to differentiate E_{total} with respect to w1 as,

$$\frac{\partial E_{total}}{\partial H1_{final}} = \frac{\partial(\frac{1}{2}(T1 - y1_{final})^2 + \frac{1}{2}(T2 - y2_{final})^2)}{\partial H1}$$

We again split this because there is no any $H1^{final}$ term in E^{toatal} as,

$$\frac{\partial E_{total}}{\partial H1_{final}} = \frac{\partial E_1}{\partial H1_{final}} + \frac{\partial E_2}{\partial H1_{final}}$$

$\frac{\partial E_1}{\partial H1_{final}}$ and $\frac{\partial E_2}{\partial H1_{final}}$ will again split because in E1 and E2 there is no H1 term. Splitting is done as,

$$\frac{\partial E_1}{\partial H1_{final}} = \frac{\partial E_1}{\partial y1} \times \frac{\partial y1}{\partial H1_{final}}$$

$$\frac{\partial E_2}{\partial H1_{final}} = \frac{\partial E_2}{\partial y2} \times \frac{\partial y2}{\partial H1\_final}$$

We again Split both $\frac{\partial E_1}{\partial y1}$ and $\frac{\partial E_2}{\partial y2}$ because there is no any y1 and y2 term in E1 and E2. We split it as,

$$\frac{\partial E_1}{\partial y1} = \frac{\partial E_1}{\partial y1_{final}} \times \frac{\partial y1_{final}}{\partial y1}$$

$$\frac{\partial E_2}{\partial y2} = \frac{\partial E_2}{\partial y2_{final}} \times \frac{\partial y2_{final}}{\partial y2}$$

Now, we find the value of $\frac{\partial E_1}{\partial y1}$ and $\frac{\partial E_2}{\partial y2}$ by putting values in equation as,

From equation

$$\frac{\partial E_1}{\partial y1} = \frac{\partial E_1}{\partial y1_{final}} \times \frac{\partial y1_{final}}{\partial y1}$$

$$= \frac{\partial(\frac{1}{2}(T1 - y1_{final})^2)}{\partial y1_{final}} \times \frac{\partial y1_{final}}{\partial y1}$$

$$= 2 \times \frac{1}{2}(T1 - y1_{final}) \times (-1) \times \frac{\partial y1_{final}}{\partial y1}$$

From equation

$$= 2 \times \frac{1}{2}(0.01 - 0.75136507) \times (-1) \times 0.186815602$$

$$\frac{\partial \mathbf{E_1}}{\partial \mathbf{y1}} = \mathbf{0.138498562}$$

From equation

$$\frac{\partial E_2}{\partial y2} = \frac{\partial E_2}{\partial y2_{final}} \times \frac{\partial y2_{final}}{\partial y2}$$

$$= \frac{\partial(\frac{1}{2}(\mathrm{T2} - \mathrm{y2_{final}})^2)}{\partial \mathrm{y2_{final}}} \times \frac{\partial \mathrm{y2_{final}}}{\partial \mathrm{y2}}$$

$$= 2 \times \frac{1}{2}(\mathrm{T2} - \mathrm{y2_{final}}) \times (-1) \times \frac{\partial \mathrm{y2_{final}}}{\partial \mathrm{y2}}$$

$$\mathrm{y2_{final}} = \frac{1}{1 + \mathrm{e^{-y2}}}$$

$$\frac{\partial y2_{final}}{\partial y2} = \frac{\partial(\frac{1}{1 + e^{-y2}})}{\partial y2}$$

$$= \frac{\mathrm{e^{-y2}}}{(1 + \mathrm{e^{-y2}})^2}$$

$$= \mathrm{e^{-y2}} \times (\mathrm{y2_{final}})^2$$

$$\mathrm{y2_{final}} = \frac{1}{1 + \mathrm{e^{-y2}}}$$

$$\mathrm{e^{-y2}} = \frac{1 - \mathrm{y2_{final}}}{\mathrm{y2_{final}}}$$

Putting the value of e^{-y2} in equation

$$= \frac{1 - \mathrm{y2_{final}}}{\mathrm{y2_{final}}} \times (\mathrm{y2_{final}})^2$$

$$= \mathrm{y2_{final}} \times (1 - \mathrm{y2_{final}})$$

$$= 0.772928465 \times (1 - 0.772928465)$$

$$\frac{\partial y2_{final}}{\partial y2} = 0.175510053$$

From equation

$$= 2 \times \frac{1}{2}(0.99 - 0.772928465) \times (-1) \times 0.175510053$$

$$\frac{\partial \mathbf{E_1}}{\partial \mathbf{y1}} = \mathbf{-0.0380982366126414}$$

Now from equation

$$\frac{\partial E_1}{\partial H1_{final}} = \frac{\partial E_1}{\partial y1} \times \frac{\partial y1}{\partial H1_{final}}$$

$$= 0.138498562 \times \frac{\partial (H1_{final} \times w_5 + H2_{final} \times w_6 + b2)}{\partial H1_{final}}$$

$$= 0.138498562 \times w5$$

$$= 0.138498562 \times 0.40$$

$$\frac{\partial \mathbf{E_1}}{\partial \mathbf{H1_{final}}} = \mathbf{0.0553994248}$$

$$\frac{\partial E_2}{\partial H1_{final}} = \frac{\partial E_2}{\partial y2} \times \frac{\partial y2}{\partial H1\_final}$$

$$= -0.0380982366126414 \times \frac{\partial (H1_{final} \times w_7 + H2_{final} \times w_8 + b2)}{\partial H1_{final}}$$

$$= -0.0380982366126414 \times w7$$

$$= -0.0380982366126414 \times 0.50$$

$$\frac{\partial \mathbf{E_2}}{\partial \mathbf{H1_{final}}} = \mathbf{-0.0190491183063207}$$

Put the value of $\frac{\partial E_1}{\partial H1_{final}}$ and $\frac{\partial E_2}{\partial H1_{final}}$ in equation as,

$$\frac{\partial E_{total}}{\partial H1_{final}} = \frac{\partial E_1}{\partial H1_{final}} + \frac{\partial E_2}{\partial H1_{final}}$$

$$= 0.0553994248 + (-0.0190491183063207)$$

$$\frac{\partial \mathbf{E_{total}}}{\partial \mathbf{H1_{final}}} = \mathbf{0.0364908241736793}$$

We have $\frac{\partial E_{total}}{\partial H1_{final}}$, we need to figure out $\frac{\partial H1\_final}{\partial H1}$, $\frac{\partial H1}{\partial w1}$ as,

$$\frac{\partial H1_{final}}{\partial H1} = \frac{\partial(\frac{1}{1+e^{-H1}})}{\partial H1}$$

$$= \frac{e^{-H1}}{(1+e^{-H1})^2}$$

$$e^{-H1} \times (H1_{final})^2$$

$$H1_{final} = \frac{1}{1+e^{-H1}}$$

$$e^{-H1} = \frac{1 - H1_{final}}{H1_{final}}$$

Putting the value of e^{-H1} in equation

$$= \frac{1 - H1_{final}}{H1_{final}} \times (H1_{final})^2$$

$$= H1_{final} \times (1 - H1_{final})$$

$$= 0.593269992 \times (1 - 0.593269992)$$

$$\frac{\partial H1_{final}}{\partial H1} = 0.2413007085923199$$

We calculate the partial derivative of the total net input to H1 with respect to w1 the same as we did for the output neuron:

$$H1 = H1_{final} \times w5 + H2_{final} \times w6 + b2$$

$$\frac{\partial y1}{\partial w1} = \frac{\partial(x1 \times w1 + x2 \times w3 + b1 \times 1)}{\partial w1}$$

$$= x1$$

$$\frac{\partial H1}{\partial w1} = 0.05$$

So, we put the values of $\frac{\partial E_{total}}{\partial H1_{final}}$, $\frac{\partial H1_{final}}{\partial H1}$, and $\frac{\partial H1}{\partial w1}$ in equation to find the final result.

$$\frac{\partial E_{total}}{\partial w1} = \frac{\partial E_{total}}{\partial H1_{final}} \times \frac{\partial H1_{final}}{\partial H1} \times \frac{\partial H1}{\partial w1}$$

$$= 0.0364908241736793 \times 0.2413007085923199 \times 0.05$$

$$\mathbf{Error_{w1}} = \frac{\partial \mathbf{E_{total}}}{\partial \mathbf{w1}} = \mathbf{0.000438568}$$

Now, we will calculate the updated weight $w1_{new}$ with the help of the following formula.

$$w1_{new} = w1 - \eta \times \frac{\partial E_{total}}{\partial w1} \text{ Here } \eta = \text{learning rate} = 0.5$$

$$= 0.15 - 0.5 \times 0.000438568$$

$$\mathbf{w1_{new} = 0.149780716}$$

In the same way, we calculate $w2_{new}$, $w3_{new}$, and w4 and this will give us the following values.

$w1_{new}$=0.149780716

$w2_{new}$=0.19956143

$w3_{new}$=0.24975114

$w4_{new}$=0.29950229

We have updated all the weights. We found the error 0.298371109 on the network when we fed forward the 0.05 and 0.1 inputs. In the first round of Backpropagation, the total error is down to 0.291027924. After repeating this process 10,000, the total error is down to 0.0000351085. At this point, the outputs neurons generate 0.159121960 and 0.984065734 i.e., nearby our target value when we feed forward the 0.05 and 0.1.

Example 1:

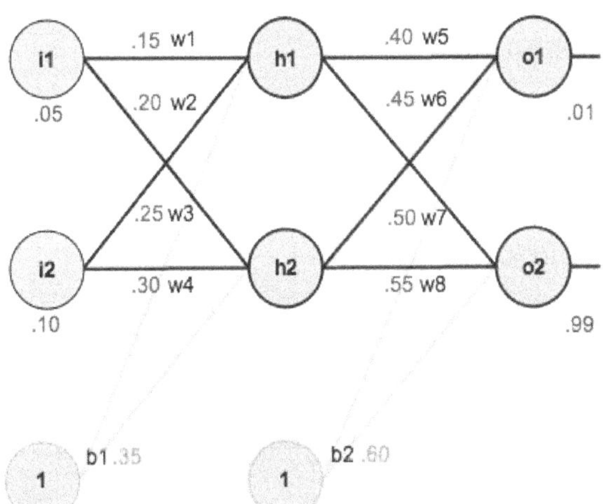

Fig. 4.12: Example 2 Backpropagation

The goal of backpropagation is to optimize the weights so that the neural network can learn how to correctly map arbitrary inputs to outputs.

For the rest of this tutorial we're going to work with a single training set: given inputs 0.05 and 0.10, we want the neural network to output 0.01 and 0.99.

The Forward Pass

To begin, lets see what the neural network currently predicts given the weights and biases above and inputs of 0.05 and 0.10. To do this we'll feed those inputs forward though the network.

We figure out the *total net input* to each hidden layer neuron, *squash* the total net input using an *activation function* (here we use the *logistic function*), then repeat the process with the output layer neurons.

Total net input is also referred to as just *net input* by some sources.

Here's how we calculate the total net input for h_1:

$$net_{h1} = w_1 * i_1 + w_2 * i_2 + b_1 * 1$$

$$net_{h1} = 0.15 * 0.05 + 0.2 * 0.1 + 0.35 * 1 = 0.3775$$

We then squash it using the logistic function to get the output of,

$$out_{h1} = \frac{1}{1+e^{-net_{h1}}} = \frac{1}{1+e^{-0.3775}} = 0.593269992$$

Carrying out the same process for $h_2$we get:

$$out_{h2} = 0.596884378$$

We repeat this process for the output layer neurons, using the output from the hidden layer neurons as inputs.

Here's the output for o_1:

$$net_{o1} = w_5 * out_{h1} + w_6 * out_{h2} + b_2 * 1$$

$$net_{o1} = 0.4 * 0.593269992 + 0.45 * 0.596884378 + 0.6 * 1 = 1.105905967$$

$$out_{o1} = \frac{1}{1+e^{-net_{o1}}} = \frac{1}{1+e^{-1.105905967}} = 0.75136507$$

And carrying out the same process for $o_2$we get:

$$out_{o2} = 0.772928465$$

Calculating the Total Error

We can now calculate the error for each output neuron using the squared error function and sum them to get the total error:

$$E_{total} = \sum \frac{1}{2}(target - output)^2$$

Some sources refer to the target as the *ideal* and the output as the *actual.*

The $\frac{1}{2}$ is included so that exponent is cancelled when we differentiate later on. The result is eventually multiplied by a learning rate anyway so it doesn't matter that we introduce a constant here [1].

For example, the target output for o_1 is 0.01 but the neural network output 0.75136507, therefore its error is:

$$E_{o1} = \frac{1}{2}(target_{o1} - out_{o1})^2 = \frac{1}{2}(0.01 - 0.75136507)^2 = 0.274811083$$

Repeating this process for o_2 (remembering that the target is 0.99) we get:

$$E_{o2} = 0.023560026$$

The total error for the neural network is the sum of these errors:

$$E_{total} = E_{o1} + E_{o2} = 0.274811083 + 0.023560026 = 0.298371109$$

The Backwards Pass

Our goal with backpropagation is to update each of the weights in the network so that they cause the actual output to be closer the target output, thereby minimizing the error for each output neuron and the network as a whole.

Output Layer

Consider w_5 We want to know how much a change in w_5 affects the total error, aka $\frac{\partial E_{total}}{\partial_{w5}}$.

$\frac{\partial E_{total}}{\partial_{w5}}$ is read as "the partial derivative of E_{total} with respect to w_5". You can also say "the gradient with respect to w_5".

By applying the chain rule we know that:

Visually, here's what we're doing:

$$\frac{\partial_{net_{o1}}}{\partial_{w5}} * \frac{\partial_{out_{o1}}}{\partial_{net_{o1}}} * \frac{\partial E_{total}}{\partial_{out_{o1}}} = \frac{\partial E_{total}}{\partial_{w5}}$$

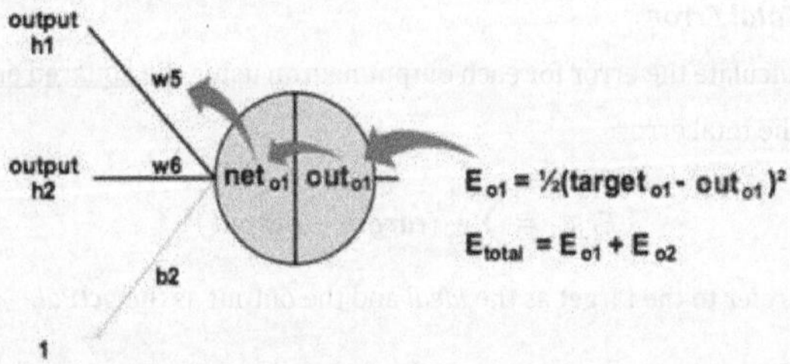

We need to figure out each piece in this equation.

First, how much does the total error change with respect to the output?

$$E_{total} = \frac{1}{2}(target_{o1} - out_{o1})^2 = \frac{1}{2}(target_{o2} - out_{o2})^2$$

$$\frac{\partial E_{total}}{\partial_{out_{o1}}} = 2 * \frac{1}{2}(target_{o1} - out_{o1})^{2-1} * -1 + 0$$

$$\frac{\partial E_{total}}{\partial_{out_{o1}}} = -(target_{o1} - out_{o1}) = -(0.01 - 0.75136507) = 0.74136507$$

$-(target - out)$ is sometimes expressed as $out - target$

When we take the partial derivative of the total error with respect to out_{o1}, the quantity $\frac{1}{2}(target_{o2} - out_{o2})^2$ becomes zero because out_{o1} does not affect it which means we're taking the derivative of a constant which is zero.

Next, how much does the output of o_1 change with respect to its total net input?

The partial derivative of the logistic function is the output multiplied by 1 minus the output:

$$out_{o1} = \frac{1}{1+e^{-net_{o1}}}$$

$$\frac{\partial_{out_{o1}}}{\partial_{net_{o1}}} = out_{o1}(1 - out_{o1}) = 0.75136507(1 - 0.75136507) = 0.186815602$$

Finally, how much does the total net input of $o1$ change with respect to w_5?

$$net_{o1} = w_5 * out_{h1} + w_6 * out_{h2} + b_2 * 1$$

$$\frac{\partial_{net_{o1}}}{\partial_{w_5}} = 1 * out_{h1} * w_5^{(1-1)} + 0 + 0 = out_{h1} = 0.593269992$$

Putting it all together:

$$\frac{\partial E_{total}}{\partial_{w_5}} = 0.74136507 * 0.186815602 * 0.593269992 = 0.082167041$$

You'll often see this calculation combined in the form of the delta rule:

$$\frac{\partial E_{total}}{\partial_{w_5}} = -(target_{o1} - out_{o1}) * out_{o1}(1 - out_{o1}) * out_{h1}$$

Alternatively, we have $\frac{\partial E_{total}}{\partial out_{o1}}$ and $\frac{\partial out_{o1}}{\partial net_{o1}}$ which can be written as, $\frac{\partial E_{total}}{\partial net_{o1}}$ aka δ_{o1} (the Greek letter delta) aka the *node delta*. We can use this to rewrite the calculation above:

$$\delta_{o1} = -(target_{o1} - out_{o1}) * out_{o1}(1 - out_{o1})$$

Therefore:

$$\frac{\partial E_{total}}{\partial_{w_5}} = \delta_{o1} out_{h1}$$

Some sources extract the negative sign from δ so it would be written as:

$$\frac{\partial E_{total}}{\partial_{w_5}} = -\delta_{o1} out_{h1}$$

To decrease the error, we then subtract this value from the current weight (optionally multiplied by some learning rate, eta, which we'll set to 0.5):

$$w_5^+ = w_5 - \eta * \frac{\partial E_{total}}{\partial_{w_5}} = 0.4 - 0.5 * 0.082167041 = 0.35891648$$

Some sources use α (alpha) to represent the learning rate, others use η (eta), and others even use ϵ(epsilon).

We can repeat this process to get the new weights w_6, w_7 and w_8:

$$w_6^+ = 0.408666186$$

$$w_7^+ = 0.511301270$$

$$w_8^+ = 0.561370121$$

We perform the actual updates in the neural network *after* we have the new weights leading into the hidden layer neurons (i.e., we use the original weights, not the updated weights, when we continue the backpropagation algorithm below).

Hidden Layer

Next, we'll continue the backwards pass by calculating new values for w_1, w_2, w_3, and w_4.

Big picture, here's what we need to figure out:

Visually:

$$\frac{\partial E_{total}}{\partial_{w1}} = \frac{\partial E_{total}}{\partial_{out_{h1}}} * \frac{\partial_{out_{h1}}}{\partial_{net_{h1}}} * \frac{\partial_{net_{h1}}}{\partial_{w1}}$$

$$\downarrow$$

$$\frac{\partial E_{total}}{\partial_{out_{h1}}} = \frac{\partial E_{o1}}{\partial_{out_{h1}}} + \frac{\partial E_{o2}}{\partial_{out_{h1}}}$$

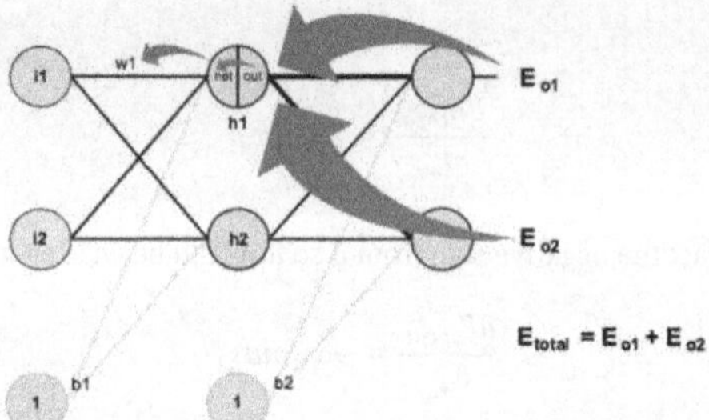

We're going to use a similar process as we did for the output layer, but slightly different to account for the fact that the output of each hidden layer neuron contributes to the output (and therefore error) of multiple output neurons. We know that out_{h1} affects both out_{o1} and out_{o2} therefore the $\frac{\partial E_{total}}{\partial_{out_{h1}}}$ needs to take into consideration its effect on the both output neurons.

Starting with $\frac{\partial E_{o1}}{\partial_{out_{h1}}}$:

We can calculate $\frac{\partial E_{o1}}{\partial_{net_{o1}}}$ using values we calculated earlier:

And $\frac{\partial_{net_{o1}}}{\partial_{out_{h1}}}$ is equal to w_5:

$$net_{o1} = w_5 * out_{h1} + w_6 * out_{h2} + b_2 * 1$$

$$\frac{\partial_{net_{o1}}}{\partial_{out_{h1}}} = w_5 = 0.40$$

Plugging them in:

Following the same process for, $\frac{\partial E_{o2}}{\partial_{out_{h1}}}$ we get:

$$\frac{\partial E_{o2}}{\partial_{out_{h1}}} = -0.019049119$$

Therefore:

Now that we have $\frac{\partial E_{total}}{\partial out_{h1}}$, we need to figure out $\frac{\partial out_{h1}}{\partial net_{h1}}$ and then $\frac{\partial net_{h1}}{\partial w}$ for each weight:

$$out_{h1} = \frac{1}{1 + e^{-net_{h1}}}$$

$\frac{\partial out_{h1}}{\partial net_{h1}}$ $= out_{h1}$ $(1\text{-}out_{h1}) = 0.59326999(1 - 0.59326999) = 0.241300709$

We calculate the partial derivative of the total net input to h_1 with respect to w_1 the same as we did for the output neuron:

$$net_{h1} = w_1 * i_1 + w_3 * i_2 + b_1 * 1$$

$$\frac{\partial net_{h1}}{\partial_{w1}} = i_1 = 0.05$$

Putting it all together:

$$\frac{\partial E_{total}}{\partial_{w1}} = 0.036350306 * 0.241300709 * 0.05 = 0.000438568$$

You might also see this written as:

$$\frac{\partial E_{total}}{\partial_{w1}} = \delta_{h1} i_1$$

We can now update w_1:

$$w_1^+ = w_1 - \eta * \frac{\partial E_{total}}{\partial_{w_1}} = 0.15 - 0.5 * 0.000438568 = 0.149780716$$

Repeating this for w_2, w_3 and w_4

$$w_2^+ = 0.19956143$$

$$w_3^+ = 0.24975114$$

$$w_4^+ = 0.29950229$$

Finally, we've updated all of our weights! When we fed forward the 0.05 and 0.1 inputs originally, the error on the network was 0.298371109. After this first round of backpropagation, the total error is now down to 0.291027924. It might not seem like much, but after repeating this process 10,000 times, for example, the error plummets to 0.0000351085. At this point, when we feed forward 0.05 and 0.1, the two outputs neurons generate 0.015912196 (vs 0.01 target) and 0.984065734 (vs 0.99 target).

CHAPTER 5

ARTIFICIAL NEURAL NETWORKS-2

5.1. Remarks on the Back-Propagation Algorithm

- Input data holds the key to the overall performance.
- Noisy data can lead to inaccurate results.
- Matrix based approach is preferred over a mini-batch.
- Gradient descent with backpropagation is not guaranteed to find the global minimum of the error function, but only a local minimum; also, it has trouble crossing plateaus in the error function landscape. This issue, caused by the non-convexity of error functions in neural networks, was long thought to be a major drawback.
- Backpropagation learning does not require normalization of input vectors; however, normalization could improve performance.
- Backpropagation possibly be sensitive to noisy data and irregularity.
- The performance of this is highly reliant on the input data.
- Needs excessive time for training.
- Backpropagation requires the derivatives of activation functions to be known at network design time.

5.2. Face Recognition Using Artificial Intelligence

- Facial Recognition is a category of biometric software that maps an individual's facial features and stores the data as a face print. The software uses deep learning algorithms to compare a live captured image to the stored face print to verify one's identity. Image processing and machine learning are the backbones of this technology. Face recognition has received substantial attention from researchers due to human activities found in various applications of security like an airport, criminal detection, face tracking, forensic, etc. Compared to other biometric traits like palm print, iris, fingerprint, etc., face biometrics can be non-intrusive.
- They can be taken even without the user's knowledge and further can be used for security-based applications like criminal detection, face tracking, airport security, and forensic surveillance systems. Face recognition involves capturing face images

from a video or a surveillance camera. They are compared with the stored database. Face recognition involves training known images, classify them with known classes, and then they are stored in the database. When a test image is given to the system it is classified and compared with the stored database.

- ***Image Processing and Machine Learning***

Image processing by computers involves the process of Computer Vision. It deals with the high-level understanding of digital images or videos. The requirement is to automate tasks that the human visual systems can do. So, a computer should be able to recognize objects such as that of a face of a human being or a lamppost or even a statue.

Image Reading

The computer reads any image as a range of values between 0 and 255. For any color image, there are 3 primary colors – Red, green, and blue. A matrix is formed for every primary color and later these matrices combine to provide a Pixel value for the individual R, G, B colors. Each element of the matrices provide data about the intensity of the brightness of the pixel.

OpenCV is a Python library that is designed to solve computer vision problems. OpenCV was originally developed in 1999 by Intel but later supported by Willow Garage. OpenCV supports a variety of programming languages such as C++, Python, Java, etc. Support for multiple platforms including Windows, Linux, and macOS. OpenCV Python is a wrapper class for the original C++ library to be used with Python. Using this, all of the OpenCV array structures get converted to/from NumPy arrays. This makes it easier to integrate it with other libraries that use NumPy. For example, libraries such as SciPy and Matplotlib.

Machine Learning

Every Machine Learning algorithm takes a dataset as input and learns from the data it basically means to learn the algorithm from the provided input and output as data. It identifies the patterns in the data and provides the desired algorithm. For instance, to identify whose face is present in a given image, multiple things can be looked at as a pattern:

- Height/width of the face.
- Height and width may not be reliable since the image could be rescaled to a smaller face or grid. However, even after rescaling, what remains unchanged are the ratios – the ratio of the height of the face to the width of the face won't change.

- Color of the face.
- Width of other parts of the face like lips, nose, etc.

There is a pattern involved - different faces have different dimensions like the ones above. Similar faces have similar dimensions. Machine Learning algorithms only understand numbers so it is quite challenging. This numerical representation of a "face" (or an element in the training set) is termed as a feature vector. A feature vector comprises of various numbers in a specific order.

As a simple example, we can map a "face" into a feature vector which can comprise various features like:

- Height of face (cm)
- Width of the face (cm)
- Average color of face (R, G, B)
- Width of lips (cm)
- Height of nose (cm)

Essentially, given an image, we can convert them into a feature vector like:

Height of face (cm) Width of the face (cm) Average color of face (RGB) Width of lips (cm) Height of nose (cm)

23.1 15.8 (255, 224, 189) 5.2 4.4

So, the image is now a vector that could be represented as (23.1, 15.8, 255, 224, 189, 5.2, 4.4). There could be countless other features that could be derived from the image, for instance, hair color, facial hair, spectacles, etc.

Machine Learning does two major functions in face recognition technology. These are given below:

1. Deriving the feature vector: it is difficult to manually list down all of the features because there are just so many. A Machine Learning algorithm can intelligently label out many of such features. For instance, a complex feature could be the ratio of the height of the nose and width of the forehead.
2. Matching algorithms: Once the feature vectors have been obtained, a Machine Learning algorithm needs to match a new image with the set of feature vectors present in the corpus.
3. Face Recognition Operations.

Face Recognition Operations

The technology system may vary when it comes to facial recognition. Different software applies different methods and means to achieve face recognition. The stepwise method is as follows:

- Face Detection: To begin with, the camera will detect and recognize a face. The face can be best detected when the person is looking directly at the camera as it makes it easy for facial recognition. With the advancements in the technology, this is improved where the face can be detected with slight variation in their posture of face facing to the camera.
- Face Analysis: Then the photo of the face is captured and analyzed. Most facial recognition relies on 2D images rather than 3D because it is more convenient to match to the database. Facial recognition software will analyze the distance between your eyes or the shape of your cheekbones.
- Image to Data Conversion: Now it is converted to a mathematical formula and these facial features become numbers. This numerical code is known a face print. The way every person has a unique fingerprint, in the same way, they have unique face print.
- Match Finding: Then the code is compared against a database of other face prints. This database has photos with identification that can be compared. The technology then identifies a match for your exact features in the provided database. It returns with the match and attached information such as name and addresses or it depends on the information saved in the database of an individual.

5.3. Face Recognition Software's

- Many renowned companies are constantly innovating and improvising to develop face recognition software that is foolproof and dependable. Some prominent software is being discussed below:

Deep Vision AI

- Deep Vision AI is a front runner company excelling in facial recognition software. The company owns the proprietorship of advanced computer vision technology that can understand images and videos automatically. It then turns the visual content into real-time analytics and provides very valuable insights.
- Deep Vision AI provides a plug and plays platform to its users worldwide. The users are given real-time alerts and faster response based upon the analysis of camera streams

through various AI-based modules. The product offers a highly accurate rate of identification of individuals on a watch list by continuous monitoring of target zones. The software is highly flexible that it can be connected to any existing camera system or can be deployed through the cloud.

- At present, Deep Vision AI offers the best performance solution in the market supporting real-time processing at +15 streams per GPU.
- Business intelligence gathering is helped by providing real-time data of customers, their frequency of visits, or enhancement of security and safety. Further, the output from the software can provide attributes like count, age, gender, etc that can enhance the understanding of consumer behaviour, changing preferences, shifts with time, and conditions that can guide future marketing efforts and strategies. The users also combine the face recognition capabilities with other AI-based features of Deep Vision AI like vehicle recognition to get more correlated data of the consumers.

Amazon Rekognition

- Amazon provides a cloud-based software solution Amazon Rekognition is a service computer vision platform. This solution allows an easy method to add image and video analysis to various applications. It uses a highly scalable and proven deep learning technology. The user is not required to have any machine learning expertise to use this software. The platform can be utilized to identify objects, text, people, activities, and scenes in images and videos. It can also detect any inappropriate content. The user gets a highly accurate facial analysis and facial search capabilities. Hence, the software can be easily used for verification, counting of people, and public safety by detection, analysis, and comparison of fac es.
- Organizations can use Amazon Rekognition Custom Labels to generate data about specific objects and scenes available in images according to their business needs. For example, a model may be easily built to classify specific machine parts on the assembly line or to detect unhealthy plants. The user simply provides the images of objects or scenes he wants to identify, and the service handles the rest.

TrueFace

- TrueFace is a leading computer vision model that helps people understanding their camera data and convert the data into actionable information. TrueFace is an on-premise computer vision solution that enhances data security and performance speeds. The platform-based solutions are specifically trained as per the requirements of individual deployment and operate effectively in a variety of ecosystems. The software places the utmost priority on the diversity of training data. It ensures equivalent performance for all users irrespective of their widely different requirements.

- Trueface has developed a suite consisting of SDK's and a dockerized container solution based on the capabilities of machine learning and artificial intelligence. The suite can convert the camera data into actionable intelligence. It can help the organizations to create a safer and smarter environment for its employees, customers, and guests using facial recognition, weapon detection, and age verification technologies.

5.4. Problems and Challenges

The face recognition technology is facing several challenges. The common problems and challenges that a face recognition system can have while detecting and recognizing faces are discussed in the following paragraphs.

- Pose: A Face Recognition System can tolerate cases with small rotation angles, but it becomes difficult to detect if the angle would be large and if the database does not contain all the angles of the face then it can impose a problem.
- Expressions: Because of the emotions, human mood varies and results in different expressions. With these facial expressions, the machine could make mistakes to find the correct person identity.
- Aging: With time and age face changes it is unique and does not remain rigid due to which it may be difficult to identify a person who is now 60 years old.
- Occlusion: Occlusion means blockage. This is due to the presence of various occluding objects such as glasses, beard, moustache, etc. on the face, and when an image is captured, the face lacks some parts. Such a problem can severely affect the classification process of the recognition system.
- Illumination: Illumination means light variations. Illumination changes can vary the overall magnitude of light intensity reflected from an object, as well as the pattern of shading and shadows visible in an image. The problem of face recognition over changes in illumination is widely recognized to be difficult for humans and algorithms. The

difficulties posed by illumination condition is a challenge for automatic face recognition systems.

- Identify similar faces: Different persons may have a similar appearance that sometimes makes it impossible to distinguish.

Disadvantages of Face Recognition

1. Danger of automated blanket surveillance.
2. Lack of clear legal or regulatory framework.
3. Violation of the principles of necessity and proportionality.
4. Violation of the right to privacy.
5. Effect on democratic political culture.

Example fig. shows face recognition.

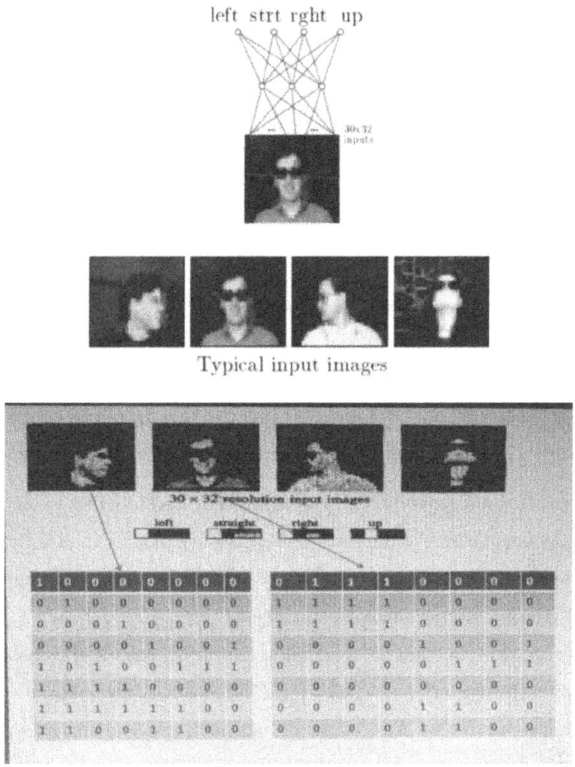

Fig. 5.1: Face Recognition System

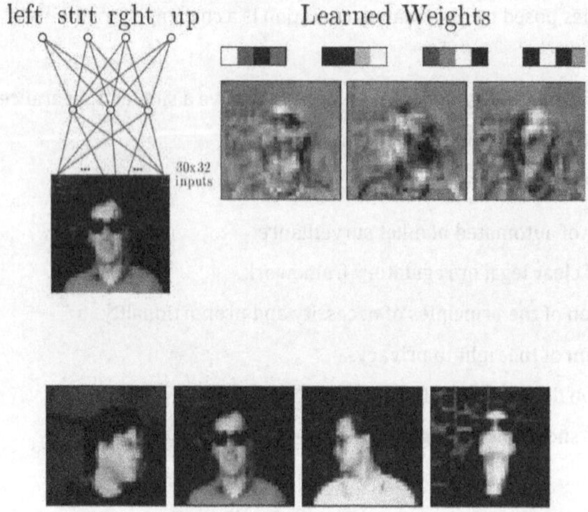

Fig. 5.2: Shows Face Recognition with L,R,S,U

5.5. Advanced Topics in Artificial Neural Networks

We know that our world is changing quickly but there are lot of concrete technology advances that you might not hear a lot about in the newspaper or on tv, that are nevertheless having a dramatic impact on our lives.

Some of these big new stories are related to the ANN (Artificial Neural Network) – a relatively new phenomenon in artificial intelligence research that's driving all sorts of progress in many fields from entertainment to medicine. As a human, we discovered that we can build better models by throwing together many of these artificial neurons and making them work together in ways that are very like or biological thought process.

- **Game playing and beyond:** You may have heard recently that a computer was able to beat a human player in the game of "Go", a game that's significantly more complex than chess. A lot of us intuitively understand this is yet another step forward along the path toward stronger artificial intelligence.
- **More precision in cancer treatment:** Cancer is one of the most confounding diseases of the western medical lexicon – but now very few kinds of cancer research are being supported by artificial neural networks as scientists get close to breaking through to new ways of treating many different kinds of tumour.

- **Progress in Neuro Science:** ANN isn't just useful in cancer research- the same principles can take all sorts of clinical data and refine it into more actionable forms. But there is a special relationship between ANN and neuroscience - because even as we are putting together these building blocks that simulate the human brain, we are learning more about how the human brain works-which is supporting new modern facilities to serve patients in new ways.
- **AI ad personalized marketing:** Another breakthrough that's supported by artificial neural networks is the uncanny ability of marketers to figure out what a given consumer wants. You may have encountered this kind of thing in a website's recommended engine. You also see ads, all this is driven by artificial neural network and machine learning algorithms that are able to make connections on their own rather than being driven by human decision-makers.
- **Everyday Interfaces:** A business is an organism and any business of significant size is going to need a bit of direction both day to day and over the long term.
- **Business Intelligence:** As soon as software became sufficiently advanced, vendors started building different enterprise software platforms to help businesses to automate everything that they used to do by hand. Rather than doing walk-throughs of facilities and trying to imagine what's going to happen in the future, today's leaders are increasingly looking at visual dashboards and seeing clearly, what they need to do to make the business work better.

CHAPTER 6

EVALUATION HYPOTHESES

6.1. Evaluation Hypotheses - Motivation

Hypothesis

A hypothesis is an explanation for something.

It is a provisional idea, an educated guess that requires some evaluation.

A good hypothesis is testable; it can be either true or false.

In science, a hypothesis must be falsifiable, meaning that there exists a test whose outcome could mean that the hypothesis is not true. The hypothesis must also be framed before the outcome of the test is known.

A good hypothesis fits the evidence and can be used to make predictions about new observations or new situations.

The hypothesis that best fits the evidence and can be used to make predictions is called a theory, or is part of a theory.

- **Hypothesis in Science**: Provisional explanation that fits the evidence and can be confirmed or disproved.

6.2. What is a Hypothesis in Machine Learning?

Machine learning, specifically supervised learning, can be described as the desire to use available data to learn a function that best maps inputs to outputs.

Technically, this is a problem called function approximation, where we are approximating an unknown target function (that we assume exists) that can best map inputs to outputs on all possible observations from the problem domain.

An example of a model that approximates the target function and performs mappings of inputs to outputs is called a hypothesis in machine learning.

The choice of algorithm (e.g. neural network) and the configuration of the algorithm (e.g. network topology and hyperparameters) define the space of possible hypothesis that the model may represent.

Learning for a machine learning algorithm involves navigating the chosen space of hypothesis toward the best or a good enough hypothesis that best approximates the target function.

Learning is a search through the space of possible hypotheses for one that will perform well, even on new examples beyond the training set.

This description is characterized as searching through and evaluating candidate hypothesis from hypothesis spaces.

The discussion of hypotheses in machine learning can be confusing for a beginner, especially when "*hypothesis*" has a distinct, but related meaning in statistics (e.g. statistical hypothesis testing) and more broadly in science (e.g. scientific hypothesis).

In this, you will discover the difference between a hypothesis in science, in statistics, and in machine learning.

After reading this, you will know:

- A scientific hypothesis is a provisional explanation for observations that is falsifiable.
- A statistical hypothesis is an explanation about the relationship between data populations that is interpreted probabilistically.
- A machine learning hypothesis is a candidate model that approximates a target function for mapping inputs to outputs.

Fig. 6.1: A Gentle Introduction to Hypotheses in Machine Learning

Overview

This tutorial is divided into four parts; they are:

1. What Is a Hypothesis?
2. Hypothesis in Statistics

3. Hypothesis in Machine Learning
4. Review of Hypothesis

What Is a Hypothesis?

A hypothesis is an explanation for something.

It is a provisional idea, an educated guess that requires some evaluation.

A good hypothesis is testable; it can be either true or false.

In science, a hypothesis must be falsifiable, meaning that there exists a test whose outcome could mean that the hypothesis is not true. The hypothesis must also be framed before the outcome of the test is known.

... not any hypothesis will do. There is one fundamental condition that any hypothesis or system of hypotheses must satisfy if it is to be granted the status of a scientific law or theory. If it is to form part of science, an hypothesis must be falsifiable.

A good hypothesis fits the evidence and can be used to make predictions about new observations or new situations.

The hypothesis that best fits the evidence and can be used to make predictions is called a theory, or is part of a theory.

- **Hypothesis in Science**: Provisional explanation that fits the evidence and can be confirmed or disproved.

What is a Hypothesis in Statistics?

Much of statistics is concerned with the relationship between observations.

Statistical hypothesis tests are techniques used to calculate a critical value called an "*effect*." The critical value can then be interpreted in order to determine how likely it is to observe the effect if a relationship does not exist.

If the likelihood is very small, then it suggests that the effect is probably real. If the likelihood is large, then we may have observed a statistical fluctuation, and the effect is probably not real.

For example, we may be interested in evaluating the relationship between the means of two samples, e.g. whether the samples were drawn from the same distribution or not, whether there is a difference between them.

One hypothesis is that there is no difference between the population means, based on the data samples.

This is a hypothesis of no effect and is called the null hypothesis and we can use the statistical hypothesis test to either reject this hypothesis, or fail to reject (retain) it. We don't say "accept" because the outcome is probabilistic and could still be wrong, just with a very low probability.

...we develop a hypothesis and establish a criterion that we will use when deciding whether to retain or reject our hypothesis. The primary hypothesis of interest in social science research is the null hypothesis.

If the null hypothesis is rejected, then we assume the alternative hypothesis that there exists some difference between the means.

- **Null Hypothesis (H0)**: Suggests no effect.
- **Alternate Hypothesis (H1)**: Suggests some effect.

Statistical hypothesis tests don't comment on the size of the effect, only the likelihood of the presence or absence of the effect in the population, based on the observed samples of data.

- **Hypothesis in Statistics**: Probabilistic explanation about the presence of a relationship between observations.

Learning for a machine learning algorithm involves navigating the chosen space of hypothesis toward the best or a good enough hypothesis that best approximates the target function.

Learning is a search through the space of possible hypotheses for one that will perform well, even on new examples beyond the training set.

This framing of machine learning is common and helps to understand the choice of algorithm, the problem of learning and generalization, and even the bias-variance trade-off. For example, the training dataset is used to learn a hypothesis and the test dataset is used to evaluate it.

A common notation is used where lowercase-h (*h*) represents a given specific hypothesis and uppercase-h (*H*) represents the hypothesis space that is being searched.

- **h (*hypothesis*)**: A single hypothesis, e.g. an instance or specific candidate model that maps inputs to outputs and can be evaluated and used to make predictions.

- **H (*hypothesis set*)**: A space of possible hypotheses for mapping inputs to outputs that can be searched, often constrained by the choice of the framing of the problem, the choice of model and the choice of model configuration.

The choice of algorithm and algorithm configuration involves choosing a hypothesis space that is believed to contain a hypothesis that is a good or best approximation for the target function. This is very challenging, and it is often more efficient to spot-check a range of different hypothesis spaces.

In most supervised machine learning algorithm, our main goal is to find out a possible hypothesis from the hypothesis space that could possibly map out the inputs to the proper outputs.

The following figure shows the common method to find out the possible hypothesis from the Hypothesis space: The following fig. shows final Hypothesis.

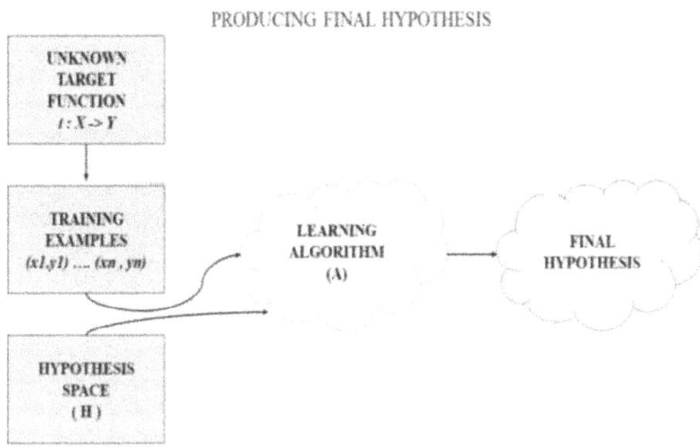

Fig. 6.2: Shows Final Hypothesis

Hypothesis Space (H)

Hypothesis space is the set of all the possible legal hypothesis. This is the set from which the machine learning algorithm would determine the best possible (only one) which would best describe the target function or the outputs.

Hypothesis (h)

A hypothesis is a function that best describes the target in supervised machine learning. The hypothesis that an algorithm would come up depends upon the data and also depends upon the restrictions and bias that we have imposed on the data. To better understand the Hypothesis Space and Hypothesis consider the following coordinate that shows the distribution of some data.

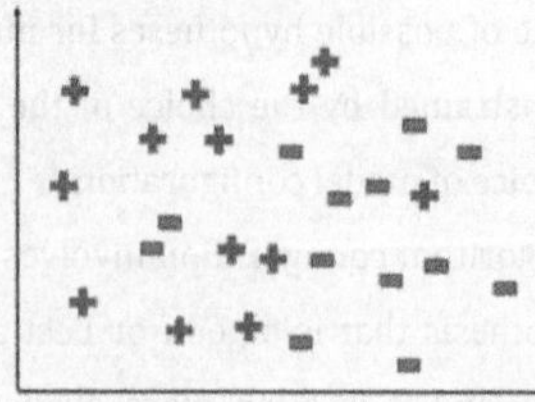

Fig. 6.3: Distribution of Data

Say suppose we have test data for which we have to determine the outputs or results. The test data is as shown below:

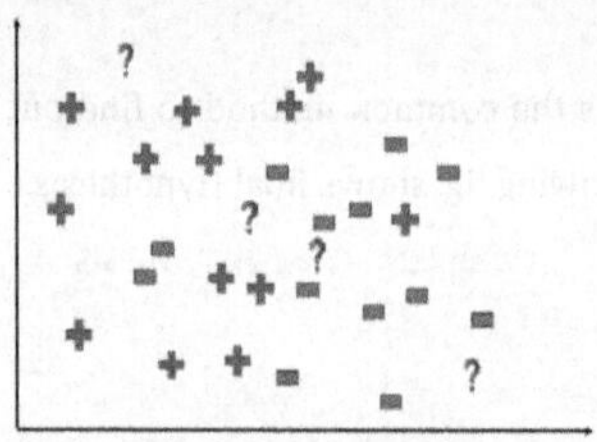

Fig. 6.4: Test Data

We can predict the outcomes by dividing the coordinate as shown below:

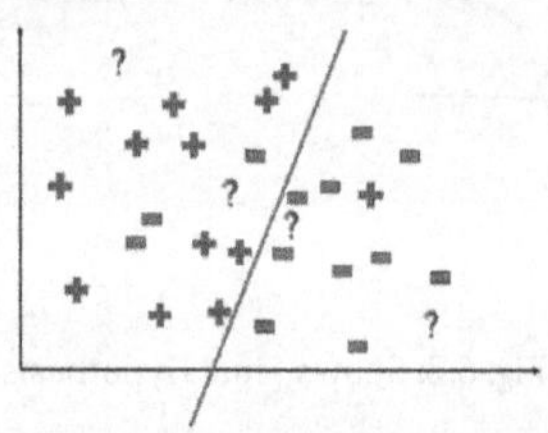

Fig. 6.5: Distribution of Data (Result)

So the test data would yield the following result:

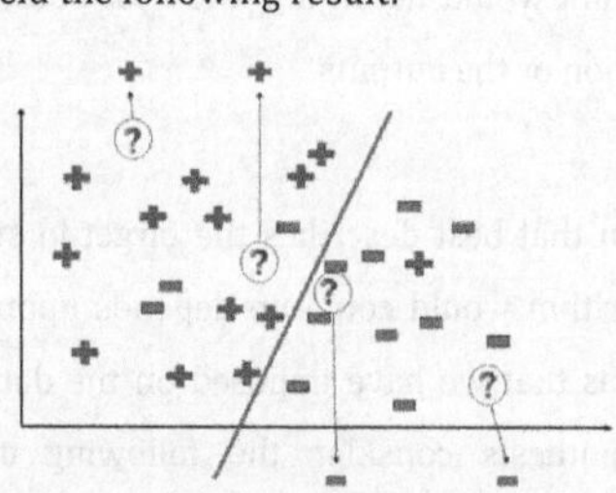

But note here that we could have divided the coordinate plane as:

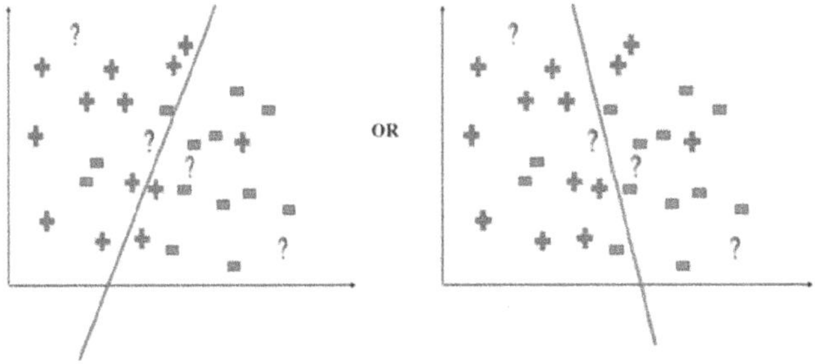

Fig. 6.6: Division of the Coordinate Plane

The way in which the coordinate would be divided depends on the data, algorithm and constraints.

- All these legal possible ways in which we can divide the coordinate plane to predict the outcome of the test data composes of the Hypothesis Space.
- Each individual possible way is known as the hypothesis.

Hence, in this example the hypothesis space would be like:

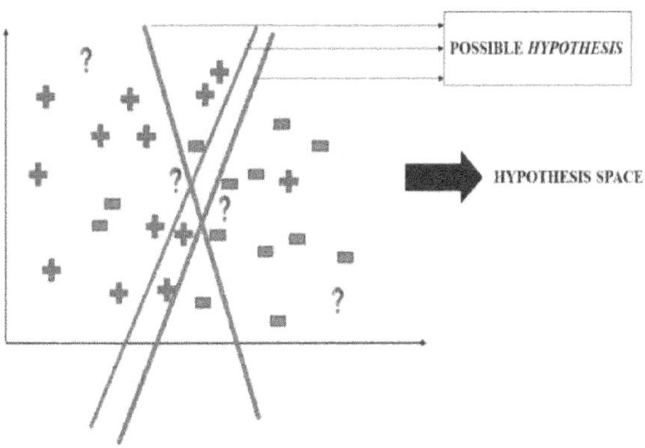

Fig. 6.7: Possible Hypothesis

Estimation Hypothesis Accuracy

- Evaluating the accuracy of hypotheses is fundamental to ML.
    - To decide whether to use this hypothesis.
    - Integral component of many learning system.

- Difficulty from limited set of data
  - Bias in the estimate
  - Variance in the estimate

Given a hypothesis *h* and a data sample,

What is the *best estimate* of the accuracy of *h*

Over unseen data?

What is *probable error* in accuracy estimate?

- Two Definitions of Error

1. ***Sample Error***

With respect to target function *f* and data sample *S*,

$$error_D(h) = \Pr_{x \in D}[f(x) \neq h(x)]$$

2. ***True Error***

With respect to target function *f* and distribution *D*,

$$error_S(h) = \frac{1}{n}\sum_{x \in S} \delta(f(x), h(x))$$

- **Problems Causing *Estimating Error***

1. *Bias*: if *S* is training set, *errorS(h)* is optimistically biased

   estimation bias = E[*errorS(h)*] - *errorD(h)*

   For unbiased estimate, *h* and *S* must be chosen independently

2. *Variance*: Even with unbiased *S*, *errorS(h)* may vary from *errorD(h)*

- Estimators

Experiment:

1. Choose sample S of size n according to distribution D
2. easure errorS(h)

   errorS(h) is a *random variable*

   errorS(h) is an *unbiased estimator* for *errorD(h)*

- ***Confidence Interval***

***if* 1. S contains *n* examples, drawn independently of *h* and each other**

2. n >= 30

then

with approximately *N%* probability, *errorD(h)* lies in interval

$$error_S(h) \pm Z_N \sqrt{\frac{error_S(h)(1-error_S(h))}{n}}$$

$N\%$:	50%	68%	80%	90%	95%	98%	99%
z_N:	0.67	1.00	1.28	1.64	1.96	2.33	2.58

6.3. Sampling Theory

In the world of Statistics, the very first thing to be done before any estimation is to create a Sample set from the entire Population Set. The Population set can be seen as the entire tree from where data is collected whereas the Sample Set can be seen as the branch in which the actual study of observations and estimation is donc. Population tree is a very large set and making the study of observations on it can be very exhausting, both time and money-wise alike. Thus to cut down on the amount of time and as well as resources, a Sample Set is created from the Population set.

Process of Sampling

1. Identifying the Population set.
2. Determination of the size of our sample set.
3. Providing a medium for the basis of selection of samples from the Population medium.
4. Picking out samples from the medium using one of many Sampling techniques like Simple Random, Systematic or Stratified Sampling.
5. Checking whether the formed sample set, contains elements actually matches the different attributes of population set, without large variations in between.
6. Checking for errors or inaccurate estimations in the formed sample set, that may or may not have occurred.
7. The set which we get after performing the above steps actually contributes to the Sample Set.

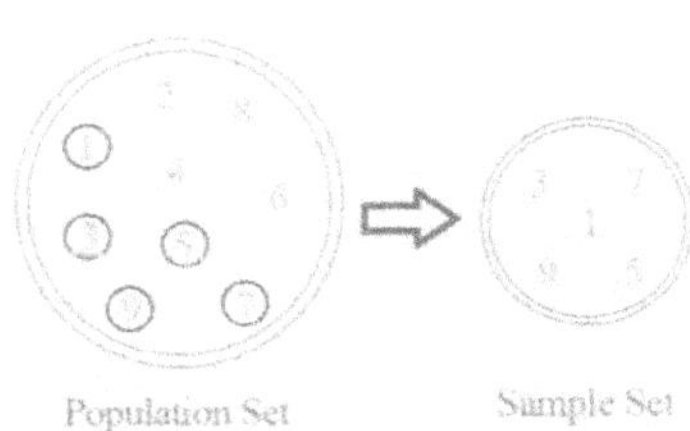

Fig. 6.8: A Simple Illustration of How Sampling is Done at It's Basic Stages

6.4. Population

Population is the whole set of variables, elements, entities which are considered for a statistical study. It is also known as the universal set from where actual inferences are drawn. Population set consists of all the attributes of individuals or elements under consideration, but doing estimations on a Population is very exhausting resources as well as time-wise alike.

Example: Consider the mean weight of all men on Earth. This here, is considered a hypothetical population because it includes all men that have ever lived on earth which includes people who will exist in the future and also people who have lived earlier before us. But there comes an anomaly, while doing such measurement which is not all men in the population tray are observable (consider men, who will exist in the future and also men, who have lived before and doesn't exist right now). Also, performing statistics on the population sample (if hypothetically possible) would require a great deal of time as well as resources, which will be exhaustive and inefficient as well.

Thus what is perform instead is to take a subset from the available population and perform statistics on them and interpolate inferences about the entire population. Taking out a subset, makes the task easier as the time required to scrutinize the subset is lesser than the time required to scrutinize the whole set of Population. Statistics is performed on the sample set to draw conclusions about the entire population tray. Calculations are considered to be a conclusion of the population set because it doesn't measure with the actual data of the population set and is not free from errors. This is obvious as sample set is used as a medium frame, having fewer members and thus some information is lost. (which results in errors).

Sampling Frame

Sampling Frame is the basis of the sample medium. It is a collection of all the sample elements taken into observation. Sometimes it might even happen that all elements in the sampling frame, didn't even take part in the actual statistics. In that case, the elements that took part in the study are called Samples and potential elements that could have been in the study but didn't take part forms the Sampling Frame. Thus, Sampling Frame is the potential list of elements on which we will perform our statistics.

Coming up with a good sampling frame is very essential because it will help in predicting the reaction of the statistics result with the population set. A sampling frame is not just a random set of handpicked elements rather it even consists of identifiers which help to identify each and every element in the set.

Example: MRCE organized a meetup of all the Geek Interns all over India at Delhi to perform a statistical study on their performances. GfG sent an invitational email to all 500 of those Interns, but since all the Interns are scattered all over India, out of 500 people of 200 show up in actual. And thus, MRCE had to perform their study on 200 students only (Sample Set). But the remaining 300 people who could have been the potential candidates in the study, but decided not to show up forms the Sampling Frame.

6.5. Methods and Types of Sampling

1. Simple Random Sampling
2. Systematic Sampling
3. Stratified Sampling

These are the most widely used Sampling Processes with each having their both advantages as well as disadvantages.

Let us look at each of these sampling methods in details:

1. **Simple Random Sampling**: Simple Random Sampling is the most elementary form of sampling. In this method, all the elements in populations are first divided into random sets of equal sizes. Random sets have no defining property among themselves, i.e. one set cannot be identified from another set based on some specific identifiers. Thus every element has an equal property of being selected.

P(of getting selected) = ½

2. The basic methods for employing SRS are:
   1) Choose the Population Set.
   2) Identify the basis of Sampling.
   3) Use of random number/session generators to pick an element from each set.

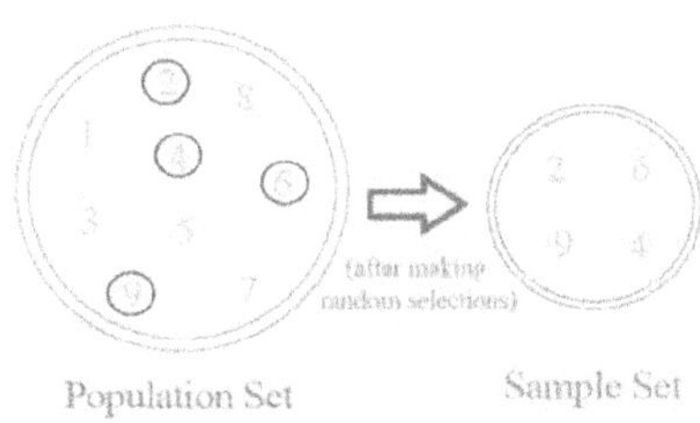

Fig. 6.9: Shows Sample Set from Population Set

3. Simple Random Sampling

Pros:

4. Less exhaustive with respect to time as it is the most elementary form of sampling.
5. Very useful for population set with very less number of elements.
6. SRS can be employed anywhere, anytime even without the use of special random generators.

Cons:

7. Not efficient for large population sets.
8. Causes the most number of errors out of the three mentioned methods of sampling.
9. There are chances of bias and then SRS won't be able to provide a correct result.
10. Does not provide a specific identifier to separate statistically similar samples.
11. **Systematic Sampling**: Systematic Sampling is also known as a type of probability sampling. It is much more accurate than SRS and also the standard error formation percentage is very low but not error-free. In this method, first, the population tray elements are arranged based on a specific order or scheme properly known as being sorted. It can be of any order, which totally depends upon the person performing the statistics. The elements are first arranged either ascendingly, descending, lexicographically or any other known methods deemed fit by the tester. Although the start point needs to be random every time. After being arranged, then the sample elements are picked based on a pre-defined interval set or function.

    Example: In a random set of numbers with elements ranging from 1 to 100. The elements are first sorted either in ascending or descending order. Then let's say every 4th element is picked to be a part of the sampling frame. This kind of sampling is known as Systematic Sampling.

P(of getting selected) = [depends upon the ordered population tray after it has been sorted]

The basic methods of employing Systematic Random Sampling are:-

1. Choosing the Population Set wisely.
2. Checking whether Systematic Sampling will be the efficient method or not.
3. If Yes, then Application of an sorting method to get an ordered pair of population elements.

4. Choosing a periodicity to crawl out elements.

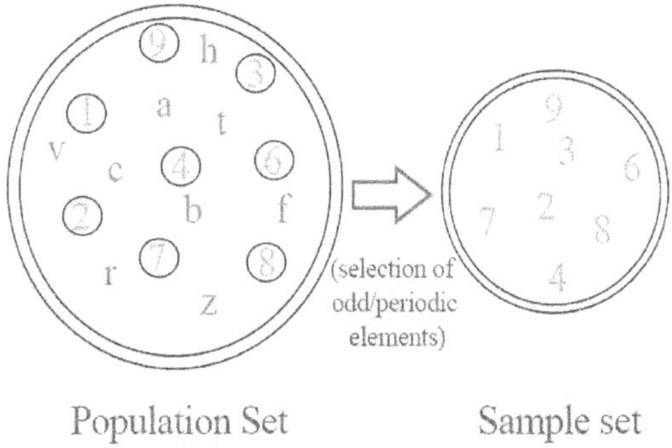

Fig. 6.10: Choosing a Periodicity to Crawl out Elements

Systematic Way of Sampling

Pros:

5. Accuracy is higher than SRS.
6. Standard probability of error is lesser.
7. No problem for bias to creep in during creation of sample frame.

Cons:

8. Not much efficient when comes to the time wise
9. Periodicity in population tray elements can lead to absurd results.
10. Systematic sampling can either provide the most accurate result or an impossible one.

Stratified Sampling: Stratified Sampling is the most complex type of Sampling Method out of all the three methods mentioned above. It is a hybrid method concerning both simple random sampling as well as systematic sampling. It is one of the most advanced types of sampling method available, providing near accurate result to the tester. In this method, the population tray is divided into sub-segments also known as stratum (singular). Each stratum can have their own unique property. After being divided into different sub-stratum, SRS or Systematic Sampling can be used to create and pick out samples for performing statistics.

The elementary methods for Stratified Sampling are:

11. Choosing the population tray wisely.
12. Checking for periodicity or any other features, so that they can be divided into different strata.

13. Dividing the population tray into sub-sets and sub-groups on the basis of selective property.
14. Using SRS or Systematic Sampling of each individual strata to form the sample frame.
15. We can even apply different sampling methods to different sub-sets.

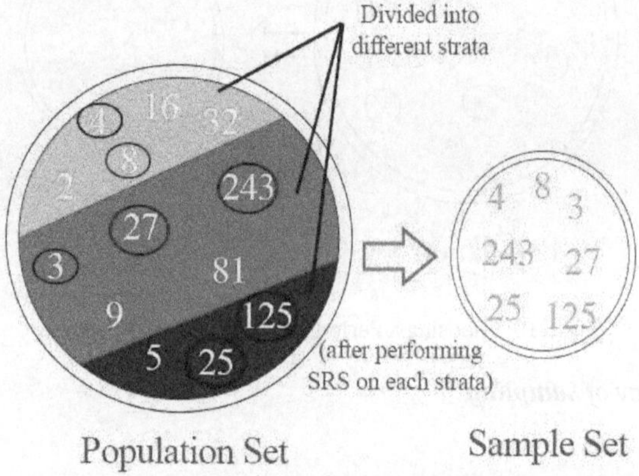

Fig. 6.11: Visual Representation of Stratified Sampling

Pros:

Provide results with high accuracy measurements.

Different results can be desired just by changing the Sampling method.

This method also compares different strata when samples are being drawn.

Cons:

- Inefficient and Expensive when comes to resources as well as money.
  - This method will fail only in rare cases where homogenity in elements is present.
- These three are the widely used methods of Sampling which are being done nowadays.

6.6. Confidence Interval

In simple terms, Confidence Interval is a range where we are certain that true value exists. The selection of a confidence level for an interval determines the probability that the confidence interval will contain the true parameter value. This range of values is generally used to deal with population-based data, extracting specific, valuable information with a certain amount of confidence, hence the term 'Confidence Interval'.

Fig. Shows how a confidence interval generally looks like.

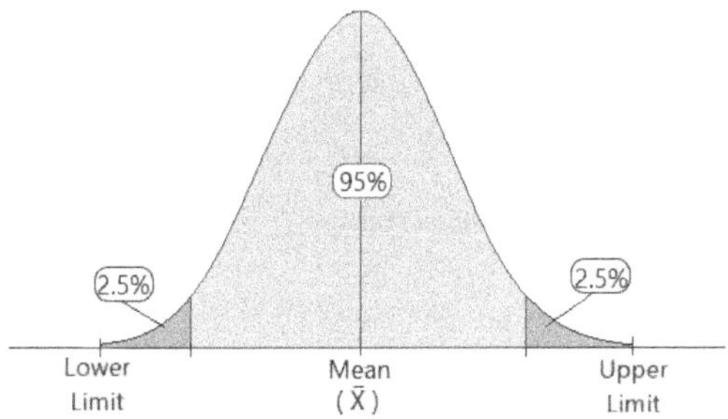

Fig. 6.12: Confidence Interval Illustration

Confidence Level

The confidence level describes the uncertainty associated with a sampling method.

Suppose we used the same sampling method (say sample mean) to compute a different interval estimate for each sample. Some interval estimates would include the true population parameter and some would not.

A 90% confidence level means that we would expect 90% of the interval estimates to include the population parameter. A 95% confidence level means that 95% of the intervals would include the population parameter.

For example, let's suppose you were surveying an average height of men in a particular city. To find that, you set a 95% confidence level and find that the 95% confidence interval is (168,182). That means if you repeated this over and over, 95 percent of the time the height of a man would fall somewhere between 168 cm and 182 cm.

6.7. Constructing a Confidence Interval

Constructing a confidence interval involves 4 steps.

Step 1: Identify the sample problem. Choose the statistic (like sample mean, etc) that you will use to estimate population parameter.

Step 2: Select a confidence level. (Usually, it is 90%, 95% or 99%)

Step 3: Find the margin of error. (Usually given) If not given, use the following formula:-

Margin of error = Critical value * Standard deviation

Step 4: Specify the confidence interval. The uncertainty is denoted by the confidence level.

And the range of the confidence interval is defined by **Eq-1**.

$$ConfidenceInterval = SampleStatistic + MarginofError \quad \textbf{(Eq-1)}$$

where,

Sample_Statistic --> Can be any kind of statistic. (e.g. sample mean)

Margin_of_Error --> generally, its (± 2.5)

Calculating a Confidence Interval

Calculation of CI requires two statistical parameters.

- **Mean (μ)** — Arithmetic mean is the average of numbers. It is defined as the sum of n numbers divided by the count of numbers till n. **(Eq-2)**

$$\mu = \frac{1+2+3+...+n}{n} \quad ..Eq2$$

- **Standard deviation (σ)** — It is the measure of how spread out the numbers are. It is defined as the summation of squared of the difference between each number and the mean. **(Eq-3)**

$$\sigma = \sqrt{\sum \frac{(x_i-\mu)^2}{n}} \quad ...Eq3$$

a) Using t-distribution

We use t-distribution when the sample size n<30.

Consider the following example. A random sample of 10 UFC fighters was taken and their weights were measured. The mean weight was found to be 240 kg. Construct a 95% confidence interval estimate for the mean weight the sample standard deviation was 25 kg. Find a confidence interval for a sample for the true mean weight of all UFC fighters.

Step 1 - Subtract 1 from your sample size. **[Eq-4]**

This gives the degrees of freedom **(df)**, required in **Step-3.**

where,

df = degree of freedom

n = sample size

Using Eq-4, we get **df = 10 – 1 = 9.**

Step 2 - Subtract the confidence interval from 1, then divide by two.

[Eq-5]

This gives the significance level **(α)**, required in **Step-3.**

$$\alpha = \frac{1-CL}{2}$$

α = Significance level

CL = Confidence Level

Using Eq-5, we get **α = (1 - .95) / 2 = 0.025**

Step 3 - Use the values of **α** and **df** in the t-distribution table and find the value of **t**.

(df)/(α)	0.1	0.05	0.025	..
∞	1.282	1.645	1.960	
1	3.078	6.314	12.706	..
2	1.886	2.920	4.303	..
:	:	:	:	..
8	1.397	1.860	2.306	..
9	1.383	1.833	2.262	.

Using the values of df and α in the t-distribution table, we get **t = 2.262.**

Step 4 - Use the t-value obtained in step 3 in the formula given for Confidence Interval with t-distribution.

$$\mu \pm t\left(\frac{\sigma}{\sqrt{n}}\right)$$

where,

μ = mean

t = chosen t-value from the table above

σ = the standard deviation

n = number of observations

So, putting the values in Eq-6, we get

$$\Rightarrow 240 \pm (2.262)^{*}(25/\sqrt{10})$$
$$\Rightarrow 240 \pm 17.883$$
$$\Rightarrow (240 - 17.883, 240 + 17.883)$$
$$\Rightarrow (222.117, 257.883)$$

where,

Lower Limit = 222.117

Upper Limit = 257.883

Therefore, we are 95% confident that the true mean weight of the UFC Fighters is between 222.117 and 257.883.

CHAPTER 7

BAYESIAN LEARNING

7.1. Introduction

Learning is an adaptive function by which our nervous system changes in relation to stimuli in the environment, thus changing our behavioral responses and permitting us to function in our environment. Learning involves a change in behavior or knowledge that results from experience. The term Machine Learning was coined by Arthur Samuel in 1959, an American pioneer in the field of computer gaming and artificial intelligence, and stated that "it gives computers the ability to learn without being explicitly programmed".

In the standard machine learning problem, we have a set of training data, inputs and observed outputs, and we want to determine some mapping between them. So, we splice together a model and generate a deterministic way of predicting a target variable y given an unseen input x. The major problem in this process is we cannot explain what's going on within the model. That's where Bayesian Machine Learning comes in. Bayesian learning can also be called as probabilistic reasoning.

"Probability theory is nothing but common sense reduced to calculation." — Pierre-Simon Laplace [1814].

Uncertainty plays an important role in our daily lives and activities as well as in business. In some cases, uncertainty even helps heighten our interest in these activities. In a business context, investment counselors cannot be sure which of two stocks will deliver the better growth over the coming year, and engineers try to reduce the likelihood that a machine will break down. Likewise, marketers maybe uncertain as to the effectiveness of an ad campaign or the eventual success of a new product. The following situations provide other examples of the role of uncertainty in our lives:

- In the last game of the World Series, the home team is down one run with the bases loaded and two out in the bottom of the ninth. The pitcher, whose batting average is only 0.105, is due up. The manager sends in a pinch hitter with a 0.320 batting average to hit for the pitcher.
- Eddie is standing at an intersection, facing the "Don't Walk" light in a city where jaywalking carries a $20 fine. After looking around to be sure there are neither cars nor police, he crosses the street.

- Arthur is 75 years old, has had three heart attacks, and works as a bomb disposal expert with his local police department. When he applies for life insurance, he is turned down as an unacceptable risk.

In each of these cases, chance was involved. The baseball manager selected the batter who was more likely to get a hit. Eddie was trying to reduce the chance that something undesirable would happen to him. Arthur's life insurance company felt that his age, health, and occupation greatly reduced the likelihood of his surviving for many more years.

Gamblers were among the first to take an interest in probabilities, followed by the insurance industry and its mortality tables that expressed the likelihood that a person of a given age would live an additional year. More recently, probabilities have proven vital in many ways to both business and the social sciences.

Bayesian probability theory answers the following fundamental question: *How do we reason?* Reasoning is central to human activity, including philosophy (what is the best way to make decisions?), cognitive science (how does the mind work?), artificial intelligence (how do we build reasoning machines?), and science (how do we test and develop theories based on experimental data?).

Basic Terminology of Probabilities

- EXPERIMENT An activity or measurement that results in an outcome.
- SAMPLE SPACE All possible outcomes of an experiment.
- EVENT One or more of the possible outcomes of an experiment; a subset of the sample space.
- PROBABILITY A number between 0 and 1 that expresses the chance that an event will occur.

$$0 \leq P(A) \leq 1$$

For any event, the probability will be no less than 0 and no greater than 1.

$$P(A) + P(A') = 1$$

Either the event will occur (A) or it will not occur A' where A' is called thecomplement of A.

In practice, multiple events occur in the space of consideration. Such probabilities are calculated based on the exclusiveness and dependency between the events.

- **MUTUALLY EXCLUSIVE EVENTS** If one event occurs, the other cannot occur. An event (e.g., A) and its complement (A') are always mutually exclusive.

- **EXHAUSTIVE EVENTS** A set of events is exhaustive if it includes all the possible outcomes of an experiment. The mutually exclusive events A and A' are exhaustive because one of them must occur. When the events within a set are both mutually exclusive and exhaustive, the sum of their probabilities is 1.0. This is because one of them must happen, and they include all of the possibilities. The entries within a relative frequency contingency table are mutually exclusive and exhaustive, and their sum will always be 1.0.
- **INTERSECTION OF EVENTS** Two or more events occurs at the same time. Such an intersection can be represented by "A and B," or "A and B and C," depending on the number of possible events involved.
- **UNION OF EVENTS** At least one of a number of possible events occurs. A union is represented by "A or B," or "A or B or C," depending on the number of events.

When Events Are Mutually Exclusive

When events are mutually exclusive, the occurrence of one means that none of the others can occur. In this case, the probability that one of the events will occur is the sum of their individual probabilities. In terms of two events, the rule can be stated as follows:

$$P(A\ or\ B) = P(A) + P(B)$$

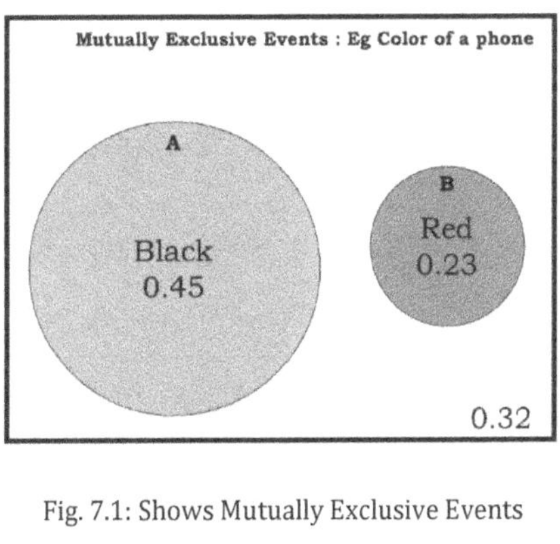

Fig. 7.1: Shows Mutually Exclusive Events

The above Figure is a relative frequency breakdown of colours of phones made in North America during the 2004 model year. As the Venn diagram indicates, the possible events are mutually exclusive. For a given phone only one colour was applied. Using the letters A and B to identify the colours Black and Red, respectively, and considering a phone selected at random from that model year, we can arrive at the following probabilities.

- Probability that the phone is either black or red:

$$P(A\ or\ B) = P(A) + P(B) = 0.45 + 0.23 = 0.68$$

- Probability that the phone is either black or some colour other than black occurred:

Although we have not specifically identified "neither black nor red" with a letter designation, it can be expressed as $P(A'\ and\ B')$. Using this identification, we can determine the probability that the randomly selected phone is either black or some colour other than black or red:

$$P(A\ or\ [A'and\ B']) = P(A) + P(A'and\ B') = 0.45 + 0.32 = 0.77$$

7.2. When Events Are Not Mutually Exclusive

When events are not mutually exclusive, two or more of them can happen at the same time. In this case, the general rule of addition can be used in calculating probabilities. In terms of two events, it can be stated as follows:

General rule of addition when events are not mutually exclusive:

$$P(A\ or\ B) = P(A) + P(B) - P(A\ and\ B)$$

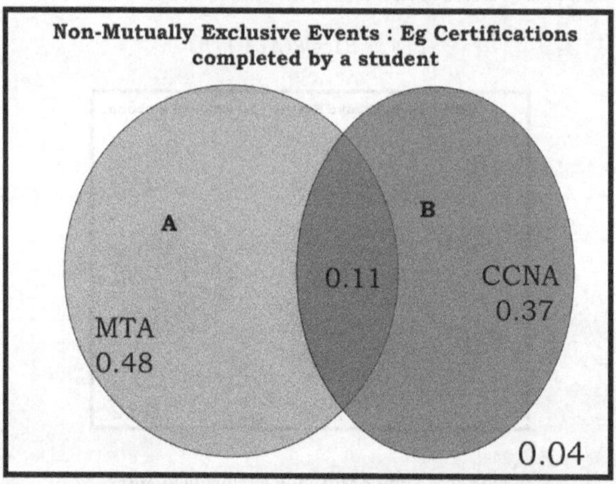

Fig. 7.2: Shows Mutually Exclusive Events

Relative frequencies for the certifications completed by students of a class are shown in the Venn diagram above. As the Venn diagram indicates, the events are not mutually exclusive. For example, a student can complete MTA Certification and also CCNA Certification, represented by the category (A and B).

In the above, the probability that a randomly selected student is MTA certified (event A) is 0.48 + 0.11, or P(A) = 0.59. The probability that this randomly selected student is CCNA Certified (event B) is 0.37 +0.11, or P(B) = 0.48. If we were to simply add P(A) = 0.59 and P(B) = 0.48, we'd get a value greater than 1 (a total of 1.07), which is not possible since a probability must be between 0 and 1. The problem is that the probability of the intersection, P(A and B) = 0.11, has been counted twice. To make up for this, we add the individual probabilities, then subtract the probability of their intersection, and the probability of a students certified as MTA or CCNA is:

$$P(A\ or\ B) = P(A) + P(B) - P(A\ and\ B) = 0.48 + 0.37 + 0.11 = 0.96$$

While addition rules are used to calculate the probability that at least one of several events will occur, in this section we'll consider rules for determining the probability that two or more of the events will all occur. These rules involve several important terms:

- **Marginal Probability:** The probability that a given event will occur. No other events are taken into consideration. A typical expression is P (A).
- **Joint Probability:** The probability that two or more events will all occur. A typical expression is P (A and B).
- **Conditional Probability:** The probability that an event will occur, given that another event has already happened. A typical expression is P (A|B), with the verbal description, "the probability of A, given B." A conditional probability maybe determined as follows:

Conditional probability of event A, given that event B has occurred:

$$P(A\,|B) = \frac{P(A\ and\ B)}{P(B)}$$

(Note: This applies only if P(B) $\neq$ 0)

The rules that follow are called multiplication rules; they determine the probability that two events will both happen or that three or more events will all happen. There are two multiplication rules, and the one that is applicable will depend on whether the events are independent or dependent. Independent Events are those events where the occurrence of one event as no effect on the probability that another will occur. Dependent Events are those where the occurrence of one event changes the probability that another will occur.

When Events Are Independent

When events are independent, their joint probability is the product of their individual probabilities. In the case of two events, the multiplication rule is as follows:

Multiplication rule when events are independent:

$$P(A \text{ and } B) = P(A) \times P(B)$$

To illustrate this rule, we'll use a device called a tree diagram, which visually summarizes the occurrence or non-occurrence of two or more events. The tree diagram is especially useful in visualizing events that occur in sequence. Figure below illustrates two consecutive tosses of a fair coin. Regardless of the result of the first toss, the probability of heads on the next toss is going to be 0.5; the tree diagram in Figure below shows all the possibilities, along with their joint probabilities.

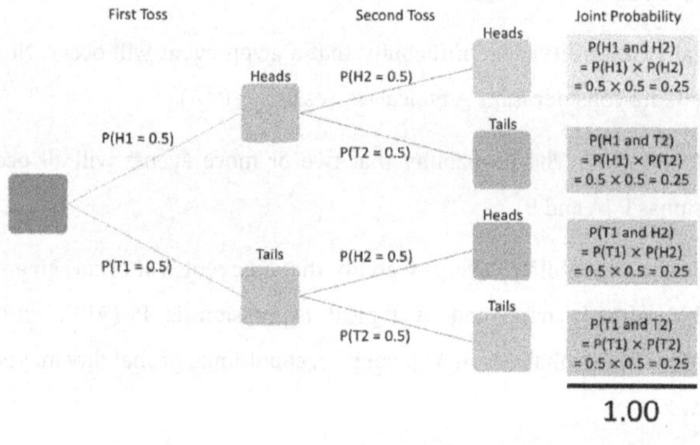

Fig. 7.3: The Possibilities, Along with their Joint Probabilities

For example, the probability of getting heads twice in a row is 0.5 ×0.5, or0.25. Likewise, the joint probability of any other given sequence (e.g., H1-T2,T1-T2, or T1-H2) will also be 0.25. Since the diagram includes all four of the possible sequences, the joint probabilities add up to 1.00.

When Events Are Not Independent

When events are not independent, the occurrence of one will influence the probability that another will take place. Under these conditions, a more general multiplication rule applies:

Multiplication rule when events are not independent:

$$P(A \text{ and } B) = P(A) \times P(B \mid A)$$

The below figure shows marginal, joint, and conditional probabilities for the student certifications. It indicates that a student certified are more likely to be male than female. The respective marginal probabilities are P (A) = 0.779 and P(A') = 0.221. Of the students, 30.4% were males whose are certified, and the joint probability for this category is P (A and B) = 0.304.

		Certification		
		B Certified	B' Not Certified	
Sex	A Male	0.304	0.475	0.779
	A' Female	0.109	0.112	0.221
		0.413	0.587	1.000

Joint probabilities

P(A and B) = 0.304
P(A and B') = 0.475
P(A' and B) = 0.109
P(A' and B') = 0.112

Marginal probabilities

P(A) = 0.779
P(A') = 0.221
P(B) = 0.413
P(B') = 0.587

Conditional probabilities

$$P(A|B) = \frac{P\ (A\ and\ B)}{P(B)} = \frac{0.304}{0.413} = 0.736$$

$$P(A'|B') = \frac{P\ (A'\ and\ B')}{P(B')} = \frac{0.112}{0.587} = 0.191$$

Fig. 7.4: Conditional Probabilities

The contingency table can be complemented by a tree diagram like the one in the previous example. Using the tree diagram, we can visually describe the two variables and probabilities related to them. The tree diagram in the figure includes the marginal, joint, and conditional probabilities. The first set of branches in the tree diagram shows the marginal probabilities. These probabilities are based on relative frequencies and have the following values:

Probability that the student is a male = P (A) = 0.779

Probability that the student is a female = P (A') = 0.221

The second set of branches in the tree diagram includes conditional probabilities dependent on the result of each initial branch.

For example, given that,

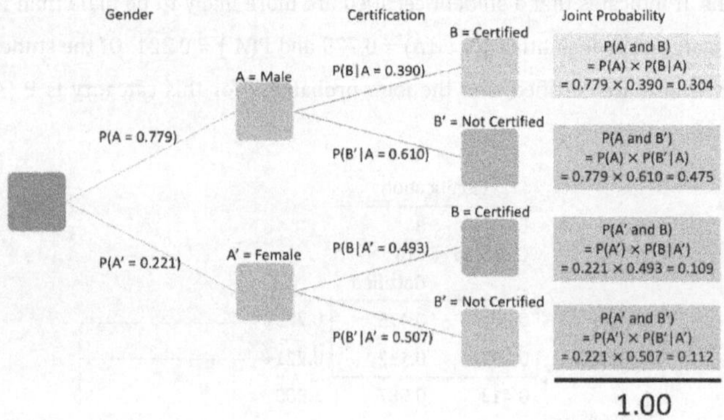

Fig. 7.5: Tree Diagram Includes Conditional Probabilities

This **tree diagram** illustrates the gender and completion of certification of the students of a class. The events are not independent, so the probabilities in the second set of branches depend on what has happened in the first set.

7.3. Bayesian Learning Methods

Bayesian learning methods is able to provide useful practical solutions and forecasting features toward solving complicated problems. **Bayesian learning** provides a natural approach to many complex data-modelling problems. Bayesian learning generates a model for **logic in the presence of uncertainty.** Bayesian methods closely match human intuition and even provides a robust model for low-level neurological processes.

Bayesian learning provides three major advantages:

1. Principled modelling of uncertainty.
2. General purpose models for unstructured data.
3. Effective algorithms for data fitting and analysis under uncertainty.

Bayesian learning is a method of statistical inference in which Bayes' theorem is used to update the probability for a hypothesis as more evidence or information becomes available.

The probability of events are calculated based on frequency of occurrence of event. This is the frequentist (or classical) definition of probability based on frequencies of events, whereas the Bayesian definition of probability is based on our knowledge of events. In the context of machine learning, we can interpret this difference as: what the data says versus what we know from the data.

Bayes Theorem provides a principled way for calculating a conditional probability. It is a deceptively simple calculation, although it can be used to easily calculate the conditional probability of events where intuition often fails.

7.4. Bayes Theorem

In the 1700s, Thomas Bayes developed a theorem that is an extension of the concept of conditional probability discussed in the previous section. In Bayes' application of conditional probability, the emphasis is on sequential events; in particular, information obtained from a second event is used to revise the probability that a first event has occurred. The theorem will be demonstrated by means of an example, and key terms will be introduced along the way.

The marginal probability is the probability of an event, irrespective of other random variables. If the random variable is independent, then it is the probability of the event directly, otherwise, if the variable is dependent upon other variables, then the marginal probability is the probability of the event summed over all outcomes for the dependent variables, called the sum rule.

The joint probability can be calculated using the conditional probability; for example:

$$P(A, B) = P(A \mid B) \times P(B)$$

This is called the product rule. Importantly, the joint probability is symmetrical, meaning that:

$$P(A, B) = P(B, A)$$

The conditional probability can be calculated using the joint probability; for example:

$$P(A \mid B) = \frac{P(A,B)}{P(B)}$$

The conditional probability is not symmetrical; for example:

$$P(A \mid B) \mathrel{!=} P(B \mid A)$$

Bayes Theorem (An Alternate Way To Calculate Conditional Probability): Principled way of calculating a conditional probability without the joint probability.

Specifically, one conditional probability can be calculated using the other conditional probability; for example:

$$P(A|B) = \frac{P(B|A) \times P(A)}{P(B)}$$

The reverse is also true; for example:

$$P(B|A) = \frac{P(A|B) \times P(B)}{P(A)}$$

This alternate approach of calculating the conditional probability is useful either when the joint probability is challenging to calculate, or when the reverse conditional probability is available or easy to calculate.

This alternate calculation of the conditional probability is referred to as Bayes Rule or Bayes Theorem, named for Reverend Thomas Bayes, who is credited with first describing it.

Often, we do not have access to the denominator directly, e.g. P(B).

We can calculate it an alternatively; for example:

- P(B) = P(B|A) * P(A) + P(B|not A) * P(not A)

This gives a formulation of Bayes Theorem that we can use that uses the alternate calculation of P(B), described below:

- $P(A \mid B) = \frac{P(B \mid A) * P(A)}{P(B \mid A) * P(A) + \mathrm{P(B|not\ A) * P(not\ A)}}$

The terms in the Bayes Theorem equation are named. In general, the result P(A|B) is referred to as the **posterior probability** and P(A) is called as the **prior probability**.

- P(A|B): Posterior probability.
- P(A): Prior probability.

Sometimes P(B|A) is referred to as the **likelihood** and P(B) is referred to as the **evidence**.

- P(B|A): Likelihood.
- P(B): Evidence.

This allows Bayes Theorem to be restated as:

- Posterior = Likelihood * Prior / Evidence

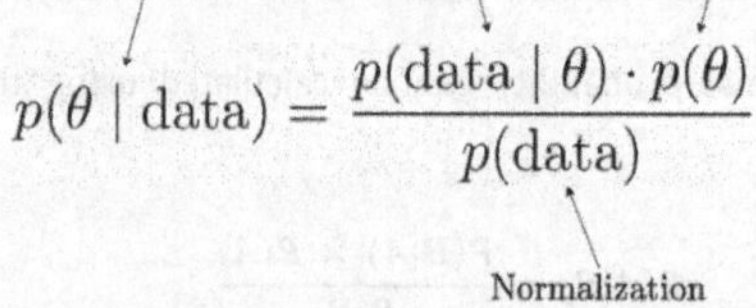

What is the Probability that There is Fire Given that there is Smoke?

Where P(Fire) is the Prior, P(Smoke|Fire) is the Likelihood, and P(Smoke) is the evidence:

- P(Fire|Smoke) = P(Smoke|Fire) * P(Fire) / P(Smoke)

You can imagine the same situation with rain and clouds.

Now that we are familiar with Bayes Theorem and the meaning of the terms, let's look at a scenario where we can calculate it.

7.5. Worked Examples for Calculating Bayes Theorem

Bayes theorem is best understood with a real-life worked example with real numbers to demonstrate the calculations.

1. Defective Phone Example

Present Information

A retailer purchases mobile phones from three different suppliers:

A, B, and C. Thirty percent of the heating elements are supplied by A, 50% by B, and 20% by C. The phones are mixed in a supply bin prior to inspection and sales. Based on past experience, 10% of the phones from A are defective, compared to only 5% of those supplied by B, and just 4% of those from C. The retailer randomly selects a phone for sales. What is the probability that the phone was supplied by A?

Solution

- Events

  A_1 = The phone was produced by A

  A_2 = The phone was produced by B

  A_3 = The phone was produced by C

- Prior probability is an initial probability based on the available present information. On this basis, $P(A_1) = 0.300$ since A supplies 30%of the mobile phones.

Additional Information

Upon testing the phone before sales, the retailer finds it to be defective.

- Events

  B = A tested phone is defective

  B'= A tested phone is not defective

- Posterior probability is the revised probability that uses the additional information. It is a conditional probability and can be expressed as $P(A_1|B)$.

A's quality record is the worst of the three suppliers, so the finding of a defective phone would tend to suggest that $P(A_1|B)$ is higher than $P(A_1)$.

From an intuitive standpoint, the posterior (revised) probability should be higher than 0.300. But how much higher? As a first step in finding out, consider the tree diagram and joint probabilities in Figure below.

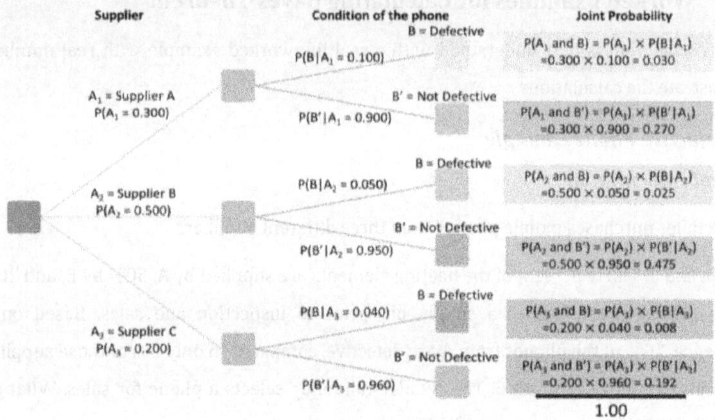

Fig. 7.6: Tree Diagram and Joint Probabilities

Because the events are dependent, the marginal probabilities in the first branches of the tree diagram are multiplied by the conditional probabilities in the second set of branches to obtain the joint probabilities of the final column. However, there is a problem: In order to construct the tree diagram, we had to use a time sequence that proceeded from the supplier source to the eventual testing of the phone.

What we really need is the reverse of this tree diagram, that is, proceeding from the present (a known defective) to the past (the probability that it was supplied by A). The joint probabilities of Figure can be used in reversing the time sequence. In doing so, it is useful to look at the joint probabilities as relative frequencies out of 1000 cases. Taking this perspective, we observe that in 63(i.e., 30 + 25 + 8) of the 1000 cases, the phone was defective, and in 30 of these the phone came from A. In other words, we have just determined that the revised probability, P $(A_1|B)$, is 30/63 = 0.476. This revised probability is among those shown in the reversed tree diagram in Figure.

Probabilities can also be revised by using Bayes' theorem. The theorem deals with sequential events, using information obtained about a second event to revise the probability that a first event has occurred.

Bayes' theorem for the revision of probability:

- Events A and B Probability of A, given that event B has occurred:
- $P(A \mid B) = \frac{P(A\ and\ B)}{P(B)} = \frac{P(A) \times P(B|A)}{[P(A) \times P(B|A)] + [P(A') \times P(B|A')]}$

General form Probability of event Ai, given that event B has occurred:

$$P(A_i|B) = \frac{P(A_i\ and\ B)}{P(B)} = \frac{P(A_i) \times P(B|A_i)}{\sum_{i=1}^{k} P(A_i) \times P(B|A_i)}$$

where A_i is the ith of k mutually exclusive and exhaustive events.

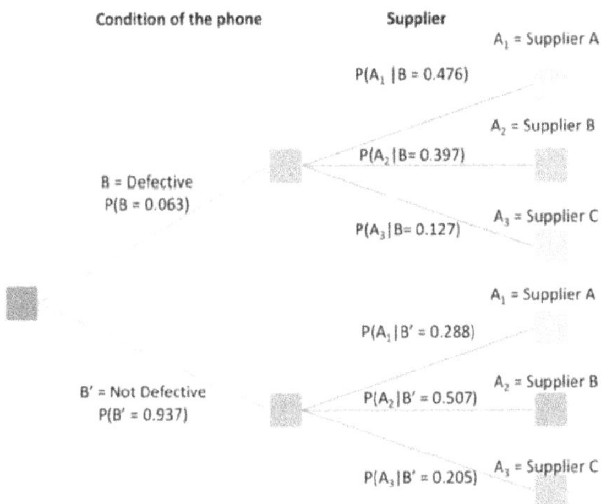

Fig. 7.7: Probability of Condition of the Phone

Applying the general form of Bayes' theorem, the heating element had to come from one of k = 3 suppliers: A (event A_1), B (event A_2), or C (event A_3). Additional information is available in the form of knowledge that the phone is defective (event B). We must use the general form of the theorem because the number of suppliers is more than two. Given that the phone is defective, Bayes' theorem is used in determining the probability that it was supplied by A:

$$P(A_i|B) = \frac{P(A_i) \times P(B|A_i)}{\sum_{i=1}^{k} P(A_i) \times P(B|A_i)}$$

$$P(A_1|B) = \frac{P(A_1) \times P(B|A_1)}{[P(A_1) \times P(B|A_1)] + [P(A_2) \times P(B|A_2)] + [P(A_3) \times P(B|A_3)]}$$

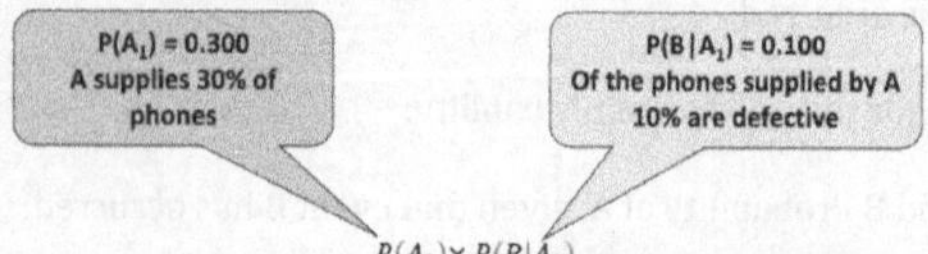

$$P(A_1|B) = \frac{P(A_1)\times P(B|A_1)}{[P(A_1)\times P(B|A_1)] + [P(A_2)\times P(B|A_2)] + [P(A_3)\times P(B|A_3)]}$$

$$= \frac{0.300 \times 0.100}{[0.300 \times 0.100] + [0.500 \times 0.050] + [0.200 \times 0.040]}$$

$$= \frac{0.030}{0.063} = 0.476$$

As in our calculations based on the tree diagrams in Figures above, the probability that the defective phone was supplied by A is found to be 0.476. If the additional information had revealed a non-defective phone, we could use the same approach in determining the probability that it had come from a given supplier. In this case, we would simply replace B with B'. For example, if we wished to find the probability that a non-defective phone had come from C, this would be calculated as,

$$P(A_3|B') = \frac{P(A_3) \times P(B'|A_3)}{[P(A_1) \times P(B'|A_1)] + [P(A_2) \times P(B'|A_2)] + [P(A_3) \times P(B'|A_3)]}$$

$$= \frac{0.200 \times 0.960}{[0.300 \times 0.900] + [0.500 \times 0.950] + [0.200 \times 0.960]}$$

$$= \frac{0.192}{0.937} = 0.205$$

The concept of additional information and revised probabilities is an important part of decision making, an activity in which both statistics and additional information are important.

2. Diagnostic Test Example

First we will define a scenario then work through a manual calculation and a calculation using the terms that may be familiar to you from the field of binary classification.

1. Diagnostic Test Scenario
2. Manual Calculation
3. Binary Classifier Terminology

Diagnostic Test Scenario

An excellent and widely used example of the benefit of Bayes Theorem is in the analysis of a medical diagnostic test.

Scenario: Consider a human population that may or may not have cancer (Cancer is True or False) and a medical test that returns positive or negative for detecting cancer (Test is Positive or Negative), e.g. like a mammogram for detecting breast cancer.

Problem: *If a randomly selected patient has the test and it comes back positive, what is the probability that the patient has cancer?*

Manual Calculation

Medical diagnostic tests are not perfect; they have error.

Sometimes a patient will have cancer, but the test will not detect it. This capability of the test to detect cancer is referred to as the **sensitivity**, or the true positive rate.

In this case, we will contrive a sensitivity value for the test. The test is good, but not great, with a true positive rate or sensitivity of 85%. That is, of all the people who have cancer and are tested, 85% of them will get a positive result from the test.

P(Test=Positive | Cancer=True) = 0.85

Given this information, our intuition would suggest that there is an 85% probability that the patient has cancer.

Our Intuitions of Probability are Wrong

This type of error in interpreting probabilities is so common that it has its own name; it is referred to as the base rate fallacy.

It has this name because the error in estimating the probability of an event is caused by ignoring the base rate. That is, it ignores the probability of a randomly selected person having cancer, regardless of the results of a diagnostic test.

In this case, we can assume the probability of breast cancer is low, and use a contrived base rate value of one person in 5,000, or (0.0002) 0.02%.

P(Cancer=True) = 0.02%.

We can correctly calculate the probability of a patient having cancer given a positive test result using Bayes Theorem.

Let's map our scenario onto the equation:

P(A|B) = P(B|A) * P(A) / P(B)

P(Cancer=True | Test=Positive) = P(Test=Positive|Cancer=True) * P(Cancer=True) / P(Test=Positive)

We know the probability of the test being positive given that the patient has cancer is 85%, and we know the base rate or the prior probability of a given patient having cancer is 0.02%; we can plug these values in:

P(Cancer=True | Test=Positive) = 0.85 * 0.0002 / P(Test=Positive)

We don't know P(Test=Positive), it's not given directly.

Instead, we can estimate it using:

P(B) = P(B|A) * P(A) + P(B|not A) * P(not A)

P(Test=Positive) =P(Test=Positive|Cancer=True) * P(Cancer=True) + P(Test=Positive|Cancer=False) * P(Cancer=False)

Firstly, we can calculate P(Cancer=False) as the complement of P(Cancer=True), which we already know.

P(Cancer=False) = 1 – P(Cancer=True)

= 1 – 0.0002

= 0.9998

Let's plugin what we have:

We can plug in our known values as follows:

P(Test=Positive) = 0.85 * 0.0002 + P(Test=Positive|Cancer=False) * 0.9998

We still do not know the probability of a positive test result given no cancer.

This requires additional information.

Specifically, we need to know how good the test is at correctly identifying people that do not have cancer. That is, testing negative result (Test=Negative) when the patient does not have cancer (Cancer=False), called the true negative rate or the **specificity**.

We will use a contrived specificity value of 95%.

P(Test=Negative | Cancer=False) = 0.95

With this final piece of information, we can calculate the false positive or false alarm rate as the complement of the true negative rate.

P(Test=Positive|Cancer=False) = 1 – P(Test=Negative | Cancer=False)

= 1 – 0.95

= 0.05

We can plug this false alarm rate into our calculation of P(Test=Positive) as follows:

P(Test=Positive) = 0.85 * 0.0002 + 0.05 * 0.9998

P(Test=Positive) = 0.00017 + 0.04999

P(Test=Positive) = 0.05016

Excellent, so the probability of the test returning a positive result, regardless of whether the person has cancer or not is about 5%.

We now have enough information to calculate Bayes Theorem and estimate the probability of a randomly selected person having cancer if they get a positive test result.

$$P(Cancer=True \mid Test=Positive) = \frac{P(Test=Positive|Cancer=True) * P(Cancer=True)}{P(Test=Positive)}$$

P(Cancer=True | Test=Positive) = 0.85 * 0.0002 / 0.05016

P(Cancer=True | Test=Positive) = 0.00017 / 0.05016

P(Cancer=True | Test=Positive) = 0.003389154704944

The calculation suggests that if the patient is informed they have cancer with this test, then there is only 0.33% chance that they have cancer.

It is a Terrible Diagnostic Test!

The example also shows that the calculation of the conditional probability requires *enough* information. For example, if we have the values used in Bayes Theorem already, we can use them directly.

This is rarely the case, and we typically have to calculate the bits we need and plug them in, as we did in this case. In our scenario we were given 3 pieces of information, the **base rate**, the **sensitivity** (or true positive rate), and the **specificity** (or true negative rate).

- **Sensitivity**: 85% of people with cancer will get a positive test result.
- **Base Rate**: 0.02% of people have cancer.
- **Specificity**: 95% of people without cancer will get a negative test result.

We did not have the P(Test=Positive), but we calculated it given what we already had available. We might imagine that Bayes Theorem allows us to be even more precise about a given scenario. For example, if we had more information about the patient (e.g. their age) and about the domain (e.g. cancer rates for age ranges), and in turn we could offer an even more accurate probability estimate.

7.6. Applications of Bayes Theorem

There are plenty of applications of the Bayes' Theorem in the real world. Bayesian Decision Theory is a statistical approach to the problem of pattern classification. Under this theory, it is assumed that the underlying probability distribution for the categories is known. Thus, we obtain an ideal Bayes Classifier against which all other classifiers are judged for performance.

- Bayes' rule is used in various occasions including a medical testing for a rare disease. With Bayes' rule, we can estimate the probability of actually having the condition given the test coming out positive.

- Besides certain circumstances, Bayes' rule can be applied to our everyday life including dating and friendships. By examining your current friendships or partners you have had, you can better understand the selection effects and modify your actions or behaviours in order to form more relationships that you think are most valuable. Applying Bayes' rule will help you analyze what you gain and what you lose by taking certain actions. Bayesian analysis can be conducted when meeting a new person with the new information collected. When we try looking for a person to have a serious relationship with, recognizing or reading the person correctly can be quite important. Especially recently, internet dating has been an viral phenomena, which is why analyzing a person correctly is highly valuable. For instance, when knowing certain characteristics about your date such as, he is quiet and loves to spend Sunday morning reading, we can guess whether or not he is a bartender, librarian, or a sales person.

- According to Kara Lilly, when trying to estimate the probability of that person being a librarian, we have to answer three questions. What is the base rate, how rare is the evidence, and how relevant is the evidence to the hypothesis? The base rate refers to the prior probability of anyone being a librarian. For example, we can analyze data and figure out the percentage of anyone that is employed as a librarian out of all the jobs in the US. The second question refers to the necessity of looking at information that is rare, not common. In this case, it would be the percentage of a person being an introvert instead of examining the percentage of a person being a male. The third question, how relevant is this evidence?, refers to connecting the information with the piece of information that we are assuming. In this case, people would assume the online date to be a librarian mostly due to his introverted characteristic. In order to see if this is true, a data analysis can be made.

- Often, people assume that Bayes' theorem can only apply to stocks or business models. However, it is clearly evident that it can be applied also in our daily lives when we try to make a decision based on the new information given.

Bayes Theorem on Concept Learning

The Bayes theorem is a method for calculating a hypothesis's probability based on its prior probability, the probabilities of observing specific data given the hypothesis, and the seen data itself. Bayes theorem calculates the probability of each possible hypothesis and outputs the most probable one. Concept learning describes the process by which experience allows us to partition objects in the world into classes for the purpose of generalization, discrimination, and inference.

In particular, consider some finite hypothesis space H defined over the instance space X, in which the objective is to learn some target concept c: X →**{0,1}**. As usual, we assume that the learner is given some sequence of training examples $((x_1, d_1)...(x_m,d_m))$ where x_i is some instance from X and where d_i is the target value of xi (i.e., $d_i = c(x_i)$). To simplify, we assume the sequence of instances $(x_1...x_m)$ is held fixed, so that the training data D can be written simply as the sequence of target values **D =** $(d_1...d_m)$.

We can design a straightforward concept learning algorithm to output the maximum a posteriori hypothesis, based on Bayes theorem, as follows:

7.7. Brute-Force MAP Learning Algorithm

1. For each hypothesis h in H, calculate the posterior probability

$$P(h|D) = \frac{P(D|h) \times P(h)}{P(D)}$$

2. Output the hypothesis h_{MAP} with the highest posterior probability

$$h_{MAP} = \underset{h \in H}{\operatorname{argmax}} P(h|D)$$

This algorithm may require significant computation, because it applies Bayes theorem to each hypothesis in H to calculate ***P(h/D)***. While this may prove impractical for large hypothesis spaces, the algorithm is still of interest because it provides a standard against which we may judge the performance of other concept learning algorithms.

In order specify a learning problem for the Brute-Force Learning Algorithm we must specify what values are to be used for ***P(h)*** and for ***P(D/h)***. We may choose the probability distributions ***P(h)*** and ***P(D/h)*** in any way we wish, to describe our prior knowledge about the learning task. Here let us choose them to be consistent with the following assumptions.

1. The training data **D** is noise free (i.e., $d_i = c(x_i)$).
2. The target concept **c** is contained in the hypothesis space H.
3. We have no a priori reason to believe that any hypothesis is more probable than any other.

Given these assumptions, what values should we specify for ***P (h)?***

Given no prior knowledge that one hypothesis is more likely than another, we assign the same prior probability to every hypothesis ***h*** in ***H.*** Furthermore, because we assume the target concept is contained in H we should require that these prior probabilities sum to 1. Together these constraints imply that we should choose.

$$P(h) = \frac{1}{|H|} \; for \; all \; h \; in \; H$$

What choice shall we make for ***P(D/h)?***

P(D/h) is the probability of observing the target values D = $(d_1 ... d_m)$ for the fixed set of instances $(x_1 ... x_m)$, given a world in which hypothesis ***h*** holds. Since we assume noise-free training data, the probability of observing classification d_i given ***h*** is just ***1*** if $d_i = h(x_i)$ and 0 if $d_i \neq h(x_i)$. Therefore,

$$P(D|h) = \begin{cases} 1 \; if \; d_i = h(x_i) \; for \; all \; d_i \; in \; D \\ 0 \; otherwise \end{cases}$$

In other words, the probability of data ***D*** given hypothesis ***h*** is 1 if ***D*** is consistent with ***h,*** and 0 otherwise.

Given these choices for ***P(h)*** and for ***P(D/h)*** we now have a fully-defined problem for the above Brute-Force Learning Algorithm. Let us consider the first step of this algorithm, which uses Bayes theorem to compute the posterior probability ***P(h/D)*** of each hypothesis ***h*** given the observed training data ***D.***

Recalling the Bayes Theorem, we have,

$$P(h|D) = \frac{P(D|h) \times P(h)}{P(D)}$$

First consider the case where ***h*** is inconsistent with the training data ***D.*** Since the above equation defines *P(D|h)* to be *0* when *h* is inconsistent with *D*, we have,

$$P(h|D) = \frac{0 \times P(h)}{P(D)} = 0 \; if \; h \; is \; inconsistent \; with \; D$$

The posterior probability of a hypothesis inconsistent with D is zero. Now consider the case where h is consistent with D. Since the above Equation defines P(D|h) to be 1 when h is consistent with D, we have,

$$P(h|D) = \frac{1 \times \frac{1}{|H|}}{P(D)}$$

$$= \frac{1 \times \frac{1}{|H|}}{\frac{|VS_{H,D}|}{|H|}}$$

$$= \frac{1}{|VS_{H,D}|} \text{if h is consistent with D}$$

where $VS_{H,D}$ is the subset of hypotheses from H that are consistent with *D*. It is easy to verify that $P(D) = \frac{|VS_{H,D}|}{|H|}$ above, because the sum over all hypotheses of *P(h/D)* must be one and because the number of hypotheses from H consistent with *D* is by definition $|VS_{H,D}|$.

To summarize, Bayes theorem implies that the posterior probability *P(h/D)* under our assumed *P(h)* and *P(D/h)* is,

$$P(h|D) = \begin{cases} \frac{1}{|VS_{H,D}|} & if\ h\ is\ consistent\ with\ D \\ 0\ otherwise \end{cases}$$

where $|VS_{H,D}|$ is the number of hypotheses from H consistent with ***D***. The evolution of probabilities associated with hypotheses is depicted schematically in Figure below. Initially all hypotheses have the same probability. As training data accumulates, the posterior probability for inconsistent hypotheses becomes zero while the total probability summing to one is shared equally among the remaining consistent hypotheses.

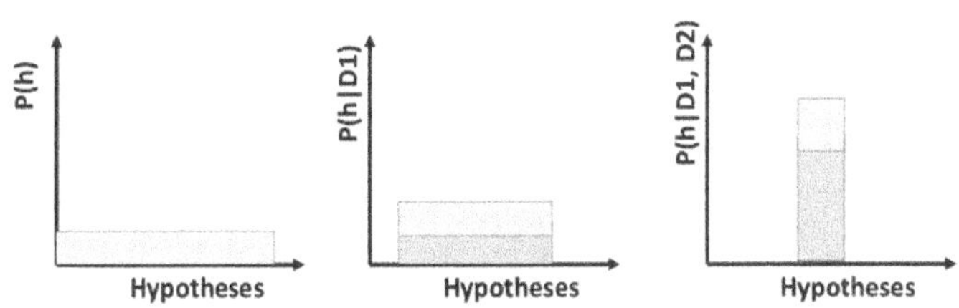

The above analysis implies that under our choice for *P(h)* and *P(D/h)*, every *consistent* hypothesis has posterior probability ($\frac{1}{|VS_{H,D}|}$), and every inconsistent hypothesis has posterior probability **0.** Every consistent hypothesis is, therefore, a MAP hypothesis.

7.8. Maximum Likelihood and Least Squared Error Hypothesis

Maximum Likelihood Estimation

Maximum Likelihood Estimation, or MLE for short, is a probabilistic framework for estimating the parameters of a model. In Maximum Likelihood Estimation, we wish to maximize the conditional probability of observing the data (*X*) given a specific probability distribution and its parameters (θ), stated formally as:

$$P(X\,;\theta)$$

Where *X* is the joint probability distribution of all observations from the problem domain from 1 to *n*.

$$P(x_1, x_2, x_3, \ldots, x_n\,;\theta)$$

This resulting conditional probability is referred to as the likelihood of observing the data given the model parameters and written using the notation *L()* to denote the likelihood function. For example:

$$L(X\,;\theta)$$

The joint probability distribution can be restated as the multiplication of the conditional probability for observing each example given the distribution parameters. Multiplying many small probabilities together can be unstable; as such, it is common to restate this problem as the sum of the natural log conditional probability.

$$\sum_{i=1}^{n} n \log(P(x_i;\theta))$$

Given the common use of log in the likelihood function, it is referred to as a log-likelihood function. It is also common in optimization problems to prefer to minimize the cost function rather than to maximize it. Therefore, the negative of the log-likelihood function is used, referred to generally as a Negative Log-Likelihood (NLL) function.

$$Minimize - \left(\sum_{i=1}^{n} n \log\big(P(x_i;\theta)\big)\right)$$

The Maximum Likelihood Estimation framework can be used as a basis for estimating the parameters of many different machine learning models for regression and classification predictive modeling. This includes the linear regression model.

7.9. Linear Regression as Maximum Likelihood

We can frame the problem of fitting a machine learning model as the problem of probability density estimation.

Specifically, the choice of model and model parameters is referred to as a modelling hypothesis h, and the problem involves finding h that best explains the data X. We can, therefore, find the modelling hypothesis that maximizes the likelihood function.

$$Maximize - \left(\sum_{i=1}^{n} n \log\big(P(x_i; h)\big) \right)$$

Supervised learning can be framed as a conditional probability problem of predicting the probability of the output given the input:

$$P(y|X)$$

As such, we can define conditional maximum likelihood estimation for supervised machine learning as follows:

$$Maximize - \left(\sum_{i=1}^{n} n \log\big(P(y_i \mid x_i; h)\big) \right)$$

Now we can replace h with our linear regression model and make some reasonable assumptions, such as the observations in the dataset are independent and drawn from the same probability distribution, and that the target variable (y) has statistical noise with a Gaussian distribution, zero mean, and the same variance for all examples.

With these assumptions, we can frame the problem of estimating y given X as estimating the mean value for y from a Gaussian probability distribution given X.

The analytical form of the Gaussian function is as follows:

$$f(x) = \frac{1}{\sqrt{2\pi\sigma^2}} e^{\frac{-1}{2\sigma^2}(y-\mu)^2}$$

Where μ is the mean of the distribution and σ^2 is the variance where the units are squared. We can use this function as our likelihood function, where μ is defined as the prediction from the model with a given set of coefficients (β) and σ is a fixed constant.

First, we can state the problem as the maximization of the product of the probabilities for each example in the dataset.

$$Maximize \prod_{i=1}^{n} \frac{1}{\sqrt{2\pi\sigma^2}} e^{\frac{-1}{2\sigma^2}(y-h(x_i,\beta))^2}$$

Where x_i is a given example and β refers to the coefficients of the linear regression model. We can transform this to a log-likelihood model as follows:

$$Maximize \sum_{i=1}^{n} log\left(\frac{1}{\sqrt{2\pi\sigma^2}} \times \frac{-1}{2\sigma^2}(y - h(x_i, \beta))^2\right)$$

It's interesting that the prediction is the mean of a distribution. It suggests that we can very reasonably add a bound to the prediction to give a prediction interval based on the standard deviation of the distribution, which is indeed a common practice.

Although the model assumes a Gaussian distribution in the prediction, there is no such expectation for the inputs to the model (X).

We can apply a search procedure to maximize this log likelihood function, or invert it by adding a negative sign to the beginning and minimize the negative log-likelihood function. This provides a solution to the linear regression model for a given dataset. This framework is also more general and can be used for curve fitting and provides the basis for fitting other regression models, such as artificial neural networks.

7.10. Least Squares and Maximum Likelihood

Interestingly, the maximum likelihood solution to linear regression presented in the previous section can be shown to be identical to the least squares solution. After derivation, the least squares equation to be minimized to fit a linear regression to a dataset looks as follows:

$$Minimize \sum_{i=1}^{n} \left(y_i - h(x_i, \beta)\right)^2$$

Where we are summing the squared errors between each target variable (y_i) and the prediction from the model for the associated input $h(x_i, \beta)$. This is often referred to as ordinary least squares. More generally, if the value is normalized by the number of examples in the dataset (averaged) rather than summed, then the quantity is referred to as the mean squared error.

$$MSE = \frac{1}{n}\sum_{i=1}^{n} (y_i - \hat{y})^2$$

Starting with the likelihood function defined in the previous section, we can show how we can remove constant elements to give the same equation as the least squares approach to solving linear regression.

$$Maximize \sum_{i=1}^{n} log\left(\frac{1}{\sqrt{2\pi\sigma^2}} \times \frac{-1}{2\sigma^2}(y - h(x_i, \beta))^2\right)$$

Key to removing constants is to focus on what does not change when different models are evaluated, e.g. when *h(xi, Beta)* is evaluated.

The first term of the calculation is independent of the model and can be removed to give:

$$Maximize \sum_{i=1}^{n} \frac{-1}{2\sigma^2}(y - h(x_i, \beta))^2$$

We can then remove the negative sign to minimize the positive quantity rather than maximize the negative quantity:

$$Minimize \sum_{i=1}^{n} \frac{1}{2\sigma^2}(y - h(x_i, \beta))^2$$

Finally, we can discard the remaining first term that is also independent of the model to give:

$$Minimize \sum_{i=1}^{n} (y - h(x_i, \beta))^2$$

We can see that this is identical to the least squares solution. In fact, under reasonable assumptions, an algorithm that minimizes the squared error between the target variable and the model output also performs maximum likelihood estimation.

7.11. Maximum Likelihood Hypothesis for Predicting Probabilities

Probability Density estimation is the problem of estimating the probability distribution for a sample of observations from a problem domain. There are many techniques for solving density estimation, although a common framework used throughout the field of machine learning is maximum likelihood estimation. Maximum likelihood estimation involves defining a likelihood function for calculating the conditional probability of observing the data sample given a probability distribution and distribution parameters. This approach can be used to search a space of possible distributions and parameters.

This flexible probabilistic framework also provides the foundation for many machine learning algorithms, including important methods such as linear regression and logistic regression for predicting numeric values and class labels respectively, but also more generally for deep learning artificial neural networks.

Probability Density Estimation

A common modelling problem involves how to estimate a joint probability distribution for a dataset.

For example, given a sample of observation (*X*) from a domain ($x_1, x_2, x_3, \ldots, x_n$), where each observation is drawn independently from the domain with the same probability distribution (so-called independent and identically distributed, i.i.d., or close to it).

Density estimation involves selecting a probability distribution function and the parameters of that distribution that best explain the joint probability distribution of the observed data (*X*).

- How do you choose the probability distribution function?
- How do you choose the parameters for the probability distribution function?

This problem is made more challenging as sample (*X*) drawn from the population is small and has noise, meaning that any evaluation of an estimated probability density function and its parameters will have some error.

There are many techniques for solving this problem, although two common approaches are:

- Maximum a Posteriori (MAP), a Bayesian method.
- Maximum Likelihood Estimation (MLE), frequentist method.

The main difference is that MLE assumes that all solutions are equally likely beforehand, whereas MAP allows prior information about the form of the solution to be harnessed.

Using MLE for Probability Estimation

We can frame the problem of fitting a machine learning model as the problem of probability density estimation. Specifically, the choice of model and model parameters is referred to as a modelling hypothesis *h*, and the problem involves finding *h* that best explains the data *X*.

$$P(X; h)$$

We can, therefore, find the modelling hypothesis that maximizes the likelihood function.

$$\text{maximize } L(X; h) = \mathit{Maximize} \sum_{i=1}^{n} \log\big(P(x_i, h)\big)$$

This provides the basis for estimating the probability density of a dataset, typically used in unsupervised machine learning algorithms; such as Clustering algorithms.

The Maximum Likelihood Estimation framework is also a useful tool for supervised machine learning. This applies to data where we have input and output variables, where the output variety may be a numerical value or a class label in the case of regression and classification predictive modelling retrospectively.

We can state this as the conditional probability of the output (y) given the input (X) given the modelling hypothesis (h).

$$Maximize\ L(y|X,h) = Maximize\ \sum_{i=1}^{n} \log(P(y_i \mid x_i, h))$$

The same Maximum Likelihood Estimation framework that is generally used for density estimation can be used to find a supervised learning model and parameters.

This provides the basis for foundational linear modelling techniques, such as:

- Linear Regression, for predicting a numerical value.
- Logistic Regression, for binary classification.

In the case of linear regression, the model is constrained to a line and involves finding a set of coefficients for the line that best fits the observed data. Fortunately, this problem can be solved analytically (e.g. directly using linear algebra).

In the case of logistic regression, the model defines a line and involves finding a set of coefficients for the line that best separates the classes. This cannot be solved analytically and is often solved by searching the space of possible coefficient values using an efficient optimization algorithm such as the BFGS algorithm or variants. Both methods can also be solved less efficiently using a more general optimization algorithm such as stochastic gradient descent.

In fact, most machine learning models can be framed under the maximum likelihood estimation framework, providing a useful and consistent way to approach predictive modelling as an optimization problem. An important benefit of the maximize likelihood estimator in machine learning is that as the size of the dataset increases, the quality of the estimator continues to improve.

7.12. Minimum Description Length Principle

The minimum description length (MDL) principle is a method for inductive inference that provides a generic solution to the model selection problem, and, more generally to the overfitting problem. – Peter Grunwald.

MDL is a principle, not a method. It allows for several methods of inductive inference and while sometimes there are clearly "better" or "worse" versions of MDL, there is no "optimal MDL".

MDL assumes that the simplest, most compact representation of the data is the best and most probable explanation of the data. The MDL principle is used to build Oracle Data Mining attribute importance models.

How does one decide among competing explanations of data given limited observations?. This is the problem of model selection. It stands out as one of the most important problems of inductive and statistical inference. The minimum description length (MDL) principle is a relatively recent method for inductive inference that provides a generic solution to the model selection problem. MDL is based on the following insight: any regularity in the data can be used to compress the data, that is, to describe it using fewer symbols than the number of symbols needed to describe the data literally. The more regularities there are, the more the data canbe compressed. Equating "learning" with "finding regularity," we can therefore say that the more we are able to compress the data, the more we have learned about the data. Formalizing this idea leads to a general theory of inductive inference with several attractive properties:

1. **Occam's razor:** MDL chooses a model that trades off goodness-of-fit on the observed data with 'complexity' or 'richness' of the model. As such, MDL embodies form of Occam's razor, a principle that is both intuitively appealing and informally applied throughout all the sciences.
2. **No overfitting, automatically:** MDL procedures automatically and inherently protect against overfitting and can be used to estimate both the parameters and the structure (e.g., number of parameters) of a model. In contrast, to avoid overfitting when estimating the structure of a model, traditional methods such as maximum likelihood must be modified and extended with additional, typically adhoc principles.
3. **Bayesian interpretation**: MDL is closely related to Bayesian inference, but avoids some of the interpretation difficulties of the Bayesian approach, especially in the realistic case when it is known a priori to the modeler that none of the models under consideration is true. In fact:
4. **No need for "underlying truth."** In contrast to other statistical methods, MDL procedures have a clear interpretation independent of whether or not there exists some underlying "true" model.
5. **Predictive interpretation**. Because data compression is formally equivalent to a form of probabilistic prediction, MDL methods can be interpreted as searching for a model with good predictive performance on unseen data.

The ideal version of MDL is given by the Kolmogorov Complexity, which is defined as the length of the shortest computer program that prints the sequence of observed data and halts. However, the Komogorov Complexity is un computable i.e. it can be shown that there exists no computer program that, for every set of data D, when given D as input, returns the shortest program that prints D). Moreover, for finite length sequences, the best program may depend on the sequence itself.

Practical versions of MDL are either based on one stage universal codes (known as refined MDL) or two-stagecodes (known as crude MDL). The refined MDL suggest that, for a given class of models, pick the model which minimizes the worst-case redundancy on the data. This leads to precisely the universal models such as mixture models and normalized maximum likelihood (NML) model.

$$Mixutre\ Model:\ q_\gamma(x^n) = \sum_{q \in Q_\gamma} \pi(q)\, q(x^n)$$

$$where\ \pi\ is\ chose\ to\ be\ minmax\ optimal\ prior\ for\ class\ Q_\gamma$$

$$NML\ Model:\ q_\gamma(x^n) = \underset{q \in Q_\gamma}{\operatorname{argmax}} \frac{q(x^n)}{\sum_{x^n} \max_{q \in Q_\gamma} q(x^n)}$$

The mixture models are usually preferred as they amenable to sequential modelling and hence to design of practical arithmetic codes based on those sequential models.

The crude MDL or two-stage code approach is based on the notion that we can specify the descriptive properties of a model for data in two stages:

1. Encode the model with some code length L(q).
2. Encode the data using the model with code length $L_q(x^n)$.

Now pick the model which minimizes the total code length of the two-stage code:

$$q_\gamma(x^n) = \underset{q \in Q_\gamma}{\operatorname{argmin}}\{L(q) + L_q(x^n)\}$$

This procedure can be used for model selection within a class.

7.13. Bayes Optimal Classifier

Global optimization is a challenging problem of finding an input that results in the minimum or maximum cost of a given objective function. Typically, the form of the objective function is complex and intractable to analyze and is often non-convex, nonlinear, high dimension, noisy, and computationally expensive to evaluate.

Bayesian Optimization provides a principled technique based on Bayes Theorem to direct a search of a global optimization problem that is efficient and effective. It works by building a probabilistic model of the objective function, called the surrogate function, that is then searched efficiently with an acquisition function before candidate samples are chosen for evaluation on the real objective function.

Bayesian Optimization is often used in applied machine learning to tune the hyper parameters of a given well-performing model on a validation dataset. The Bayes optimal classifier is a probabilistic model that makes the most likely prediction for a new example, given the training dataset.

This model is also referred to as the Bayes optimal learner, the Bayes classifier, Bayes optimal decision boundary, or the Bayes optimal discriminant function.

- **Bayes Classifier**: Probabilistic model that makes the most probable prediction for new examples.

Specifically, the Bayes optimal classifier answers the question:

What is the most probable classification of the new instance given the training data?

This is different from the MAP framework that seeks the most probable hypothesis (model). Instead, we are interested in making a specific prediction.

The equation below demonstrates how to calculate the conditional probability for a new instance (v_i) given the training data (D), given a space of hypotheses (H).

$$P(v_j|D) = \sum_{h \in H} P\left(v_j|h_i\right) \times P(h_i|D)$$

Where v_j is a new instance to be classified, H is the set of hypotheses for classifying the instance, h_i is a given hypothesis, $P(v_j|h_i)$ is the posterior probability for v_i given hypothesis h_i, and $P(h_i|D)$ is the posterior probability of the hypothesis h_i given the data D.

Selecting the outcome with the maximum probability is an example of a Bayes optimal classification. Any model that classifies examples using this equation is a Bayes optimal classifier and no other model can outperform this technique, on average. Because the Bayes classifier is optimal, the Bayes error is the minimum possible error that can be made.

- **Bayes Error:** The minimum possible error that can be made when making predictions.

The Naive Bayes classifier is an example of a classifier that adds some simplifying assumptions and attempts to approximate the Bayes Optimal Classifier.

7.14. Naive Bayes Classifier Algorithm

- Naive Bayes algorithm is a supervised learning algorithm, which is based on Bayes theorem and used for solving classification problems.
- It is mainly used in text classification that includes a high-dimensional training dataset.
- Naive Bayes Classifier is one of the simple and most effective Classification algorithms which helps in building the fast machine learning models that can make quick predictions.
- It is a probabilistic classifier, which means it predicts on the basis of the probability of an object.
- Some popular examples of Naive Bayes Algorithm are spam filtration, Sentimental analysis, and classifying articles.
- The Naive Bayes algorithm is comprised of two words Naive and Bayes, Which can be described as:
- Naive: It is called Naive because it assumes that the occurrence of a certain feature is independent of the occurrence of other features. Such as if the fruit is identified on the bases of color, shape, and taste, then red, spherical, and sweet fruit is recognized as an apple. Hence each feature individually contributes to identify that it is an apple without depending on each other.
- Bayes: It is called Bayes because it depends on the principle of Bayes' Theorem.
- **Bayes' Theorem**:
- Bayes' theorem is also known as Bayes' Rule or Bayes' law, which is used to determine the probability of a hypothesis with prior knowledge. It depends on the conditional probability.
- The formula for Bayes' theorem is given as:

$$P(A|B) = \frac{P(B|A)P(A)}{P(B)}$$

- Naive Bayes Classifier Algorithm.

Where,

- P(A|B) is Posterior probability: Probability of hypothesis A on the observed event B.
- P(B|A) is Likelihood probability: Probability of the evidence given that the probability of a hypothesis is true.

- P(A) is Prior Probability: Probability of hypothesis before observing the evidence.
- P(B) is Marginal Probability: Probability of Evidence.

Steps

- Find the P(A)- prior probability.
- Convert the given dataset into frequency tables.
- Generate Likelihood table by finding the probabilities of given features. (Conditional probabilities).
- Now, use Bayes theorem to calculate the posterior probability.

Advantages of Naive Bayes Classifier

- Naive Bayes is one of the fast and easy ML algorithms to predict a class of datasets.
- It can be used for Binary as well as Multi-class Classifications.
- It performs well in Multi-class predictions as compared to the other Algorithms.
- It is the most popular choice for text classification problems.

Disadvantages of Naive Bayes Classifier

- Naive Bayes assumes that all features are independent or unrelated, so it cannot learn the relationship between features.

Applications of Naive Bayes Classifier

- It is used for Credit Scoring.
- It is used in medical data classification.
- It can be used in real-time predictions because Naive Bayes Classifier is an eager learner.
- It is used in Text classification such as Spam filtering and Sentiment analysis.

NAIVE BAYES CLASSIFIER – EXAMPLE - 1

Day	Outlook	Temperature	Humidity	Wind	PlayTennis
D1	Sunny	Hot	High	Weak	No
D2	Sunny	Hot	High	Strong	No
D3	Overcast	Hot	High	Weak	Yes
D4	Rain	Mild	High	Weak	Yes
D5	Rain	Cool	Normal	Weak	Yes
D6	Rain	Cool	Normal	Strong	No
D7	Overcast	Cool	Normal	Strong	Yes
D8	Sunny	Mild	High	Weak	No
D9	Sunny	Cool	Normal	Weak	Yes
D10	Rain	Mild	Normal	Weak	Yes
D11	Sunny	Mild	Normal	Strong	Yes
D12	Overcast	Mild	High	Strong	Yes
D13	Overcast	Hot	Normal	Weak	Yes
D14	Rain	Mild	High	Strong	No

Outlook = Sunny, Temperature = Cool, Humidity = High, Wing =Strong)

Calculate prior probability(P)-> Y & N

Day	Outlook	Temperature	Humidity	Wind	PlayTennis
D1	Sunny	Hot	High	Weak	No
D2	Sunny	Hot	High	Strong	No
D3	Overcast	Hot	High	Weak	Yes
D4	Rain	Mild	High	Weak	Yes
D5	Rain	Cool	Normal	Weak	Yes
D6	Rain	Cool	Normal	Strong	No
D7	Overcast	Cool	Normal	Strong	Yes
D8	Sunny	Mild	High	Weak	No
D9	Sunny	Cool	Normal	Weak	Yes
D10	Rain	Mild	Normal	Weak	Yes
D11	Sunny	Mild	Normal	Strong	Yes
D12	Overcast	Mild	High	Strong	Yes
D13	Overcast	Hot	Normal	Weak	Yes
D14	Rain	Mild	High	Strong	No

P(PlayTennis = yes) =9/14 =.64

P(PlayTennis = no) = 5/14 = .36

Calculate the Conditional Probability->Each Attribute

Day	Outlook	Temperature	Humidity	Wind	PlayTennis
D1	Sunny	Hot	High	Weak	No
D2	Sunny	Hot	High	Strong	No
D3	Overcast	Hot	High	Weak	Yes
D4	Rain	Mild	High	Weak	Yes
D5	Rain	Cool	Normal	Weak	Yes
D6	Rain	Cool	Normal	Strong	No
D7	Overcast	Cool	Normal	Strong	Yes
D8	Sunny	Mild	High	Weak	No
D9	Sunny	Cool	Normal	Weak	Yes
D10	Rain	Mild	Normal	Weak	Yes
D11	Sunny	Mild	Normal	Strong	Yes
D12	Overcast	Mild	High	Strong	Yes
D13	Overcast	Hot	Normal	Weak	Yes
D14	Rain	Mild	High	Strong	No

Outlook	Y	N
sunny	2/9	3/5
overcast	4/9	0
rain	3/9	2/5
Tempreature		
hot	2/9	2/5
mild	4/9	2/5
cool	3/9	1/5

Humidity	Y	N
high	3/9	4/5
normal	6/9	1/5

Windy		
Strong	3/9	3/5
Weak	6/9	2/5

Classify the new ex->Y or N

(Outlook = sunny, Temperature = cool, Humidity = high, Wing = strong

$$v_{NB} = \underset{v_j \epsilon \{yes,no\}}{argmax} P(v_j) \prod_i P(a_i | v_j)$$

$$= \underset{v_j \epsilon \{yes,no\}}{argmax} P(v_j) P(Outlook = sunny|v_j) P(Temperature = cool|v_j)$$

$$P(Humidity\ high|v_j) P(Wind = strong||v_j)$$

$$v_{NB}(yes) = P(yes) P(sunny|yes) P(cool|yes) P(high|yes) P(strong|yes) = 0.053$$

$$v_{NB}(no) = P(no) P(sunny|no) P(cool|no) P(high|no) P(strong|no) = .0206$$

$$v_{NB}(yes) = \frac{v_{NB}(yes)}{v_{NB}(yes)+v_{NB}(no)} = 0.205 \qquad v_{NB}(no) = \frac{v_{NB}(no)}{v_{NB}(yes)+v_{NB}(no)} = 0.795$$

Ex 2: Calculate Prior Probability (M) & P(H)

No	Color	Legs	Height	Smelly	Species
1	White	3	Short	Yes	M
2	Green	2	Tall	No	M
3	Green	3	Short	Yes	M
4	White	3	Short	Yes	M
5	Green	2	Short	No	H
6	White	2	Tall	No	H
7	White	2	Tall	No	H
8	White	2	Short	Yes	H

New Instance

(Color = Green, Legs = 2, Height = Tall, and Smelly = No)

$$P(M) = \frac{4}{8} = 0.5 \quad P(H) = \frac{4}{8} = 0.5$$

- Estimate Conditional probabilities of each attributes {color, legs, height, smelly} for the species classes: {M, H} using the data given in the table.
- Using these probabilities estimate the probability values for the new instance - {Color = Green, legs = 2, Height = Tall, and Smelly = No).

No	Color	Legs	Height	Smelly	Species
1	White	3	Short	Yes	M
2	Green	2	Tall	No	M
3	Green	3	Short	Yes	M
4	White	3	Short	Yes	M
5	Green	2	Short	No	H
6	White	2	Tall	No	H
7	White	2	Tall	No	H
8	White	2	Short	Yes	H

Calculate for All Attributes (Conditional Probabilities)->Possible Outcome, Possible Values

No	Color	Legs	Height	Smelly	Species
1	White	3	Short	Yes	M
2	Green	2	Tall	No	M
3	Green	3	Short	Yes	M
4	White	3	Short	Yes	M
5	Green	2	Short	No	H
6	White	2	Tall	No	H
7	White	2	Tall	No	H
8	White	2	Short	Yes	H

Color	M	H
White	2/4	3/4
Green	2/4	1/4

Legs	M	H
2	1/4	4/4
3	3/4	0/4

Height	M	H
Tall	3/4	2/4
Short	1/4	2/4

Smelly	M	H
Yes	3/4	1/4
No	1/4	3/4

Calculate the Probability of New Instance->Classify Whether M or H (Using Prior & Conditional)

$P(M) = \frac{4}{8} = 0.5 \quad P(H) = \frac{4}{8} = 0.5$

Color	M	H
White	2/4	3/4
Green	2/4	1/4

Legs	M	H
2	1/4	4/4
3	3/4	0/4

Height	M	H
Tall	3/4	2/4
Short	1/4	2/4

Smelly	M	H
Yes	3/4	1/4
No	1/4	3/4

$p(M|New\ Instance) = p(M) * p(Color = Green|M) * p(Legs = 2|M) * p(Height = tall|M) * p(Smelly = no\ |M)$

$p(M|New\ Instance) = 0.5 * \frac{2}{4} * \frac{1}{4} * \frac{3}{4} * \frac{1}{4} = 0.0117$

$P(M) = \frac{4}{8} = 0.5 \quad P(H) = \frac{4}{8} = 0.5$

Color	M	H
White	2/4	3/4
Green	2/4	1/4

Legs	M	H
2	1/4	4/4
3	3/4	0/4

Height	M	H
Tall	3/4	2/4
Short	1/4	2/4

Smelly	M	H
Yes	3/4	1/4
No	1/4	3/4

$p(M|New\ Instance) = p(M) * p(Color = Green|M) * p(Legs = 2|M) * p(Height = tall|M) * p(Smelly = no\ |M)$

$p(M|New\ Instance) = 0.5 * \frac{2}{4} * \frac{1}{4} * \frac{3}{4} * \frac{1}{4} = 0.0117$

$p(H|New\ Instance) = p(H) * p(Color = Green|H) * p(Legs = 2|H) * p(Height = tall|H) * p(Smelly = no\ |H)$

$p(H|New\ Instance) = 0.5 * \frac{1}{4} * \frac{4}{4} * \frac{2}{4} * \frac{3}{4} = 0.047$

$$p(M|New\ Instance) = p(M) * p(Color = Green|M) * p(Legs = 2|M) * p(Height = tall|M) * p(Smelly = no\ |M)$$

$$p(M|New\ Instance) = 0.5 * \frac{2}{4} * \frac{1}{4} * \frac{3}{4} * \frac{1}{4} = 0.0117$$

$$p(H|New\ Instance) = p(H) * p(Color = Green|H) * p(Legs = 2|H) * p(Height = tall|H) * p(Smelly = no\ |H)$$

$$p(H|New\ Instance) = 0.5 * \frac{1}{4} * \frac{4}{4} * \frac{2}{4} * \frac{3}{4} = 0.047$$

$$p(H|New\ Instance) > p(M|New\ Instance)$$

Hence the new instance belongs to special H.

EX: 3

Problem: If the weather is sunny, then the Player should play or not?

Solution: To solve this, first consider the below dataset:

	Outlook	Play
0	Rainy	Yes
1	Sunny	Yes
2	Overcast	Yes
3	Overcast	Yes
4	Sunny	No
5	Rainy	Yes
6	Sunny	Yes
7	Overcast	Yes
8	Rainy	No
9	Sunny	No
10	Sunny	Yes
11	Rainy	No
12	Overcast	Yes
13	Overcast	Yes

Frequency Table for the Weather Conditions

Weather	Yes	No
Overcast	5	0
Rainy	2	2
Sunny	3	2
Total	10	5

Likelihood Table Weather Condition

Weather	No	Yes	
Overcast	0	5	5/14= 0.35
Rainy	2	2	4/14=0.29
Sunny	2	3	5/14=0.35
All	4/14=0.29	10/14=0.71	

Applying Bayes'Theorem

P(Yes|Sunny)= P(Sunny|Yes)*P(Yes)/P(Sunny)

P(Sunny|Yes)= 3/10= 0.3

P(Sunny)= 0.35

P(Yes)=0.71

So P(Yes|Sunny) = 0.3*0.71/0.35= **0.60**

P(No|Sunny)= P(Sunny|No)*P(No)/P(Sunny)

P(Sunny|NO)= 2/4=0.5

P(No)= 0.29

P(Sunny)= 0.35

So P(No|Sunny)= 0.5*0.29/0.35 = **0.41**

So as we can see from the above calculation that **P(Yes|Sunny)>P(No|Sunny)**

Hence on a Sunny day, Player can play the game.

Disadvantages of Naive Bayes Classifier

- Naive Bayes assumes that all features are independent or unrelated, so it cannot learn the relationship between features.

7.15. Text Classification Using Naive Bayes Classifier

- Text Classification is an example of supervised machine learning task since a labelled dataset containing text documents and their labels is used for train a classifier.
- The Naive Bayes classifier is a simple classifier that classifies based on probabilities of events. It is the applied commonly to text classification.... With the training set, we can train a Naive Bayes classifier which we can use to automatically categorize a new sentence.

- **Binary Classification**: When we have to categorize given data into 2 distinct classes. Example – On the basis of given health conditions of a person, we have to determine whether the person has a certain disease or not.
- **Multiclass Classification**: The number of classes is more than 2. For Example – On the basis of data about different species of flowers, we have to determine which specie does our observation belong to.

EX Fig: Binary and Multiclass Classification. Here x1 and x2 are our variables upon which the class is predicted.

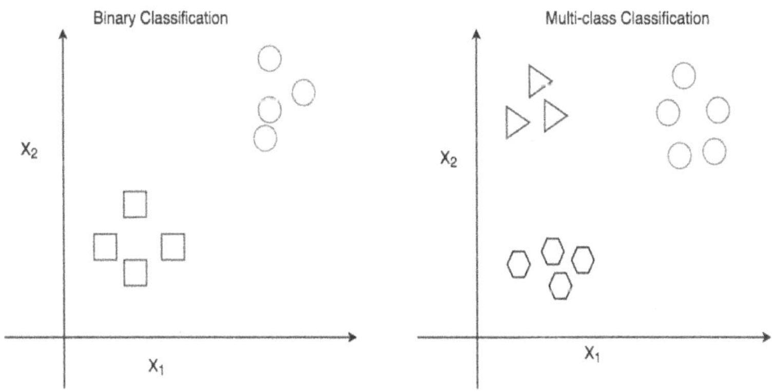

Fig. 7.8: Binary and Multiclass Classification

How does classification works?

- Suppose we have to predict whether a given patient has a certain disease or not, on the basis of 3 variables, called features.
- Which means there are two possible outcomes:
- The patient has the said disease. Basically a result labeled "Yes" or "True".
- The patient is disease free. A result labeled "No" or "False".
- This is a binary classification problem.
- We have a set of observations called training data set, which comprises of sample data with actual classification results. We train a model, called Classifier on this data set, and use that model to predict whether a certain patient will have the disease or not.

Example 1

Naïve Bayes Model – Text Classification Example

- Dataset for the text classification with training and test data is given below.
- The goal is to classify the test data into the right class as h or —h (read as not h).

	Document ID	Keywords in the document	Class h
Training Set	1	Love Happy Joy Joy Happy	Yes
	2	Happy Love Kick Joy Happy	Yes
	3	Love Move Joy Good	Yes
	4	Love Happy Joy Love Pain	Yes
	5	Joy Love Pain Kick Pain	No
	6	Pain Pain Love kick	No
Testing Set	7	Love Pain Joy Love Kick	?

Formula

Naïve Bayes Model – Text Classification Example

- The probability of the document 'd' being in class 'c' is computed as follows,

$$p(c|d) \propto p(c) \prod_{1 \le k \le n_d} p(t_k|c)$$

- Where, $p(t_k|c)$ is the conditional probability of term t_k occurring in a document of class c.

- **TO FIND P(H) & P(-H)->**

Naïve Bayes Model – Text Classification Example

$$p(c|d) \propto p(c) \prod_{1 \le k \le n_d} p(t_k|c)$$

- The prior probabilities of a document being classified using the six documents are,

$$P(h) = \frac{4}{6} = \frac{2}{3}$$

$$and$$

$$p(-h) = \frac{2}{6} = \frac{1}{3}$$

- That is there is $\frac{2}{3}$ prior probability that a document will be classified as h and $\frac{1}{3}$ probability of not h.

Ex: Totally Class 'h' has 19 Wordsout of that 5 are 'Love'

	Document ID	Keywords in the document	Class h
Training Set	1	Love Happy Joy Joy Happy	Yes
	2	Happy Love Kick Joy Happy	Yes
	3	Love Move Joy Good	Yes
	4	Love Happy Joy Love Pain	Yes
	5	Joy Love Pain Kick Pain	No
	6	Pain Pain Love kick	No
Testing Set	7	Love Pain Joy Love Kick	?

Class h
$P(Love \mid h) = 5/19$
$P(Pain \mid h) = 1/19$
$P(Joy \mid h) = 5/19$
$P(Kick \mid h) = 1/19$

Keywords in the document	Class h
Love Happy Joy Joy Happy	Yes
Happy Love Kick Joy Happy	Yes
Love Move Joy Good	Yes
Love Happy Joy Love Pain	Yes

Document ID	Keywords in the document	Class h
1	Love Happy Joy Joy Happy	Yes
2	Happy Love Kick Joy Happy	Yes
3	Love Move Joy Good	Yes
4	Love Happy Joy Love Pain	Yes

Class h
$P(Love \mid h) = 5/19$

Ex: TOTALLY CLASS '-h' has 9 words out of that 2 are 'love'

Class h	Class -h
$P(Love \mid h) = 5/19$	$P(Love \mid -h) = 2/9$
$P(Pain \mid h) = 1/19$	$P(Pain \mid -h) = 4/9$
$P(Joy \mid h) = 5/19$	$P(Joy \mid -h) = 1/9$
$P(Kick \mid h) = 1/19$	$P(Kick \mid -h) = 2/9$

5	Joy Love Pain Kick Pain	No
6	Pain Pain Love kick	No

↓

5	Joy Love Pain Kick Pain	No
6	Pain Pain Love kick	No

Class -h
$P(Love \mid -h) = 2/9$
$P(Pain \mid -h) = 4/9$
$P(Joy \mid -h) = 1/9$
$P(Kick \mid -h) = 2/9$

	Document ID	Keywords in the document	Class h
Training Set	1	Love Happy Joy Joy Happy	Yes
	2	Happy Love Kick Joy Happy	Yes
	3	Love Move Joy Good	Yes
	4	Love Happy Joy Love Pain	Yes
	5	Joy Love Pain Kick Pain	No
	6	Pain Pain Love kick	No
Testing Set	7	Love Pain Joy Love Kick	?

Conditional Probability

- The conditional probability for each term is the relative frequency of the term occurring in each class of the documents 'h class' and 'not h class'.

Testing Example:

Love Pain Joy Love Kick = ?

Class h	Class -h
$P(Love \mid h) = 5/19$	$P(Love \mid -h) = 2/9$
$P(Pain \mid h) = 1/19$	$P(Pain \mid -h) = 4/9$
$P(Joy \mid h) = 5/19$	$P(Joy \mid -h) = 1/9$
$P(Kick \mid h) = 1/19$	$P(Kick \mid -h) = 2/9$

Testing Instance

Testing Example:

Love Pain Joy Love Kick = ?

$$p(c|d) \propto p(c) \prod_{1 \le k \le n_d} p(t_k|c)$$

Class h	Class -h
$P(Love \mid h) = 5/19$	$P(Love \mid -h) = 2/9$
$P(Pain \mid h) = 1/19$	$P(Pain \mid -h) = 4/9$
$P(Joy \mid h) = 5/19$	$P(Joy \mid -h) = 1/9$
$P(Kick \mid h) = 1/19$	$P(Kick \mid -h) = 2/9$

$$P(h|d_7) = P(h) * (P(Love|h) * (P(Love|h) * P(Pain|h) * P(Joy|h) * P(Kick|h)$$
$$= (2/3) * (5/19) * (5/19) * (1/19) * (5/19) * (1/19) = \mathbf{0.0000067}$$

Testing Example

Testing Example:
Love Pain Joy Love Kick = ?

$$p(c|d) \propto p(c) \prod_{1 \le k \le n_d} p(t_k|c)$$

Class h	Class -h
$P(Love \mid h) = 5/19$	$P(Love \mid -h) = 2/9$
$P(Pain \mid h) = 1/19$	$P(Pain \mid -h) = 4/9$
$P(Joy \mid h) = 5/19$	$P(Joy \mid -h) = 1/9$
$P(Kick \mid h) = 1/19$	$P(Kick \mid -h) = 2/9$

$$p(-h|d7) = p(-h) * P(Love| -h) * P(Love| -h) * P(Pain| -h) * P(Joy| -h) * P(Kick| -h)$$
$$= (1/3) * (2/9) * (2/9) * (4/9) * (1/9) * (2/9) = \mathbf{0.00018}$$

Compare

$$P(h|d_7) = \mathbf{0.0000067}$$

$$p(-h|d7) = \mathbf{0.00018}$$

Testing Example:
Love Pain Joy Love Kick = No

Class label for testing example is: **No**

Conclusion

As per the

Testing Set	7	Love Pain Joy Love Kick	?

- P(-h) is > p(h). So our given testing instance does not belongs to'h'.
- Hence its belongs to (-h).
- That is class 'h' label is 'No'.

Note

To Maintain the Probability < 1 Always

- Laplace smoothing is a smoothing technique that helps tackle the problem of zero probability in the Naive Bayes machine learning algorithm.

- Using higher alpha values will push the likelihood towards a value of 0.5, i.e., the probability of a word equal to 0.5 for both the positive and negative reviews.
- So we are maintaining alpha value as 1 in both (numerator and denominator).

7.16. Bayesian Belief Network (BBN)

Concept

- Bayesian Belief Network is a graphical representation of different probabilistic relationships among random variables in a particular set. It is a classifier with no dependency on attributes i.e it is condition independent.
- Due to its feature of joint probability, the probability in Bayesian Belief Network is derived, based on a condition — P(attribute/parent) i.e probability of an attribute, true over parent attribute.
- (Note: A classifier assigns data in a collection to desired categories.)
- A Bayesian Belief Network (BBN), or simply Bayesian Network, is a statistical model used to describe the conditional dependencies between different random variables.
- A Bayesian network (also known as a Bayes network, belief network, or decision network) is a probabilistic graphical model that represents a set of variables and their conditional dependencies.

Working

- A Bayesian network is made of nodes and arcs. Let's understand what is Bayesian belief network explained in simple words.
- Each node represents the random variables, and a variable can be discrete or continuous.
- Directed arrows or arcs correspond to the causal relationship between the variables. These directed links connect the pair of nodes in the graphical model.
- In these links, one node directly affects the other node, and if there is no direct link, the variables are independent of each other.
- Graphical and visual networks provide a model to visualize the structure of the probabilities and develop designs for new models as well.
- Relationships determine the type of relationship and the presence or absence of it between variables.
- Computations calculate complex probability problems efficiently.

- Bayesian networks can investigate and tell you whether a particular feature is taken into a note for the decision-making process and can force to include that feature if necessary. This network will ensure that all known features are investigated for deciding on a problem.
- Bayesian Networks are more extensible than other networks and learning methods. Adding a new piece in the network requires only a few probabilities and a few edges in the graph. So, it is an excellent network for adding a new piece of data to an existing probabilistic model.
- The graph of a Bayesian Network is useful. It is readable to both computers and humans; both can interpret the information, unlike some networks like neural networks, which humans can't read.
- The most significant disadvantage is that there is no universally acknowledged method for constructing networks from data. There have been many developments in this regard, but there hasn't been a conqueror in a long time.
- The design of Bayesian Networks is hard to make compared to other networks. It needs a lot of effort. Hence, only the person creating the network can exploit causal influences. Neural networks are an advantage compared to this, as they learn different patterns and aren't limited to only the creator.
- The Bayesian network fails to define cyclic relationships—for example, deflection of airplane wings and fluid pressure field around it. The deflection depends on the pressure, and the pressure is dependent on the deflection. It is a tightly coupled problem which this network fails to define and make decisions.
- The network is expensive to build.
- It performs poorly on high dimensional data.

  To build a Bayesian network, you have to ask three questions yourself:
- Variables: what are the random variables in my problem?
- Conditional dependencies: what are the relationships between the variables, and are they independent or dependent?
- Probability Dispersals: how is the probability of each variable distributed in my problem?

Bayesian Belief Network

Bayesian belief network is key computer technology for dealing with probabilistic events and to solve a problem which has uncertainty. We can define a Bayesian network as:

"A Bayesian network is a probabilistic graphical model which represents a set of variables and their conditional dependencies using a directed acyclic graph."

It is also called a **Bayes network, belief network, decision network**, or **Bayesian model**. Bayesian networks are probabilistic, because these networks are built from a **probability distribution**, and also use probability theory for prediction and anomaly detection.

Real world applications are probabilistic in nature, and to represent the relationship between multiple events, we need a Bayesian network. It can also be used in various tasks including **prediction, anomaly detection, diagnostics, automated insight, reasoning, time series prediction**, and **decision making under uncertainty**.

Bayesian Network can be used for building models from data and experts opinions, and it consists of two parts:

- **Directed Acyclic Graph**
- **Table of conditional probabilities**

The generalized form of Bayesian network that represents and solve decision problems under uncertain knowledge is known as an **Influence diagram**.

A Bayesian network graph is made up of nodes and Arcs (directed links), where:

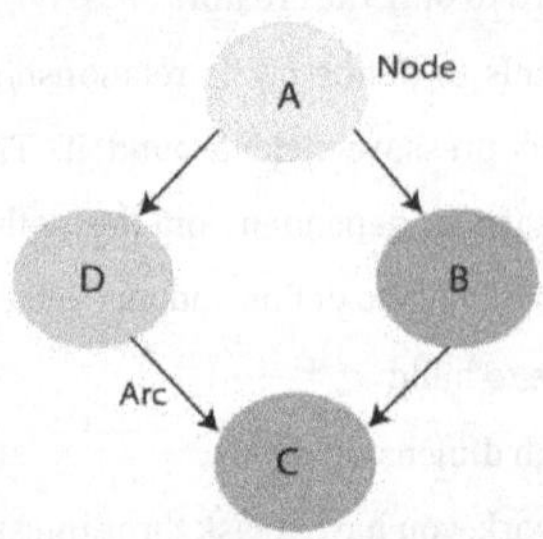

Fig. 7.9: Bayesian Network Graph

- Each **node** corresponds to the random variables, and a variable can be **continuous** or **discrete**.
- **Arc or directed arrows** represent the causal relationship or conditional probabilities between random variables. These directed links or arrows connect the pair of nodes in the graph.

These links represent that one node directly influence the other node, and if there is no directed link that means that nodes are independent with each other.

- In the above diagram, A, B, C, and D are random variables represented by the nodes of the network graph.
- If we are considering node B, which is connected with node A by a directed arrow, then node A is called the parent of Node B.
- Node C is independent of node A.

Note: The Bayesian network graph does not contain any cyclic graph. Hence, it is known as a directed acyclic graph or DAG.

The Bayesian Network has Mainly Two Components

- Causal Component
- Actual numbers

Each node in the Bayesian network has condition probability distribution P(Xi |Parent(Xi)), which determines the effect of the parent on that node.

Bayesian network is based on Joint probability distribution and conditional probability. So let's first understand the joint probability distribution:

Joint Probability Distribution

If we have variables x1, x2, x3,....., xn, then the probabilities of a different combination of x1, x2, x3.. xn, are known as Joint probability distribution.

P[x1, x2, x3,....., xn], it can be written as the following way in terms of the joint probability distribution.

= P[x1| x2, x3,....., xn]P[x2, x3,....., xn]

= P[x1| x2, x3,....., xn]P[x2|x3,....., xn]....P[xn-1|xn]P[xn].

In general for each variable Xi, we can write the equation as:

P(Xi|Xi-1,........., X1) = P(Xi |Parents(Xi))

Ex: A Bayesian Network Graph is Made Up of Nodes and Arcs (Directed Links)

Example: Harry installed a new burglar alarm at his home to detect burglary. The alarm reliably responds at detecting a burglary but also responds for minor earthquakes. Harry has two neighbors David and Sophia, who have taken a responsibility to inform Harry at work when they hear the alarm. David always calls Harry when he hears the alarm, but sometimes he got confused with the phone ringing and calls at that time too. On the other hand, Sophia likes to listen to high music, so sometimes she misses to hear the alarm. Here we would like to compute the probability of Burglary Alarm.

Problem

Calculate the probability that alarm has sounded, but there is neither a burglary, nor an earthquake occurred, and David and Sophia both called the Harry.

Solution

- The Bayesian network for the above problem is given below. The network structure is showing that burglary and earthquake is the parent node of the alarm and directly affecting the probability of alarm's going off, but David and Sophia's calls depend on alarm probability.
- The network is representing that our assumptions do not directly perceive the burglary and also do not notice the minor earthquake, and they also not confer before calling.
- The conditional distributions for each node are given as conditional probabilities table or CPT.
- Each row in the CPT must be sum to 1 because all the entries in the table represent an exhaustive set of cases for the variable.
- In CPT, a boolean variable with k boolean parents contains 2^K probabilities. Hence, if there are two parents, then CPT will contain 4 probability values.

List of All Events Occurring in this Network

- **Burglary (B)**
- **Earthquake(E)**
- **Alarm(A)**
- **David Calls(D)**
- **Sophia calls(S)**

We can write the events of problem statement in the form of probability: **P[D, S, A, B, E]**, can rewrite the above probability statement using joint probability distribution.

P[D, S, A, B, E]= P[D | S, A, B, E]. P[S, A, B, E]

=P[D | S, A, B, E]. P[S | A, B, E]. P[A, B, E]

= P [D| A]. P [S| A, B, E]. P[A, B, E]

= P[D | A]. P[S | A]. P[A| B, E]. P[B, E]

= P[D | A]. P[S | A]. P[A| B, E]. P[B |E]. P[E]

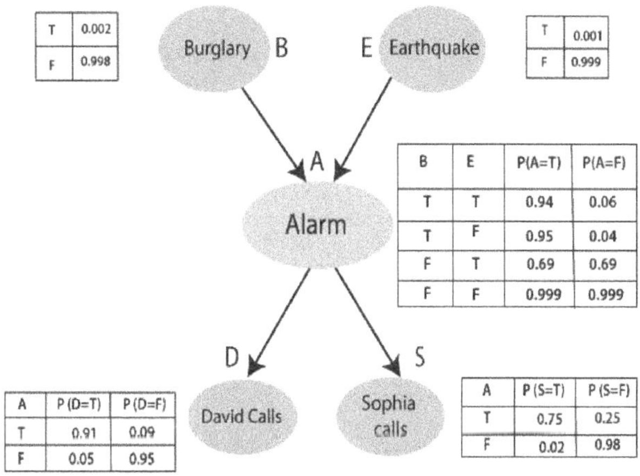

Let's take the observed probability for the Burglary and earthquake component: P(B= True) = 0.002, which is the probability of burglary.

P(B= False)= 0.998, which is the probability of no burglary.

P(E= True)= 0.001, which is the probability of a minor earthquake.

P(E= False)= 0.999, Which is the probability that an earthquake not occurred.

We can provide the conditional probabilities as per the below tables.

Conditional Probability Table for Alarm A

The Conditional probability of Alarm A depends on Burglar and earthquake:

B	E	P(A= True)	P(A= False)
True	True	0.94	0.06
True	False	0.95	0.04
False	True	0.31	0.69
False	False	0.001	0.999

Conditional Probability Table for David Calls

The Conditional probability of David that he will call depends on the probability of Alarm.

A	P(D= True)	P(D= False)
True	0.91	0.09
False	0.05	0.95

Conditional Probability Table for Sophia Calls

The Conditional probability of Sophia that she calls is depending on its Parent Node "Alarm."

A	P(S= True)	P(S= False)
True	0.75	0.25
False	0.02	0.98

From the formula of joint distribution, we can write the problem statement in the form of probability distribution:

P(S, D, A, ¬B, ¬E) = P (S|A) *P (D|A)*P (A|¬B ^ ¬E) *P (¬B) *P (¬E).

= 0.75* 0.91* 0.001* 0.998*0.999

= 0.00068045.

Hence, a Bayesian network can answer any query about the domain by using Joint distribution.

The Semantics of Bayesian Network

There are two ways to understand the semantics of the Bayesian network, which is given below:

1. To understand the network as the representation of the Joint probability distribution.
2. It is helpful to understand how to construct the network.

7.17. Gibbs Algorithm

Gibbs sampling is a particular form of Markov Chain Monte Carlo (MCMC) algorithm for approximating joint and marginal distribution by sampling from conditional distributions. Gibbs algorithm can be used when the joint distribution is not explicitly known or is difficult to sample from directly, but the conditional distribution is known or easy to sample from. Even when the joint distribution is known, the computational burden needed to calculate it may be huge. In such scenarios also Gibbs algorithm comes in aid. Gibbs algorithm can generate a sequence of samples from conditional individual distributions, which constitutes a Markov chain, to approximate the joint distribution.

Characteristics of Gibbs Sampling algorithm.

1. It is a form of Markov Chain Monte Carlo (MCMC) algorithm.
2. It samples from the conditional distribution while other parameters are fixed.
3. It updates a single parameter at a time.

Gibbs Sampling Algorithm

- Suppose $p(x,y)$ is a p.d.f. or p.m.f. that is difficult to sample from directly.
- Suppose, though, that we *can* easily sample from the conditional distributions $p(x|y)$ and $p(y|x)$.

The Gibbs sampler proceeds as follows:

First set x and y to some initial starting values, then sample $x|y$, then sample $y|x$, then $x|y$, and so on.

Step 0. Set (x0, y0) to some starting value.

Step 1. Sample $x1 \sim p(x|y0)$, that is, from the conditional distribution $X \mid Y = y0$.

Current state: $(x1, y0)$

Sample $y1 \sim p(y|x1)$, that is, from the conditional distribution

$Y \mid X = x1$.

Current state: $(x1, y1)$

Step 2. Sample $x2 \sim p(x|y1)$, that is, from the conditional distribution $X \mid Y = y1$.

Current state: $(x2, y1)$

Sample $y2 \sim p(y|x2)$, that is, from the conditional distribution $Y \mid X = x2$.

Current state: $(x2, y2)$.

Repeat iterations 1 and 2, M times.

This procedure defines a sequence of pairs of random variables (X0, Y0), (X1, Y1), (X2, Y2), (X3, Y3).

Applications of Gibbs Sampling

Gibbs sampling algorithm has been widely used in machine learning in the form of Bayesian Networks, Statistical Inference, Bioinformatics, Econometrics. The Gibbs sampling can simulate the target distribution by constructing a Gibbs sequence which converges to a stationary distribution that is independent of the starting value. The stationary distribution is the target distribution.

The major advantages of Gibbs Sampling include,

1. Approximation of joint and marginal distribution.
2. Estimation of unknown parameters.
3. Compute an integral (e.g. Mean, Median etc.,).

7.18. Naive Bayes Classifier

Naive Bayes classifiers are a collection of classification algorithms based on **Bayes' Theorem**. It is not a single algorithm but a family of algorithms where all of them share a common principle, i.e. every pair of features being classified is independent of each other.

Classification is a predictive modelling problem that involves assigning a label to a given input data sample.

The problem of classification predictive modelling can be framed as calculating the conditional probability of a class label given a data sample, for example:

$$P(Class|Data) = \frac{P(Data|Class) \times P(Class)}{P(Data)}$$

Where P(class|data) is the probability of class given the provided data.

This calculation can be performed for each class in the problem and the class that is assigned the largest probability can be selected and assigned to the input data. In practice, it is very challenging to calculate full Bayes Theorem for classification.

The priors for the class and the data are easy to estimate from a training dataset, if the dataset is suitability representative of the broader problem.

The conditional probability of the observation based on the class P(data|class) is not feasible unless the number of examples is extraordinarily large, e.g. large enough to effectively estimate the probability distribution for all different possible combinations of values. This is almost never the case, we will not have sufficient coverage of the domain.

As such, the direct application of Bayes Theorem also becomes intractable, especially as the number of variables or features (n) increases.

Naive Bayes Classifier Algorithm

The solution to using Bayes Theorem for a conditional probability classification model is to simplify the calculation.

The Bayes Theorem assumes that each input variable is dependent upon all other variables. This is a cause of complexity in the calculation. We can remove this assumption and consider each input variable as being independent from each other.

This changes the model from a dependent conditional probability model to an independent conditional probability model and dramatically simplifies the calculation.

This means that we calculate P(data|class) for each input variable separately and multiple the results together, for example:

$$P(Class|x_1, x_2, \dots, x_n) = \frac{P(x_1|Class) \times P(x_2|Class) \times \dots \times P(Class)}{P(x_1, x_2, \dots, x_n)}$$

We can also drop the probability of observing the data as it is a constant for all calculations, for example:

$$P(Class|x_1, x_2, \dots, x_n) = P(x_1|Class) \times P(x_2|Class) \times \dots \times P(Class)$$

This simplification of Bayes Theorem is common and widely used for classification predictive modeling problems and is generally referred to as Naive Bayes.

The word "*naive*" is French and typically has a diaeresis (umlaut) over the "i", which is commonly left out for simplicity, and "Bayes" is capitalized as it is named for Reverend Thomas Bayes.

Consider a fictional dataset that describes the weather conditions for playing a game of golf. Given the weather conditions, each tuple classifies the conditions as fit("Yes") or unfit("No") for playing golf.

Here is a tabular representation of our dataset.

	Outlook	**Temperature**	**Humidity**	**Windy**	**Play Golf**
0	Rainy	Hot	High	False	No
1	Rainy	Hot	High	True	No
2	Overcast	Hot	High	False	Yes
3	Sunny	Mild	High	False	Yes
4	Sunny	Cool	Normal	False	Yes
5	Sunny	Cool	Normal	True	No
6	Overcast	Cool	Normal	True	Yes
7	Rainy	Mild	High	False	No
8	Rainy	Cool	Normal	False	Yes
9	Sunny	Mild	Normal	False	Yes
10	Rainy	Mild	Normal	True	Yes
11	Overcast	Mild	High	True	Yes
12	Overcast	Hot	Normal	False	Yes
13	Sunny	Mild	High	True	No

The dataset is divided into two parts, namely, **feature matrix** and the **response vector**.

- Feature matrix contains all the vectors(rows) of dataset in which each vector consists of the value of **dependent features**. In above dataset, features are 'Outlook', 'Temperature', 'Humidity' and 'Windy'.
- Response vector contains the value of **class variable** (prediction or output) for each row of feature matrix. In above dataset, the class variable name is 'Play golf'.

Assumption

The fundamental Naive Bayes assumption is that each feature makes an:

- Independent
- Equal

Contribution to the outcome.

With relation to our dataset, this concept can be understood as:

- We assume that no pair of features are dependent. For example, the temperature being 'Hot' has nothing to do with the humidity or the outlook being 'Rainy' has no effect on the winds. Hence, the features are assumed to be **independent**.
- Secondly, each feature is given the same weight (or importance). For example, knowing only temperature and humidity alone can't predict the outcome accurately. None of the attributes is irrelevant and assumed to be contributing **equally** to the outcome.

Note: The assumptions made by Naive Bayes are not generally correct in real-world situations. In-fact, the independence assumption is never correct but often works well in practice.

Now, before moving to the formula for Naive Bayes, it is important to know about Bayes' theorem.

Bayes' Theorem

Bayes' Theorem finds the probability of an event occurring given the probability of another event that has already occurred. Bayes' theorem is stated mathematically as the following equation:

$$P(A|B) = \frac{P(B|A) \times P(A)}{P(B)}$$

Where A and B are events and P(B) ≠ 0.

- Basically, we are trying to find probability of event A, given the event B is true. Event B is also termed as **evidence**.
- P(A) is the **priori** of A (the prior probability, i.e. Probability of event before evidence is seen). The evidence is an attribute value of an unknown instance (here, it is event B).
- P(A|B) is a posteriori probability of B, i.e. probability of event after evidence is seen.

Now, with regards to our dataset, we can apply Bayes' theorem in following way:

$$P(y|X) = \frac{P(X|y) \times P(y)}{P(X)}$$

Where, y is class variable and X is a dependent feature vector (of size *n*) where:

$$X = (x_1, x_2, x_3, \ldots, x_n)$$

Just to clear, an example of a feature vector and corresponding class variable can be: (refer 1st row of dataset).

X = (Rainy, Hot, High, False)

y = No

So basically, P(y|X) here means, the probability of "Not playing golf" given that the weather conditions are "Rainy outlook", "Temperature is hot", "high humidity" and "no wind".

Naive Assumption

Now, it is time to put a naive assumption to the Bayes' theorem, which is, **independence** among the features. So now, we split **evidence** into the independent parts.

Now, if any two events A and B are independent, then,

$$P(A,B) = P(A) \times P(B)$$

Hence, we reach to the result:

$$P(y|x_1, x_2, x_3, \ldots, x_n) = \frac{P(x_1|y) \times P(x_2|y) \times P(x_3|y) \times \ldots \times P(x_n|y) \times P(y)}{P(x_1) \times P(x_2) \times P(x_3) \times \ldots \times P(x_n)}$$

Which can be expressed as:

$$P(y|x_1, x_2, x_3, \ldots, x_n) = \frac{P(y) \times \prod_{i=1}^{n} P(x_i|y)}{P(x_1) \times P(x_2) \times P(x_3) \times \ldots \times P(x_n)}$$

Now, as the denominator remains constant for a given input, we can remove that term:

$$P(y|x_1, x_2, x_3, \ldots, x_n) \propto P(y) \times \prod_{i=1}^{n} P(x_i|y)$$

Now, we need to create a classifier model. For this, we find the probability of given set of inputs for all possible values of the class variable *y* and pick up the output with maximum probability. This can be expressed mathematically as:

$$y = \underset{y}{\operatorname{argmax}} \left\{ P(y) \times \prod_{i=1}^{n} P(x_i|y) \right\}$$

So, finally, we are left with the task of calculating P(y) and $P(x_i|y)$.

Please note that P(y) is also called **class probability** and $P(x_i|y)$ is called **conditional probability**. The different naive Bayes classifiers differ mainly by the assumptions they make regarding the distribution of $P(x_i|y)$.

Let us try to apply the above formula manually on our weather dataset. For this, we need to do some pre computations on our dataset.

We need to find $P(x_i|y_j)$ for each x_i in X and y_j in y. All these calculations have been demonstrated in the tables below:

OUTLOOK	Yes	No	P(Y)	P(N)
Sunny	2	3	2/9	3/5
Overcast	4	0	4/9	0/5
Rainy	3	2	3/9	2/5
Total	9	5	9/9	5/5

TEMPERATURE	Yes	No	P(Y)	P(N)
Hot	2	2	2/9	2/5
Mild	4	2	4/9	2/5
Cool	3	1	3/9	1/5
Total	9	5	9/9	5/5

HUMIDITY	Yes	No	P(Y)	P(N)
High	3	4	3/9	4/5
Normal	6	1	6/9	1/5
Total	9	5	9/9	5/5

WIND	Yes	No	P(Y)	P(N)
False	6	2	6/9	2/5
True	3	3	3/9	3/5
Total	9	5	9/9	5/5

	Play	P(Play)
Yes	9	9/14
No	5	5/14
Total	14	14/14

So, in the figure above, we have calculated $P(x_i|y_j)$ for each x_i in X and y_j in y manually in the tables. For example, probability of playing golf given that the temperature is cool, i.e P(temp = cool | play golf = Yes) = 3/9.

Also, we need to find class probabilities (P(y)) which has been calculated in the fifth table. For example, P(play golf = Yes) = 9/14.

So now, we are done with our pre-computations and the classifier is ready!

Let us test it on a new set of features (let us call it today):

today = (Sunny, Hot, Normal, False)

So, probability of playing golf is given by:

$$P(Yes|today) = \frac{P(Sunny: Outlook|Yes) \times P(Hot: Tempertature|Yes) \times P(Normal: Humidity|Yes) \times P(No: Wind|Yes) \times P(Yes)}{P(today)}$$

and probability to not play golf is given by:

$$P(No|today) = \frac{P(Sunny: Outlook|No) \times P(Hot: Tempertature|No) \times P(Normal: Humidity|No) \times P(No: Wind|No) \times P(No)}{P(today)}$$

Since, P(today) is common in both probabilities, we can ignore P(today) and find proportional probabilities as:

$$P(Yes|today) \propto \frac{2}{9} \times \frac{2}{9} \times \frac{6}{9} \times \frac{6}{9} \times \frac{9}{14} \approx 0.0141$$

and

$$P(No|today) \propto \frac{3}{5} \times \frac{2}{5} \times \frac{1}{5} \times \frac{2}{5} \times \frac{5}{14} \approx 0.0068$$

Now, since

$$P(Yes|today) + P(No|today) = 1$$

These numbers can be converted into a probability by making the sum equal to 1 (normalization):

$$P(Yes|today) = \frac{0.0141}{0.0141 + 0.0068} = 0.67$$

and

$$P(No|today) = \frac{0.0068}{0.0141 + 0.0068} = 0.33$$

Since

$$P(Yes|today) > P(No|today)$$

So, prediction that golf would be played is 'Yes'.

The method that we discussed above is applicable for discrete data. In case of continuous data, we need to make some assumptions regarding the distribution of values of each feature. The different naive Bayes classifiers differ mainly by the assumptions they make regarding the distribution of $P(x_i|y)$.

Now, we discuss one of such classifiers here.

7.19. Gaussian Naive Bayes Classifier

In Gaussian Naive Bayes, continuous values associated with each feature are assumed to be distributed according to a **Gaussian distribution.** A Gaussian distribution is also called Normal distribution. When plotted, it gives a bell shaped curve which is symmetric about the mean of the feature values as shown below:

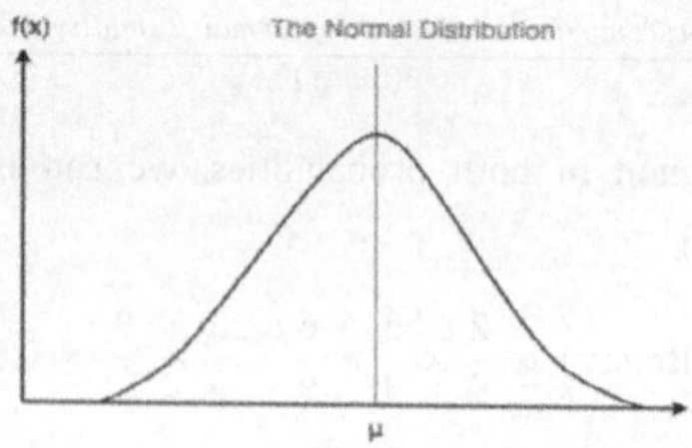

The likelihood of the features is assumed to be Gaussian, hence, conditional probability is given by:

$$P(x_i|y) = \frac{1}{\sqrt{2\pi\sigma_y^2}} exp^{\left(-\frac{(x_i - \mu_y)^2}{2\sigma_y^2}\right)}$$

Naive Bayes and Text Classification

This section will introduce some of the main concepts and procedures that are needed to apply the naive Bayes model to text classification tasks. Although the examples are mainly concerning a two-class problem — classifying text messages as *spam* or *good* — the same approaches are applicable to multi-class problems such as classification of documents into different topic areas (e.g., "Computer Science", "Biology", "Statistics", "Economics", "Politics", etc.).

The Bag of Words Model

One of the most important sub-tasks in pattern classification are *feature extraction* and *selection*; the three main criteria of good features are listed below:

- ***Salient.*** The features are important and meaningful with respect to the problem domain.
- ***Invariant.*** Invariance is often described in context of image classification: The features are insusceptible to distortion, scaling, orientation, etc. A nice example is given by C. Yao *and others* in *Rotation-Invariant Features for Multi-Oriented Text Detection in Natural Images.*

- ***Discriminatory.*** The selected features bear enough information to distinguish well between patterns when used to train the classifier.

Prior to fitting the model and using machine learning algorithms for training, we need to think about how to best represent a text document as a feature vector. A commonly used model in ***Natural Language Processing*** is the so-called *bag of words* model. The idea behind this model really is as simple as it sounds. First comes the creation of the ***vocabulary*** — the collection of all different words that occur in the training set and each word is associated with a count of how it occurs. This vocabulary can be understood as a set of non-redundant items where the order doesn't matter. Let D_1 and D_2 be two documents in a training dataset:

- D_1: "Each state has its own laws."
- D_2: "Every country has its own culture."

Based on these two documents, the vocabulary could be written as,

V={each:1,state:1,has:2,its:2,own:2,laws:1,every:1,country:1,culture:1}

The vocabulary can then be used to construct the *d*-dimensional feature vectors for the individual documents where the dimensionality is equal to the number of different words in the vocabulary (d=|V|). This process is called ***vectorization***.

Table 1: Bag of Words Representation of Two Sample Documents D_1 and D_2.

	each	**state**	**has**	**its**	**own**	**laws**	**every**	**country**	**culture**
X_{D1}	1	1	1	1	1	1	0	0	0
X_{D2}	0	0	1	1	1	0	1	1	1
Total	1	1	2	2	2	1	1	1	1

Given the example in Table 1 one question is whether the 1s and 0s of the feature vectors are binary counts (1 if the word occurs in a particular document, 0 otherwise) or absolute counts (how often the word occurs in each document). The answer depends on which probabilistic model is used for the naive Bayes classifier.

Tokenization

Tokenization describes the general process of breaking down a text corpus into individual elements that serve as input for various natural language processing algorithms. Usually, tokenization is accompanied by other optional processing steps, such as the removal of stop words and punctuation characters, stemming or lemmatizing, and the construction of *n grams*. Below is an example of a simple but typical tokenization step that splits a sentence into individual words, removes punctuation, and converts all letters to lowercase.

Table 2: Example of Tokenization

A swimmer likes swimming, thus he swims.

↓

a	swimmer	likes	swimming	thus	he	swims

Stop Words

Stop words are words that are particularly common in a text corpus and thus considered as rather un-informative (e.g., words such as *so, and, or, the,* ..."). One approach to stop word removal is to search against a language-specific stop word dictionary. An alternative approach is to create a *stop list* by sorting all words in the entire text corpus by frequency. The stop list — after conversion into a *set* of non-redundant words — is then used to remove all those words from the input documents that are ranked among the top *n* words in this stop list.

Table 3: Example of Stop Word Removal

A swimmer likes swimming, thus he swims.

↓

swimmer	likes	swimming	,	he	.

Fig. 7.10: Example of Lemmatization

Stemming and Lemmatization

Stemming describes the process of transforming a word into its root form. The original stemming algorithm was developed my Martin F. Porter in 1979 and is hence known as *Porter stemmer.*

Stemming can create non-real words, such as "thu" in the example above. In contrast to stemming, *lemmatization* aims to obtain the canonical (grammatically correct) forms of the words, the so-called *lemmas.* Lemmatization is computationally more difficult and expensive than stemming, and in practice, both stemming and lemmatization have little impact on the performance of text classification [9]. The following Fig. Shows Example of Porter Stemming.

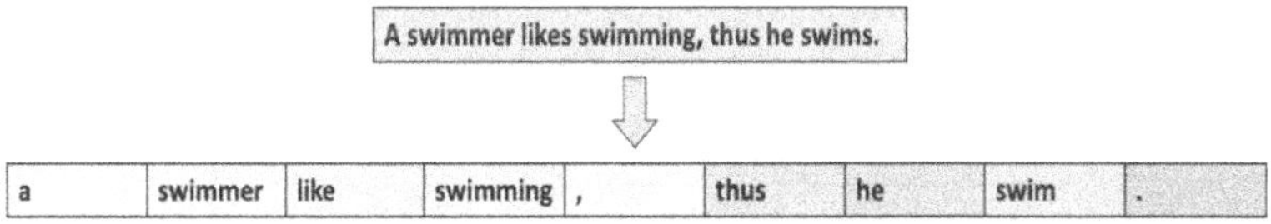

N-Grams

In the *n-gram* model, a token can be defined as a sequence of *n* items. The simplest case is the so-called *unigram* (1-gram) where each word consists of exactly one word, letter, or symbol. All previous examples were unigrams so far. Choosing the optimal number *n* depends on the language as well as the particular application. For example, Andelka Zecevic found in his study that *n*-grams with 3≤n≤7 were the best choice to determine authorship of Serbian text documents. In a different study, the *n*-grams of size 4≤n≤8 yielded the highest accuracy in authorship determination of English text books and Kanaris *and others* report that *n*-grams of size 3 and 4 yield good performances in anti-spam filtering of e-mail messages.

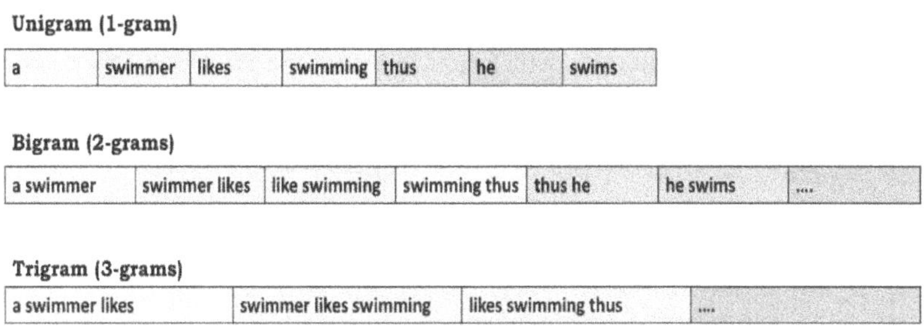

Fig. 7.11: Diagram for N-Grams

The Decision Rule for Spam Classification

In context of spam classification the decision rule of a naive Bayes classifier based on the posterior probabilities can be expressed as,

$$\text{if } P(\omega = spam|x) \geq P(\omega = good|x) \text{classify as spam, else classify as good.}$$

The posterior probability is the product of the class-conditional probability and the prior probability; the evidence term in the denominator can be dropped since it is constant for both classes.

$$P(\omega = spam|x) = P(x|\omega = spam) \times P(spam)$$

$$P(\omega = good|x) = P(x|\omega = good) \times P(good)$$

The prior probabilities can be obtained via the maximum-likelihood estimate based on the frequencies of spam and ham messages in the training dataset.

$$\hat{P}(\omega = spam) = \frac{\#\ of\ spam\ messages}{Total\ \#\ of\ messages}$$

$$\hat{P}(\omega = good) = \frac{\#\ of\ good\ messages}{Total\ \#\ of\ messages}$$

Assuming that the words in every document are conditionally independent (according to the *Naïve* assumption), two different models can be used to compute the class-conditional probabilities: The *Multi-variate Bernoulli* model and the *Multinomial* model. We will use the Multinomial model for this example.

7.20. Multinomial Naive Bayes

Term Frequency

A alternative approach to characterize text documents — rather than binary values — is the *term frequency (tf(t,d))*. The term frequency is typically defined as the number of times a given term *t* (i.e., word or token) appears in a document *d* (this approach is sometimes also called *raw frequency*). In practice, the term frequency is often normalized by dividing the raw term frequency by the document length.

$$Normalized\ Term\ Frequency = \frac{tf(t,d)}{n_d}$$

Where

- tf(t,d): Raw term frequency (the count of term t in document d).
- n_d: The total number of terms in document d.

The term frequencies can then be used to compute the maximum-likelihood estimate based on the training data to estimate the class-conditional probabilities in the multinomial model:

$$\hat{P}(x_i|\omega_j) = \frac{\sum tf(x_i, d\ \in \omega_j) + a}{\sum N_{d\ \in \omega_j} + a \times V}$$

Where

- x_i: A word from the feature vector **xx** of a particular sample.
- $\sum tf(x_i, d \in \omega_j)$: The sum of raw term frequencies of word x_i from all documents in the training sample that belong to class ω_j.
- $\sum N_{d \in \omega_j}$: The sum of all term frequencies in the training dataset for class ω_j.
- α: An additive smoothing parameter (α=1 for Laplace smoothing).
- V: The size of the vocabulary (number of different words in the training set).

The class-conditional probability of encountering the text x can be calculated as the product from the likelihoods of the individual words (under the *naive* assumption of conditional independence).

$$P(x, \omega_j) = P(x_1|\omega_j) \times P(x_2|\omega_j) \times \ldots\ldots \times P(x_n|\omega_j)$$

$$P(x, \omega_j) = \prod_{i=1}^{m} P(x_i|\omega_j)$$

Term Frequency - Inverse Document Frequency (Tf-idf)

The *term frequency - inverse document frequency (Tf-idf)* is another alternative for characterizing text documents. It can be understood as a weighted *term frequency*, which is especially useful if stop words have not been removed from the text corpus. The Tf-idf approach assumes that the importance of a word is inversely proportional to how often it occurs across all documents. Although Tf-idf is most commonly used to rank documents by relevance in different text mining tasks, such as page ranking by search engines, it can also be applied to text classification via naive Bayes.

$$\mathrm{Tf - idf = tfn(t, d) \cdot idf(t)}$$

Let tfn(d,f) be the normalized term frequency, and idf, the inverse document frequency, which can be calculated as follows.

$$\mathrm{idf(t)} = \log\left(\frac{n_d}{n_d(t)}\right)$$

Where

- n_d: The total number of documents.
- $n_d(t)$: The number of documents that contain the term t.

7.21. Bayesian Belief Networks

Probabilistic models can define relationships between variables and be used to calculate probabilities. Fully conditional models may require an enormous amount of data to cover all possible cases, and probabilities may be intractable to calculate in practice. Simplifying assumptions such as the conditional independence of all random variables can be effective, such as in the case of Naive Bayes, although it is a drastically simplifying step.

An alternative is to develop a model that preserves known conditional dependence between random variables and conditional independence in all other cases. Bayesian networks are a probabilistic graphical model that explicitly capture the known conditional dependence with directed edges in a graph model. All missing connections define the conditional independencies in the model.

As such Bayesian Networks provide a useful tool to visualize the probabilistic model for a domain, review all of the relationships between the random variables, and reason about causal probabilities for scenarios given available evidence.

The networks are not exactly Bayesian by definition, although given that both the probability distributions for the random variables (nodes) and the relationships between the random variables (edges) are specified subjectively, the model can be thought to capture the "belief" about a complex domain.

A Bayesian Belief Network, or simply "*Bayesian Network*," provides a simple way of applying Bayes Theorem to complex problems. "A Bayesian network is a probabilistic graphical model which represents a set of variables and their conditional dependencies using a directed acyclic graph. "It is also called a **Bayes network, belief network, decision network**, or **Bayesian model**. Bayesian networks are probabilistic, because these networks are built from a **probability distribution**, and also use probability theory for prediction and anomaly detection.

The networks are not exactly Bayesian by definition, although given that both the probability distributions for the random variables (nodes) and the relationships between the random variables (edges) are specified subjectively, the model can be thought to capture the "*belief*" about a complex domain.

Bayesian probability is the study of subjective probabilities or belief in an outcome, compared to the frequentist approach where probabilities are based purely on the past occurrence of the event.

A Bayesian Network captures the joint probabilities of the events represented by the model. Central to the Bayesian network is the notion of conditional independence.

Independence refers to a random variable that is unaffected by all other variables. A dependent variable is a random variable whose probability is conditional on one or more other random variables.

Conditional independence describes the relationship among multiple random variables, where a given variable may be conditionally independent of one or more other random variables. This does not mean that the variable is independent per se; instead, it is a clear definition that the variable is independent of specific other known random variables.

A probabilistic graphical model, such as a Bayesian Network, provides a way of defining a probabilistic model for a complex problem by stating all of the conditional independence assumptions for the known variables, whilst allowing the presence of unknown (latent) variables.

As such, both the presence and the absence of edges in the graphical model are important in the interpretation of the model. Bayesian networks provide useful benefits as a probabilistic model.

For Example:

- **Visualization.** The model provides a direct way to visualize the structure of the model and motivate the design of new models.
- **Relationships.** Provides insights into the presence and absence of the relationships between random variables.
- **Computations.** Provides a way to structure complex probability calculations.

Real world applications are probabilistic in nature, and to represent the relationship between multiple events, we need a Bayesian network. It can also be used in various tasks including prediction, anomaly detection, diagnostics, automated insight, reasoning, time series prediction, and decision making under uncertainty.

Bayesian Network can be used for building models from data and experts opinions, and it consists of two parts:

- Directed Acyclic Graph.
- Table of conditional probabilities.

The generalized form of Bayesian network that represents and solve decision problems under uncertain knowledge is known as an Influence diagram.

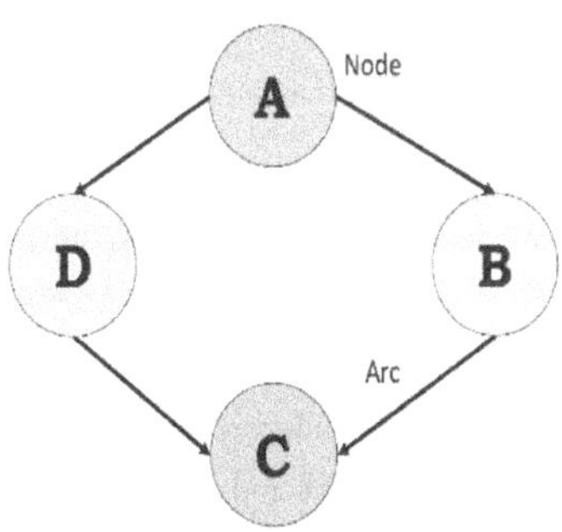

Fig. 7.12: Bayesian Network Graph

A Bayesian network graph is made up of nodes and Arcs (directed links), where:

- Each **node** corresponds to the random variables, and a variable can be **continuous** or **discrete**.

- **Arc or directed arrows** represent the causal relationship or conditional probabilities between random variables. These directed links or arrows connect the pair of nodes in the graph. These links represent that one node directly influence the other node, and if there is no directed link that means that nodes are independent with each other.
    - In the above diagram, A, B, C, and D are random variables represented by the nodes of the network graph.
    - If we are considering node B, which is connected with node A by a directed arrow, then node A is called the parent of Node B.
    - Node C is independent of node A.

The Bayesian network graph does not contain any cyclic graph. Hence, it is known as a **directed acyclic graph or DAG.**

Example of a Bayesian Network

We can make Bayesian Networks concrete with a small example.

Consider a problem with three random variables: A, B, and C. A is dependent upon B, and C is dependent upon B.

We can state the conditional dependencies as follows:

- A is conditionally dependent upon B, e.g. P(A|B)
- C is conditionally dependent upon B, e.g. P(C|B)

We know that C and A have no effect on each other.

We can also state the conditional independencies as follows:

- A is conditionally independent from C: P(A|B, C)
- C is conditionally independent from A: P(C|B, A)

Notice that the conditional dependence is stated in the presence of the conditional independence. That is, A is conditionally independent of C, or A is conditionally dependent upon B in the presence of C.

We might also state the conditional independence of A given C as the conditional dependence of A given B, as A is unaffected by C and can be calculated from A given B alone.

- P(A|C, B) = P(A|B)

We can see that B is unaffected by A and C and has no parents; we can simply state the conditional independence of B from A and C as P(B, P(A|B), P(C|B)) or P(B).

We can also write the joint probability of A and C given B or conditioned on B as the product of two conditional probabilities.

For example:

- P(A, C | B) = P(A|B) * P(C|B)

The model summarizes the joint probability of P(A, B, C), calculated as:

- P(A, B, C) = P(A|B) * P(C|B) * P(B)

We can draw the graph as follows:

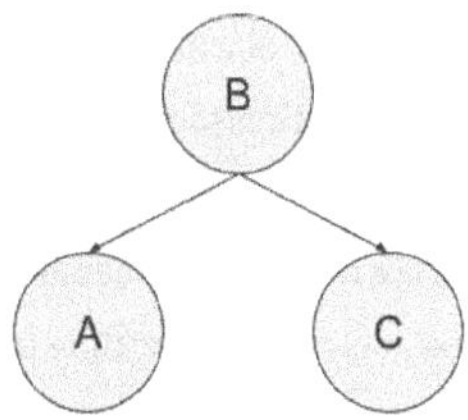

Example of a Simple Bayesian Network

Notice that the random variables are each assigned a node, and the conditional probabilities are stated as directed connections between the nodes. Also notice that it is not possible to navigate the graph in a cycle, e.g. no loops are possible when navigating from node to node via the edges.

Also notice that the graph is useful even at this point where we don't know the probability distributions for the variables.

The Bayesian network has mainly two components:

- **Causal Component**
- **Actual numbers**

Each node in the Bayesian network has condition probability distribution **$P(X_i|Parent(X_i))$**, which determines the effect of the parent on that node.

Bayesian network is based on Joint probability distribution and conditional probability. So let's first understand the joint probability distribution:

Joint probability distribution:

If we have variables $x_1, x_2, x_3, \ldots, x_n$, then the probabilities of a different combination of $x_1, x_2, x_3 .. x_n$, are known as Joint probability distribution.

$P[x_1, x_2, x_3, \ldots, x_n]$, it can be written as the following way in terms of the joint probability distribution.

$= P[x_1| x_2, x_3, \ldots, x_n]P[x_2, x_3, \ldots, x_n]$

$= P[x_1| x_2, x_3, \ldots, x_n]P[x_2|x_3, \ldots, x_n] \ldots P[x_{n-1}|x_n]P[x_n]$.

In general for each variable Xi, we can write the equation as:

$P(X_i|X_{i-1},........., X_1) = P(X_i |Parents(X_i))$

Explanation of Bayesian Network

Let's understand the Bayesian network through an example by creating a directed acyclic graph.

Example: Rufus installed a new burglar alarm at his home to detect burglary. The alarm reliably responds at detecting a burglary but also responds for minor earthquakes. Rufus has two neighbours Vikas and Chintu, who have taken a responsibility to inform Rufus at work when they hear the alarm. Vikas always calls Rufus when he hears the alarm, but sometimes he got confused with the phone ringing and calls at that time too. On the other hand, Chintu likes to listen to high music, so sometimes she misses to hear the alarm. Here we would like to compute the probability of Burglary Alarm.

Problem

Calculate the probability that alarm has sounded, but there is neither a burglary, nor an earthquake occurred, and Vikas and Chintu both called the Rufus.

Solution

- The Bayesian network for the above problem is given below. The network structure is showing that burglary and earthquake is the parent node of the alarm and directly affecting the probability of alarm's going off, but Vikas and Chintu's calls depend on alarm probability.
- The network is representing that our assumptions do not directly perceive the burglary and also do not notice the minor earthquake, and they also not confer before calling.
- The conditional distributions for each node are given as conditional probabilities table or CPT.
- Each row in the CPT must be sum to 1 because all the entries in the table represent an exhaustive set of cases for the variable.
- In CPT, a boolean variable with k boolean parents contains 2^K probabilities. Hence, if there are two parents, then CPT will contain 4 probability values.

List of All Events Occurring in this Network

- **Burglary (B)**
- **Earthquake(E)**
- **Alarm(A)**

- **Vikas Calls(V)**
- **Chintu calls(C)**

We can write the events of problem statement in the form of probability: **P[V, C, A, B, E]**, can rewrite the above probability statement using joint probability distribution:

P[V, C, A, B, E]= P[V | C, A, B, E]× P[C, A, B, E]

=P[V|C,A,B,E]×P[C|A,B,E]× P[A,B,E]

= P [V|A]× P [C|A,B,E]× P[A,B,E]

= P[V|A]× P[C|A]×P[A|B,E]×P[B,E]

= P[V|A]×P[C|A]×P[A|B,E]×P[B|E] ×P[E]

Let's take the observed probability for the Burglary and earthquake component:

P(B= True) = 0.002, which is the probability of burglary.

P(B= False)= 0.998, which is the probability of no burglary.

P(E= True)= 0.001, which is the probability of a minor earthquake.

P(E= False)= 0.999, Which is the probability that an earthquake not occurred.

We can provide the conditional probabilities as per the below tables:

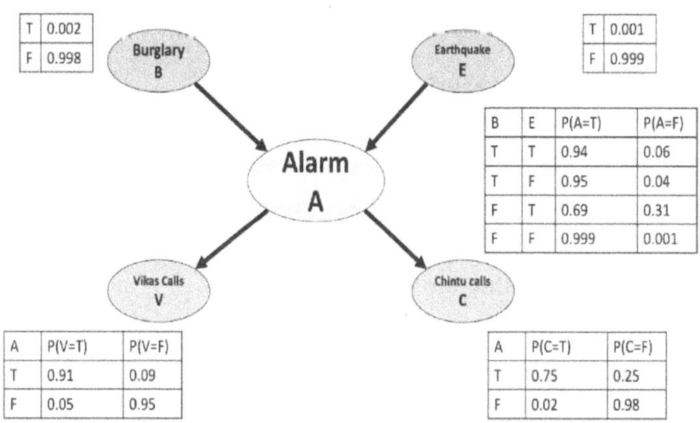

Conditional Probability Table for Alarm A

The Conditional probability of Alarm A depends on Burglar and earthquake:

B	E	P(A= True)	P(A= False)
True	True	0.94	0.06
True	False	0.95	0.04
False	True	0.31	0.69
False	False	0.001	0.999

Conditional Probability Table for Vikas Calls

The Conditional probability of Vikas that he will call depends on the probability of Alarm.

A	P(V= True)	P(V= False)
True	0.91	0.09
False	0.05	0.95

Conditional Probability Table for Chintu Calls

The Conditional probability of Chintu that she calls is depending on its Parent Node "Alarm."

A	P(S= True)	P(S= False)
True	0.75	0.25
False	0.02	0.98

From the formula of joint distribution, we can write the problem statement in the form of probability distribution:

P(C, V, A, ¬B, ¬E) = P (C|A) *P (V|A)*P (A|¬B ^ ¬E) *P (¬B) *P (¬E).

= 0.75* 0.91* 0.001* 0.998*0.999

= 0.00068045.

Hence, a Bayesian network can answer any query about the domain by using Joint distribution.

The Semantics of Bayesian Network

There are two ways to understand the semantics of the Bayesian network, which is given below:

1. **To understand the network as the representation of the Joint probability distribution.**

   It is helpful to understand how to construct the network.

2. **To understand the network as an encoding of a collection of conditional independence statements.**

   It is helpful in designing inference procedure.

7.22. Expectation Maximization (EM) Algorithm

In most of the real-life problem statements of **Machine learning**, it is very common that we have many relevant features available to build our model but only a small portion of them are observable. Since we do not have the values for the not observed (latent) variables, the **Expectation-Maximization** algorithm tries to use the existing data to determine the optimum values for these variables and then finds the model parameters.

Expectation maximization (EM) is an approach that is used in many ways to find maximum likelihood estimates of parameters in probabilistic models. EM is an iterative optimization algorithm to estimate some unknown parameters given some measurement data. Most commonly used to estimate parameters of a probabilistic model (e.g., Gaussian mixture distributions). EM has also been used to discover hidden variables and to estimate missing data.

The intuition behind EM is an old one: alternate between estimating the unknowns and the hidden variables. This idea has been around for a long time. However, in 1977, Dempster, et al., proved convergence and explained the relationship to maximum likelihood estimation. EM is a latent variable model.

What is Meant by the Latent Variable Model?

A latent variable model consists of **observable** variables along with **unobservable** variables. Observed variables are those variables in the dataset that can be measured whereas unobserved (latent/hidden) variables are inferred from the observed variables.

- It can be used to find the **local maximum likelihood (MLE)** parameters or **maximum a posteriori (MAP)** parameters for latent variables in a statistical or mathematical model.
- It is used to predict these missing values in the dataset, provided we know the general form of probability distribution associated with these latent variables.
- In simple words, the basic idea behind this algorithm is to use the observable samples of latent variables to predict the values of samples that are unobservable for learning. This process is repeated until the convergence of the values occurs.

Detailed Explanation of the EM Algorithm

EM algorithm alternates between performing two major steps an expectation (E) step, which computes an expectation of the likelihood by including the latent variables as if they were observed, and a maximization (M) step, which computes the maximum likelihood estimates of the parameters by maximizing the expected likelihood found on the E step. The parameters found on the M step are then used to begin another E step, and the process is repeated.

Here is the Algorithm you have to Follow

- Given a set of incomplete data, start with a set of initialized parameters.
- **Expectation step (E – step):** In this expectation step, by using the observed available data of the dataset, we can try to estimate or guess the values of the missing data. Finally, after this step, we get complete data having no missing values.
- **Maximization step (M – step):** Now, we have to use the complete data, which is prepared in the expectation step, and update the parameters.
- Repeat step 2 and step 3 until we converge to our solution.

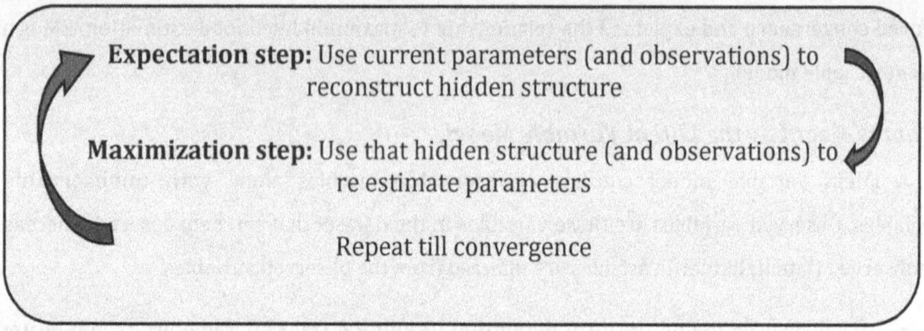

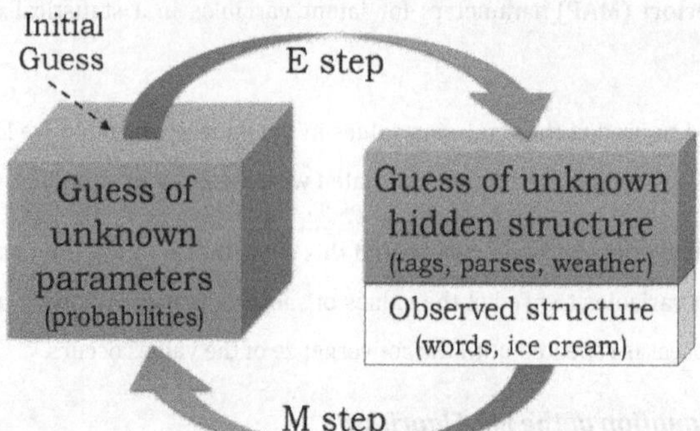

Fig. 7.13: Shows EM Steps

EM forms the basis of important algorithms such as hidden Markov modeling and is used in many fields including human language technology and image processing. The Expectation-Maximization algorithm aims to use the available observed data of the dataset to estimate the missing data of the latent variables and then using that data to update the values of the parameters in the maximization step.

Let us understand the EM algorithm in a detailed manner:

- **Initialization Step:** In this step, we initialized the parameter values with a set of initial values, then give the set of incomplete observed data to the system with the assumption that the observed data comes from a specific model **i.e, probability distribution.**
- **Expectation Step:** In this step, by using the observed data to estimate or guess the values of the missing or incomplete data. It is used to update the variables.
- **Maximization Step:** In this step, we use the complete data generated in the **"Expectation"** step to update the values of the parameters i.e, **update the hypothesis**.
- **Checking of convergence Step:** Now, in this step, we checked whether the values are converging or not, if yes, then stop otherwise repeat these two steps i.e, the **"Expectation"** step and **"Maximization"** step until the convergence occurs.

Flow Chart for EM Algorithm

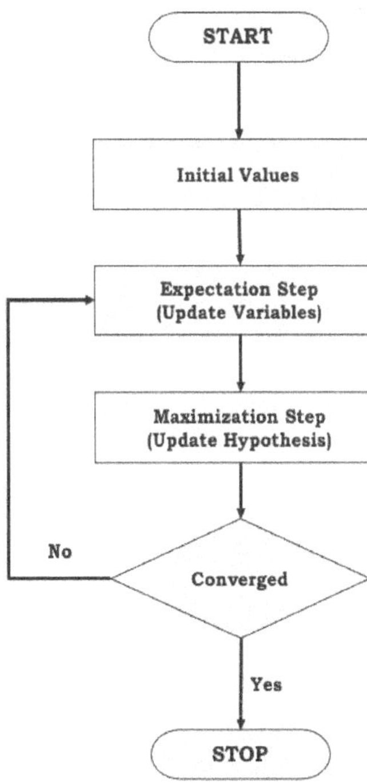

Worked Example

We will take a coin flipping example and solve using EM. Assume that we have two coins, C1 and C2 and the bias of C1 is θ_1 (i.e., probability of getting heads with C1) and the bias of C2 is θ_2 (i.e., probability of getting heads with C2). We want to find θ_1, θ_2 by performing a number of trials (i.e., coin tosses).

We choose 5 times one of the coins and we toss the chosen coin 10 times.

$$\theta_1 = \frac{number\ of\ heads\ using\ C1}{Total\ number\ of\ flips\ for\ C1}$$

$$\theta_2 = \frac{number\ of\ heads\ using\ C2}{Total\ number\ of\ flips\ for\ C2}$$

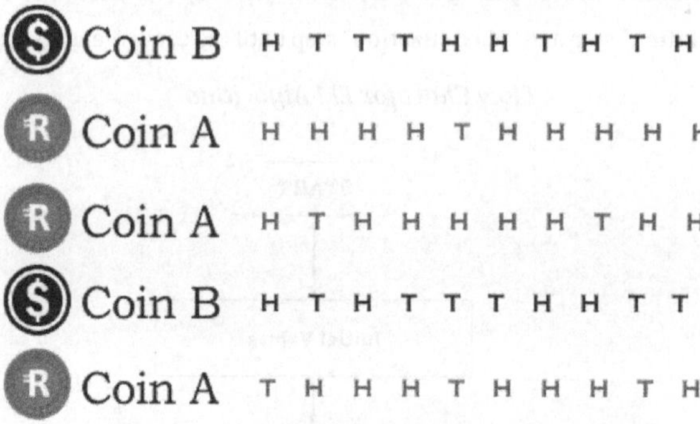

	COIN A	COIN B
Trial 1		5H, 5 T
Trial 2	9H, 1T	
Trial 3	8H, 2T	
Trial 4		4H, 6T
Trial 5	24H, 3T	9H, 11T

$$\theta_1 = \frac{24}{24+6} = 0.8$$

$$\theta_2 = \frac{9}{9+11} = 0.45$$

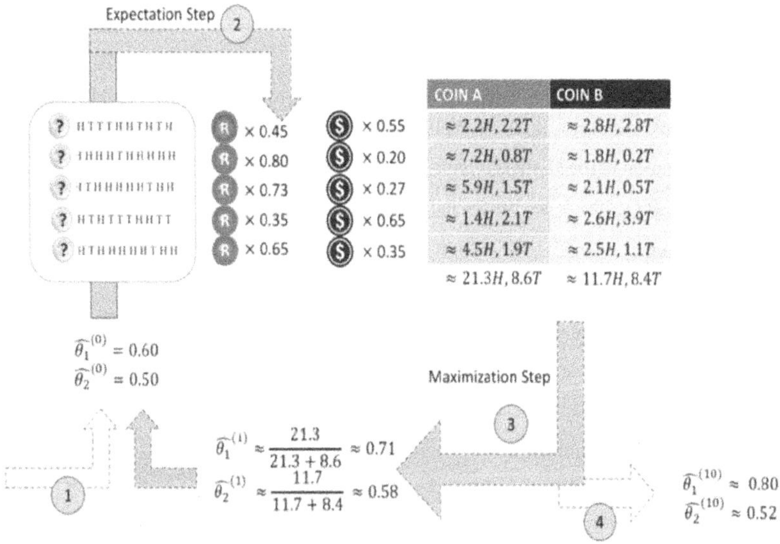

Generic form of the EM Algorithm

Initialize

$\theta_x = \{\Sigma_1, \Sigma_2, \Sigma_3, \mu_1, \mu_2, \mu_3\}$

$\theta_z = \{\pi_1, \pi_2, \pi_3\}$

Until Convergence (Repeat E & M Steps)

{

E: Expectation Step

$$\gamma\,(Z_{nk}) = \frac{\pi_k N(x_n|\mu_k, \Sigma_k)}{\sum_{l=1}^{3} \pi_l N(x_n|\mu_l, \Sigma_l)}$$

M: Maximization Step

$$\pi_k = \frac{\sum_{n=1}^{N} \gamma(Z_{nk})}{N}$$

$$\mu_k = \frac{\sum_{n=1}^{N} \gamma(Z_{nk}) x_n}{\sum_{n=1}^{N} \gamma(Z_{nk})}$$

$$\Sigma_k = \frac{\sum_{n=1}^{N} \gamma(Z_{nk})(x_n - \mu_k)(x_n - \mu_k)^T}{\sum_{n=1}^{N} \gamma(Z_{nk})}$$

}

Advantages and Disadvantages of EM Algorithm

Advantages

- The basic two steps of the EM algorithm i.e, E-step and M-step are often pretty easy for many of the machine learning problems in terms of implementation.
- The solution to the M-steps often exists in the closed-form.
- It is always guaranteed that the value of likelihood will increase after each iteration.

Disadvantages

- It has **slow convergence**.
- It converges to the **local optimum** only.
- It takes both forward and backward probabilities into account. This thing is in contrast to that of numerical optimization which considers only **forward probabilities**.

Applications of EM Algorithm

The latent variable model has several real-life applications in Machine learning:

- Used to calculate the **Gaussian density** of a function.
- Helpful to fill in the **missing data** during a sample.
- It finds plenty of use in different domains such as Natural **Language Processing (NLP)**, **Computer Vision,** etc.
- Used in image reconstruction in the field of **Medicine and Structural Engineering**.
- Used for estimating the parameters of the **Hidden Markov Model (HMM)** and also for some other mixed models like **Gaussian Mixture Models**, etc.
- Used for finding the values of latent variables.

CHAPTER 8

COMPUTATIONAL LEARNING THEORY

8.1. Introduction

Computational learning theory, or statistical learning theory, refers to mathematical frameworks for quantifying learning tasks and algorithms.

These are sub-fields of machine learning that a machine learning practitioner does not need to know in great depth in order to achieve good results on a wide range of problems. Nevertheless, it is a sub-field where having a high-level understanding of some of the more prominent methods may provide insight into the broader task of learning from data.

Theorems that characterize classes of learning problems or specific algorithms in terms of computational complexity or ***sample complexity***, i.e. the number of training examples necessary or sufficient to learn hypotheses of a given accuracy. Complexity of a learning problem depends on:

- Size or expressiveness soft the hypothesis space.
- Accuracy to which target concept must be approximated.
- Probability with which the learner must produce a successful hypothesis.
- Manner in which training examples are presented, e.g. randomly or by query to an oracle.

COLT seeks to use the tools of theoretical computer science to quantify learning problems. This includes characterizing the difficulty of learning specific tasks.

Computational learning theory may be thought of as an extension or sibling of statistical learning theory, or *SLT* for short, that uses formal methods to quantify learning algorithms.

- **Computational Learning Theory** (*CoLT*): Formal study of learning tasks.
- **Statistical Learning Theory** (*SLT*): Formal study of learning algorithms.

This division of learning tasks vs. learning algorithms is arbitrary, and in practice, there is a lot of overlap between the two fields. One can extend statistical learning theory by taking computational complexity of the learner into account. This field is called computational learning theory or COLT. This theoretical framework known as computational learning theory, also some-times called statistical learning theory.

The focus in computational learning theory is typically on supervised learning tasks. Formal analysis of real problems and real algorithms is very challenging. As such, it is common to reduce the complexity of the analysis by focusing on binary classification tasks and even simple binary rule-based systems. As such, the practical application of the theorems may be limited or challenging to interpret for real problems and algorithms.

The main unanswered question in learning is this: How can we be sure that our learning algorithm has produced a hypothesis that will predict the correct value for previously unseen inputs?

Questions explored in computational learning theory might include:

- How do we know a model has a good approximation for the target function?
- What hypothesis space should be used?
- How do we know if we have a local or globally good solution?
- How do we avoid overfitting?
- How many data examples are needed?

As a machine learning practitioner, it can be useful to know about computational learning theory and some of the main areas of investigation. The field provides a useful grounding for what we are trying to achieve when fitting models on data, and it may provide insight into the methods.

Computational learning theory provides a formal framework in which it is possible to precisely formulate and address questions regarding the performance of different learning algorithms. Thus, careful comparisons of both the predictive power and the computational efficiency of competing learning algorithms can be made. Three key aspects that must be formalized are:

- The way in which the learner interacts with its environment.
- The definition of success in completing the learning task.
- A formal definition of efficiency of both data usage (sample complexity) and processing time (time complexity).

It is important to remember that the theoretical learning models are abstractions of real-life problems. Close connections with experimentalists are useful to help validate or modify these abstractions so that the theoretical results reflect empirical performance. The computational learning theory research has therefore close connections to machine learning research.

Besides the model's predictive capability, the computational learning theory also addresses other important features such as simplicity, robustness to variations in the learning scenario, and an ability to create insights to empirically observed phenomena.

There are many subfields of study, although perhaps two of the most widely discussed areas of study from computational learning theory are:

- PAC Learning.
- VC Dimension.

Tersely, we can say that PAC Learning is the theory of machine learning problems and VC dimension is the theory of machine learning algorithms.

You may encounter the topics as a practitioner and it is useful to have a thumbnail idea of what they are about. Let's take a closer look at each.

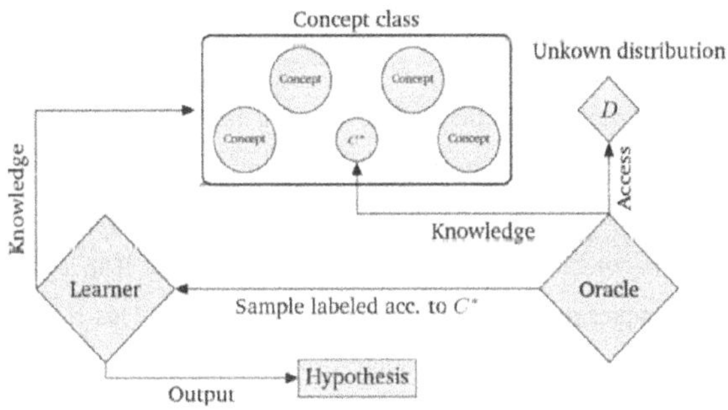

Fig. 8.1: Concept Class

Computational Learning Theory in Machine Learning

These are sub-fields of machine learning that a machine learning practitioner does not need to know in great depth in order to achieve good results on a wide range of problems. Nevertheless, it is a sub-field where having a high-level understanding of some of the more prominent methods may provide insight into the broader task of learning from data.

Prototypical Concept Learning Task

Given:

Instances X (set of instance or objects in world)

Target concept c (subset of instance space)

Hypothesis H (collection of concepts over X)

Training data D (example from instance space)

Determine:

A hypothesis h in H such that h(x) = c(x) for all x in D? (Training error)

A hypothesis h in H such that h(x) = c(x) for all x in X? (True error)

All machine learning tasks seek to minimize the errors. Trying to minimize the errors with the given training and test data leads to overfitting of models as shown in figure below.

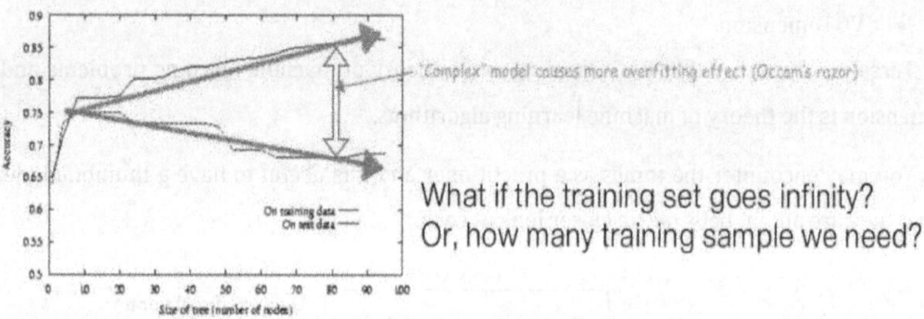

Additionally, Theoretical results in machine learning mainly deal with a type of inductive learning called supervised learning. In supervised learning, an algorithm is given samples that are labeled in some useful way. For example, the samples might be descriptions of mushrooms, and the labels could be whether or not the mushrooms are edible. The algorithm takes these previously labeled samples and uses them to induce a classifier. This classifier is a function that assigns labels to samples, including samples that have not been seen previously by the algorithm. The goal of the supervised learning algorithm is to optimize some measure of performance such as minimizing the number of mistakes made on new samples.

In addition to performance bounds, computational learning theory studies the time complexity and feasibility of learning. In computational learning theory, a computation is considered feasible if it can be done in polynomial time.

There are two kinds of time complexity results:

- Positive results – Showing that a certain class of functions is learnable in polynomial time.
- Negative results – Showing that certain classes cannot be learned in polynomial time.

Negative results often rely on commonly believed, but yet unproven assumptions, such as:

- Computational complexity – P ≠ NP (the P versus NP problem).
- Cryptographic – One-way functions exist.

What is the Difference between Computational Learning Theory and Statistical Learning Theory?

While both frameworks use similar mathematical analysis, the primary difference between CoLT and SLT are their objectives. CoLT focuses on studying "learnability," or what functions/features are necessary to make a given task learnable for an algorithm. Whereas SLT is primarily focused on studying and improving the accuracy of existing training programs.

What is Machine Learning Theory?

Machine Learning Theory, also known as Computational Learning Theory, aims to understand the fundamental principles of learning as a computational process. This field seeks to understand at a precise mathematical level what capabilities and information are fundamentally needed to learn different kinds of tasks successfully, and to understand the basic algorithmic principles involved in getting computers to learn from data and to improve performance with feedback. The goals of this theory are both to aid in the design of better automated learning methods and to understand fundamental issues in the learning process itself.

Machine Learning Theory draws elements from both the Theory of Computation and Statistics and involves tasks such as:

- Creating mathematical models that capture key aspects of machine learning, in which one can analyze the inherent ease or difficulty of different types of learning problems.
- Proving guarantees for algorithms (under what conditions will they succeed, how much data and computation time is needed) and developing machine learning algorithms that probably meet desired criteria.
- Mathematically analyzing general issues, such as: "Why is Occam's Razor a good idea?", "When can one be confident about predictions made from limited data?", "How much power does active participation add over passive observation for learning?", and "What kinds of methods can learn even in the presence of large quantities of distracting information?"

What is 'Probably Approximately Correct' Learning?

PAC learning, also known as Probably Approximately Correct learning is a theoretical machine learning framework created by Leslie Valiant. PAC learning aims to quantify the difficulty involved in a learning task and it might be considered to be the main sub-field of computational learning theory.

PAC learning bothers about the amount of computational effort that is needed in order to identify a hypothesis (fit model) that is a close match for the unknown target function.

PAC Learning (Theory of Learning Problems)

It is Probably Approximately Correct Learning, or commission learning refers to a theoretical machine learning framework developed by Leslie Valiant. PAC learning seeks to quantify the issue of a learning task. It could be thought about as the premier sub-field of computational learning theory.

Consider that we tend to try to approximate unknown underlying mapping performance from inputs to outputs in supervised learning. We don't intend to understand what this mapping performance appears like. However, we tend to suspect it exists and have samples of knowledge made by the performer.

PAC learning worries with the quantity of computational effort needed to seek out a hypothesis (fit model) that's an exact match for the unknown target performance. The idea is that a hypothesis is observed that supports the predictions it makes on new knowledge, e.g., supports its generalization error. A hypothesis that gets most or an extensive range of predictions correct, e.g., features a tiny generalization error, is a fair approximation for the target performance.

This probabilistic language offers the concept its name: "probability roughly correct." That is, a hypothesis seeks to "approximate" a target performance and is "probably" smart if it's an occasional generalization error. A commission learning algorithmic rule refers to an associate algorithmic rule that returns a hypothesis that's commission.

Using formal strategies, a minimum generalization error is such for a supervised learning task. The concept will then be accustomed to estimate the expected range of samples from the matter domain that might be needed to see whether or not a hypothesis was commissioned or not. It provides a way to estimate the number of samples required to seek out a commission hypothesis. Additionally, a hypothesis is economical beneath the commission framework if the associate algorithm will notice a commission hypothesis in polynomial time.

Definition: Consider a concept class ***C*** defined over a set of instances ***X*** of length ***n*** and a learner ***L*** using hypothesis space ***H***. ***C*** is ***PAC-learnable*** by ***L*** using ***H*** if for all $c \in C$, distributions ***D*** over ***X***, ε such that $0<\varepsilon<1/2$, and δ such that $0<\delta<1/2$, learner ***L*** will, with probability at least $(1-\delta)$, output a hypothesis $h \in H$ such that $error_D(h) \leq \varepsilon$, in time that is ***polynomial*** in $1/\varepsilon$, $1/\delta$, ***n***, and ***size(c)***.

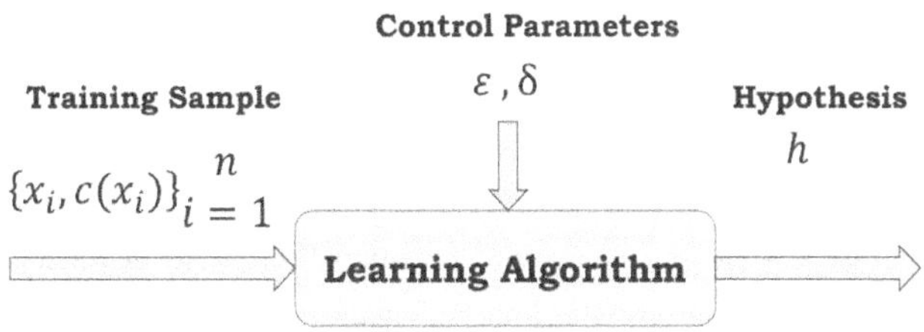

Fig. 8.2: Shows Learning Algorithm

What is VC Dimension?

The Vapnik–Chervonenkis theory (VC Theory) is a theoretical machine learning framework created by Vladimir Vapnik and Alexey Chervonenkis.

It aims to quantity the capability of a learning algorithm and could be considered to be the main sub-field of statistical learning theory.

One of the main elements of the VC theory is the Vapnik-Chervonenkis dimension (VC dimension). It quantifies the complexity of a hypothesis space. It comes up with an estimation of the capability or capacity of a classification machine learning algorithm for a particular dataset (number and dimensionality of examples).

VC Dimension (Theory of Learning Algorithms)

VC theory learning seeks to quantify the aptitude of an algorithmic learning rule. It could be thought-about the premier sub-field of applied math learning theory. VC theory includes several parts, most notably the VC dimension.

The VC dimension quantifies the complexities of a hypothesis house, e.g., the models that would be work given an illustration and learning algorithmic rule. It is a measure of the capacity of a classification algorithm. It is defined as the cardinality (size) of the largest set of points that the algorithm can shatter. Shatter means to correctly classify regardless of the labeling.

One way to think about a hypothesis house's complexities (space of models that would be fit) relies on the number of distinct hypotheses it contains and maybe however the house could be navigated. The VC dimension could be an innovative approach that instead measures the number of examples from the targeted downside, which will be discriminated by hypotheses within the house.

The VC dimension estimates the aptitude or capability of a classification machine learning algorithmic rule for a particular dataset (number and spatial property of examples). Formally, the VC dimension is that the most extensive range of examples from the coaching dataset that the house of hypotheses from the algorithmic rule will "shatter."

Within the case of a dataset, a Shatter or a shattered set means that points within the featured house are selected or separated from one another exploitation hypotheses within the home. The labels of examples within the separate teams are unit correct (whatever they happen to be). Whether a gaggle of points is shattered by associate algorithmic rule depends on the hypothesis house and the range of topics.

For example, a line (hypothesis space) is accustomed to shattering 3 points, not four points. Any placement of 3 points on a second plane with category labels zero or one is "correctly" split by a brand with a line, e.g., shattered. But, placements of 4 points on a plane with binary category labels that can't be separated adequately by a title with a line, e.g., can't be shattered. Instead, another "algorithm" should be used, like ovals. The VC dimension is employed as a part of the commission learning framework.

8.2. Probably Learning and Approximately Correct Hypothesis

PAC Learning (Theory of Learning Problems)

Probably approximately correct learning, or PAC learning, refers to a theoretical machine learning framework developed by Leslie Valiant.

PAC learning seeks to quantify the difficulty of a learning task and might be considered the premier sub-field of computational learning theory.

Consider that in supervised learning, we are trying to approximate an unknown underlying mapping function from inputs to outputs. We don't know what this mapping function looks like, but we suspect it exists, and we have examples of data produced by the function.

PAC learning is concerned with how much computational effort is required to find a hypothesis (fit model) that is a close match for the unknown target function.

What Is a Hypothesis in Machine Learning?

The idea is that a bad hypothesis will be found out based on the predictions it makes on new data, e.g. based on its generalization error.

A hypothesis that gets most or a large number of predictions correct, e.g. has a small generalization error, is probably a good approximation for the target function.

The underlying principle is that any hypothesis that is seriously wrong will almost certainly be "found out" with high probability after a small number of examples, because it will make an incorrect prediction. Thus, any hypothesis that is consistent with a sufficiently large set of training examples is unlikely to be seriously wrong: that is, TELY it must be probably approximately correct.

This probabilistic language gives the theorem its name: "probability approximately correct." That is, a hypothesis seeks to "approximate" a target function and is "probably" good if it has a low generalization error.

A PAC learning algorithm refers to an algorithm that returns a hypothesis that is PAC.

Using formal methods, a minimum generalization error can be specified for a supervised learning task. The theorem can then be used to estimate the expected number of samples from the problem domain that would be required to determine whether a hypothesis was PAC or not. That is, it provides a way to estimate the number of samples required to find a PAC hypothesis.

The goal of the PAC framework is to understand how large a data set needs to be in order to give good generalization. It also gives bounds for the computational cost of learning.

Additionally, a hypothesis space (machine learning algorithm) is efficient under the PAC framework if an algorithm can find a PAC hypothesis (fit model) in polynomial time.

A hypothesis space is said to be efficiently PAC-learnable if there is a polynomial time algorithm that can identify a function that is PAC.

8.3. Sample Complexity for the Finite Hypothesis Space

The growth in the number of required training examples with problem size is called the *sample complexity* of the learning problem. We consider only *consistent learners*, which are those that maintain a training error of 0. We can derive a bound on the number of training examples required by *any* consistent learner. Every consistent learner outputs a hypothesis belonging to the version space. Therefore, we need to bound the number of examples needed to assure that the version space contains no unacceptable hypothesis.

The version space $|VS_{H,D}|$ is said to be *ε-exhausted* with respect to c and $\mathcal{D}$ if every hypothesis h in $VS_{H,D}$ has error less than ε with respect to c and $\mathcal{D}$.

$$(\forall h \in VS_{H,D}) error_{\mathcal{D}}(h) < \varepsilon$$

Sample Complexity for Infinite Hypothesis Space

So far, we have been using |H| in our equation for sample complexity. Only works for finite H. It can also lead to weak (i.e., too loose/high) bounds. We now show how to handle infinite H by using the Vapnik-Chervonenkis dimension.

A *dichotomy* of a set S is a partition of S into two disjoint subsets. There are $2^{|S|}$ possible dichotomies in instance set S. A set of instances is *shattered* by hypothesis space H if and only if for every dichotomy of S there exists some hypothesis in H consistent with this dichotomy. The ability of H to shatter a set of instances is a measure of its capacity to represent target concepts over them.

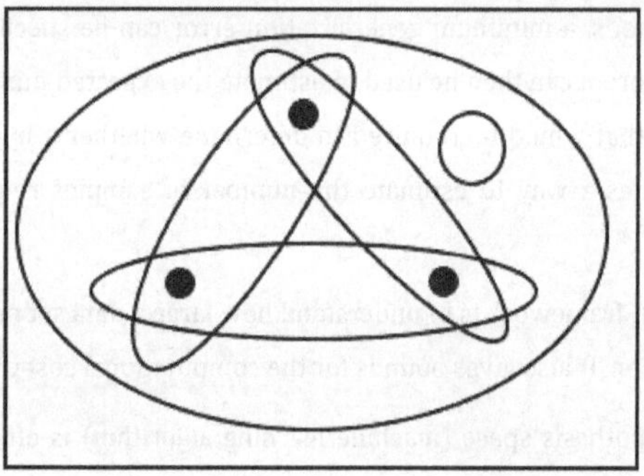

Fig. 8.3: Vapnik-Chervonenkis Dimension

The *Vapnik-Chervonenkis dimension*, VC(H), of hypothesis space H defined over instance space X is the size of the largest finite subset of X shattered by H. If arbitrarily large finite sets of X can be shattered by H, then $VC(H) \equiv \infty$.

$$\text{For any finite H we have that} \begin{cases} VC(H) = d \\ |H| \geq 2^d \\ VC(H) \leq log_2|H| \end{cases}$$

8.4. The Mistake Bound Model of Learning

Computational learning theory studies other models (other than PAC) were:

- The order of the training examples is varied.
- There is noise in the data.
- The definition of success is different.
- The learner makes different assumptions about the distribution of instances, etc.

In these scenarios, we use the ***mistake bound*** model of learning in which the learner is evaluated by the total number of mistakes it makes before it converges to the correct hypothesis.

The learner receives a sequence of training examples similar to Instance based earning. Upon receiving each example x, the learner must predict the target value class label c(x). In this scenario, How many mistakes will the learner make before it learns the target concept? e. g. Learning fraudulent credit card purchases.

Find S,

- Instances drawn at random from X according to distribution $\mathcal{D}$.
- Learner must classify each instance before receiving correct classification from teacher.
- Consider Find-S when H= conjunction of boolean literals.
    1. Initialize h to the most specific hypothesis $l_1 \wedge \neg l_1 \wedge l_2 \wedge \neg l_2 \ldots l_n \wedge \neg l_n$.
    2. For each positive training instance x, remove from h any literal that is not satisfied by x.
    3. Output hypothesis h.
- How many mistakes before converging to correct h?.
- *n+1. The first hypothesis eliminates n terms, each subsequent mistake will eliminate at least one more term.*

CHAPTER 9

INSTANCE-BASED LEARNING

9.1. Introduction

The Machine Learning systems which are categorized as **instance-based learning** are the systems that learn the training examples by heart and then generalizes to new instances based on some similarity measure. It is called instance-based because it builds the hypotheses from the training instances. It is also known as **memory-based learning** or **lazy-learning.** The time complexity of this algorithm depends upon the size of training data. The worst-case time complexity of this algorithm is **O (n)**, where n is the number of training instances.

For example, If we were to create a spam filter with an instance-based learning algorithm, instead of just flagging emails that are already marked as spam emails, our spam filter would be programmed to also flag emails that are very similar to them. This requires a measure of resemblance between two emails. A similarity measure between two emails could be the same sender or the repetitive use of the same keywords or something else.

Advantages

1. Instead of estimating for the entire instance set, local approximations can be made to the target function.
2. This algorithm can adapt to new data easily, one which is collected as we go.

Disadvantages

1. Classification costs are high.
2. Large amount of memory required to store the data, and each query involves starting the identification of a local model from scratch.

Instance-based methods are sometimes referred to as lazy learning methods because they delay processing until a new instance must be classified. A key advantage of lazy learning is that instead of estimating the target function once for the entire instance space, these methods can estimate it locally and differently for each new instance to be classified.

9.2. k-Nearest Neighbour Algorithm

K-Nearest Neighbours is one of the most basic yet essential classification algorithms in Machine Learning. It belongs to the supervised learning domain and finds intense application in pattern recognition, data mining and intrusion detection. It is widely disposable in real-life scenarios since it is non-parametric, meaning, it does not make any underlying assumptions about the distribution of data. The basic idea of the K-Nearest Neighbor Classifier is "If it walks like a duck, quacks like a duck, then it's probably a duck".

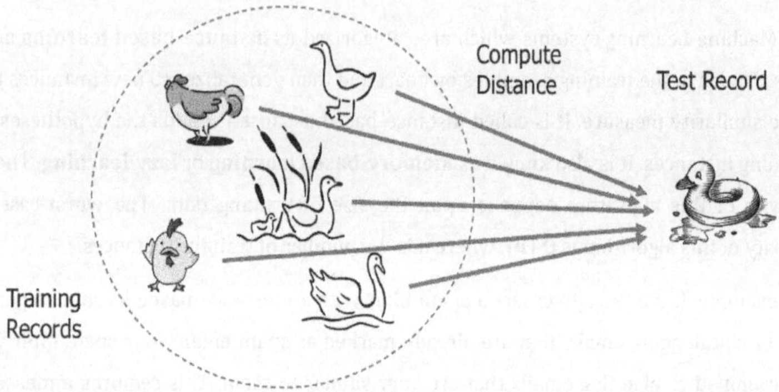

Fig. 9.1: Basic Idea K-Nearest Neighbor Classifier

We are given some prior data (also called training data), which classifies coordinates into groups identified by an attribute. To identify the class to which a given test data belongs, the K-Nearest Neighbor classifier computes the distance or similarity between previously known training samples. K closest training samples are identified as neighbors. Their class labels are analyzed. The test sample is then labelled based on the majority class label identified from its closes training samples. As an example, consider the following table of data points containing two features:

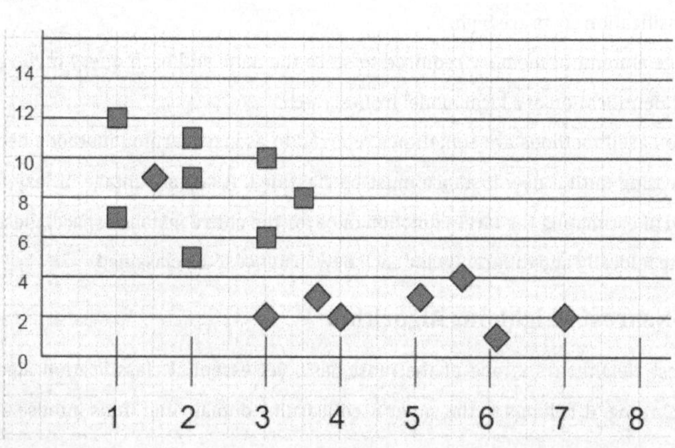

Now, given another set of data points (also called testing data), allocate these points a group by analyzing the training set. Note that the unclassified points are marked as 'White'.

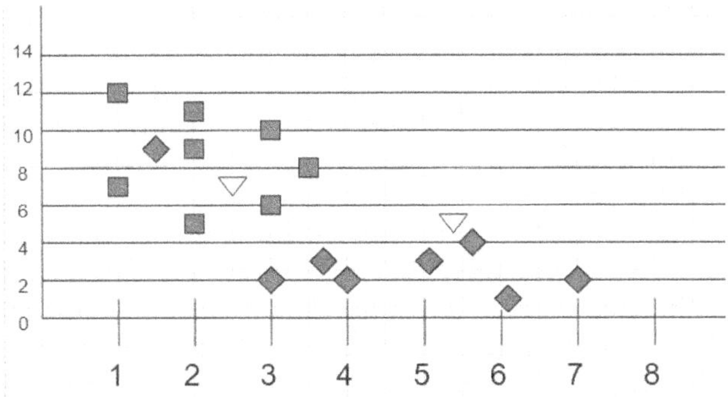

Fig. 9.2: Shows Group by Analyzing the Training Set

Intuition

If we plot these points on a graph, we may be able to locate some clusters or groups. Now, given an unclassified point, we can assign it to a group by observing what group its nearest neighbours belong to. This means a point close to a cluster of points classified as 'Red' has a higher probability of getting classified as 'Red'.

Intuitively, we can see that the first point (2.5, 7) should be classified as 'Green' and the second point (5.5, 4.5) should be classified as 'Red'.

Algorithm

- k-Nearest Neighbor Learning algorithm assumes all instances correspond to points in the n-dimensional space R_n.
- The nearest neighbors of an instance are defined in terms of Euclidean distance.
- Euclidean distance between the instances $x_i = <x_{i1},\ldots,x_{in}>$ and $x_j = <x_{j1},\ldots,x_{jn}>$ are:

$$d(x_i, x_j) = \sqrt{\sum_{r=1}^{n} (x_{ir} - x_{jr})^2}$$

- For a given query instance x_q, $f(x_q)$ is calculated the function values of k-nearest neighbor of x_q.
- Store all training examples $<x_i,f(x_i)>$.
- Calculate $f(x_q)$ for a given query instance x_q using k-nearest neighbor.

- Nearest neighbor: (k=1)
  - Locate the nearest training example x_n, and estimate $f(x_q)$.
  - $f(x_q) \leftarrow f(x_n)$.
- k-Nearest neighbor:
  - Locate k nearest training examples, and estimate $f(x_q)$.
  - If the target function is real-valued, take mean of f-values of k nearest neighbors.

$$f(x_q) = \frac{\sum_{i=1}^{k} f(x_i)}{k}$$

  - If the target function is discrete-valued, take a vote among f-values of k nearest neighbors.

K can be kept as an odd number so that we can calculate a clear majority in the case where only two groups are possible (e.g. Red/Blue). With increasing K, we get smoother, more defined boundaries across different classifications. Also, the accuracy of the above classifier increases as we increase the number of data points in the training set.

Additional- K-Nearest Neighbor (KNN) Algorithm for Machine Learning

- K-Nearest Neighbor is one of the simplest Machine Learning algorithms based on Supervised Learning technique.
- K-NN algorithm assumes the similarity between the new case/data and available cases and put the new case into the category that is most similar to the available categories.
- K-NN algorithm stores all the available data and classifies a new data point based on the similarity. This means when new data appears then it can be easily classified into a well suite category by using K- NN algorithm.
- K-NN algorithm can be used for Regression as well as for Classification but mostly it is used for the Classification problems.
- K-NN is a **non-parametric algorithm**, which means it does not make any assumption on underlying data.
- It is also called a **lazy learner algorithm** because it does not learn from the training set immediately instead it stores the dataset and at the time of classification, it performs an action on the dataset.
- KNN algorithm at the training phase just stores the dataset and when it gets new data, then it classifies that data into a category that is much similar to the new data.

- **Example:** Suppose, we have an image of a creature that looks similar to cat and dog, but we want to know either it is a cat or dog. So for this identification, we can use the KNN algorithm, as it works on a similarity measure. Our KNN model will find the similar features of the new data set to the cats and dogs images and based on the most similar features it will put it in either cat or dog category.

Fig. 9.3: KNN Classifier

Why do we need a K-NN Algorithm?

Suppose there are two categories, i.e., Category A and Category B, and we have a new data point x1, so this data point will lie in which of these categories. To solve this type of problem, we need a K-NN algorithm. With the help of K-NN, we can easily identify the category or class of a particular dataset. Consider the below diagram:

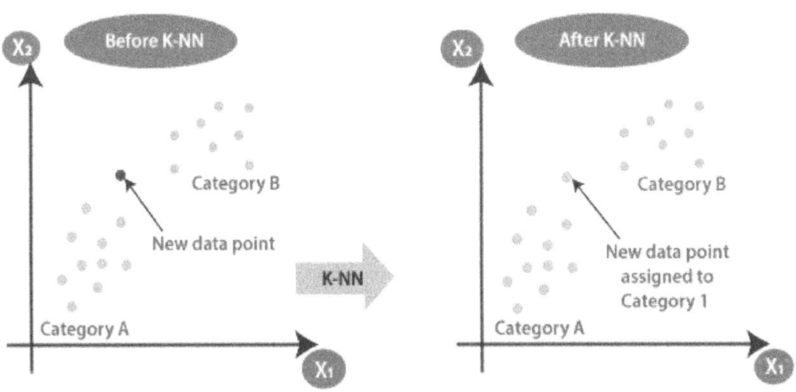

Fig. 9.4: Before and After Applying K-NN

How does K-NN Work?

The K-NN working can be explained on the basis of the below algorithm:

- **Step-1:** Select the number K of the neighbors.
- **Step-2:** Calculate the Euclidean distance of **K number of neighbors.**
- **Step-3:** Take the K nearest neighbors as per the calculated Euclidean distance.
- **Step-4:** Among these k neighbors, count the number of the data points in each category.
- **Step-5:** Assign the new data points to that category for which the number of the neighbor is maximum.
- **Step-6:** Our model is ready.

Suppose we have a new data point and we need to put it in the required category. Consider the below image:

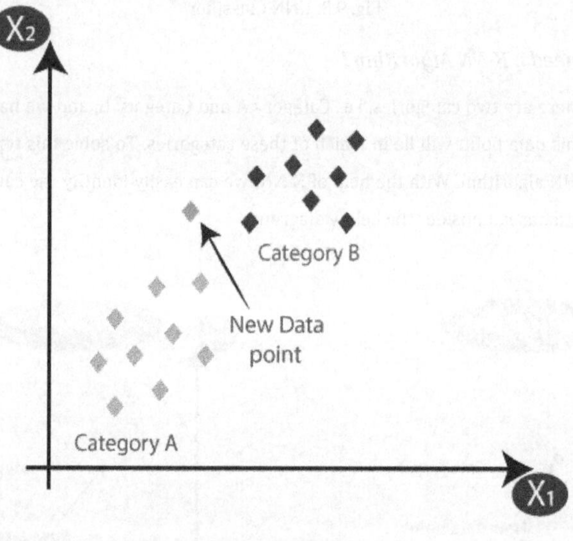

Fig. 9.5: Shows Classification

- Firstly, we will choose the number of neighbors, so we will choose the k=5.
- Next, we will calculate the **Euclidean distance** between the data points. The Euclidean distance is the distance between two points, which we have already studied in geometry. It can be calculated as,

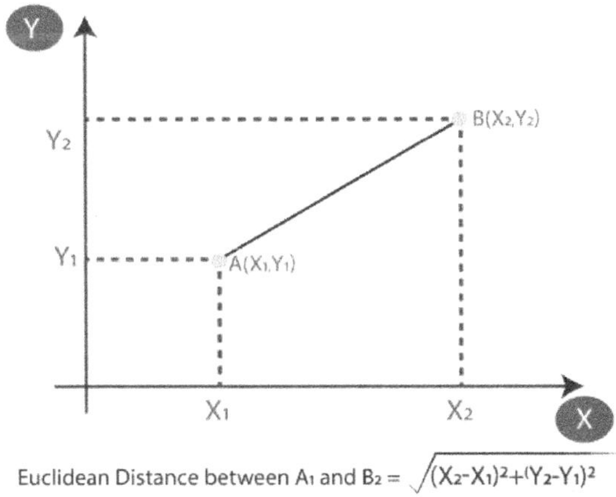

Fig. 9.6: Euclidean Distance between the Data Points

- By calculating the Euclidean distance we got the nearest neighbors, as three nearest neighbors in category A and two nearest neighbors in category B. Consider the below image.

Fig. 9.7: Shows Classification

- As we can see the 3 nearest neighbors are from category A, hence this new data point must belong to category A.

How to Select the Value of K in the K-NN Algorithm?

Below are some points to remember while selecting the value of K.

K-NN Algorithm

- There is no particular way to determine the best value for "K", so we need to try some values to find the best out of them. The most preferred value for K is 5.
- A very low value for K such as K=1 or K=2, can be noisy and lead to the effects of outliers in the model.
- Large values for K are good, but it may find some difficulties.

Advantages of KNN Algorithm

- It is simple to implement.
- It is robust to the noisy training data.
- It can be more effective if the training data is large.

Disadvantages of KNN Algorithm

- Always needs to determine the value of K which may be complex some time.
- The computation cost is high because of calculating the distance between the data points for all the training samples.

K-Means Clustering Algorithm

K-Means Clustering is an unsupervised learning algorithm that is used to solve the clustering problems in machine learning or data science. In this topic, we will learn what is K-means clustering algorithm, how the algorithm works, along with the Python implementation of k-means clustering.

What is K-Means Algorithm?

K-Means Clustering is an Unsupervised Learning algorithm which groups the unlabeled dataset into different clusters. Here K defines the number of pre-defined clusters that need to be created in the process, as if K=2, there will be two clusters, and for K=3, there will be three clusters, and so on.

It is an iterative algorithm that divides the unlabeled dataset into k different clusters in such a way that each dataset belongs only one group that has similar properties.

It allows us to cluster the data into different groups and a convenient way to discover the categories of groups in the unlabeled dataset on its own without the need for any training.

It is a centroid-based algorithm, where each cluster is associated with a centroid. The main aim of this algorithm is to minimize the sum of distances between the data point and their corresponding clusters.

The algorithm takes the unlabeled dataset as input, divides the dataset into k-number of clusters, and repeats the process until it does not find the best clusters. The value of k should be predetermined in this algorithm.

The k-means Clustering

Algorithm Mainly Performs Two Tasks

- Determines the best value for K center points or centroids by an iterative process.
- Assigns each data point to its closest k-center. Those data points which are near to the particular k-center, create a cluster.

Hence each cluster has data points with some commonalities, and it is away from other clusters.

The below diagram explains the working of the K-means Clustering Algorithm:

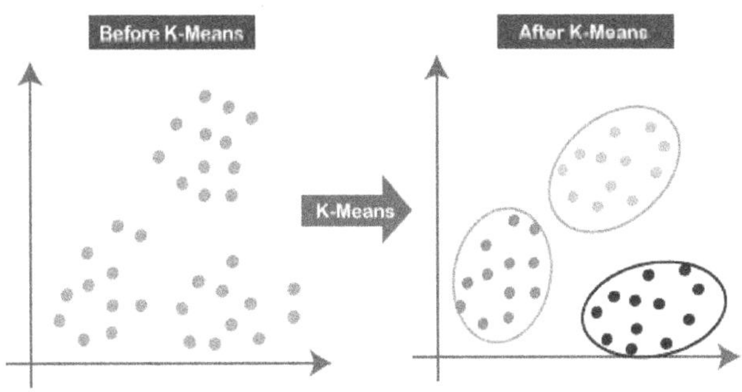

Fig. 9.8: The Working of the K-means Clustering Algorithm

How does the K-Means Algorithm Work?

The working of the K-Means algorithm is explained in the below steps:

Step-1: Select the number K to decide the number of clusters.

Step-2: Select random K points or centroids. (It can be other from the input dataset).

Step-3: Assign each data point to their closest centroid, which will form the predefined K clusters.

Step-4: Calculate the variance and place a new centroid of each cluster.

Step-5: Repeat the third steps, which means reassign each data point to the new closest centroid of each cluster.

Step-6: If any reassignment occurs, then go to step-4 else go to FINISH.

Step-7: The model is ready.

Suppose we have two variables M1 and M2. The x-y axis scatter plot of these two variables is given below:

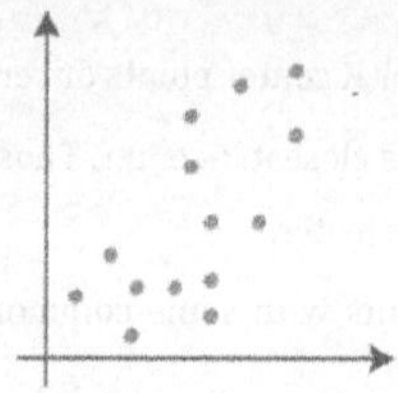

Fig. 9.9: The x-y Axis Scatter Plot of These Two Variables

- Let's take number k of clusters, i.e., K=2, to identify the dataset and to put them into different clusters. It means here we will try to group these datasets into two different clusters.
- We need to choose some random k points or centroid to form the cluster. These points can be either the points from the dataset or any other point. So, here we are selecting the below two points as k points.
- Which are not the part of our dataset. Consider the below image.

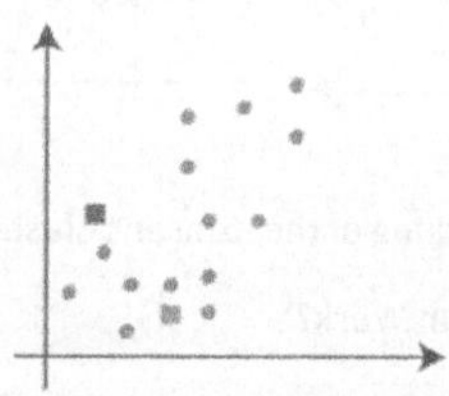

Fig. 9.10: The Scatter Plot to its Closest K-point or Centroid

- Now we will assign each data point of the scatter plot to its closest K-point or centroid. We will compute it by applying some mathematics that we have studied to calculate the distance between two points. So, we will draw a median between both the centroids. Consider the below image.

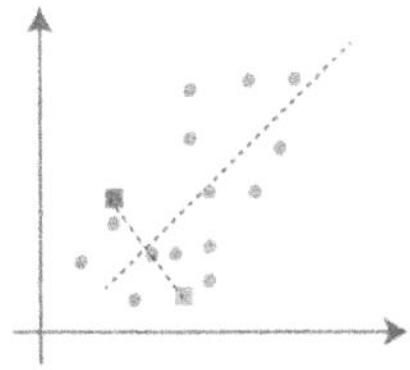

Fig. 9.11: Visualization

From the above image, it is clear that points left side of the line is near to the K1 or blue centroid, and points to the right of the line are close to the yellow centroid. Let's color them as blue and yellow for clear visualization.

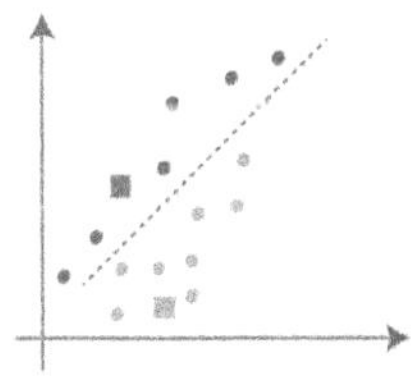

Fig. 9.12: Classification

- As we need to find the closest cluster, so we will repeat the process by choosing **a new centroid**. To choose the new centroids, we will compute the center of gravity of these centroids, and will find new centroids as below.

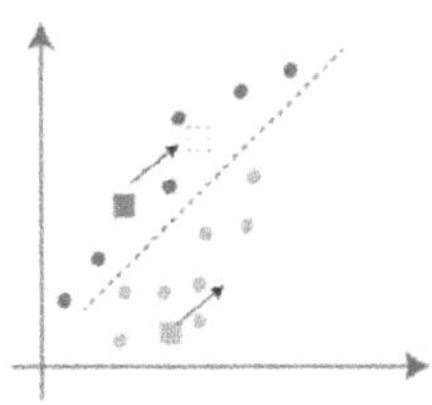

Next, we will reassign each data point to the new centroid. For this, we will repeat the same process of finding a median line. The median will be like below image.

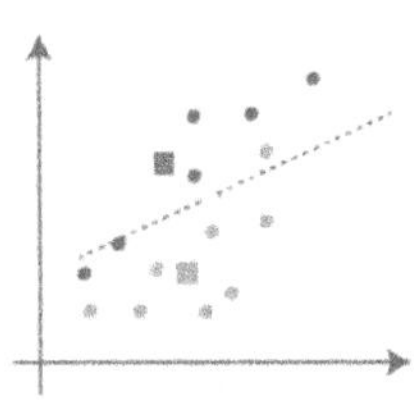

From the above image, we can see, one yellow point is on the left side of the line, and two blue points are right to the line. So, these three points will be assigned to new centroids.

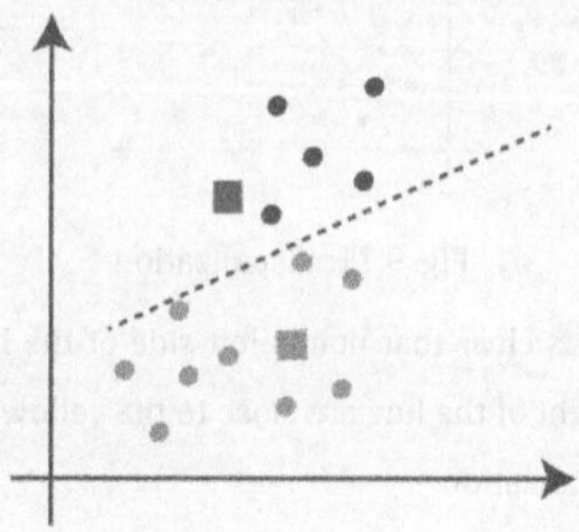

As reassignment has taken place, so we will again go to the step-4, which is finding new centroids or K-points.

- We will repeat the process by finding the center of gravity of centroids, so the new centroids will be as shown in the below image.

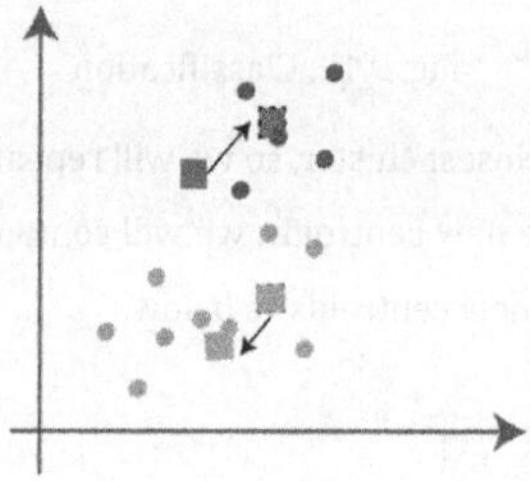

- As we got the new centroids so again will draw the median line and reassign the data points. So, the image will be:

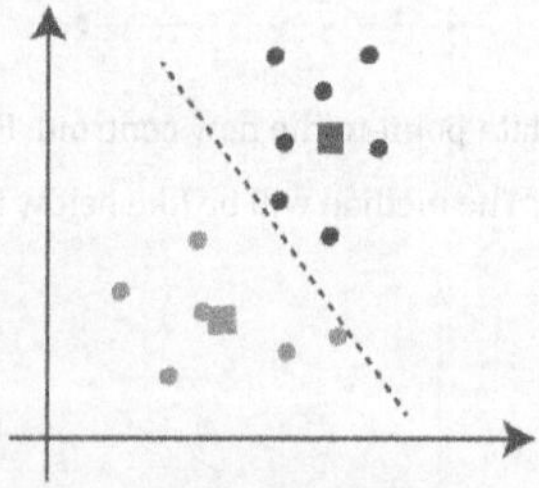

- We can see in the above image; there are no dissimilar data points on either side of the line, which means our model is formed. Consider the below image.

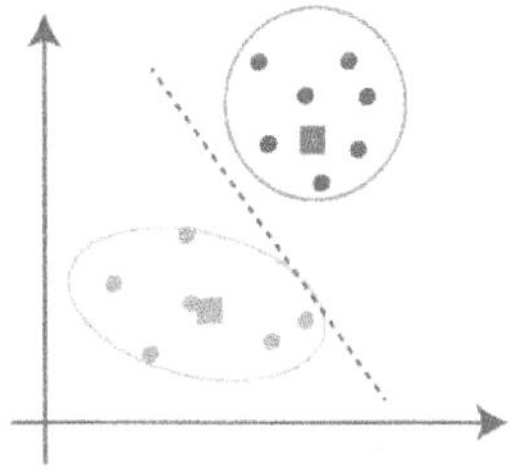

As our model is ready, so we can now remove the assumed centroids, and the two final clusters will be as shown in the below image.

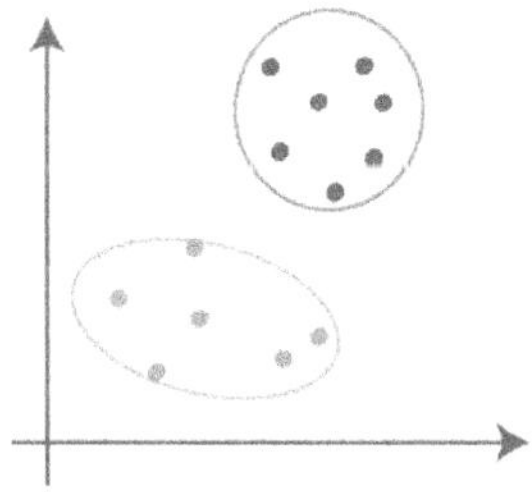

Fig. 9.13: K-Means Clustering

How to choose the value of "K number of clusters" in K-means Clustering?

The performance of the K-means clustering algorithm depends upon highly efficient clusters that it forms. But choosing the optimal number of clusters is a big task. There are some different ways to find the optimal number of clusters, but here we are discussing the most appropriate method to find the number of clusters or value of K. The method is given below:

Elbow Method

The Elbow method is one of the most popular ways to find the optimal number of clusters. This method uses the concept of WCSS value. **WCSS** stands for **Within Cluster Sum of Squares**, which defines the total variations within a cluster. The formula to calculate the value of WCSS (for 3 clusters) is given below:

$$WCSS = \sum_{P_i \text{ in Cluster1}} distance(P_i\ C_1)^2 + \sum_{P_i \text{ in Cluster2}} distance(P_i\ C_2)^2 + \sum_{P_i \text{ in CLuster3}} distance(P_i\ C_3)^2$$

In the above formula of WCSS,

$\sum_{P_i \text{ in Cluster1}}$ distance $(P_i\ C_1)^2$: It is the sum of the square of the distances between each data point and its centroid within a cluster 1 and the same for the other two terms.

To measure the distance between data points and centroid, we can use any method such as Euclidean distance or Manhattan distance.

To find the optimal value of clusters, the elbow method follows the below steps.

- It executes the K-means clustering on a given dataset for different K values (ranges from 1-10).
- For each value of K, calculates the WCSS value.
- Plots a curve between calculated WCSS values and the number of clusters K.
- The sharp point of bend or a point of the plot looks like an arm, then that point is considered as the best value of K.

Since the graph shows the sharp bend, which looks like an elbow, hence it is known as the elbow method. The graph for the elbow method looks like the below image:

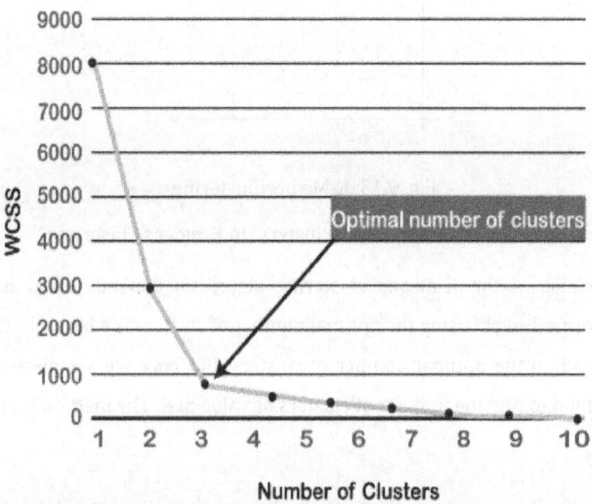

Fig. 9.14: The Graph for the Elbow Method

Note: We can choose the number of clusters equal to the given data points. If we choose the number of clusters equal to the data points, then the value of WCSS becomes zero, and that will be the endpoint of the plot.

9.3. Locally Weighted Regression

Linear regression is a supervised learning algorithm used for computing linear relationships between input (X) and output (Y).

The Steps Involved in Ordinary Linear Regression Are:

Training phase: *Compute to minimize the cost.*

Predict output: *for given query point*

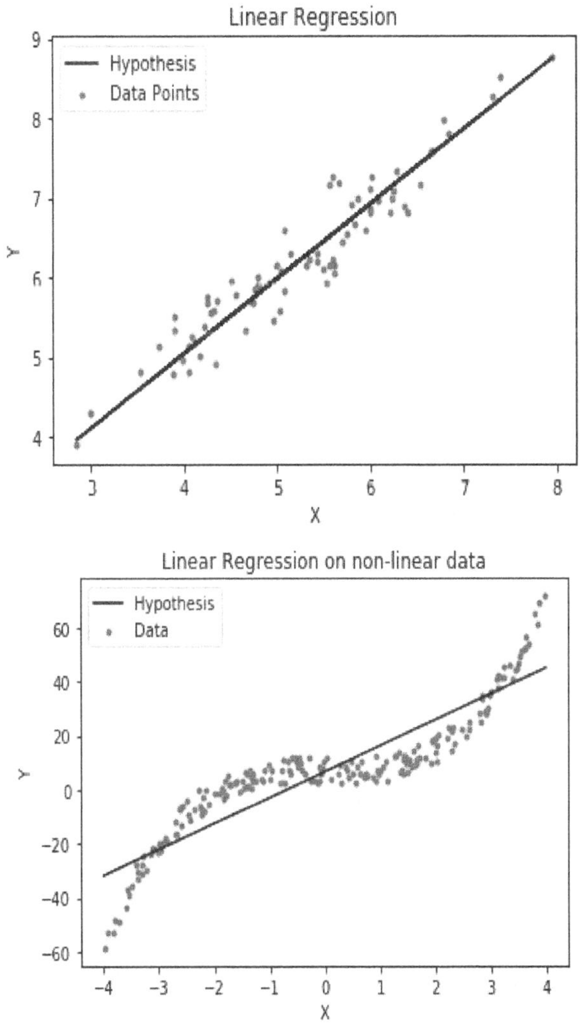

Fig. 9.15: Linear Regression

As evident from the image b, this algorithm cannot be used for making predictions when there exists a non-linear relationship between X and Y. In such cases, locally weighted linear regression is used.

Locally weighted linear regression is a non-parametric algorithm, that is, the model does not learn a fixed set of parameters as is done in ordinary linear regression. Rather parameters \ theta are computed individually for each query point x. While computing \ theta, a higher "preference" is given to the points in the training set lying in the vicinity of x than the points lying far away from x.

KNN forms local approximation to f for each query point x_q. It would be advantageous to form an explicit approximation f(x) for region surrounding x_q. Locally weighted regression uses nearby or distance-weighted training examples to form this local approximation to f. We might approximate the target function in the neighborhood surrounding x, using a linear function, a quadratic function, a multilayer neural network.

- The phrase "locally weighted regression" is called.
    - Local because the function is approximated based only on data near the query point.
    - Weighted because the contribution of each training example is weighted by its distance from the query point.
    - Regression because this is the term used widely in the statistical learning community for the problem of approximating real-valued functions.

Given a new query instance x_q, the general approach in locally weighted regression is to construct an approximation f that fits the training examples in the neighbourhood surrounding x_q.

This approximation is then used to calculate the value $f(x_q)$, which is output as the estimated target value for the query instance. Given a new query instance xq, the general approach in locally weighted regression is to construct an approximation f that fits the training examples in the neighbourhood surrounding x_q.

This approximation is then used to calculate the value $f(x_q)$, which is output as the estimated target value for the query instance. f is approximated near x_q using a linear function of the form,

$$\hat{f}(x) = w_0 + w_1 a_1(x) + \cdots + w_n a_n(x)$$

$a_i(x)$ denotes the value of the ith attribute of the instance x.

Minimize the squared error:

$$E_3(x_q) \equiv \frac{1}{2} \sum_{k\ Nearest\ Neighbors\ of\ x_q} \left(f(x) - \hat{f}(x)\right)^2 K\left(d(x_q, x)\right)$$

Kernel Function K is the function of distance that is used to determine the weight of each training example.

$$\Delta w_j = \eta \sum_{k\ Nearest\ Neighbors\ of\ x_q} K\left(d(x_q, x)\right)\left(f(x) - \hat{f}(x)\right) a_j(x)$$

9.4. Radial Basis Functions

A Radial basis function is a function whose value depends only on the distance from the origin. In effect, the function must contain only real values. Alternative forms of radial basis functions are defined as the distance from another point denoted C, called a center. A radial basis function network is a type of supervised artificial neural network that uses supervised machine learning (ML) to function as a nonlinear classifier. Nonlinear classifiers use sophisticated functions to go further in analysis than simple linear classifiers that work on lower-dimensional vectors.

A radial basis function network is also known as a radial basis network. Using a set of prototypes along with other training examples, neurons look at the distance between an input and a prototype, using what is called an input vector.

The activation functions of artificial neurons drive outputs that can be represented in different ways to show how the network classifies data points. The radial basis function network uses radial basis functions as its activation functions. Like other kinds of neural networks, radial basis function networks have input layers, hidden layers and output layers. However, radial basis function networks often also include a nonlinear activation function of some kind. Output weights can be trained using gradient descent. Some consider an RBF approach to be relatively "intuitive" and a good way to address specialized ML problems.

Their main features are:

1. They are two-layer feed-forward networks.
2. The hidden nodes implement a set of radial basis functions (e.g. Gaussian functions).
3. The output nodes implement linear summation functions as in an MLP.

4. The network training is divided into two stages: first the weights from the input to hidden layer are determined, and then the weights from the hidden to output layer.
5. The training/learning is very fast.
6. The networks are very good at interpolation.

A Radial basis function works by defining itself by the distance from its origin or center. This is done by incorporating the absolute value of the function. Absolute values are defined as the value without its associated sign (positive or negative). For example, the absolute value of -4, is 4. Accordingly, the radial basis function is a function in which its values are defined as:

$$\varphi(x) = \varphi(\|x\|)$$

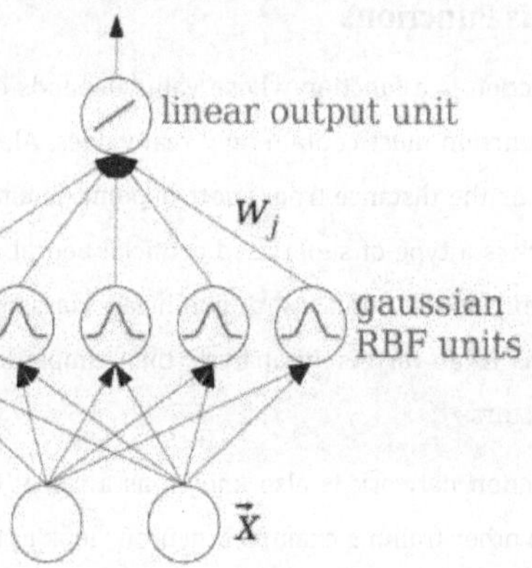

The Gaussian variation of the Radial Basis Function, often applied in Radial Basis Function Networks, is a popular alternative. The formula for a Gaussian with a one-dimensional input is:

$$f(x) = \frac{1}{\sigma\sqrt{2\pi}} e^{-\frac{(x=\mu)^2}{2\sigma^2}}$$

The RBF Network output is defined as,

$$Output = \sum_j w_j \times e^{\left(-\frac{\|\vec{x}-\mu_j\|^2}{\sigma_j^2}\right)}$$

Applications of the Radial Basis Function

Radial basis functions make up the core of the Radial Basis Function Network, or RBFN. This particular type of neural network is useful in cases where data may need to be classified in a non-linear way. RBFNs work by incorporating the Radial basis function as a neuron and using it as a way of comparing input data to training data. An input vector is processed by multiple Radial basis function neurons, with varying weights, and the sum total of the neurons produce a value of similarity. If input vectors match the training data, they will have a high similarity value. Alternatively, if they do not match the training data, they will not be assigned a high similarity value. Comparing similarity values with different classifications of data allows for non-linear classification.

9.5. Case-based Reasoning

Case-based reasoning (CBR) is an experience-based approach to solving new problems by adapting previously successful solutions to similar problems. Addressing memory, learning, planning and problem solving, CBR provides a foundation for a new technology of intelligent computer systems that can solve problems and adapt to new situations.

In CBR, the "intelligent" reuse of knowledge from already-solved problems, or cases, relies on the premise that the more similar two problems are, the more similar their solutions will be.

CBR developed its roots in the work of artificial intelligence theorist and cognitive psychologist, Roger Schank, and his students at Yale in the late 20th century. The researchers studied the problem-solving ability of humans and found that most people assemble solutions based on earlier experiences with similar situations.

With applications spanning fields ranging from machine learning to medicine to law, CBR is accomplished by gathering case histories and implemented by identifying significant features that describe a case. CBR systems can "learn" by acquiring new knowledge as cases. This, along with the application of database techniques, makes it easier to maintain large volumes of information.

Four Step Process for CBR

In general, the case-based reasoning process entails:

1. **Retrieve:** Gathering from memory an experience closest to the current problem.
2. **Reuse:** Suggesting a solution based on the experience and adapting it to meet the demands of the new situation.
3. **Revise:** Evaluating the use of the solution in the new context.
4. **Retain:** Storing this new problem-solving method in the memory system.

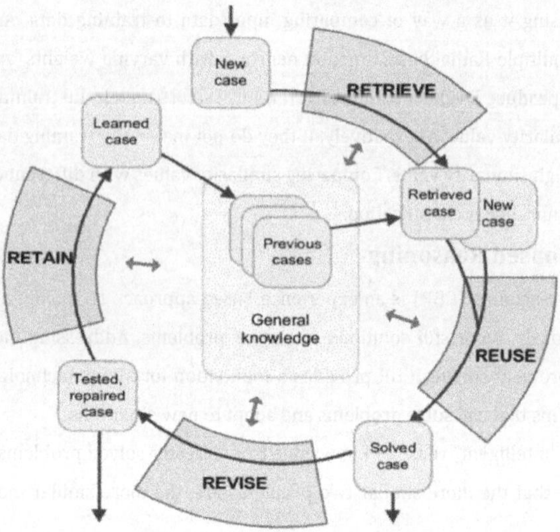

Fig. 9.16: Four Step Process for CBR

Comparison to Other Techniques

Case-based reasoning has several differences from other AI approaches, such as knowledge-based systems (KBS). Rather than relying completely on general knowledge of a problem domain or making associations along generalized relationships between problem descriptors and conclusions, CBR employs the specific knowledge of previously experienced, concrete problem situations. CBR also offers incremental, sustained learning in that each time a problem is solved a new experience is retained and can be applied for future problems.

Advantages and Disadvantages of CBR

Scientists cite both advantages and disadvantages to CBR. On the plus side, remembering past experiences helps learners avoid repeating previous mistakes, and the reasoner can discern what features of a problem are significant and focus on them.

Further, CBR is intuitive because it reflects how people work. Because no knowledge must be elicited to create rules or methods, development is easier. Another benefit is that systems learn by acquiring new cases through use, and this makes maintenance easier.

CBR also enables the reasoner to propose solutions to problems quickly. The reasoner can propose solutions in areas that he or she does not fully understand, evaluate solutions when no algorithmic method is available and interpret open-ended and ill-defined concepts.

On the negative side, critics claim that the main premise of CBR is based on anecdotal evidence and that adapting the elements of one case to another may be complex and potentially lead to inaccuracies. However, recent work has enhanced CBR by using a statistical framework. This makes it possible to produce case-based predictions with a higher level of confidence.

9.6. Remarks on Lazy and Eager Learning

When a machine learning algorithm builds a model soon after receiving training data set, it is called eager learning. It is called eager; because, when it gets the data set, the first thing it does - build the model. Then it forgets the training data. Later, when an input data comes, it uses this model to evaluate it. Most machine learning algorithms are eager learners.

On the contrary, when a machine learning algorithm does not build a model immediately after receiving the training data, rather waits till it is provided with an input data to evaluate, it is called lazy learning. It is called lazy; because, it delays building a model, if it builds any, until it is absolutely necessary. When it gets training data, it only stores them. Later, when input data comes, only then it uses this stored data to evaluate the result. Lazy learning algorithm do not learn a discriminative function from the training data but "memorizes" the training dataset instead. On the contrary eager learning algorithm learns its model weights (parameters) during training time.

There is a different set of pros and cons associated with eager and lazy learning. It is obvious that lazy learning would take less time during training but more time during prediction. Each time you want to make a prediction, you are searching for the nearest neighbour in the entire training set (note that there are tricks such as Ball Trees and KDtrees to speed this up a bit.

Eager learning builds a model for the whole data set, meaning it generalizes the data set, at the beginning. It might suffer accuracy compare to lazy learning that has more options in terms of the availability of the whole data set as well as the mechanisms to make use of it.

Some examples are:

Lazy: K - Nearest Neighbour, Case - Based Reasoning.

Eager: Decision Tree, SVM, logistic regression.

CHAPTER 10

GENETIC ALGORITHM

10.1. Genetic Algorithm

Genetic Algorithm (GA) is a search-based optimization technique based on the principles of **Genetics and Natural Selection**. It is frequently used to find optimal or near-optimal solutions to difficult problems which otherwise would take a lifetime to solve. It is frequently used to solve optimization problems, in research, and in machine learning.

10.2. Genetic Algorithms - Motivation, Genetic Algorithms, An Illustrative Example

Introduction to Optimization

Optimization is the process of **making something better**. In any process, we have a set of inputs and a set of outputs as shown in the following figure.

Fig. 10.1: Process Diagram

Optimization refers to finding the values of inputs in such a way that we get the "best" output values. The definition of "best" varies from problem to problem, but in mathematical terms, it refers to maximizing or minimizing one or more objective functions, by varying the input parameters.

The set of all possible solutions or values which the inputs can take make up the search space. In this search space, lies a point or a set of points which gives the optimal solution. The aim of optimization is to find that point or set of points in the search space.

Genetic Algorithms (GAs) are adaptive heuristic search algorithms that belong to the larger part of evolutionary algorithms. Genetic algorithms are based on the ideas of natural selection and genetics. These are intelligent exploitation of random search provided with historical data to direct the search into the region of better performance in solution space. **They are commonly used to generate high-quality solutions for optimization problems and search problems.**

Genetic algorithms simulate the process of natural selection which means those species who can adapt to changes in their environment are able to survive and reproduce and go to next generation. In simple words, they simulate "survival of the fittest" among individual of consecutive generation for solving a problem. **Each generation consist of a population of individuals** and each individual represents a point in search space and possible solution. Each individual is represented as a string of character/integer/float/bits. This string is analogous to the Chromosome.

Foundation of Genetic Algorithms

Genetic algorithms are based on an analogy with genetic structure and behavior of chromosomes of the population. Following is the foundation of GAs based on this analogy:

1. Individual in population compete for resources and mate.
2. Those individuals who are successful (fittest) then mate to create more offspring than others.
3. Genes from "fittest" parent propagate throughout the generation, that is sometimes parents create offspring which is better than either parent.
4. Thus each successive generation is more suited for their environment.

What are Genetic Algorithms?

Nature has always been a great source of inspiration to all mankind. Genetic Algorithms (GAs) are search based algorithms based on the concepts of natural selection and genetics. GAs are a subset of a much larger branch of computation known as **Evolutionary Computation**.

GAs were developed by John Holland and his students and colleagues at the University of Michigan, most notably David E. Goldberg and has since been tried on various optimization problems with a high degree of success.

In GAs, we have a **pool or a population of possible solutions** to the given problem. These solutions then undergo recombination and mutation (like in natural genetics), producing new children, and the process is repeated over various generations. Each individual (or candidate solution) is assigned a fitness value (based on its objective function value) and the fitter individuals are given a higher chance to mate and yield more "fitter" individuals. This is in line with the Darwinian Theory of "Survival of the Fittest".

In this way we keep "evolving" better individuals or solutions over generations, till we reach a stopping criterion.

Genetic Algorithms are sufficiently randomized in nature, but they perform much better than random local search (in which we just try various random solutions, keeping track of the best so far), as they exploit historical information as well.

Advantages of GAs

GAs have various advantages which have made them immensely popular. These include:

- Does not require any derivative information (which may not be available for many real-world problems).
- Is faster and more efficient as compared to the traditional methods.
- Has very good parallel capabilities.
- Optimizes both continuous and discrete functions and also multi-objective problems.
- Provides a list of "good" solutions and not just a single solution.
- Always gets an answer to the problem, which gets better over the time.
- Useful when the search space is very large and there are a large number of parameters involved.

Limitations of GAs

Like any technique, GAs also suffer from a few limitations. These include:

- GAs are not suited for all problems, especially problems which are simple and for which derivative information is available.
- Fitness value is calculated repeatedly which might be computationally expensive for some problems.
- Being stochastic, there are no guarantees on the optimality or the quality of the solution.
- If not implemented properly, the GA may not converge to the optimal solution.

GA - Motivation

Genetic Algorithms have the ability to deliver a "good-enough" solution "fast-enough". This makes genetic algorithms attractive for use in solving optimization problems. The reasons why GAs are needed are as follows:

Solving Difficult Problems

In computer science, there is a large set of problems, which are **NP-Hard.** What this essentially means is that, even the most powerful computing systems take a very long time (even years!) to solve that problem. In such a scenario, GAs prove to be an efficient tool to provide **usable near-optimal solutions** in a short amount of time.

Failure of Gradient based Methods

Traditional calculus based methods work by starting at a random point and by moving in the direction of the gradient, till we reach the top of the hill. This technique is efficient and works very well for single-peaked objective functions like the cost function in linear regression. But, in most real-world situations, we have a very complex problem called as landscapes, which are made of many peaks and many valleys, which causes such methods to fail, as they suffer from an inherent tendency of getting stuck at the local optima as shown in the following figure.

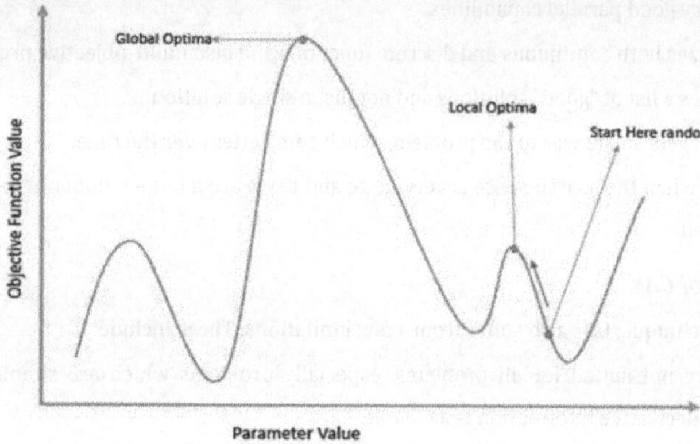

Fig. 10.2: Shows Local Optima

Getting a Good Solution Fast

Some difficult problems like the Travelling Salesperson Problem (TSP), have real-world applications like path finding and VLSI Design. Now imagine that you are using your GPS Navigation system, and it takes a few minutes (or even a few hours) to compute the "optimal" path from the source to destination. Delay in such real world applications is not acceptable and therefore a "good-enough" solution, which is delivered "fast" is what is required.

Search Space

The populations of individuals are maintained within search space. Each individual represents a solution in search space for given problem. Each individual is coded as a finite length vector (analogous to chromosome) of components. These variable components are analogous to Genes. Thus a chromosome (individual) is composed of several genes (variable components).

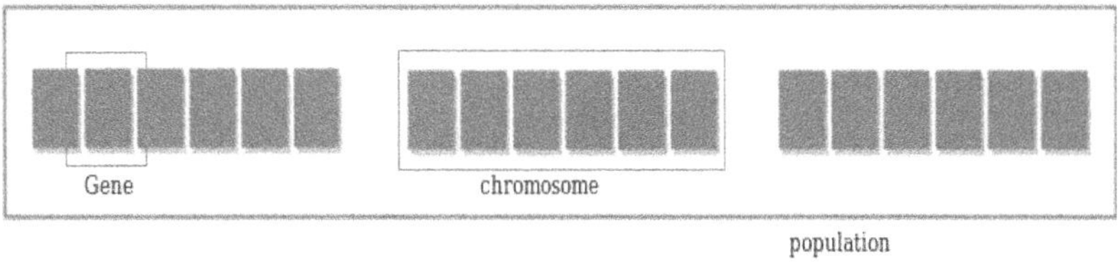

Fig. 10.3: Shows Gene, Chromosome and Population

Fitness Score

A Fitness Score is given to each individual which **shows the ability of an individual to "compete"**. The individual having optimal fitness score (or near optimal) are sought.

The GAs maintains the population of n individuals (chromosome/solutions) along with their fitness scores. The individuals having better fitness scores are given more chance to reproduce than others. The individuals with better fitness scores are selected who mate and produce **better offspring** by combining chromosomes of parents. The population size is static so the room has to be created for new arrivals. So, some individuals die and get replaced by new arrivals eventually creating new generation when all the mating opportunity of the old population is exhausted. It is hoped that over successive generations better solutions will arrive while least fit die.

Each new generation has on average more "better genes" than the individual (solution) of previous generations. Thus each new generations have better **"partial solutions"** than previous generations. Once the offspring produced having no significant difference from offspring produced by previous populations, the population is converged. The algorithm is said to be converged to a set of solutions for the problem.

10.3. Operators of Genetic Algorithms

Once the initial generation is created, the algorithm evolves the generation using following operators:

1. **Selection Operator:** The idea is to give preference to the individuals with good fitness scores and allow them to pass their genes to successive generations.
2. **Crossover Operator:** This represents mating between individuals. Two individuals are selected using selection operator and crossover sites are chosen randomly. Then the genes at these crossover sites are exchanged thus creating a completely new individual (offspring).

For example:

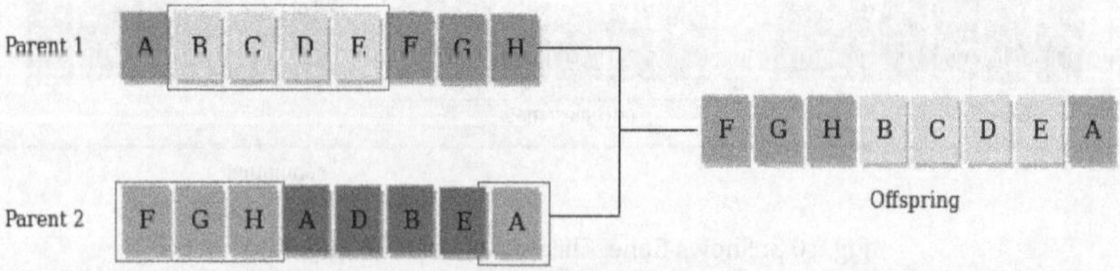

Fig. 10.4: Shows Offspring

3. **Mutation Operator:** The key idea is to insert random genes in offspring to maintain the diversity in the population to avoid premature convergence. For example:

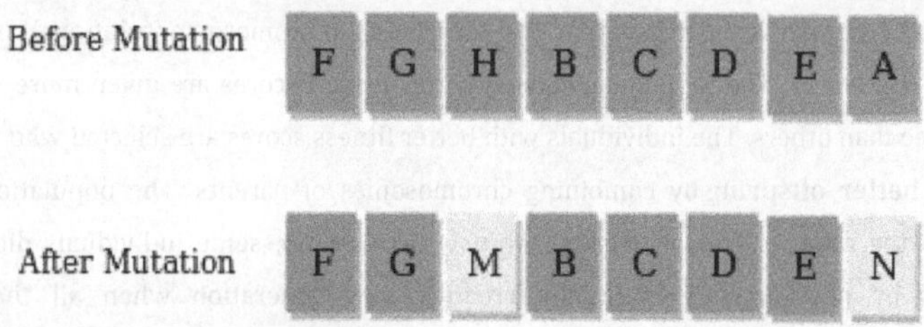

Fig. 10.5: Shows Mutation

The whole algorithm can be summarized as:

1. Randomly initialize populations p
2. Determine fitness of population
3. Until convergence repeat
   a) Select parents from population
   b) Crossover and generate new population
   c) Perform mutation on new population
   d) Calculate fitness for new population

Example Problem and Solution Using Genetic Algorithms

Given a target string, the goal is to produce target string starting from a random string of the same length. In the following implementation, following analogies are made:

- Characters A-Z, a-z, 0-9, and other special symbols are considered as genes.
- A string generated by these characters is considered as chromosome/solution/ Individual.

Fitness score is the number of characters which differ from characters in target string at a particular index. So individual having lower fitness value is given more preference.

Additional

Genetic Algorithms - Fundamentals

This section additionally introduces the basic terminology required to understand GAs. Also, a generic structure of GAs is presented in both **pseudo-code and graphical forms**. The reader is advised to properly understand all the concepts introduced in this section and keep them in mind when reading other sections of this tutorial as well.

Basic Terminology

Before beginning a discussion on Genetic Algorithms, it is essential to be familiar with some basic terminology which will be used throughout this tutorial.

- **Population** – It is a subset of all the possible (encoded) solutions to the given problem. The population for a GA is analogous to the population for human beings except that instead of human beings, we have Candidate Solutions representing human beings.
- **Chromosomes** – A chromosome is one such solution to the given problem.
- **Gene** – A gene is one element position of a chromosome.
- **Allele** – It is the value a gene takes for a particular chromosome.

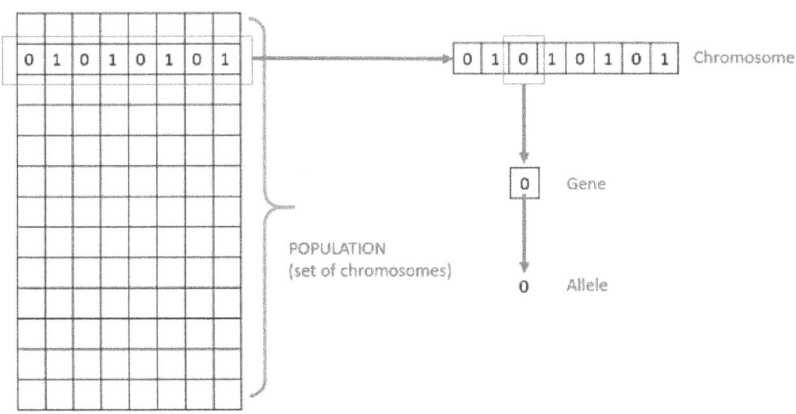

Fig. 10.6: Shows Population

- **Genotype** – Genotype is the population in the computation space. In the computation space, the solutions are represented in a way which can be easily understood and manipulated using a computing system.
- **Phenotype** – Phenotype is the population in the actual real world solution space in which solutions are represented in a way they are represented in real world situations.
- **Decoding and Encoding** – For simple problems, the **phenotype and genotype** spaces are the same. However, in most of the cases, the phenotype and genotype spaces are different. Decoding is a process of transforming a solution from the genotype to the phenotype space, while encoding is a process of transforming from the phenotype to genotype space. Decoding should be fast as it is carried out repeatedly in a GA during the fitness value calculation.

  For example, consider the 0/1 Knapsack Problem. The Phenotype space consists of solutions which just contain the item numbers of the items to be picked.

  However, in the genotype space it can be represented as a binary string of length n (where n is the number of items). A **0 at position x** represents that **x^th** item is picked while a 1 represents the reverse. This is a case where genotype and phenotype spaces are different.

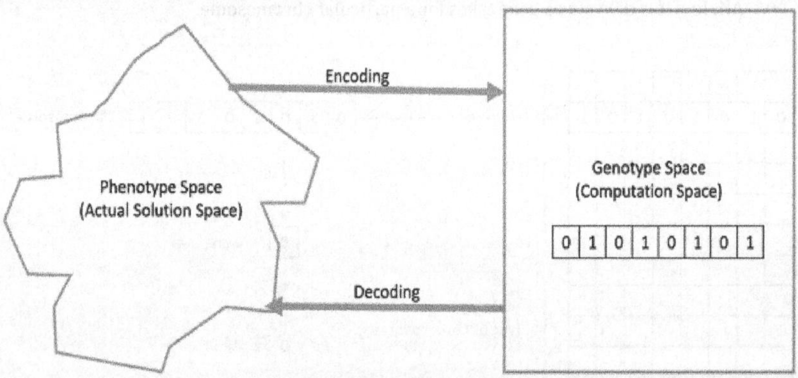

Fig. 10.7: Shows Decoding, Encoding

- **Fitness Function** – A fitness function simply defined is a function which takes the solution as input and produces the suitability of the solution as the output. In some cases, the fitness function and the objective function may be the same, while in others it might be different based on the problem.

- **Genetic Operators** – These alter the genetic composition of the offspring. These include crossover, mutation, selection, etc.

Basic Structure

The basic structure of a GA is as follows:

We start with an initial population (which may be generated at random or seeded by other heuristics), select parents from this population for mating. Apply crossover and mutation operators on the parents to generate new off-springs. And finally these off-springs replace the existing individuals in the population and the process repeats. In this way genetic algorithms actually try to mimic the human evolution to some extent.

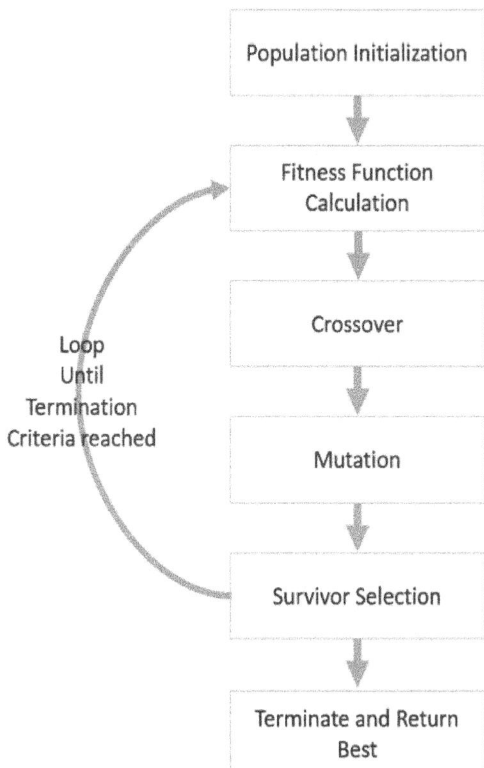

Fig. 10.8: Basic Structure of GA

A generalized **pseudo-code** for a GA is explained in the following program:

```
GA()
initialize population
find fitness of population
while (termination criteria is reached) do
parent selection
crossover with probability pc
mutation with probability pm
decode and fitness calculation
survivor selection
find best
return best
```

Genotype Representation

One of the most important decisions to make while implementing a genetic algorithm is deciding the representation that we will use to represent our solutions. It has been observed that improper representation can lead to poor performance of the GA.

Therefore, choosing a proper representation, having a proper definition of the mappings between the phenotype and genotype spaces is essential for the success of a GA.

In this section, we present some of the most commonly used representations for genetic algorithms. However, representation is highly problem specific and the reader might find that another representation or a mix of the representations mentioned here might suit his/her problem better.

Binary Representation

This is one of the simplest and most widely used representation in GAs. In this type of representation the genotype consists of bit strings.

For some problems when the solution space consists of Boolean decision variables – yes or no, the binary representation is natural. Take for example the 0/1 Knapsack Problem. If there are n items, we can represent a solution by a binary string of n elements, where the xth element tells whether the item x is picked (1) or not (0).

0	0	1	0	1	1	1	0	0	1

For other problems, specifically those dealing with numbers, we can represent the numbers with their binary representation. The problem with this kind of encoding is that different bits have different significance and therefore mutation and crossover operators can have undesired consequences. This can be resolved to some extent by using **Gray Coding,** as a change in one bit does not have a massive effect on the solution.

Real Valued Representation

For problems where we want to define the genes using continuous rather than discrete variables, the real valued representation is the most natural. The precision of these real valued or floating point numbers is however limited to the computer.

0.5	0.2	0.6	0.8	0.7	0.4	0.3	0.2	0.1	0.9

Integer Representation

For discrete valued genes, we cannot always limit the solution space to binary 'yes' or 'no'. For example, if we want to encode the four distances - North, South, East and West, we can encode them as **{0,1,2,3}**. In such cases, integer representation is desirable.

1	2	3	4	3	2	4	1	2	1

Permutation Representation

In many problems, the solution is represented by an order of elements. In such cases permutation representation is the most suited.

A classic example of this representation is the travelling salesman problem (TSP). In this the salesman has to take a tour of all the cities, visiting each city exactly once and come back to the starting city. The total distance of the tour has to be minimized. The solution to this TSP is naturally an ordering or permutation of all the cities and therefore using a permutation representation makes sense for this problem.

1	5	9	8	7	4	2	3	6	0

Genetic Algorithms - Population

Population is a subset of solutions in the current generation. It can also be defined as a set of chromosomes. There are several things to be kept in mind when dealing with GA population:

- The diversity of the population should be maintained otherwise it might lead to premature convergence.

- The population size should not be kept very large as it can cause a GA to slow down, while a smaller population might not be enough for a good mating pool. Therefore, an optimal population size needs to be decided by trial and error.

The population is usually defined as a two dimensional array of – **size population, size x, chromosome size**.

Population Initialization

There are two primary methods to initialize a population in a GA. They are:

- **Random Initialization** – Populate the initial population with completely random solutions.
- **Heuristic initialization** – Populate the initial population using a known heuristic for the problem.

It has been observed that the entire population should not be initialized using a heuristic, as it can result in the population having similar solutions and very little diversity. It has been experimentally observed that the random solutions are the ones to drive the population to optimality. Therefore, with heuristic initialization, we just seed the population with a couple of good solutions, filling up the rest with random solutions rather than filling the entire population with heuristic based solutions.

It has also been observed that heuristic initialization in some cases, only effects the initial fitness of the population, but in the end, it is the diversity of the solutions which lead to optimality.

10.4. Population Models

There are two population models widely in use:

Steady State

In steady state GA, we generate one or two off-springs in each iteration and they replace one or two individuals from the population. A steady state GA is also known as **Incremental GA**.

Generational

In a generational model, we generate 'n' off-springs, where n is the population size, and the entire population is replaced by the new one at the end of the iteration.

Genetic Algorithms - Fitness Function

The fitness function simply defined is a function which takes a **candidate solution to the problem as input and produces as output** how "fit" our how "good" the solution is with respect to the problem in consideration.

Calculation of fitness value is done repeatedly in a GA and therefore it should be sufficiently fast. A slow computation of the fitness value can adversely affect a GA and make it exceptionally slow.

In most cases the fitness function and the objective function are the same as the objective is to either maximize or minimize the given objective function. However, for more complex problems with multiple objectives and constraints, an **Algorithm Designer** might choose to have a different fitness function.

A fitness function should possess the following characteristics:

- The fitness function should be sufficiently fast to compute.
- It must quantitatively measure how fit a given solution is or how fit individuals can be produced from the given solution.

In some cases, calculating the fitness function directly might not be possible due to the inherent complexities of the problem at hand. In such cases, we do fitness approximation to suit our needs.

The following image shows the fitness calculation for a solution of the 0/1 Knapsack. It is a simple fitness function which just sums the profit values of the items being picked (which have a 1), scanning the elements from left to right till the knapsack is full.

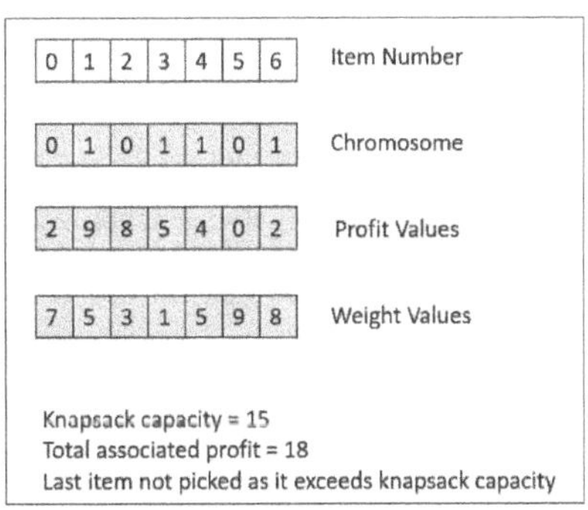

Fig. 10.9: Fitness Calculation

Genetic Algorithms - Parent Selection

Parent Selection is the process of selecting parents which mate and recombine to create off-springs for the next generation. Parent selection is very crucial to the convergence rate of the GA as good parents drive individuals to a better and fitter solutions.

However, care should be taken to prevent one extremely fit solution from taking over the entire population in a few generations, as this leads to the solutions being close to one another in the solution space thereby leading to a loss of diversity. **Maintaining good diversity** in the population is extremely crucial for the success of a GA. This taking up of the entire population by one extremely fit solution is known as **premature convergence** and is an undesirable condition in a GA.

Fitness Proportionate Selection

Fitness Proportionate Selection is one of the most popular ways of parent selection. In this every individual can become a parent with a probability which is proportional to its fitness. Therefore, fitter individuals have a higher chance of mating and propagating their features to the next generation. Therefore, such a selection strategy applies a selection pressure to the more fit individuals in the population, evolving better individuals over time.

Consider a circular wheel. The wheel is divided into **n pies**, where n is the number of individuals in the population. Each individual gets a portion of the circle which is proportional to its fitness value.

Two implementations of fitness proportionate selection are possible:

Roulette Wheel Selection

In a roulette wheel selection, the circular wheel is divided as described before. A fixed point is chosen on the wheel circumference as shown and the wheel is rotated. The region of the wheel which comes in front of the fixed point is chosen as the parent. For the second parent, the same process is repeated.

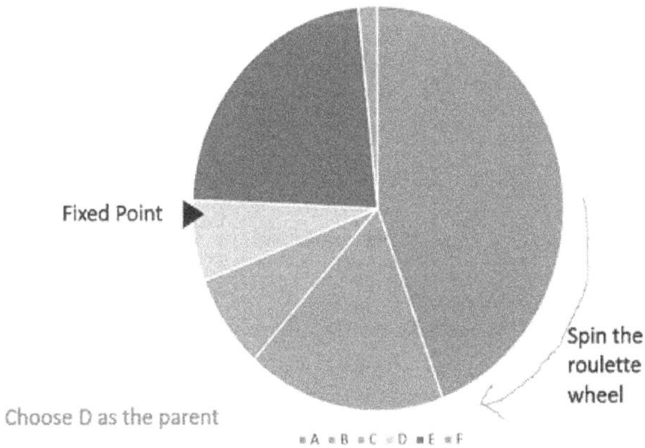

Chromosome	Fitness Value
A	8.2
B	3.2
C	1.4
D	1.2
E	4.2
F	0.3

Fig. 10.10: Shows Roulette Wheel Selection

It is clear that a fitter individual has a greater pie on the wheel and therefore a greater chance of landing in front of the fixed point when the wheel is rotated. Therefore, the probability of choosing an individual depends directly on its fitness.

Implementation wise, we use the following steps:

- Calculate S = the sum of a finesses.
- Generate a random number between 0 and S.
- Starting from the top of the population, keep adding the finesses to the partial sum P, till P<S.
- The individual for which P exceeds S is the chosen individual.

10.5. Stochastic Universal Sampling (SUS)

Stochastic Universal Sampling is quite similar to Roulette wheel selection, however instead of having just one fixed point, we have multiple fixed points as shown in the following image. Therefore, all the parents are chosen in just one spin of the wheel. Also, such a setup encourages the highly fit individuals to be chosen at least once.

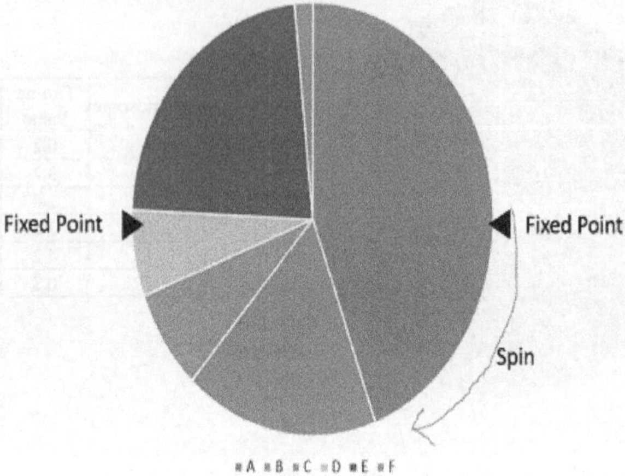

Chromosome	Fitness Value
A	8.2
B	3.2
C	1.4
D	1.2
E	4.2
F	0.3

Fig. 10.11: Stochastic Universal Sampling

It is to be noted that fitness proportionate selection methods don't work for cases where the fitness can take a negative value.

Tournament Selection

In K-Way tournament selection, we select K individuals from the population at random and select the best out of these to become a parent. The same process is repeated for selecting the next parent. Tournament Selection is also extremely popular in literature as it can even work with negative fitness values.

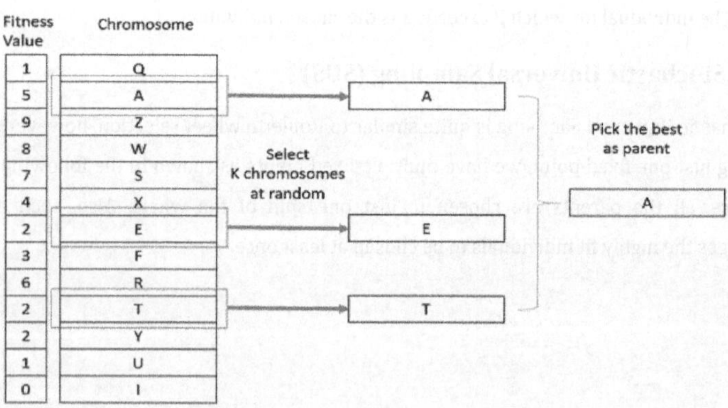

Fig. 10.12: Shows Random Selection

Rank Selection

Rank Selection also works with negative fitness values and is mostly used when the individuals in the population have very close fitness values (this happens usually at the end of the run). This leads to each individual having an almost equal share of the pie (like in case of fitness proportionate selection) as shown in the following image and hence each individual no matter how fit relative to each other has an approximately same probability of getting selected as a parent. This in turn leads to a loss in the selection pressure towards fitter individuals, making the GA to make poor parent selections in such situations.

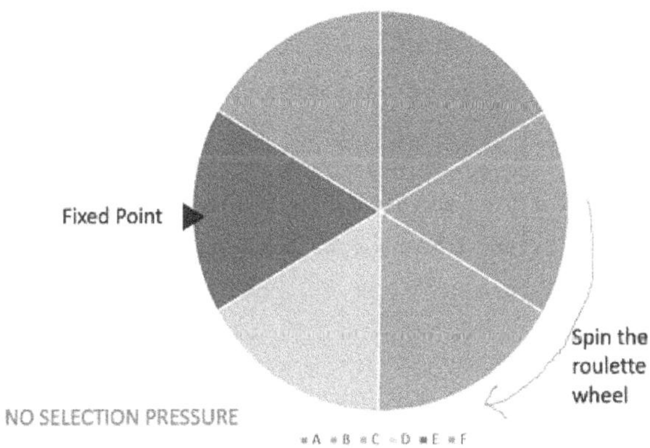

Chromosome	Fitness Value
A	8.1
B	8.0
C	8.05
D	7.95
E	8.02
F	7.99

Fig. 10.13: Rank Selection

In this, we remove the concept of a fitness value while selecting a parent. However, every individual in the population is ranked according to their fitness. The selection of the parents depends on the rank of each individual and not the fitness. The higher ranked individuals are preferred more than the lower ranked ones.

Chromosome	Fitness Value	Rank
A	8.1	1
B	8.0	4
C	8.05	2
D	7.95	6
E	8.02	3
F	7.99	5

Random Selection

In this strategy we randomly select parents from the existing population. There is no selection pressure towards fitter individuals and therefore this strategy is usually avoided.

Genetic Algorithms - Crossover

In this chapter, we will discuss about what a Crossover Operator is along with its other modules, their uses and benefits.

Introduction to Crossover

The crossover operator is analogous to reproduction and biological crossover. In this more than one parent is selected and one or more off-springs are produced using the genetic material of the parents. Crossover is usually applied in a GA with a high probability – p_c.

Crossover Operators

In this section we will discuss some of the most popularly used crossover operators. It is to be noted that these crossover operators are very generic and the GA Designer might choose to implement a problem-specific crossover operator as well.

One Point Crossover

In this one-point crossover, a random crossover point is selected and the tails of its two parents are swapped to get new off-springs.

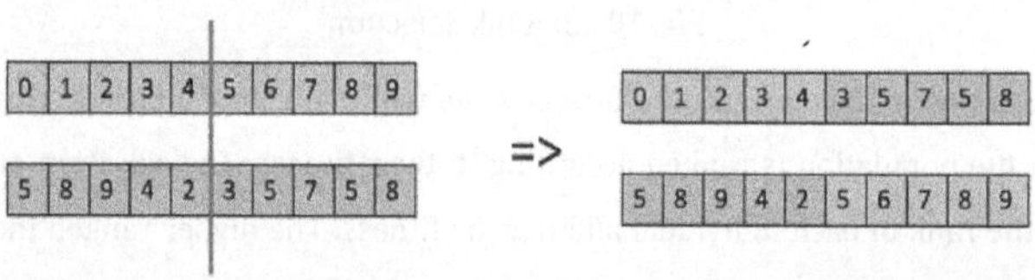

Multi Point Crossover

Multi point crossover is a generalization of the one-point crossover wherein alternating segments are swapped to get new off-springs.

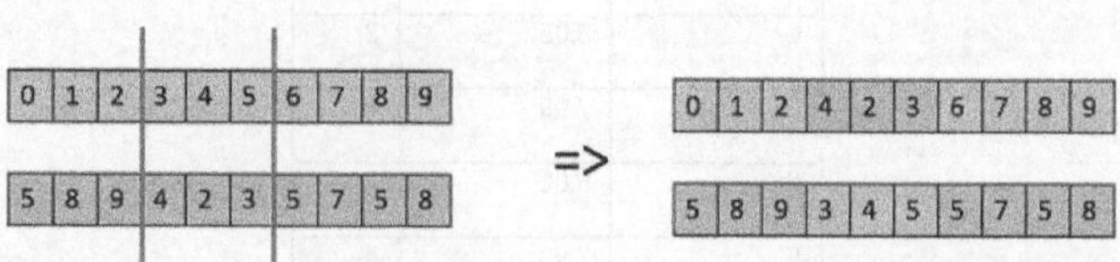

Uniform Crossover

In a uniform crossover, we don't divide the chromosome into segments, rather we treat each gene separately. In this, we essentially flip a coin for each chromosome to decide whether or not it'll be included in the off-spring. We can also bias the coin to one parent, to have more genetic material in the child from that parent.

Whole Arithmetic Recombination

This is commonly used for integer representations and works by taking the weighted average of the two parents by using the following formulae:

- Child1 = $\alpha.x + (1-\alpha).y$
- Child2 = $\alpha.x + (1-\alpha).y$

Obviously, if $\alpha = 0.5$, then both the children will be identical as shown in the following image.

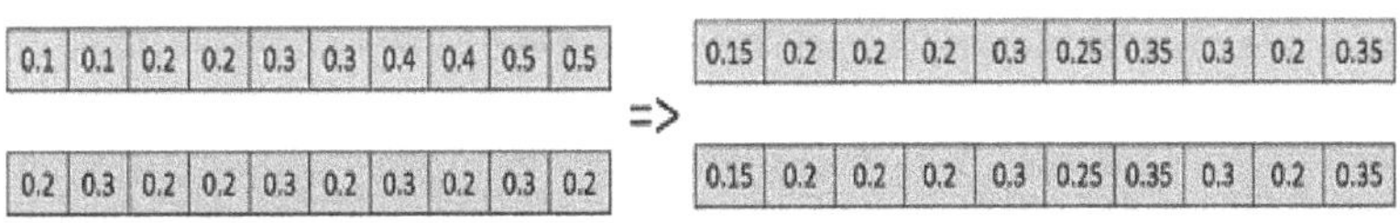

Davis' Order Crossover (OX1)

OX1 is used for permutation based crossovers with the intention of transmitting information about relative ordering to the off-springs. It works as follows:

- Create two random crossover points in the parent and copy the segment between them from the first parent to the first offspring.
- Now, starting from the second crossover point in the second parent, copy the remaining unused numbers from the second parent to the first child, wrapping around the list.
- Repeat for the second child with the parent's role reversed.

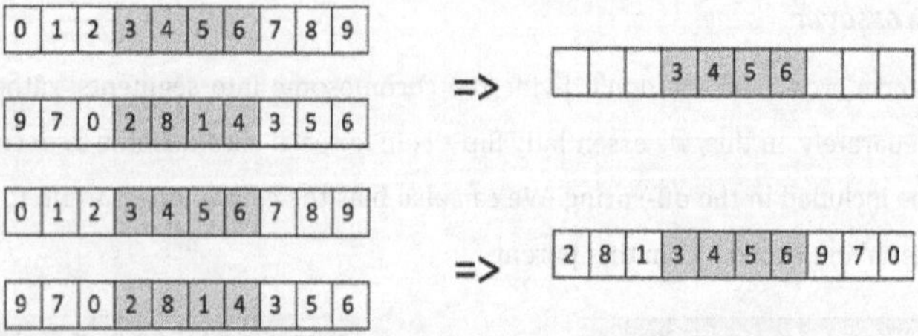

Repeat the same procedure to get the second child

There exist a lot of other crossovers like Partially Mapped Crossover (PMX), Order based crossover (OX_2), Shuffle Crossover, Ring Crossover, etc.

Genetic Algorithms - Mutation

Introduction to Mutation

In simple terms, mutation may be defined as a small random tweak in the chromosome, to get a new solution. It is used to maintain and introduce diversity in the genetic population and is usually applied with a low probability – p_m. If the probability is very high, the GA gets reduced to a random search.

Mutation is the part of the GA which is related to the "exploration" of the search space. It has been observed that mutation is essential to the convergence of the GA while crossover is not.

Mutation Operators

In this section, we describe some of the most commonly used mutation operators. Like the crossover operators, this is not an exhaustive list and the GA designer might find a combination of these approaches or a problem-specific mutation operator more useful.

Bit Flip Mutation

In this bit flip mutation, we select one or more random bits and flip them. This is used for binary encoded GAs.

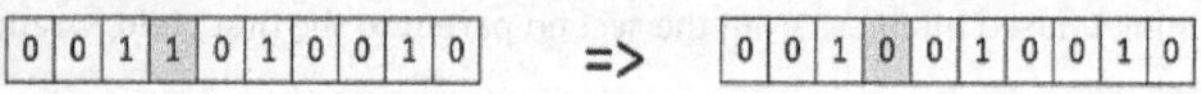

Random Resetting

Random Resetting is an extension of the bit flip for the integer representation. In this, a random value from the set of permissible values is assigned to a randomly chosen gene.

Swap Mutation

In swap mutation, we select two positions on the chromosome at random, and interchange the values. This is common in permutation based encodings.

1	2	3	4	5	6	7	8	9	0	=>	1	6	3	4	5	2	7	8	9	0

Scramble Mutation

Scramble mutation is also popular with permutation representations. In this, from the entire chromosome, a subset of genes is chosen and their values are scrambled or shuffled randomly.

0	1	2	3	4	5	6	7	8	9	=>	0	1	3	6	4	2	5	7	8	9

Inversion Mutation

In inversion mutation, we select a subset of genes like in scramble mutation, but instead of shuffling the subset, we merely invert the entire string in the subset.

0	1	2	3	4	5	6	7	8	9	=>	0	1	6	5	4	3	2	7	8	9

Genetic Algorithms - Survivor Selection

The Survivor Selection Policy determines which individuals are to be kicked out and which are to be kept in the next generation. It is crucial as it should ensure that the fitter individuals are not kicked out of the population, while at the same time diversity should be maintained in the population.

Some GAs employ **Elitism.** In simple terms, it means the current fittest member of the population is always propagated to the next generation. Therefore, under no circumstance can the fittest member of the current population be replaced.

The easiest policy is to kick random members out of the population, but such an approach frequently has convergence issues, therefore the following strategies are widely used.

Age based Selection

In Age-Based Selection, we don't have a notion of a fitness. It is based on the premise that each individual is allowed in the population for a finite generation where it is allowed to reproduce, after that, it is kicked out of the population no matter how good its fitness is.

For instance, in the following example, the age is the number of generations for which the individual has been in the population. The oldest members of the population i.e. P4 and P7 are kicked out of the population and the ages of the rest of the members are incremented by one.

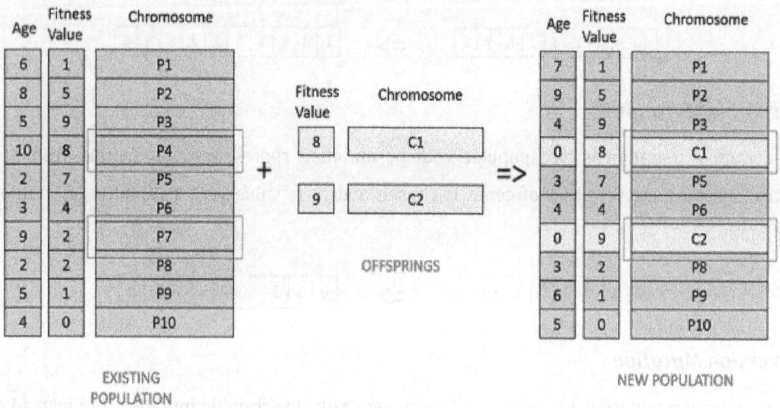

Fitness based Selection

In this fitness based selection, the children tend to replace the least fit individuals in the population. The selection of the least fit individuals may be done using a variation of any of the selection policies described before – tournament selection, fitness proportionate selection, etc.

For example, in the following image, the children replace the least fit individuals P1 and P10 of the population. It is to be noted that since P1 and P9 have the same fitness value, the decision to remove which individual from the population is arbitrary.

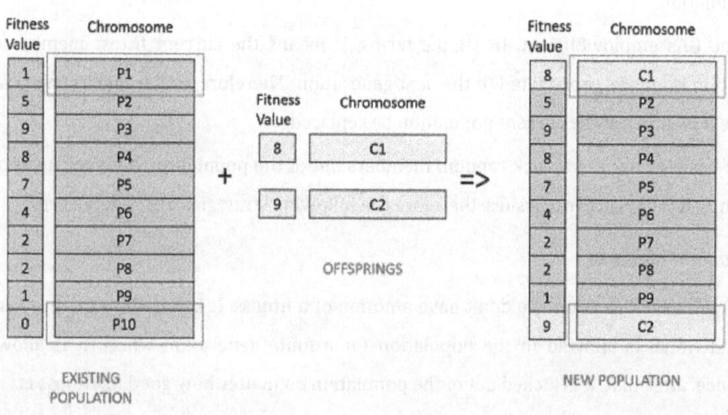

Genetic Algorithms - Termination Condition

The termination condition of a Genetic Algorithm is important in determining when a GA run will end. It has been observed that initially, the GA progresses very fast with better solutions coming in every few iterations, but this tends to saturate in the later stages where the improvements are very small. We usually want a termination condition such that our solution is close to the optimal, at the end of the run.

Usually, we keep one of the following termination conditions:

- When there has been no improvement in the population for X iterations.
- When we reach an absolute number of generations.
- When the objective function value has reached a certain pre-defined value.

For example, in a genetic algorithm we keep a counter which keeps track of the generations for which there has been no improvement in the population. Initially, we set this counter to zero. Each time we don't generate off-springs which are better than the individuals in the population, we increment the counter.

However, if the fitness any of the off-springs is better, then we reset the counter to zero. The algorithm terminates when the counter reaches a predetermined value.

Like other parameters of a GA, the termination condition is also highly problem specific and the GA designer should try out various options to see what suits his particular problem the best.

Models of Lifetime Adaptation

Till now in this tutorial, whatever we have discussed corresponds to the Darwinian model of evolution - natural selection and genetic variation through recombination and mutation. In nature, only the information contained in the individual's genotype can be transmitted to the next generation. This is the approach which we have been following in the tutorial so far.

However, other models of lifetime adaptation - **Lamarckian Model** and **Baldwinian Model** also do exist. It is to be noted that whichever model is the best, is open for debate and the results obtained by researchers show that the choice of lifetime adaptation is highly problem specific.

Often, we hybridize a GA with local search - like in Memetic Algorithms. In such cases, one might choose do go with either Lamarckian or Baldwinian Model to decide what to do with individuals generated after the local search.

10.6. Lamarckian Model

The Lamarckian Model essentially says that the traits which an individual acquires in his/her lifetime can be passed on to its offspring. It is named after French biologist Jean-Baptiste Lamarck.

Even though, natural biology has completely disregarded Lamarckism as we all know that only the information in the genotype can be transmitted. However, from a computation view point, it has been shown that adopting the Lamarckian model gives good results for some of the problems.

In the Lamarckian model, a local search operator examines the neighborhood (acquiring new traits), and if a better chromosome is found, it becomes the offspring.

Baldwinian Model

The Baldwinian model is an intermediate idea named after James Mark Baldwin (1896). In the Baldwin model, the chromosomes can encode a tendency of learning beneficial behaviors. This means, that unlike the Lamarckian model, we don't transmit the acquired traits to the next generation, and neither do we completely ignore the acquired traits like in the Darwinian Model.

The Baldwin Model is in the middle of these two extremes, wherein the tendency of an individual to acquire certain traits is encoded rather than the traits themselves.

In this Baldwinian Model, a local search operator examines the neighborhood (acquiring new traits), and if a better chromosome is found, it only assigns the improved fitness to the chromosome and does not modify the chromosome itself. The change in fitness signifies the chromosomes capability to "acquire the trait", even though it is not passed directly to the future generations.

Effective Implementation

GAs are very general in nature, and just applying them to any optimization problem wouldn't give good results. In this section, we describe a few points which would help and assist a GA designer or GA implementer in their work.

Introduce Problem-specific Domain Knowledge

It has been observed that the more problem-specific domain knowledge we incorporate into the GA; the better objective values we get. Adding problem specific information can be done by either using problem specific crossover or mutation operators, custom representations, etc.

The following image shows Michalewicz's (1990) view of the EA:

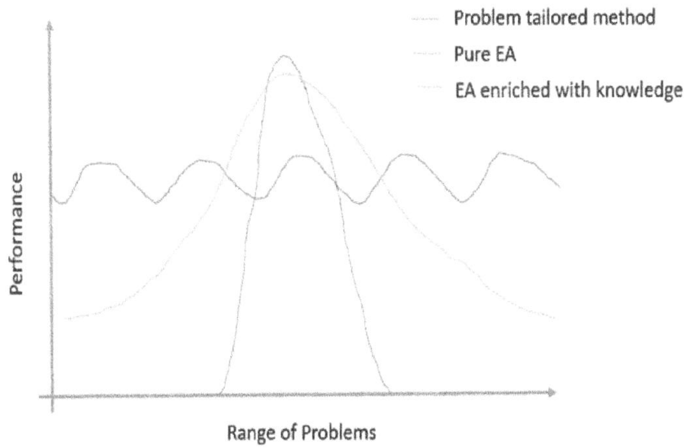

Fig. 10.14: Michalewicz's (1990) View of the EA

Reduce Crowding

Crowding happens when a highly fit chromosome gets to reproduce a lot, and in a few generations, the entire population is filled with similar solutions having similar fitness. This reduces diversity which is a very crucial element to ensure the success of a GA. There are numerous ways to limit crowding.

Some of them are:

- **Mutation** to introduce diversity.
- Switching to **rank selection** and **tournament selection** which have more selection pressure than fitness proportionate selection for individuals with similar fitness.
- **Fitness Sharing** – In this an individual's fitness is reduced if the population already contains similar individuals.

Randomization Helps!

It has been experimentally observed that the best solutions are driven by randomized chromosomes as they impart diversity to the population. The GA implementer should be careful to keep sufficient amount of randomization and diversity in the population for the best results.

Hybridize GA with Local Search

Local search refers to checking the solutions in the neighborhood of a given solution to look for better objective values.

It may be sometimes useful to hybridize the GA with local search. The following image shows the various places in which local search can be introduced in a GA.

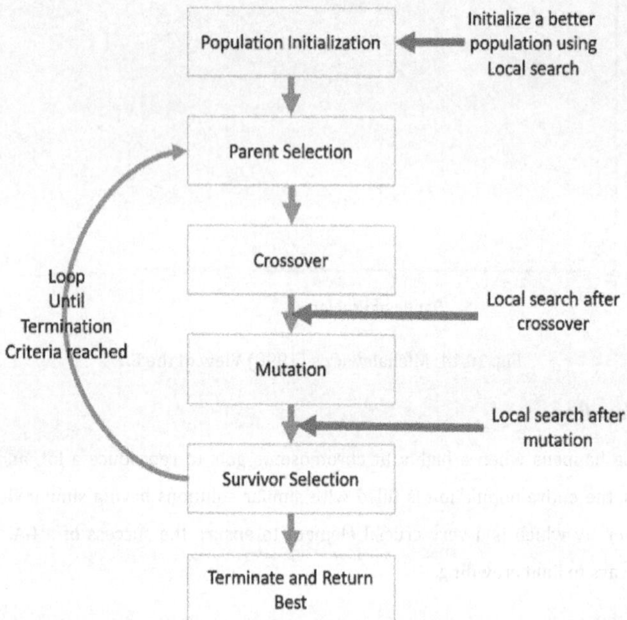

Fig. 10.15: The Various Places in which Local Search can be Introduced in a GA

Variation of Parameters and Techniques

In genetic algorithms, there is no "one size fits all" or a magic formula which works for all problems. Even after the initial GA is ready, it takes a lot of time and effort to play around with the parameters like population size, mutation and crossover probability etc. to find the ones which suit the particular problem.

Genetic Algorithms - Advanced Topics

In this section, we introduce some advanced topics in Genetic Algorithms. A reader looking for just an introduction to GAs may choose to skip this section.

Constrained Optimization Problems

Constrained Optimization Problems are those optimization problems in which we have to maximize or minimize a given objective function value that is subject to certain constraints. Therefore, not all results in the solution space are feasible, and the solution space contains feasible regions as shown in the following image.

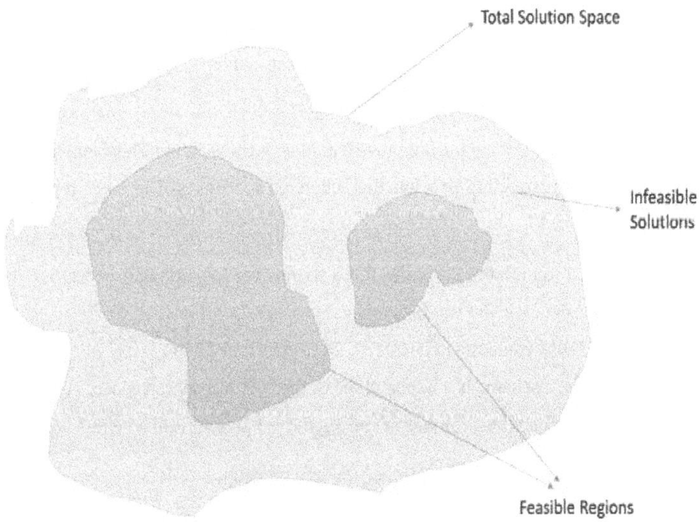

Fig. 10.16: Feasible Regions

In such a scenario, crossover and mutation operators might give us solutions which are infeasible. Therefore, additional mechanisms have to be employed in the GA when dealing with constrained Optimization Problems.

Some of the most common methods are:

- Using **penalty functions** which reduces the fitness of infeasible solutions, preferably so that the fitness is reduced in proportion with the number of constraints violated or the distance from the feasible region.
- Using **repair functions** which take an infeasible solution and modify it so that the violated constraints get satisfied.
- **Not allowing infeasible solutions** to enter into the population at all.
- Use a **special representation or decoder functions** that ensures feasibility of the solutions.

Basic Theoretical Background

In this section, we will discuss about the Schema and NFL theorem along with the building block hypothesis.

Schema Theorem

Researchers have been trying to figure out the mathematics behind the working of genetic algorithms, and Holland's Schema Theorem is a step in that direction. Over the year's various improvements and suggestions have been done to the Schema Theorem to make it more general.

In this section, we don't delve into the mathematics of the Schema Theorem, rather we try to develop a basic understanding of what the Schema Theorem is. The basic terminology to know are as follows:

- A **Schema** is a "template". Formally, it is a string over the alphabet = {0,1,*},
  Where * is don't care and can take any value.
  Therefore, *10*1 could mean 01001, 01011, 11001, or 11011
  Geometrically, a schema is a hyper-plane in the solution search space.
- **Order** of a schema is the number of specified fixed positions in a gene.

Schema	Order
***	0
101	3
*11	2
1**	1

- **Defining length** is the distance between the two furthest fixed symbols in the gene.

Schema	Defining Length
****	0
11	1
1*0*	2
1111	3

The schema theorem states that this schema with above average fitness, short defining length and lower order is more likely to survive crossover and mutation.

Building Block Hypothesis

Building Blocks are low order, low defining length schemata with the above given average fitness. The building block hypothesis says that such building blocks serve as a foundation for the GAs success and adaptation in GAs as it progresses by successively identifying and recombining such "building blocks".

No Free Lunch (NFL) Theorem

Wolpert and Macready in 1997 published a paper titled "No Free Lunch Theorems for Optimization." It essentially states that if we average over the space of all possible problems, then all non-revisiting black box algorithms will exhibit the same performance.

It means that the more we understand a problem, our GA becomes more problem specific and gives better performance, but it makes up for that by performing poorly for other problems.

GA based Machine Learning

Genetic Algorithms also find application in Machine Learning. **Classifier systems** are a form of **genetics-based machine learning** (GBML) system that are frequently used in the field of machine learning. GBML methods are a niche approach to machine learning.

There are two categories of GBML systems:

- **The Pittsburg Approach** – In this approach, one chromosome encoded one solution, and so fitness is assigned to solutions.
- **The Michigan Approach** – One solution is typically represented by many chromosomes and so fitness is assigned to partial solutions.

It should be kept in mind that the standard issue like crossover, mutation, Lamarckian or Darwinian, etc. are also present in the GBML systems.

Genetic Algorithms - Application Areas

Genetic Algorithms are primarily used in optimization problems of various kinds, but they are frequently used in other application areas as well.

In this section, we list some of the areas in which Genetic Algorithms are frequently used. These are:

- **Optimization** – Genetic Algorithms are most commonly used in optimization problems wherein we have to maximize or minimize a given objective function value under a given set of constraints. The approach to solve Optimization problems has been highlighted throughout the tutorial.

- **Economics** – GAs are also used to characterize various economic models like the cobweb model, game theory equilibrium resolution, asset pricing, etc.
- **Neural Networks** – GAs are also used to train neural networks, particularly recurrent neural networks.
- **Parallelization** – GAs also have very good parallel capabilities, and prove to be very effective means in solving certain problems, and also provide a good area for research.
- **Image Processing** – GAs are used for various digital image processing (DIP) tasks as well like dense pixel matching.
- **Vehicle routing problems** – With multiple soft time windows, multiple depots and a heterogeneous fleet.
- **Scheduling applications** – GAs are used to solve various scheduling problems as well, particularly the time tabling problem.
- **Machine Learning** – As already discussed, genetics based machine learning (GBML) is a niche area in machine learning.
- **Robot Trajectory Generation** – GAs have been used to plan the path which a robot arm takes by moving from one point to another.
- **Parametric Design of Aircraft** – GAs have been used to design aircrafts by varying the parameters and evolving better solutions.
- **DNA Analysis** – GAs have been used to determine the structure of DNA using spectrometric data about the sample.
- **Multimodal Optimization** – GAs are obviously very good approaches for multimodal optimization in which we have to find multiple optimum solutions.
- **Traveling salesman problem and its applications** – GAs have been used to solve the TSP, which is a well-known combinatorial problem using novel crossover and packing strategies.

Why Use Genetic Algorithms

- They are Robust.
- Provide optimisation over large space state.
- Unlike traditional AI, they do not break on slight change in input or presence of noise.

Application of Genetic Algorithms

- Genetic algorithms have many applications, some of them are:
- Recurrent Neural Network

- Mutation testing
- Code breaking
- Filtering and signal processing
- Learning fuzzy rule base etc

10.7. Understanding Hypothesis Space Search

In most supervised machine learning algorithm, our main goal is to find out a possible hypothesis from the hypothesis space that could possibly map out the inputs to the proper outputs.

The following figure shows the common method to find out the possible hypothesis from the Hypothesis space:

PRODUCING FINAL HYPOTHESIS

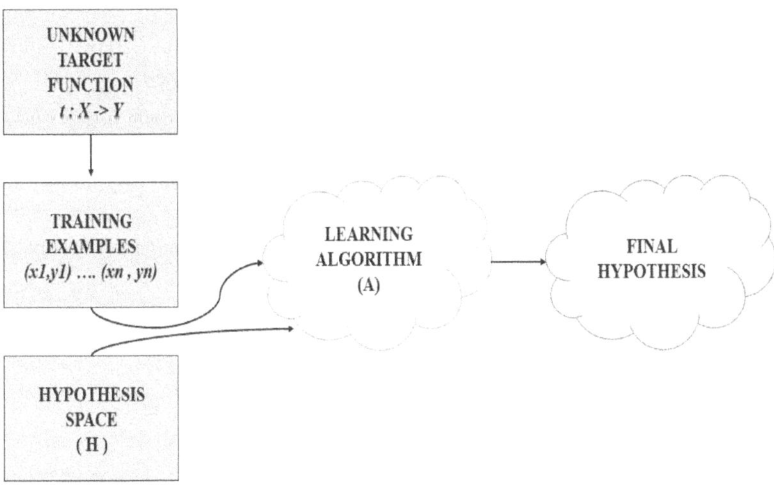

Fig. 10.17: Hypothesis Space

Hypothesis Space (H)

Hypothesis space is the set of all the possible legal hypothesis. This is the set from which the machine learning algorithm would determine the best possible (only one) which would best describe the target function or the outputs.

Hypothesis (h)

A hypothesis is a function that best describes the target in supervised machine learning. The hypothesis that an algorithm would come up depends upon the data and also depends upon the restrictions and bias that we have imposed on the data. To better understand the Hypothesis Space and Hypothesis consider the following coordinate that shows the distribution of some data:

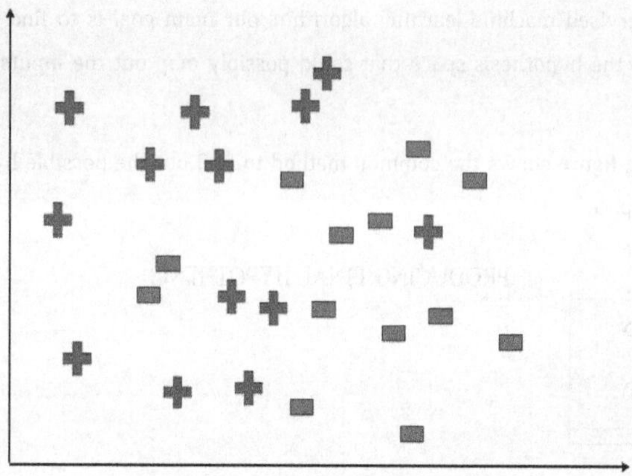

Fig. 10.18: Shows Distribution of Data

Say suppose we have test data for which we have to determine the outputs or results. The test data is as shown below.

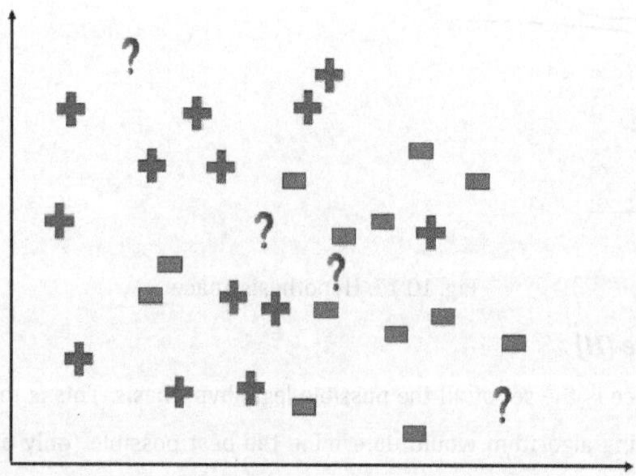

Fig. 10.19: Shows the Test Data

We can predict the outcomes by dividing the coordinate as shown below.

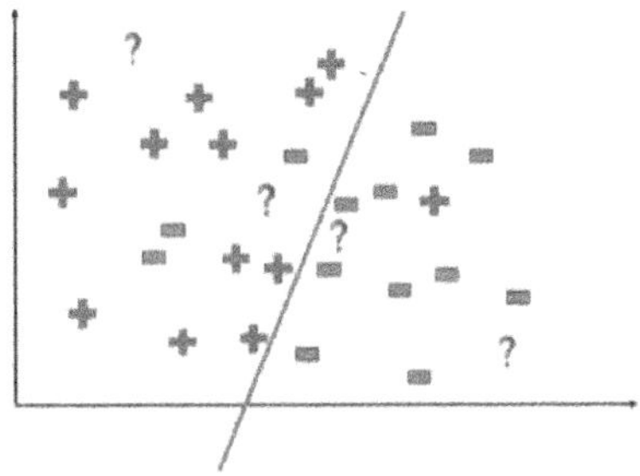

Fig. 10.20: Shows the Output After Classification Data

So the test data would yield the following result:

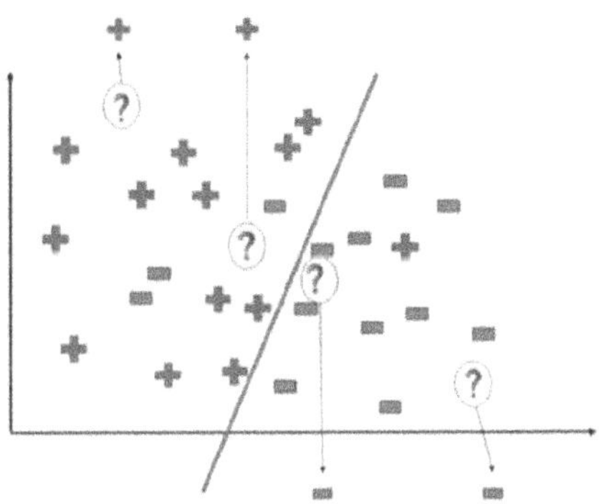

But note here that we could have divided the coordinate plane as:

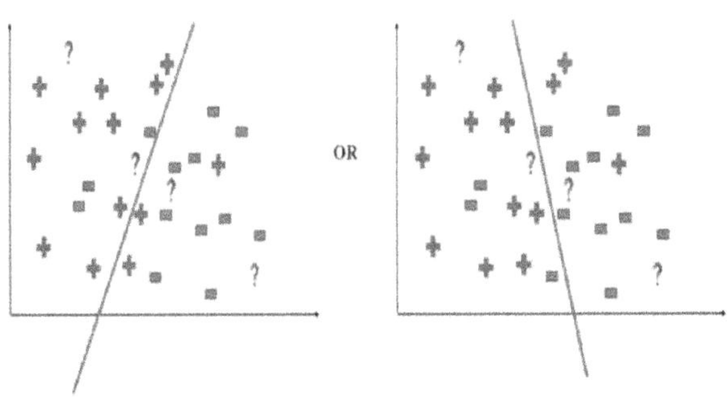

The way in which the coordinate would be divided depends on the data, algorithm and constraints.

- All these legal possible ways in which we can divide the coordinate plane to predict the outcome of the test data composes of the Hypothesis Space.
- Each individual possible way is known as the hypothesis.

Hence, in this example the hypothesis space would be like:

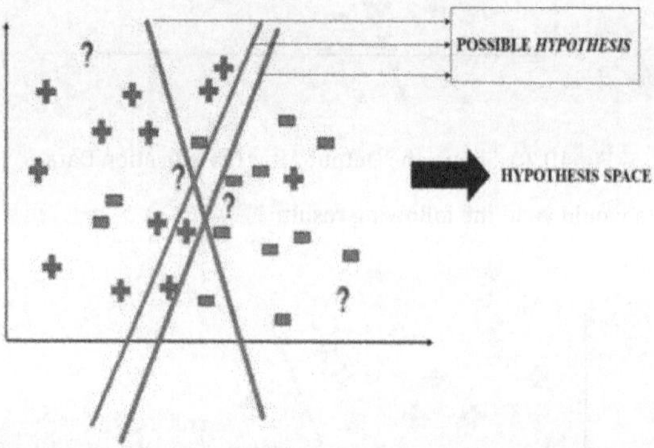

Fig. 10.21: Shows Possible Hypothesis

Hypothesis Space Search

- Randomized beam search method to seek maximally fit hypothesis.
- GAs vs. Backprop - GD moves smoothly from one hypothesis to a new one which is very similar.
- GAs move much more abruptly - replacing a parent with an offspring that maybe radically different.
- GA is therefore less likely to fall into the same kind of local minima that plague GD.
- GAs have their own problems – Crowding.

10.8. Simple Genetic Algorithm (SGA)

Introduction

Simple Genetic Algorithm (SGA) is one of the three types of strategies followed in Genetic algorithm.

1. SGA starts with the creation of an initial population of size N.
2. Then, we evaluate the goodness/fitness of each of the solutions/individuals.

After that, the convergence criterion is checked, if it meets then we converge the algorithm otherwise go for the next steps:

1. Select Np individuals from the previous population.
2. Create the mating pool randomly.
3. Perform Crossover.
4. Perform Mutation in offspring solutions.
5. Perform inversion in offspring solutions.
6. Replace the old solutions of the last generation with the newly created solutions and go to step (2).

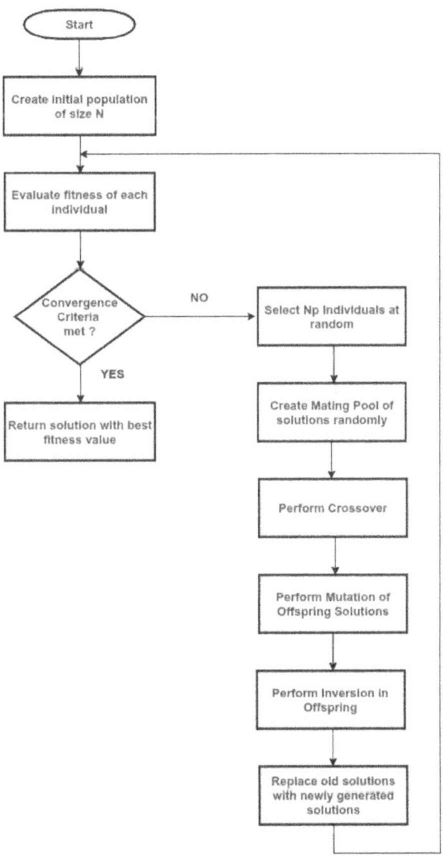

Fig. 10.22: Shows Simple Genetic Algorithm Block Diagram

Important Parameters While Solving Problems in Simple Genetic Algorithm

1. Initial Population N
2. Mating pool size Np
3. Convergence threshold
4. Crossover
5. Mutation
6. Inversion

Features

7. Computationally Expensive.
8. Biased towards more highly fit individuals.
9. Performs well when the initial population is large enough.

Applications

10. Learning robot behaviour using Simple Genetic Algorithm.
11. In the finance industry.
12. Neural networks.
13. Soft computing Applications like Fuzzy logic, Neuro computing.
14. Optimization problems.

10.9. Genetic Programming (GP)

In artificial intelligence, **genetic programming (GP)** is a technique of evolving programs, starting from a population of unfit (usually random) programs, fit for a particular task by applying operations analogous to natural genetic processes to the population of programs.

The operations are: selection of the fittest programs for reproduction (crossover) and mutation according to a predefined fitness measure, usually proficiency at the desired task. The crossover operation involves swapping random parts of selected pairs (parents) to produce new and different offspring that become part of the new generation of programs. Mutation involves substitution of some random part of a program with some other random part of a program. Some programs not selected for reproduction are copied from the current generation to the new generation. Then the selection and other operations are recursively applied to the new generation of programs.

Typically, members of each new generation are on average more fit than the members of the previous generation, and the best-of-generation program is often better than the best-of-generation programs from previous generations. Termination of the recursion is when some individual program reaches a predefined proficiency or fitness level.

It may and often does happen that a particular run of the algorithm results in premature convergence to some local maximum which is not a globally optimal or even good solution. Multiple runs (dozens to hundreds) are usually necessary to produce a very good result. It may also be necessary to increase the starting population size and variability of the individuals to avoid pathologies.

Program Representation

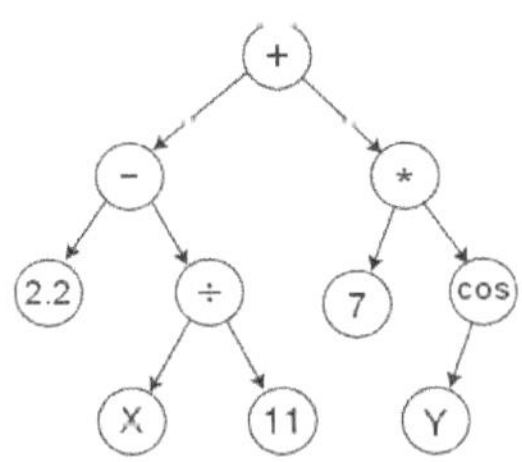

$$\left(2.2 - \left(\frac{X}{11}\right)\right) + \left(7 * \cos(Y)\right)$$

A function represented as a tree structure.

Genetic Representation

GP evolves computer programs, traditionally represented in memory as tree structures Trees can be easily evaluated in a recursive manner. Every tree node has an operator function and every terminal node has an operand, making mathematical expressions easy to evolve and evaluate. Thus traditionally GP favors the use of programming languages that naturally embody tree structures (for example, Lisp; other functional programming languages are also suitable).

Non-tree representations have been suggested and successfully implemented, such as linear genetic programming which suits the more traditional imperative languages. The commercial GP software Discipulus uses automatic induction of binary machine code ("AIM") to achieve better performance. μGPuses directed multigraphs to generate programs that fully exploit the syntax of a given assembly language. Multi expression programming uses Three-address code for encoding solutions. Other program representations on which significant research and development have been conducted include programs for stack-based virtual machines, [33] [34] [35] and sequences of integers that are mapped to arbitrary programming languages via grammars. Cartesian genetic programming is another form of GP, which uses a graph representation instead of the usual tree based representation to encode computer programs.

Most representations have structurally noneffective code (introns). Such non-coding genes may seem to be useless because they have no effect on the performance of any one individual. However, they alter the probabilities of generating different offspring under the variation operators, and thus alter the individual's variational properties. Experiments seem to show faster convergence when using program representations that allow such non-coding genes, compared to program representations that do not have any non-coding genes.

Selection

Selection is a process whereby certain individuals are selected from the current generation that would serve as parents for the next generation. The individuals are selected probabilistically such that the better performing individuals have a higher chance of getting selected. The most commonly used selection method in GP is tournament selection, although other methods such as fitness proportionate selection, lexicase selection, and others have been demonstrated to perform better for many GP problems.

Elitism, which involves seeding the next generation with the best individual (or best *n* individuals) from the current generation, is a technique sometimes employed to avoid regression.

Crossover

In Genetic Programming two fit individuals are chosen from the population to be parents for one or two children. In tree genetic programming, these parents are represented as inverted lisp like trees, with their root nodes at the top. In subtree crossover in each parent a subtree is randomly chosen. (Highlighted with yellow in the animation.) In the root donating parent (in the animation on the left) the chosen subtree is removed and replaced with a copy of the randomly chosen subtree from the other parent, to give a new child tree. Sometimes two child crossover is used, in which case the removed subtree (in the animation on the left) is not simply deleted but is copied to a copy of the second parent (here on the right) replacing (in the copy) its randomly chosen subtree. Thus this type of subtree crossover takes two fit trees and generates two child trees.

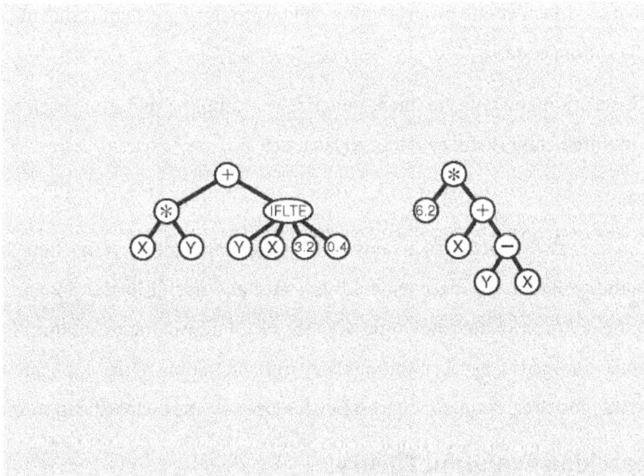

Mutation

There are many types of mutation in genetic programming. They start from a fit syntactically correct parent and aim to randomly create a syntactically correct child. In the animation a subtree is randomly chosen (highlighted by yellow). It is removed and replaced by a randomly generated subtree.

Other mutation operators select a leaf (external node) of the tree and replace it with a randomly chosen leaf. Another mutation is to select at random a function (internal node) and replace it with another function with the same arity (number of inputs). Hoist mutation randomly chooses a subtree and replaces it with a subtree within itself. Thus hoist mutation is guaranteed to make the child smaller. Leaf and same arity function replacement ensure the child is the same size as the parent. Whereas subtree mutation (in the animation) may, depending upon the function and terminal sets, have a bias to either increase or decrease the tree size. Other subtree based mutations try to carefully control the size of the replacement subtree and thus the size of the child tree. Fig. Shows mutation.

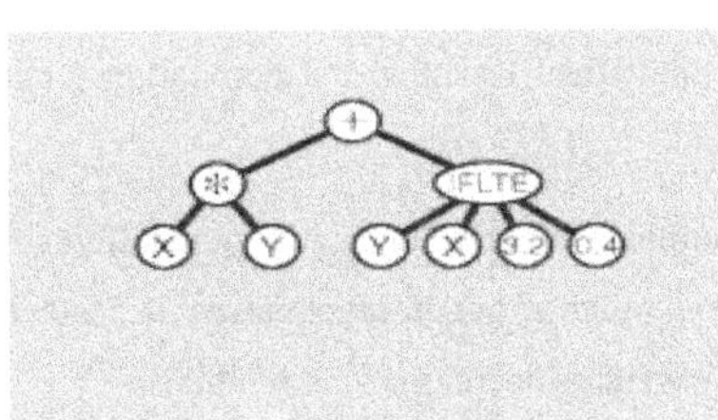

Animation of creating genetic programming child by mutating parent removing subtree and replacing with random code.

Similarly there are many types of linear genetic programming mutation, each of which tries to ensure the mutated child is still syntactically correct.

Applications

GP has been successfully used as an automatic programming tool, a machine learning tool and an automatic problem-solving engine. GP is especially useful in the domains where the exact form of the solution is not known in advance or an approximate solution is acceptable (possibly because finding the exact solution is very difficult). Some of the applications of GP are curve fitting, data modeling, symbolic regression, feature selection, classification, etc.

10.10. Lamarckian Evolution Theory

Lamarckian Evolution Theory

The Lamarckian theory states the characteristic individual acquire during their lifetime pass them to their children. This theory is named after French biologist Jean Baptiste Lamarck. According to Lamarck's theory, learning is an important part of the evolution of species (or for our purpose in the Evolutionary algorithm). This theory is discredited in a biological context but can be used in genetic algorithms in machine learning.

Baldwin Effect

Baldwin proposed that individual learning can explain evolutionary phenomena that appear to require Lamarckian inheritance of acquired characteristics. The ability of individuals to learn can guide the evolutionary process. In effect, learning smooths the fitness landscape, thus facilitating evolution.

Baldwin Effect is first demonstrated by Hinton and Nolan in the context of machine learning in 1987. They take simple Neural Networks (NNs). In one experiment they take NNs of fixed weights while other NNs set to trainable. They concluded that,

- When there is no individual learning, the population (collection of NNs) failed to improve over time.
- When learning is applied in early stages, the population contains many individuals with many trainable weights, but in later stages, it achieved high fitness with the number of trainable weights decreases in individuals.

G-prop Algorithm

G-Prop is an evolutionary hybrid algorithm. It is a hybrid of Backpropagation (BP) and Multi-layer Perceptron (MLP). Below is the G-Prop algorithm.

- Generate the initial model with random weight values and hidden layer sizes uniformly distributed from 2 to a maximum of a given value.
- For G generations:

Evaluate the new individuals: train them using the training set and obtain their fitness according to the number of correct classifications on the validation set and the hidden layer size.

Select the n best individuals in the population based on the value fitness function and combine them, using mutation, crossover, addition, elimination, and substitution of hidden neurons.

Replace the n worst individuals by the new individuals.

Use the best individuals on the test set to obtain a testing error.

Fitness Function: The fitness function is defined as the ability to classify/approximate the validation set to segregate the best individual while training for each generation. In the case of two individuals having the same fitness function, the individual with the lowest hidden layer parameter terms better because the number of parameters is proportional to the speed of training.

The Lamarckian approach uses no special fitness function, instead, it uses a local search genetic operator (similar to Quick Propagation) that is designed to improve the individuals, saving the individual trained weights back to the population.

For the Baldwin effect, the process of using fitness function is followed:

In the first step, we calculate the classification/ approximation ability of an individual on the validation set before training.

Then it is trained and its ability is calculated using the following criteria:

The best individual (MLP/ANN) is that with higher classification/approximation ability after training.

If both MLPs show the same accuracy. Then the best is that whose classification/ approximation ability before training is higher, this is because the intuition is that the MLP is more likely to have high accuracy when trained again.

If both MLPs has equal accuracy before and after training, then the best model is the smaller (the model which has less trainable parameters).

10.11. Additional Explanation

Genetic Algorithm

A genetic algorithm is a search-based algorithm used for solving optimization problems in machine learning. This algorithm is important because it solves difficult problems that would take a long time to solve. It has been used in various real-life applications such as data center, electronic circuit design, code-breaking, image processing, and artificial creativity.

This article will take the reader through the basics of this algorithm and explains how it works. It also explains how it has been applied in various fields and highlights some of its limitations.

Motivation

Genetic Algorithm (GA) Explained

The following are some of the basic terminologies that can help us to understand genetic algorithms:

- **Population:** This is a subset of all the probable solutions that can solve the given problem.
- **Chromosomes:** A chromosome is one of the solutions in the population.
- **Gene:** This is an element in a chromosome.
- **Allele:** This is the value given to a gene in a specific chromosome.
- **Fitness function:** This is a function that uses a specific input to produce an improved output. The solution is used as the input while the output is in the form of solution suitability.
- **Genetic operators:** In genetic algorithms, the best individuals mate to reproduce an offspring that is better than the parents. Genetic operators are used for changing the genetic composition of this next generation.

A genetic algorithm (GA) is a heuristic search algorithm used to solve search and optimization problems. This algorithm is a subset of evolutionary algorithms, which are used in computation. Genetic algorithms employ the concept of genetics and natural selection to provide solutions to problems.

These algorithms have better intelligence than random search algorithms because they use historical data to take the search to the best performing region within the solution space.

GAs are also based on the behavior of chromosomes and their genetic structure. Every chromosome plays the role of providing a possible solution. The fitness function helps in providing the characteristics of all individuals within the population. The greater the function, the better the solution.

Advantages of Genetic Algorithm

- It has excellent parallel capabilities.
- It can optimize various problems such as discrete functions, multi-objective problems, and continuous functions.
- It provides answers that improve over time.
- A genetic algorithm does not need derivative information.

How Genetic Algorithms Work

Genetic algorithms use the evolutionary generational cycle to produce high-quality solutions. They use various operations that increase or replace the population to provide an improved fit solution.

Genetic algorithms follow the following phases to solve complex optimization problems.

Initialization

The genetic algorithm starts by generating an initial population. This initial population consists of all the probable solutions to the given problem. The most popular technique for initialization is the use of random binary strings.

Fitness Assignment

The fitness function helps in establishing the fitness of all individuals in the population. It assigns a fitness score to every individual, which further determines the probability of being chosen for reproduction. The higher the fitness score, the higher the chances of being chosen for reproduction.

Selection

In this phase, individuals are selected for the reproduction of offspring. The selected individuals are then arranged in pairs of two to enhance reproduction. These individuals pass on their genes to the next generation.

The main objective of this phase is to establish the region with high chances of generating the best solution to the problem (better than the previous generation). The genetic algorithm uses the fitness proportionate selection technique to ensure that useful solutions are used for recombination.

Reproduction

This phase involves the creation of a child population. The algorithm employs variation operators that are applied to the parent population. The two main operators in this phase include crossover and mutation.

1. **Crossover:** This operator swaps the genetic information of two parents to reproduce an offspring. It is performed on parent pairs that are selected randomly to generate a child population of equal size as the parent population.
2. **Mutation:** This operator adds new genetic information to the new child population. This is achieved by flipping some bits in the chromosome. Mutation solves the problem of local minimum and enhances diversification. The following image shows how mutation is done.

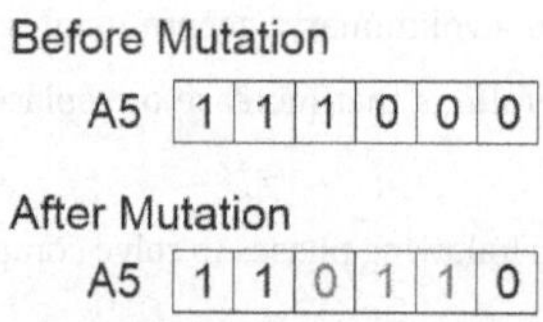

Replacement

Generational replacement takes place in this phase, which is a replacement of the old population with the new child population. The new population consists of higher fitness scores than the old population, which is an indication that an improved solution has been generated.

Termination

After replacement has been done, a stopping criterion is used to provide the basis for termination. The algorithm will terminate after the threshold fitness solution has been attained. It will identify this solution as the best solution in the population.

Application Areas

Genetic algorithms are applied in the following fields:

- **Transport:** Genetic algorithms are used in the traveling salesman problem to develop transport plans that reduce the cost of travel and the time taken. They are also used to develop an efficient way of delivering products.
- **DNA Analysis:** They are used in DNA analysis to establish the DNA structure using spectrometric information.

- **Multimodal Optimization:** They are used to provide multiple optimum solutions in multimodal optimization problems.
- **Aircraft Design:** They are used to develop parametric aircraft designs. The parameters of the aircraft are modified and upgraded to provide better designs.
- **Economics:** They are used in economics to describe various models such as the game theory, cobweb model, asset pricing, and schedule optimization.

Limitations of Genetic Algorithms

- They are not effective in solving simple problems.
- Lack of proper implementation may make the algorithm converge to a solution that is not optimal.
- The quality of the final solution is not guaranteed.
- Repetitive calculation of fitness values may make some problems to experience computational challenges.

Genetic Algorithm

The problem addressed by GAS is to search a space of candidate hypotheses to identify the best hypothesis. In GAS the "best hypothesis" is defined as the one that optimizes a predefined numerical measure for the problem at hand, called the hypothesis ***Fitness.***

For example,

- If the learning task is the problem of approximating an unknown function given training examples of its input and output, then fitness could be defined as the accuracy of the hypothesis over this training data.
- If the task is to learn a strategy for playing chess, fitness could be defined as the number of games won by the individual when playing against other individuals in the current population.

A Genetic Algorithm

Fitness: A function that assigns an evaluation score, given a hypothesis.

Fitness-threshold: A threshold specifying the termination criterion.

p: The number of hypotheses to be included in the population.

r: The fraction of the population to be replaced by Crossover at each step.

m: The mutation rate.

- Initialize population: P ←Generate **p** hypotheses at random.
- Evaluate: For each h in P, compute Fitness(h)'.
- While [max Fitness(h)]<Fitness-threshold do.

  h

Create a new generation, Ps:

1. **Select:** Probabilistically select (1-r) p members of P to add to Ps. The probability Pr(hi) of selecting hypothesis hi from P is given by,

$$\mathbf{Pr}(h_i) = \frac{\boldsymbol{Fitness}(h_i)}{\sum_{j=1}^{p} \boldsymbol{Fitness}(h_j)}$$

2. **Crossover:** Probabilistically select pairs of hypotheses from P, according to &(hi) given above. For each pair, (hl, h2), produce two offspring by applying the Crossover operator. Add all offspring to Ps.
3. **Mutate:** Choose m percent of the members of P, with uniform probability. For each, invert one randomly selected bit in its representation.
4. **Update:** P ←Ps.
5. **Evaluate:** for each h in P, compute Fitness(h)
   - Return the hypothesis from P that has the highest fitness.

Note

*A prototypical genetic algorithm. A population containing **p** hypotheses is maintained. On each iteration, the successor population **Ps** is formed by probabilistically selecting current hypotheses according to their fitness and by adding new hypotheses. New hypotheses are created by applying a crossover operator to pairs of most fit hypotheses and by creating single point mutations in the resulting generation of hypotheses. This process is iterated until sufficiently fit hypotheses are discovered. Typical crossover and mutation operators are defined in a subsequent table.*

Representing Hypothesis

Hypotheses in GAs are often represented by bit strings, so that they can be easily manipulated by genetic operators such as mutation and crossover. The hypotheses represented by these bit strings can be quite complex. For example, sets of if-then rules can easily be represented in this way, by choosing an encoding of rules that allocates specific substrings for each rule precondition and post condition.

To see how if-then rules can be encoded by bit strings, first consider how we might use a bit string to describe a constraint on the value of a single attribute.

- To pick an example, consider the attribute ***Outlook,*** which can take on any of the three values ***Sunny, Overcast,*** or ***Rain.***
- One obvious way to represent a constraint on ***Outlook*** is to use a bit string of length three, in which each bit position corresponds to one of its three possible values.
- Placing a 1 in some position indicates that the attribute is allowed to take on the corresponding value. For example, the string 010represents the constraint that ***Outlook*** must take on the second of these values, or ***Outlook* = *Overcast.***
- Similarly, the string 011 represents the more general constraint that allows two possible values, or ***(Outlook* = *Overcast v Rain).***
- Note 111 represents the most general possible constraint, indicating that we don't care which of its possible values the attribute takes on.

Given this method for representing constraints on a single attribute, conjunctions of constraints on multiple attributes can easily be represented by concatenating the corresponding bit strings.

For Example

- Consider a second attribute, ***Wind,*** that can take on the value ***Strong*** or ***Weak.***
- *A* rule precondition such as ***(Outlook* = *Overcast*** V ***Rain) A (Wind* = *Strong)*** can then be represented by the following bit string of length five:

Outlook	***Wind***
011	10

- Rule post conditions (such as ***PlayTennis*= *yes)*** can be represented in a similar fashion. Thus, an entire rule can be described by concatenating the bit strings describing the rule preconditions, together with the bit string describing the rule post condition.
- For example, the rule
  - ***IF Wind* = *Strong*** THEN ***PlayTennis*= *yes***
  - Would be represented by the string

Outlook	***Wind***	***PlayTennis***
111	10	10

- Where the first three bits describe the "don't care" constraint on ***Outlook,*** the next two bits describe the constraint on ***Wind,*** and the final two bits describe the rule post condition (here we assume ***PlayTennis*** can take on the values ***Yes*** or ***No).***

Genetic Operators

The generation of successors in a GA is determined by a set of operators that recombine and mutate selected members of the current population. The two most common operators are ***crossover*** and ***mutation.***

The ***crossover operator*** produces two new offspring from two parent strings, by copying selected bits from each parent. The bit at position i in each offspring is copied from the bit at position ***I*** in one of the two parents. To illustrate, consider the ***single-point crossover*** operator at the top Consider the topmost of the two offspring in this case. This offspring takes its first five bits from the first parent and its remaining six bits from the second parent, because the crossover mask 11 11 1000000 specifies these choices for each of the bit positions. The second offspring uses the same crossover mask, but switches the roles of the two parents. Therefore, it contains the bits that were not used by the first offspring. In single-point crossover, the crossover mask is always constructed so that it begins with a string containing ***n*** contiguous Is, followed by the necessary number of 0s to complete the string. This results in offspring in which the first n bits are contributed by one parent and the remaining bits by the second parent.

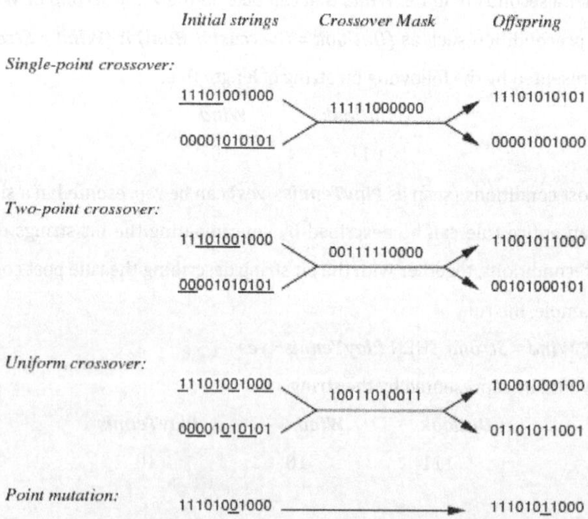

Fitness Function and Selection

The fitness function defines the criterion for ranking potential hypotheses and for probabilistically selecting them for inclusion in the next generation population.

Fitness proportionate selection:

$$\Pr(h_i) = \frac{Fitness(h_i)}{\sum_{j=1}^{p} Fitness(h_j)}$$

Tournament selection:

- Pick h1, h2 at random with uniform prob.
- With probability p, select the more fit.

Rank selection:

- Sort all hypotheses by fitness.
- Probability of selection is proportional to rank.

10.12. An Illustrative Example

To illustrate, consider a hypothesis space in which rule pre conditions are conjunctions of constraints over two Boolean attributes, *a1* and *a2*. The rule post-condition is described by a single bit that indicates the predicted value of the target attribute c. Thus, the hypothesis consisting of the two rules.

$$\text{IF } a_1 = T \wedge a_2 = F \text{ THEN } c = T; \quad \text{IF } a_2 = T \text{ THEN } c = F$$

Would be represented by the string,

$$\begin{array}{cccccc} a_1 & a_2 & c & a_1 & a_2 & c \\ 10 & 01 & 1 & 11 & 10 & 0 \end{array}$$

Note: the length of the bit string grows with the number of rules in the hypothesis.

Hypothesis Space Search

- GA search can move very abruptly (as compared to Backpropagation, for Example), replacing a parent hypothesis by an offspring that may be radically different from the parent.
- The problem of ***Crowding***: when one individual is more fit than others, this individual and closely related one will take up a large fraction of the population.

- ***Solutions:***
    a. Use tournament or rank selection instead of roulette selection.
    b. Fitness sharing.
    c. Restrict ion on the kinds of individuals allowed to recombine to form offsprings.

Genetic Programming

Genetic programming (GP) is a form of evolutionary computation in which the individuals in the evolving population are computer programs rather than bit strings.

Representing Programs

Programs manipulated by a Genetic Program are typically represented by trees corresponding to the parse tree of the program.

Each function call is represented by anode in the tree, and the arguments to the function are given by its descendant nodes. For example, we illustrate this tree representation for the Function to apply genetic programming to a particular domain, the user must define the primitive functions to be considered (e.g., sin, cos, +, -, exponential~), as well as the terminals (e.g., *x*, *y*, constants such as 2). The genetic programming algorithm then uses an evolutionary search to explore the vast space of programs that can be described using these primitives.

$$\sin(x) + \sqrt{x^2 + y}$$

Population of programs represented by trees	**Crossover**
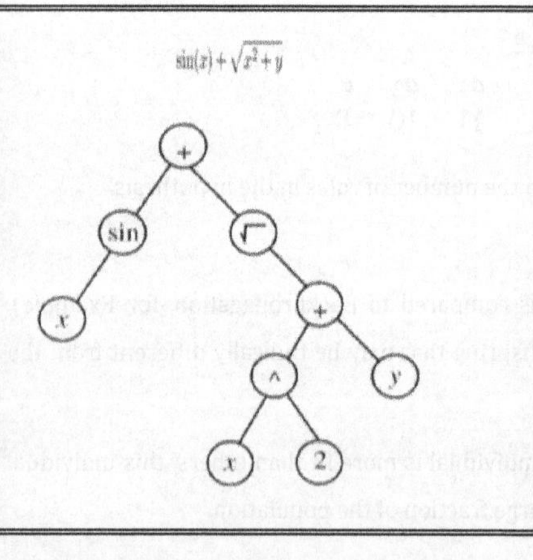	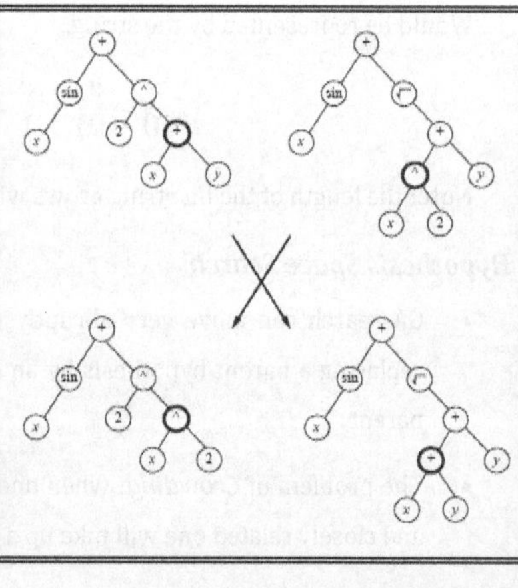

10.13. Illustrative Example

The task is to develop a general algorithm for stacking the blocks into a single stack that spells the word "universal, "independent of the initial configuration of blocks in the world.

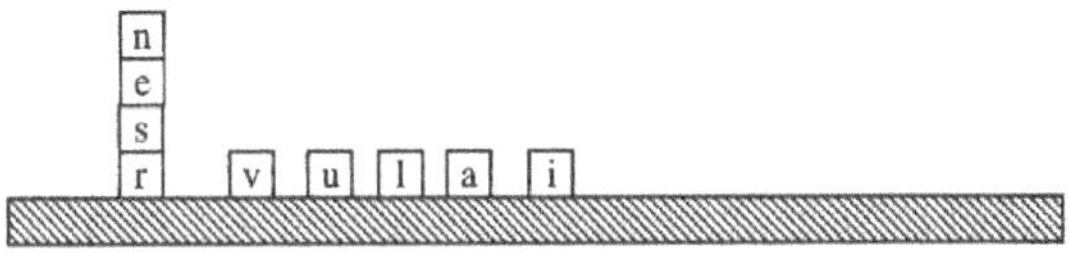

The actions available for manipulating blocks allow moving only a single block at a time. In particular, the top block on the stack can be moved to the table surface, or a block on the table surface can be moved to the top of the stack.

As in most GP applications, the choice of problem representation has a significant impact on the ease of solving the problem. The primitive functions used to compose programs for this task include the following three terminal arguments:

- CS (current stack), which refers to the name of the top block on the stack, or F if there is no current stack.
- TB (top correct block), which refers to the name of the topmost block on the stack, such that it and those blocks beneath it are in the correct order.
- NN (next necessary), which refers to the name of the next block needed above TB in the stack, in order to spell the word "universal," or F if no more blocks are needed.

As can be seen, this particular choice of terminal arguments provides a natural representation for describing programs for manipulating blocks for this task. Imagine, in contrast, the relative difficulty of the task if we were to instead define the terminal arguments to be the x and y coordinates of each block.

In addition to these terminal arguments, the program language in this application included the following primitive functions:

- ***(MS x)*** (move to stack), if block x is on the table, this operator moves x to the top of the stack and returns the value T. Otherwise, it does nothing and returns the value F.
- ***(MT x)*** (move to table), if block x is somewhere in the stack, this moves the block at the top of the stack to the table and returns the value T. Otherwise, it returns the value F.
- ***(EQ x y)*** (equal), which returns T if x equals y, and returns F otherwise.
- ***(NOT x)***, which returns ***T*** if ***x = F***, and returns ***F*** if ***x = T***.
- ***(DU x y)*** (do until), which executes the expression ***x*** repeatedly until expression returns the value ***T***.

To allow the system to evaluate the fitness of any given program, Koza provided a set of 166 training example problems representing a broad variety of initial block configurations, including problems of differing degrees of difficulty.

The fitness of any given program was taken to be the number of these examples solved by the algorithm. The population was initialized to a set of 300 random programs. After 10 generations, the system discovered the following program, which solves all 166 problems.

(EQ (DU (MT CS) (NOT CS)) (DU (MS NN) (NOT NN)))

Notice this program contains a sequence of two DU, or "Do Until" statements. The first repeatedly moves the current top of the stack onto the table, until the stack becomes empty. The second "Do Until" statement then repeatedly moves the next necessary block from the table onto the stack. The role played by the top level EQ expression here is to provide a syntactically legal way to sequence these two "Do Until" loops.

Parallelizing Genetic Algorithm

- GAs are naturally suited to parallel implementation. Different approaches were tried:
    - **Coarse Grain:** subdivides the population into distinct groups of individuals (*demes*) and conducts a GA search in each deme. Transfer between demes occurs (though infrequently) by a migration process in which individuals from one deme are copied or transferred to other demes.
    - **Fine Grain:** One processor is assigned per individual in the population and recombination takes place among neighboring individuals.

Models of Evolution and Learning

- As a kind of evolutionary algorithm, the genetic algorithms allow learning through experience. Basically, new strategies are generated from the previous ones to seek and find new solutions with a better fit.
- Thus, it consists of an optimization of the fitness function through the algorithm's implementation.

Lamarckian Evolution Theory

The Lamarckian theory states the characteristic individual acquire during their lifetime pass them to their children. This theory is named after French biologist Jean Baptiste Lamarck. According to Lamarck's theory, learning is an important part of the evolution of species (or for our purpose in the Evolutionary algorithm). This theory is discredited in a biological context but can be used in genetic algorithms in machine learning.

Fig. 10.23: Evolutionary Algorithm Example

Baldwin Effect

Baldwin proposed that individual learning can explain evolutionary phenomena that appear to require Lamarckian inheritance of acquired characteristics. The ability of individuals to learn can guide the evolutionary process. In effect, learning smoothes the fitness landscape, thus facilitating evolution.

Baldwin Effect is first demonstrated by Hinton and Nolan in the context of machine learning in 1987. They take simple Neural Networks (NNs). In one experiment they take NNs of fixed weights while other NNs set to trainable. They concluded that:

- When there is no individual learning, the population (collection of NNs) failed to improve over time.
- When learning is applied in early stages, the population contains many individuals with many trainable weights, but in later stages, it achieved high fitness with the number of trainable weights decreases in individuals.

G-prop Algorithm

G-Prop is an evolutionary hybrid algorithm. It is a hybrid of Backpropagation (BP) and Multi-layer Perception (MLP). Below is the G-Prop algorithm.

- Generate the initial model with random weight values and hidden layer sizes uniformly distributed from 2 to a maximum of a given value.
- For G generations:
    - Evaluate the new individuals: train them using the training set and obtain their fitness according to the number of correct classifications on the validation set and the hidden layer size.

- Select the *n* best individuals in the population based on the value fitness function and combine them, using mutation, crossover, addition, elimination, and substitution of hidden neurons.
- Replace the *n* worst individuals by the new individuals.

- Use the best individuals on the test set to obtain a testing error.

Fitness Function: The fitness function is defined as the ability to classify/approximate the validation set to segregate the best individual while training for each generation. In the case of two individuals having the same fitness function, the individual with the lowest hidden layer parameter terms better because the number of parameters is proportional to the speed of training.

- The Lamarckian approach uses no special fitness function, instead, it uses a local search genetic operator (similar to Quick Propagation) that is designed to improve the individuals, saving the individual trained weights back to the population.
- For the Baldwin effect, the process of using fitness function is followed:
    - In the first step, we calculate the classification/approximation ability of an individual on the validation set before training.
    - Then it is trained and its ability is calculated using the following criteria:
        - The best individual (MLP/ANN) is that with higher classification/ approximation ability after training.
        - If both MLPs show the same accuracy. Then the best is that whose classification/approximation ability before training is higher, this is because the intuition is that the MLP is more likely to have high accuracy when trained again.
        - If both MLPs has equal accuracy before and after training, then the best model is the smaller (the model which has less trainable parameters).

Parallel Genetic Algorithm

Parallel genetic algorithm is such an algorithm that uses multiple genetic algorithms to solve a single task. All these algorithms try to solve the same task and after they've completed their job, the best individual of every algorithm is selected, then the best of them is selected, and this is the solution to a problem. This is one of the most popular approach to parallel genetic algorithms, even though there are others. This approach is often called 'island model' because populations are isolated from each other, like real-life creature populations may be isolated living on different islands. Fig. illustrates that.

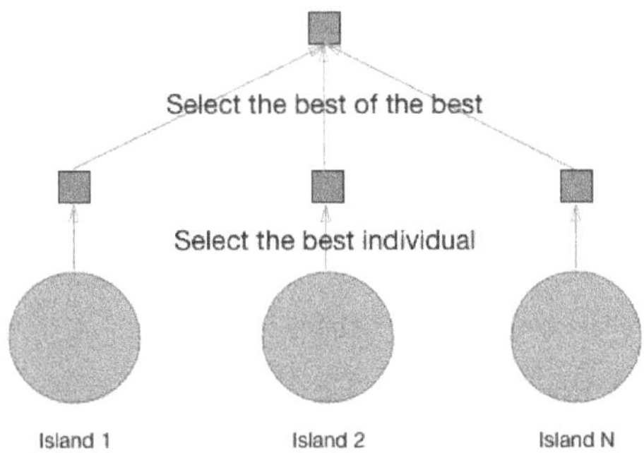

Fig. 10.24: Parallel Genetic Algorithm

These genetic algorithms do not depend on each other, as a result, they can run in parallel, taking advantage of a multicourse CPU. Each algorithm has its own set of individual, as a result these individuals may differ from individuals of another algorithm, because they have different mutation/crossover history.

Also it describes a parallel genetic algorithm that uses two independent algorithms to improve its performance. The difference between these two algorithms is the way individuals are selected for mutation and crossover. Moreover, some creatures, with the highest fitting, are allowed to 'migrate' from one algorithm to another. While this may be sufficient sometimes, but when a task is very hard to solve or an individual is a complex entity, we may need even more diversity within individuals.

In order to achieve this we may use as many algorithms as possible (say, two times more than the number of CPU cores we have) and variety almost every property of an algorithm. As a result, each algorithm has its own set of individuals that was created using methods that differ from those used by other algorithms. This is also an 'island model', even though 'islands' are more different from each other. The only restriction is that all algorithms use the same fitting function to assess individuals so that it is possible to compare individuals that belong to different algorithms. As a result, these genetic algorithms may differ in the following aspects:

- How new individuals are created.
- How individuals mutate and how they are selected for mutation.
- How individuals crossover and how they are selected for crossover.
- How much individuals are taking part in a single crossover event and how much individuals are created as a result.

- How much individuals survive after each algorithm iteration and how these creatures are selected.
- How much individuals each generation contain.
- How much generations an algorithm walks through.

By varying these characteristics it is possible to make many different genetic algorithms that solve the same task but have entirely different individuals.

It is important to note that these independent genetic algorithms have the same structure as any other conventional genetic algorithm, so that they can be extracted from a parallel genetic algorithm and be used on their own.

Crossover between Algorithms

So, what do we have? We have several genetic algorithms that are running independently and have their own sets of individuals. We can select individuals that belong to different algorithms and cross them over. As a result, features that appear in individuals of one algorithm will be available to another one. This allows to create such individuals that could not be created by any of the algorithms alone, bringing even more diversity to them and spreading convenient features.

Let's illustrate this with an example. Say we have three independent genetic algorithms and we want to crossover them in pairs. We take the first algorithm and randomly select the second element of a pair. So, we create as much pairs as many algorithms we have, in each pair the first element is chosen sequentially, and the second one is random. Then we perform crossover on populations of these two algorithms taking individuals from both of them. We pick individuals for crossover in such a way, that individuals from different algorithms are crossed over together. We use crossover mechanisms that are used by the first algorithm of a pair and this algorithm receives all of the individuals that were created as a result of a crossover; the second algorithm of a pair is simply a donor that provides its individuals. Therefore, each algorithm receives new individuals when it is the first element of a pair. If a crossover algorithm requires more than two individuals, additional individuals may be taken from any of the algorithms of a pair, it is only recommended that no algorithm dominate here. It is also possible to use special crossover technique when it comes to crossover between algorithms, that is applied only for crossover between algorithms.

It is recommended to use crossover between algorithms somewhere in the middle on the process (or even multiple times), not at the very beginning or at the end. At the very beginning each algorithm has fresh individuals that were not affected by mutations or crossover, as a result their features that are specific to a particular algorithm are not brightly expressed. At the very end, there are no more generations that may affect new individuals produced within crossover, as a result they will not compete with other individuals in order to determine which one is better.

A parallel genetic algorithm may take a little more time than a non-parallel one, that is because is uses several computation threads which, in turn, cause the Operation System to perform context switching more frequently. Nevertheless, parallel genetic algorithm tend to produce better results and more optimal individuals than a non-parallel one.

CHAPTER 11

LEARNING SETS OF RULES

11.1. Learning Sets of Rules

One of the most expressive and human readable representations for learned hypotheses is sets of if-then rules. We explore several algorithms for learning such sets of rules. One important special case involves learning sets of rules containing variables, called first-order Horn clauses. Because sets of first-order Horn clause scan be interpreted as programs in the logic programming language PROLOG, learning them is often called inductive logic programming (ILP).

As an example of first-order rule sets, consider the following two rules that jointly describe the target concept Ancestor. Here we use the predicateParent (x, y) to indicate that y is the mother or father of x, and the predicateAncestor(x, y) to indicate that y is an ancestor of x related by an arbitrary number of family generations.

$$IF \quad Parent\ (x,y) \qquad THEN \quad Ancestor\ (x,y)$$

$$IF \quad Parent\ (x,z) \land Ancestor\ (z,y) \qquad THEN \quad Ancestor\ (x,y)$$

Note these two rules compactly describe a recursive function that would be very difficult to represent using a decision tree or other propositional representation. One way to see the representational power of first-order rules is to consider the general purpose programming language PROLOG, In PROLOG programs are sets of first-order rules such as the two shown above (rules of this form are also called ***Horn clauses)***.

11.2. Sequential Covering Algorithms

Sequential Covering Algorithm

Sequential Covering is a popular algorithm based on Rule-Based Classification used for learning a disjunctive set of rules. The basic idea here is to learn one rule, remove the data that it covers, and then repeat the same process in this way; it covers all the rules involved with it in a sequential manner during the training phase.

Algorithm Involved

Sequential_covering (Target_attribute, Attributes, Examples, Threshold)

Learned_rules = {}

```
Rule = Learn-One-Rule(Target_attribute, Attributes, Examples)

while Performance(Rule, Examples) > Threshold :
Learned_rules = Learned_rules + Rule
    Examples = Examples - {examples correctly classified by Rule}
    Rule = Learn-One-Rule(Target_attribute, Attributes, Examples)

Learned_rules = sort Learned_rules according to performance over Examples
return Learned_rules
```

Sequential Learning is a powerful algorithm for generating rule-based classifiers in Machine Learning. It uses 'Learn-One-Rule' algorithm as its base to learn a sequence of disjunctive rules.

The sequential covering algorithm for learning a disjunctive set of rules. ***LEARN-ONE-RULE*** *m*ust return a single rule that covers at least some of the *Examples*. ***PERFORMANCE*** is a user-provided subroutine to evaluate rule quality. This covering algorithm learns rules until it can no longer learn a rule whose performance is above the given *Threshold*.

Working on the Algorithm

The algorithm involves a set of 'ordered rules' or 'list of decisions' to be made.

Step 1 – Create an empty decision list, 'R'.

Step 2 – 'Learn-One-Rule' Algorithm It extracts the best rule for a particular class 'y', where a rule is defined as: (Fig).

General Form of Rule

Ri : (Condition1 ... Condition **i) -->Yi**

In the beginning,

Step 2.a – if all training examples ∈ class 'y', then it's classified as **positive example.**

Step 2.b – else if all training examples∉ class 'y', then it's classified as **negative example**.

Step 3 – The rule becomes **'desirable'** when it covers a majority of the positive examples.

Step 4 – When this rule is obtained, delete all the training data associated with that rule.

(I.e. when the rule is applied to the dataset, it covers most of the training data, and has to be removed).

Step 5 – The new rule is added to the bottom of decision list, 'R'.

General to Specific Beam Search

One effective approach to implementing LEARN-ONE-RULE is to organize the hypothesis space search in the same general fashion as the ID3 algorithm, but to follow only the most promising branch in the tree at each step.

The general-to-specific search suggested above for the LEARN-ONE-RULE Algorithm is a greedy depth-first search with no backtracking. As with any greedy search, there is a danger that a suboptimal choice will be made at any step. To reduce this risk, we can extend the algorithm to perform a ***beam search;*** that is, a search in which the algorithm maintains a list of the k best candidates at each step, rather than a single best candidate. On each search step, descendants (specializations) are generated for each of these k best candidates, and the resulting set is again reduced to the k most promising members. Beam search keeps track of the most promising alternatives to the current top-rated hypothesis, so that all of their successors can be considered at each search step.

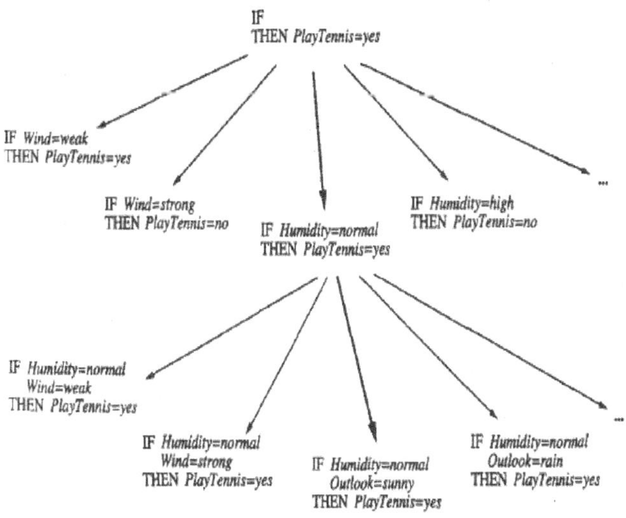

Fig. 11.1: IF...THEN Rule

The search for rule preconditions as **LEARN-ONE-RULE** proceeds from general to specific. At each step, the preconditions of the best rule are specialized in all possible ways. Rule post conditions **are** determined by the examples found to satisfy the preconditions. This figure illustrates a beam search of width 1.

11.3. Learn-One-Rule Algorithm

1. *Initialize a set of most general complexes.*
2. *Evaluate performances of those complexes over the example set.*
    - *Count how many positive and negative examples it covers.*
    - *Evaluate their performances.*
3. *Sort complexes according to their performances.*
4. *If the best complex satisfies some* **threshold**, *form the hypothesis and* **return.**
5. *Otherwise, pick k best performing complexes for the next generation.*
6. *Specializing all k complexes in the set to find new set of less general complexes.*
7. *Go to step 2.*

The number k is the beam factor of the search, meaning the maximum number of complexes to be specialized.

Variations

The SEQUENTIAL-COVERING algorithm, together with the LEARN-ONE-RULE- Algorithm, learns a set of if-then rules that covers the training examples. Many variations on this approach have been explored. For example, in some cases it might be desirable to have the program learn only rules that cover positive examples and to include a "default" that assigns a negative classification to instances not covered by any rule.

11.4. Learning Rule Sets: Summary

The SEQUENTIAL-COVERING algorithm described above and the decision tree learning algorithms which suggest a variety of possible methods for learning sets of rules. We consider several key dimensions in the design space of such rule learning algorithms. First, *sequential covering* algorithms learn one rule at a time, removing the covered examples and repeating the process on the remaining examples. In contrast, decision tree algorithms such as ID3 learn the entire set of disjoints simultaneously as part of the single search for an acceptable decision tree. We might, therefore, call algorithms such as ID3 *simultaneous covering* algorithms, in contrast to sequential covering algorithms such as CN2. Which should we prefer?

- ID3 chooses attributes by comparing the partitions of the data they generate.
- CN2 chooses among alternative attribute-value pairs by comparing the subsets of data they cover.
- Thus, CN2 makes a larger number of independent choices. So it is better if there is plenty of data.

A final dimension is the particular definition of rule **PERFORMANCE** used to guide the search in **LEARN-ONE-RULE.** Various evaluation functions have been used. Some common evaluation functions include:

Relative frequency: Let ***n*** denote the number of examples the rule matches and let ***nc*** denote the number of these that it classifies correctly. The relative frequency estimate of rule performance is Relative frequency is used to evaluate rules in the AQ program.

$$\frac{n_c}{n}$$

M-estimate of accuracy: This accuracy estimate is biased toward the default accuracy expected of the rule. It is often preferred when data is scarce and the rule must be evaluated based on few examples. As above, let ***n*** and ***nc*** denote the number of examples matched and correctly predicted by the rule.

Let ***p*** be the prior probability that a randomly drawn example from the entire data set will have the classification assigned by the rule (e.g., if 12 out of 100 examples have the value predicted by the rule, then p = .12). Finally, let m be the weight, or equivalent number of examples for weighting this prior ***p.*** The m-estimate of rule accuracy is ***Entropy.***

$$\frac{n_c + mp}{n + m}$$

This is the measure used by the **PERFORMANCE** subroutine in the algorithm. Let ***S*** be the set of examples that match the rule preconditions. Entropy measures the uniformity of the target function values for this set of examples. We take the negative of the entropy so that better rules will have higher scores.

$$-Entropy(S) = \sum_{i=1}^{c} p_i \log_2 p_i$$

11.5. Learning First-Order Rules

In this section, we consider learning rules that contain variables-in particular, learning first-order Horn theories. Our motivation for considering such rules is that they are much more expressive than propositional rules. Inductive learning of first-order rules or theories is often referred to as ***Inductive logic programming*** (or LP for short), because this process can be viewed as automatically inferring **PROLOG** programs from examples. **PROLOG** is a general purpose, Turing-equivalent programming language in which programs are expressed as collections of Horn clauses.

First-Order Horn Clauses

To see the advantages of first-order representations over propositional (variable free) representations, consider the task of learning the simple target concept ***Daughter (x, y),*** defined over pairs of people ***x*** and ***y.*** The value of ***Daughter (x, y)*** is ***True*** when ***x*** is the daughter of ***y,*** and ***False*** otherwise. Suppose each person in the data is described by the attributes ***Name, Mother, Father, Male, Female.***

Hence, each training example will consist of the description of two people in terms of these attributes, along with the value of the target attribute ***Daughter.*** For example, the following is a positive example in which Sharon is the daughter of Bob:

(Namel= Sharon,	***Motherl= Louise,***	***Fatherl= Bob,***
Malel= False,	***Female1 = True,***	
Name2 = Bob,	***Mother2 = Nora,***	***Father2 = Victor,***
Male2 = True,	***Female2 = False,***	***Daughterl.2 = True)***

Where the subscript on each attribute name indicates which of the two persons is being described. Now if we were to collect a number of such training examples for the target concept ***Daughter l,2*** and provide them to a propositional rule learner such as CN2 or C4.5, the result would be a collection of very specific rules such as,

IF ***(Father1 = Bob) A (Name2 = Bob) A (Femalel= True)***

THEN ***daughter 1,2= True***

Although it is correct, this rule is so specific that it will rarely, if ever, be useful in classifying future pairs of people. The problem is that propositional representations offer no general way to describe the essential ***relations*** among the values of the attributes. In contrast, a program using first-order representations could learn the following general rule:

IF Father(y, x) ^Female(y), THEN ***Daughter(x, y)***

Where **x** and ***y*** are variables that can be bound to any person.

First-order Horn clauses may also refer to variables in the preconditions that do not occur in the postconditions. For example, one rule for ***GrandDaughter*** might be,

IF ***Father(y, z)*** A ***Mother(z, x) A Female(y)***

THEN ***GrandDaughter(x, y)***

Note the variable ***z*** in this rule, which refers to the father of ***y***, is not present in the rule post-conditions. Whenever such a variable occurs only in the pre-conditions, it is assumed to be existentially quantified; that is, the rule preconditions are satisfied as long as there exists at least one binding of the variable that satisfies the corresponding literal.

First Order Logic: Terminology

All Expressions in First Order Logic are Composed of

- constants – e.g. bob, 23, a
  - variables – e.g. X,Y,Z
  - predicate symbols – e.g. female, father
  - predicates take on the values True or False only
  - function symbols – e.g. age – functions can take on any constant as a value
  - connectives – e.g. $\wedge$, $\vee$, $\neg$, $\rightarrow$ (or $\leftarrow$) – quantifiers – e.g. $\forall$, $\exists$
- A term is,
  - any constant – e.g. bob.
  - any variable – e.g X.
  - any function applied to any term – e.g. age(bob).
- A literal is any predicate or negated predicate applied to any terms – e.g. female(sue), ¬father(X,Y).
  - A ground literal is a literal that contains no variables – e.g. female(sue).
  - A positive literal is a literal that does not contain a negated predicate – e.g. female(sue).
  - A negative literal is a literal that contains a negated predicate – e.g ¬father(X,Y).

A clause is any disjunction of literals M1 $\vee$ ···$\vee$ Mn whose variables are universally quantified (with wide scope).

11.6. Learning Sets of First-Order Rules: FOIL

FOIL (Quinlan, 1990) is the natural extension of SEQUENTIAL-COVERING and LEARN-ONE-RULE to first order rule learning. FOIL learns first order rules which are similar to Horn clauses with two exceptions:

- Literals may not contain function symbols (reduces complexity of hypothesis space).
- Literals in body of clause may be negated (hence, more expressive than Horn clauses).

Like SEQUENTIAL-COVERING, FOIL learns one rule at time and removes positive examples covered by the learned rule before attempting to learn a further rule. Unlike SEQUENTIAL-COVERING and LEARN-ONE-RULE, FOIL only tries to learn rules that predict when the target literal is true and propositional version sought rules that predicted both true and false values of target attribute it performs a simple hill-climbing search (beam search of width one).

FOIL Searches its Hypothesis Space Via Two Nested Loops

- The outer loop at each iteration adds a new rule to an overall disjunctive hypothesis (i.e.rule1 ∨rule2 ∨...) This loop may be viewed as a specific-to-general search starting with the empty disjunctive hypothesis which covers no positive instances stopping when the hypothesis is general enough to cover all positive examples.
- The inner loop works out the detail of each specific rule, adding conjunctive constraints to the rule precondition on each iteration. This loop may be viewed as a general-to-specific search starting with the most general precondition (empty) stopping when the hypothesis is specific enough to exclude all negative examples.

FOIL: Algorithm

FOIL(Target predicate,Predicates,Examples)

- Pos ← positive Examples
- Neg ← negative Examples • Learned rules ← {}
- while Pos, do

Learn a NewRule

- NewRule ← most general rule possible (no preconditions)
- NewRuleNeg ← Neg
- while NewRuleNeg, do

Add a new literal to specialize NewRule

1. Candidate literals ← generate candidates based on Predicates.
2. Best literal ← argmaxL∈Candidate literals Foil Gain(L,NewRule).
3. add Best literal to NewRule preconditions.
4. NewRuleNeg ← subset of NewRuleNeg that satisfies NewRule preconditions.
    - Learned rules ← Learned rules+NewRule
    - Pos ← Pos – {members of Pos covered by NewRule}
        - Return Learned rules

Generating Candidate Specializations in FOIL

Suppose we are learning a rule of the form:

$$P(x1, x\ 2..., x\ k) \leftarrow L1 \ldots L\ n$$

- Then candidate specialisations add a new literal of the form:
    - Q (v1..., v r), where
        - Q is any predicate in the rule or training data.
        - At least one of the vi in the created literal must already exist as a variable in the rule.
- Equal (Xj,Xk), where x j and x k are variables already present in the rule.
- The negation of either of the above forms of literals.

Example

Suppose we are trying to learn granddaughter (X, Y), given instances described by the predicates father and female:

- FOIL starts with the most general rule: granddaughter (X, Y) ←
- The above procedure generates candidate additional literals:

  equal (X, Y), female(X), female(Y), father (X, Y), father (Y, X), father (X, Z), father (Z, X), father (Y, Z), father (Z, Y)

  Plus, the negations of each of these,
- Suppose FOIL now chooses father (Y, Z) as most promising:

  granddaughter (X, Y) ← father (Y, Z)
- New candidate literals to specialise this rule includes those from above,

  plus equal (Z, X), equal (Z, Y), female(Z), female(Y), father (Z, W), father (W, Z)

plus, their negations.

If FOIL next selects father(Z,X), then female(Y) the rule

$$granddaughter(X,Y) \leftarrow father(Y,Z) \land father(Z,X) \land female(Y)$$

is generated.

- Assuming this rule covers only positive examples, no more specialisations for the current rule is sought. If more positive examples remain, search for another rule begins.

FOIL: Performance Evaluation Measure

- How do we decide which is the best literal to add when specialising a rule?

- To do this FOIL considers each possible binding of variables in the candidate rule specialisation to constants in the training examples.
- For example, suppose we have the training data:

  Granddaughter (bill, Joan) ***father (joan, joe)*** ***father (tom, joe)***

  female(joan) ***father(joe,bill)***

and we also assume ("closed world assumption") that any literals.

- Involving predicates granddaughter, father, and female.
- Involving constants bill, joan, joe, and tom.
- Not in the training data are false. E.g. ¬granddaughter(bill,tom) is also true.
  - Given the initial rule: granddaughter(X,Y) ←

    FOIL considers all possible bindings of X and Y to the constants bill, joan, joe, and tom. Note that only {X /bill,Y / joan } is a positive binding (i.e. corresponds to a positive training example). The other 15 bindings of constants to X and Y are negative.

At each stage of rule specialisation, candidate specialisations are preferred according to whether they possess more positive and fewer negative bindings.

- The precise evaluation measure used by FOIL is:

$$Foil\_Gain(L, R) \equiv t\ (log_2 \frac{p_1}{p_1 + n_1} - log_2 \frac{p_0}{p_0 + n_0}$$

Where

- L is the candidate literal to add to rule R
- $p0$ = number of positive bindings of R
- $n0$ = number of negative bindings of R
- $p1$ = number of positive bindings of R + L
- $n1$ = number of negative bindings of R + L
- t is the number of positive bindings of R also covered by R + L

  • Note, in information-theoretic terms:

$-log_2 \frac{p_0}{p_0+n_0}$ - is minimum number of bits to encode the classification of a positive binding covered by R.

$-log_2 \frac{p_1}{p_1+n_1}$ - is minimum number of bits to encode the classification of a positive binding covered by R + L.

- t is number of positive bindings covered by R that remain covered by R + L.
- So, Foil Gain (R, L) is reduction due to L in total number of bits required to encode the classification of all positive bindings of R.

11.7. Induction as Inverted Deduction

A second, quite different approach to inductive logic programming is based on the simple observation that induction is just the inverse of deduction! In general, machine learning involves building theories that explain the observed data. Given some data D and some partial background knowledge B, learning can be described as generating a hypothesis h that, together with B, explains D. Put more precisely, assume as usual that the training data D is a set of training examples, each of the form (xi, f (xi)). Here xi denotes the ith training instance and f (xi) denotes its target value. Then learning is the problem of discovering a hypothesis h, such that the classification f (xi) of each training instance xi follows deductively from the hypothesis h, the description of xi, and any other background knowledge Bknown to the system.

$$(\forall \langle x_i, f(x_i) \rangle \in D)\ (B \wedge h \wedge x_i) \vdash f(x_i)$$

The expression X F Y is read "Y follows deductively from X," or alternatively "X entails Y." Expression describes the constraint that must be satisfied by the learned hypothesis h; namely, for every training instance xi, the target classification f(xi) must follow deductively from B, h, and xi.

11.8. Inverting Resolution

It is easiest to introduce the resolution rule in propositional form, though it is readily extended to first-order representations. Let ***L*** be an arbitrary propositional literal, and let *P* and *R* be arbitrary propositional clauses.

$$\frac{\begin{array}{ccc} P & \vee & L \\ \neg L & \vee & R \end{array}}{\begin{array}{ccc} P & \vee & R \end{array}}$$

The resolution rule is which should be read as follows: Given the two clauses above the line, conclude the clause below the line. Intuitively, the resolution rule is quite sensible. Given the two assertions ***P** Vl* and ***-L*** *v R,* it is obvious that either ***L*** or ***-L*** must be false. Therefore, either *P* or *R* must be true. Thus, the conclusion ***P*** *v R* of there solution rule is intuitively satisfying.

PROGOL

PROGOL uses a sequential covering algorithm to learn a set of expressions from H that cover the data. For each example ***(xi,***f***(xi))*** that is not yet covered by these learned expressions, it first searches for the most specific hypothesis ***hi*** within H such that **(B A *hi A xi)* l- *f (xi).*** More precisely, it approximates this by calculating the most specific hypothesis among those that entail f ***(xi)*** within ***k*** applications of the resolution rule (where k is a user-specified parameter).

PROGOL then performs a general-to-specific search of the hypothesis space bounded by the most general possible hypothesis and by the specific bound ***hi*** calculated in step 2. Within this set of hypotheses, it seeks the hypothesis having minimum description length (measured by the number of literals). This part of the search is guided by an A*-like heuristic that allows pruning without running the risk of pruning away the shortest hypothesis.

Additional Explanation

Sequential Covering Algorithm

Sequential Covering is a popular algorithm based on Rule-Based Classification used for learning a disjunctive set of rules. The basic idea here is to learn one rule, remove the data that it covers, then repeat the same process. In this process, In this way, it covers all the rules involved with it in a sequential manner during the training phase.

Algorithm Involved

```
Sequential_covering (Target_attribute, Attributes, Examples, Threshold):
Learned_rules = {}
    Rule = Learn-One-Rule(Target_attribute, Attributes, Examples)

    while Performance(Rule, Examples) > Threshold :
Learned_rules = Learned_rules + Rule
        Examples = Examples - {examples correctly classified by Rule}
        Rule = Learn-One-Rule(Target_attribute, Attributes, Examples)

Learned_rules = sort Learned_rules according to performance over Examples
   return Learned_rules
```

The Sequential Learning algorithm takes care of to some extent, the low coverage problem in the Learn-One-Rule algorithm covering all the rules in a sequential manner.

Working on the Algorithm

The algorithm involves a set of 'ordered rules' or 'list of decisions' to be made.

Step 1 - *create an empty decision list, 'R'.*

Step 2 - *'Learn-One-Rule' Algorithm.*

It extracts the best rule for a particular class 'y', where a rule is defined as: (Fig).

General Form of Rule

In the beginning,

Step 2.a - *if all training examples ∈ class 'y', then it's classified as* **positive example**.

Step 2.b - *else if all training examples ∉ class 'y', then it's classified as* **negative example**.

Step 3 - *The rule becomes* **'desirable'** *when it covers a majority of the positive examples.*

Step 4 - *When this rule is obtained, delete all the training data associated with that rule.*

(i.e. when the rule is applied to the dataset, it covers most of the training data, and has to be removed)

Step 5 - *The new rule is added to the bottom of decision list, 'R'. (Fig).*

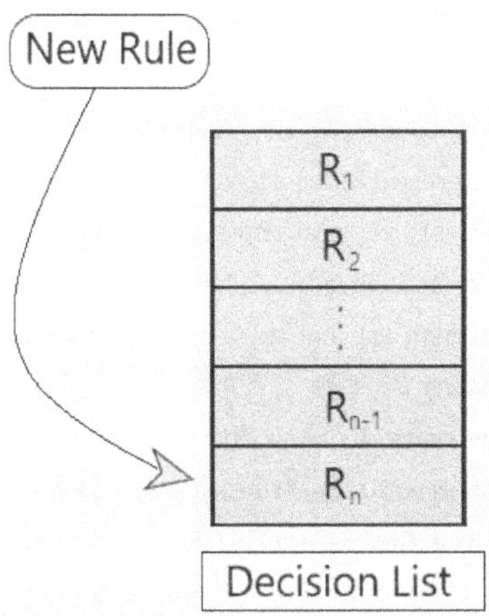

Fig. 11.2: Decision List 'R'

Below, is a visual representation describing the working of the algorithm.

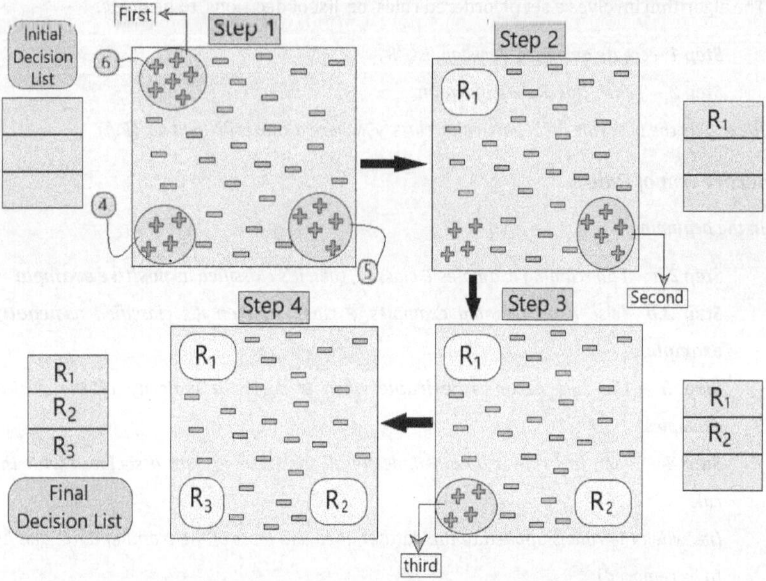

Fig. 11.3: Visual Representation of Working of the Algorithm

- Let us understand step by step how the algorithm is working in the example shown in Fig.
- First, we created an empty decision list. During Step 1, we see that there are three sets of positive examples present in the dataset. So, as per the algorithm, we consider the one with maximum no of positive example. *(6, as shown in Step 1 of Fig).*
- Once we cover these 6 positive examples, we get our first rule R_1, which is then pushed into the decision list and those positive examples are removed from the dataset. *(as shown in Step 2 of Fig).*
- Now, we take the next majority of positive examples *(5, as shown in Step 2 of Fig)* and follow the same process until we get rule R_2. (Same for R_3).
- In the end, we obtain our final decision list with all the desirable rules.

Sequential Learning is a powerful algorithm for generating rule-based classifiers in Machine Learning. It uses 'Learn-One-Rule' algorithm as its base to learn a sequence of disjunctive rules.

Rule based Classification

- **IF-THEN Rules:**
  - Rule-based classifier makes use of a set of IF-THEN rules for classification. We can express a rule in the following from.
  - IF condition THEN conclusion.
  - Let us consider a rule R1.
  - R1: IF age = youth AND student = yes.
  - THEN buy_computer = yes.
- **Points to remember:**
  - The IF part of the rule is called rule antecedent or precondition.
  - The THEN part of the rule is called rule consequent.
  - The antecedent part the condition consist of one or more **attribute** tests and these tests are logically ANDed.
  - The consequent part consists of class prediction.
- **Note – We can also write rule R1 as follows:**
  - R1: (age = youth) ^ (student = yes))(buys computer = yes).
  - If the condition holds true for a given tuple, then the antecedent is satisfied.
  - Rule Extraction.
  - Here we will learn how to build a rule-based **classifier** by extracting IF-THEN rules from a decision tree.
- **Points to remember:**
- **To extract a rule from a decision tree:**
  - One rule is created for each path from the root to the leaf node.
  - To form a rule antecedent, each splitting criterion is logically ANDed.
  - The leaf node holds the class prediction, forming the rule consequent.
  - Rule Induction Using Sequential Covering Algorithm.
  - Sequential Covering Algorithm can be used to extract IF-THEN rules form the training data. We do not require to generate a decision tree first. In this algorithm, each rule for a given class covers many of the tuples of that class.
  - Some of the sequential Covering Algorithms are AQ, CN2, and RIPPER. As per the general strategy the rules are learned one at a time. For each time rules are learned, a tuple covered by the rule is removed and the process continues for the rest of the tuples. This is because the path to each leaf in a decision tree corresponds to a rule.

- Note – The Decision tree induction can be considered as learning a set of rules simultaneously.
- The Following is the sequential learning Algorithm where rules are learned for one class at a time. When learning a rule from a class Ci, we want the rule to cover all the tuples from class C only and no tuple form any other class.
- Algorithm: Sequential Covering.

Input:

D, a data set class-labeled tuples.

Att_vals, the set of all attributes and their possible values.

Output: A Set of IF-THEN rules.

Method:

```
Rule_set={ }; // initial set of rules learned is empty

for each class c do

 repeat
 Rule = Learn_One_Rule(D, Att_valls, c);
  remove tuples covered by Rule form D;
  until termination condition;

Rule_set=Rule_set+Rule; // add a new rule to rule-set
end for
return Rule_Set;
```

Rule Pruning

The rule is pruned is due to the following reason:

The Assessment of quality is made on the original set of training data. The rule may perform well on training data but less well on subsequent data. That's why the rule pruning is required.

The rule is pruned by removing conjunct. The rule R is pruned, if pruned version of R has greater quality than what was assessed on an independent set of tuples.

FOIL is one of the simple and effective method for rule pruning. For a given rule R,

$$FOIL\_Prune = pos - neg / pos + neg$$

Where pos and neg is the number of positive tuples covered by R, respectively.

Note – This value will increase with the accuracy of R on the pruning set. Hence, if the FOIL_Prune value is higher for the pruned version of R, then we prune R.

Sequential Covering

Introduction

This is the most popular algorithm implementing Rule Learning. In the scope of this page, only the algorithm for **propositional training examples** is discussed. A covering algorithm, in the context of propositional learning systems, is an algorithm that develops a cover for the set of positive examples - that is, a set of hypotheses that account for all the positive examples but none of the negative examples. This is called sequential covering because it learn one rule at a time and repeat this process to gradually cover the full set of positive examples. The most effective approach to **Learn-One-Rule** is beam search.

Algorithm

The algorithm - given a set of examples:

1. *Start with an empty **Cover***
2. *Using **Learn-One-Rule** to find the best hypothesis.*
3. *If the Just-Learnt-Rule satisfies the threshold then*
    - *Put Just-Learnt-Rule to the **Cover**.*
    - *Remove examples covered by Just-Learnt-Rule.*
    - *Go to step 2.*
4. *Sort the **Cover** according to its performance over examples.*
5. *Return: **Cover**.*

Example

An example of a set of propositional examples in this system is as follow:

Id	Size	Colour	Shape	Weight	Expensive
1	Big	Red	Square	Heavy	Yes
2	Small	Blue	Triangle	Light	Yes
3	Small	Blue	Square	Light	No
4	Big	Green	Triangle	Heavy	No
5	Big	Blue	Square	Light	No
6	Big	Green	Square	Heavy	Yes
7	Small	Red	Triangle	Light	Yes

The final set of rules is like follow:

Expensive = Yes if:

Colour = Red. (covers example 1,7)

Or (Colour = Green & Shape = Square). (covers example 6)

Or (Colour = Blue & Shape = Triangle). (covers example 2)

Visualization

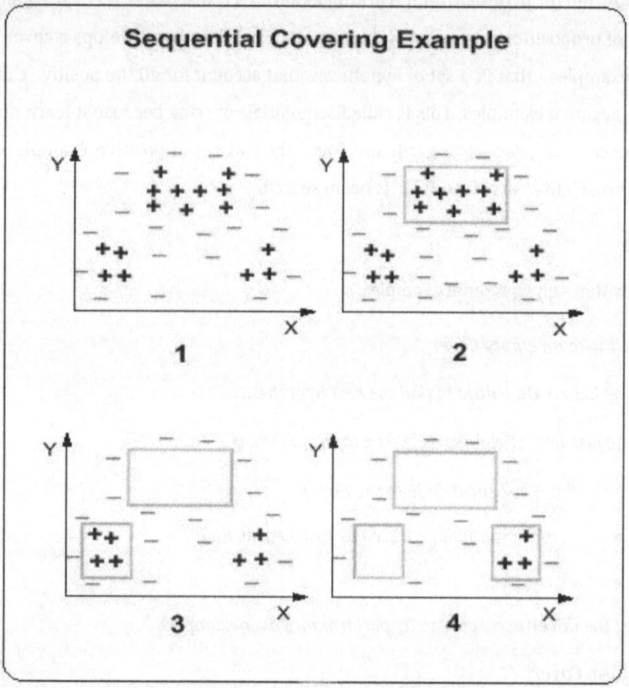

Fig. 11.4: Sequential Covering Examples

Properties

One characteristic of this algorithm is it requires high accuracy, meaning the prediction should be correct with high probability. Another is that it is possibly low coverage, meaning that it does not make prediction for all examples. There might be some examples that do not classified by the algorithm.

CHAPTER 12

REINFORCEMENT LEARNING

12.1. Introduction

Reinforcement Learning is a feedback-based Machine learning technique in which an agent learns to behave in an environment by performing the actions and seeing the results of actions. For each good action, the agent gets positive feedback, and for each bad action, the agent gets negative feedback or penalty.

In Reinforcement Learning, the agent learns automatically using feedbacks without any labeled data, unlike learning. Since there is no labeled data, so the agent is bound to learn by its experience only. RL solves a specific type of problem where decision making is sequential, and the goal is long-term, such as **game-playing, robotics**, etc.

The agent interacts with the environment and explores it by itself. The primary goal of an agent in reinforcement learning is to improve the performance by getting the maximum positive rewards. The agent learns with the process of hit and trial, and based on the experience, it learns to perform the task in a better way. Hence, we can say that ***"Reinforcement learning is a type of machine learning method where an intelligent agent (computer program) interacts with the environment and learns to act within that."*** How a Robotic dog learns the movement of his arms is an example of Reinforcement learning. It is a core part of Artificial intelligence, and all AI agent works on the concept of reinforcement learning. Here we do not need to pre-program the agent, as it learns from its own experience without any human intervention.

Example: Suppose there is an AI agent present within a maze environment, and his goal is to find the diamond. The agent interacts with the environment by performing some actions, and based on those actions, the state of the agent gets changed, and it also receives a reward or penalty as feedback.

- The agent continues doing these three things **(take action, change state/remain in the same state, and get feedback)**, and by doing these actions, he learns and explores the environment.
- The agent learns that what actions lead to positive feedback or rewards and what actions lead to negative feedback penalty. As a positive reward, the agent gets a positive point, and as a penalty, it gets a negative point.

12.2. Reinforcement Learning

Reinforcement learning is an area of Machine Learning. It is about taking suitable action to maximize reward in a particular situation. It is employed by various software and machines to find the best possible behavior or path it should take in a specific situation. Reinforcement learning differs from supervised learning in a way that in supervised learning the training data has the answer key with it so the model is trained with the correct answer itself whereas in reinforcement learning, there is no answer but the reinforcement agent decides what to do to perform the given task. In the absence of a training dataset, it is bound to learn from its experience.

Example: The problem is as follows: We have an agent and a reward, with many hurdles in between. The agent is supposed to find the best possible path to reach the reward. The following problem explains the problem more easily. The fig. shows example for Reinforcement learning.

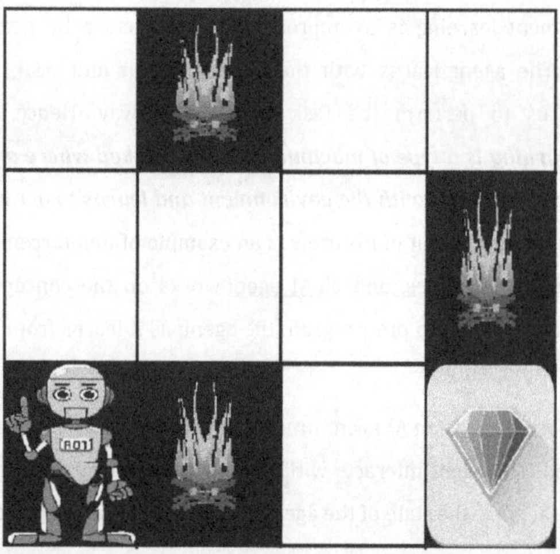

The above image shows the robot, diamond, and fire. The goal of the robot is to get the reward that is the diamond and avoid the hurdles that are fired. The robot learns by trying all the possible paths and then choosing the path which gives him the reward with the least hurdles. Each right step will give the robot a reward and each wrong step will subtract the reward of the robot. The total reward will be calculated when it reaches the final reward that is the diamond.

Main Points in Reinforcement Learning

- Input: The input should be an initial state from which the model will start.
- Output: There are many possible outputs as there are a variety of solutions to a particular problem.
- Training: The training is based upon the input, The model will return a state and the user will decide to reward or punish the model based on its output.
- The model keeps continues to learn.
- The best solution is decided based on the maximum reward.
  - Reinforcement Learning is a feedback-based Machine learning technique in which an agent learns to behave in an environment by performing the actions and seeing the results of actions. For each good action, the agent gets positive feedback, and for each bad action, the agent gets negative feedback or penalty.
  - In Reinforcement Learning, the agent learns automatically using feedbacks without any labeled data, unlike supervised learning.
  - Since there is no labeled data, so the agent is bound to learn by its experience only.
  - RL solves a specific type of problem where decision making is sequential, and the goal is long-term, such as **game-playing, robotics**, etc.
  - The agent interacts with the environment and explores it by itself. The primary goal of an agent in reinforcement learning is to improve the performance by getting the maximum positive rewards.
  - The agent learns with the process of hit and trial, and based on the experience, it learns to perform the task in a better way. Hence, we can say that ***"Reinforcement learning is a type of machine learning method where an intelligent agent (computer program) interacts with the environment and learns to act within that."*** How a Robotic dog learns the movement of his arms is an example of Reinforcement learning.
  - It is a core part of Artificial intelligence, and all AI agent works on the concept of reinforcement learning. Here we do not need to pre-program the agent, as it learns from its own experience without any human intervention.

- **Example:** Suppose there is an AI agent present within a maze environment, and his goal is to find the diamond. The agent interacts with the environment by performing some actions, and based on those actions, the state of the agent gets changed, and it also receives a reward or penalty as feedback.
- The agent continues doing these three things **(take action, change state/remain in the same state, and get feedback)**, and by doing these actions, he learns and explores the environment.
- The agent learns that what actions lead to positive feedback or rewards and what actions lead to negative feedback penalty. As a positive reward, the agent gets a positive point, and as a penalty, it gets a negative point. The below image shows about RL.

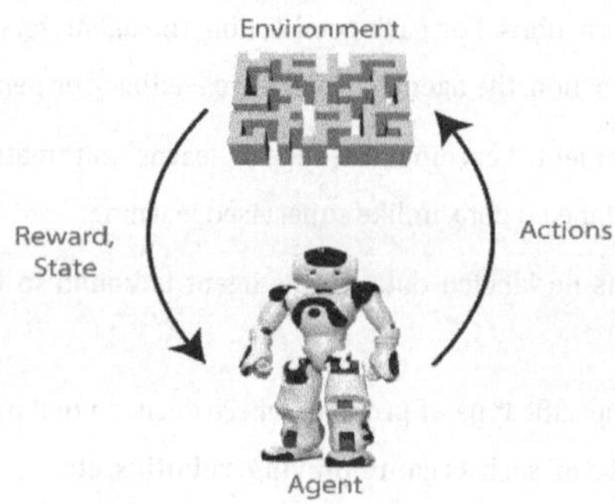

Fig. 12.1: RL Steps

Terms Used in Reinforcement Learning

- **Agent():** An entity that can perceive/explore the environment and act upon it.
- **Environment():** A situation in which an agent is present or surrounded by. In RL, we assume the stochastic environment, which means it is random in nature.
- **Action():** Actions are the moves taken by an agent within the environment.
- **State():** State is a situation returned by the environment after each action taken by the agent.
- **Reward():** A feedback returned to the agent from the environment to evaluate the action of the agent.
- **Policy():** Policy is a strategy applied by the agent for the next action based on the current state.

- **Value():** It is expected long-term retuned with the discount factor and opposite to the short-term reward.
- **Q-value():** It is mostly similar to the value, but it takes one additional parameter as a current action (a).

Key Features of Reinforcement Learning

- In RL, the agent is not instructed about the environment and what actions need to be taken.
- It is based on the hit and trial process.
- The agent takes the next action and changes states according to the feedback of the previous action.
- The agent may get a delayed reward.
- The environment is stochastic, and the agent needs to explore it to reach to get the maximum positive rewards.

12.3. Approaches to Implement Reinforcement Learning

There are mainly three ways to implement reinforcement-learning in ML, which are:

1. Value-based

The value-based approach is about to find the optimal value function, which is the maximum value at a state under any policy. Therefore, the agent expects the long-term return at any state(s) under policy π.

2. Policy-based

Policy-based approach is to find the optimal policy for the maximum future rewards without using the value function. In this approach, the agent tries to apply such a policy that the action performed in each step helps to maximize the future reward.

The policy-based approach has mainly two types of policy:

- **Deterministic:** The same action is produced by the policy (π) at any state.
- **Stochastic:** In this policy, probability determines the produced action.

3. Model-based

In the model-based approach, a virtual model is created for the environment, and the agent explores that environment to learn it. There is no particular solution or algorithm for this approach because the model representation is different for each environment.

Elements of Reinforcement Learning

There are four main elements of Reinforcement Learning, which are given below:

1. Policy
2. Reward Signal
3. Value Function
4. Model of the environment

1. **Policy:** A policy can be defined as a way how an agent behaves at a given time. It maps the perceived states of the environment to the actions taken on those states. A policy is the core element of the RL as it alone can define the behavior of the agent. In some cases, it may be a simple function or a lookup table, whereas, for other cases, it may involve general computation as a search process. It could be deterministic or a stochastic policy:

   For deterministic policy: a = π(s)
   For stochastic policy: π(a | s) = P[At =a | St = s]

2. **Reward Signal:** The goal of reinforcement learning is defined by the reward signal. At each state, the environment sends an immediate signal to the learning agent, and this signal is known as a **reward signal**. These rewards are given according to the good and bad actions taken by the agent. The agent's main objective is to maximize the total number of rewards for good actions. The reward signal can change the policy, such as if an action selected by the agent leads to low reward, then the policy may change to select other actions in the future.
3. **Value Function:** The value function gives information about how good the situation and action are and how much reward an agent can expect. A reward indicates the **immediate signal for each good and bad action**, whereas a value function specifies **the good state and action for the future**. The value function depends on the reward as, without reward, there could be no value. The goal of estimating values is to achieve more rewards.
4. **Model:** The last element of reinforcement learning is the model, which mimics the behavior of the environment. With the help of the model, one can make inferences about how the environment will behave. Such as, if a state and an action are given, then a model can predict the next state and reward.

The model is used for planning, which means it provides a way to take a course of action by considering all future situations before actually experiencing those situations. The approaches for solving the RL problems **with the help of the model** are termed as the **model-based approach**. Comparatively, an approach **without using a model** is called a **model-free approach**.

How does Reinforcement Learning Work?

To understand the working process of the RL, we need to consider two main things:

- **Environment:** It can be anything such as a room, maze, football ground, etc.
- **Agent:** An intelligent agent such as AI robot.

Let's take an example of a maze environment that the agent needs to explore. Consider the below image.

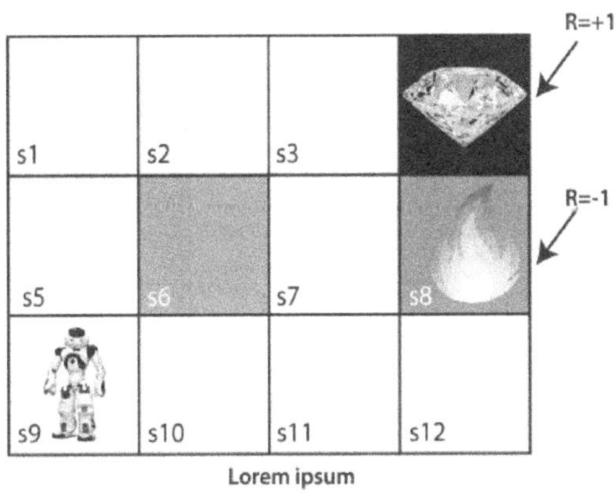

Fig. 12.2: RL Example

In the above image, the agent is at the very first block of the maze. The maze is consisting of an S_6 block, which is a **wall**, S_8 a **fire pit**, and S_4 a **diamond block.**

The agent cannot cross the S_6 block, as it is a solid wall. If the agent reaches the S_4 block, then get the **+1 reward;** if it reaches the fire pit, then gets **-1 reward point**. It can take four actions: **move up, move down, move left, and move right.**

The agent can take any path to reach to the final point, but he needs to make it in possible fewer steps. Suppose the agent considers the path **S9-S5-S1-S2-S3**, so he will get the +1-reward point.

The agent will try to remember the preceding steps that it has taken to reach the final step. To memorize the steps, it assigns 1 value to each previous step. Consider the below step.

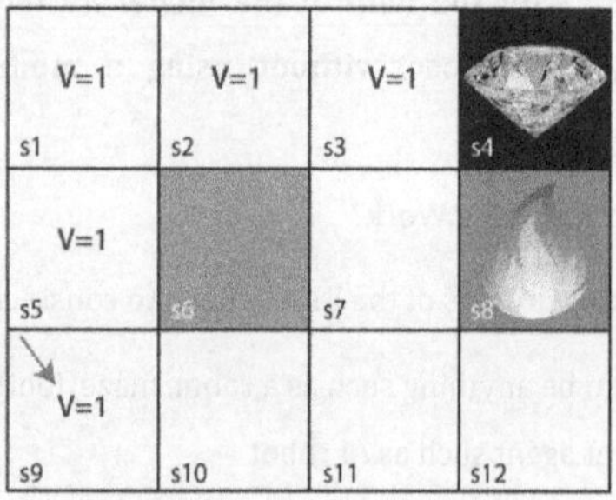

Now, the agent has successfully stored the previous steps assigning the 1 value to each previous block. But what will the agent do if he starts moving from the block, which has 1 value block on both sides? Consider the below diagram.

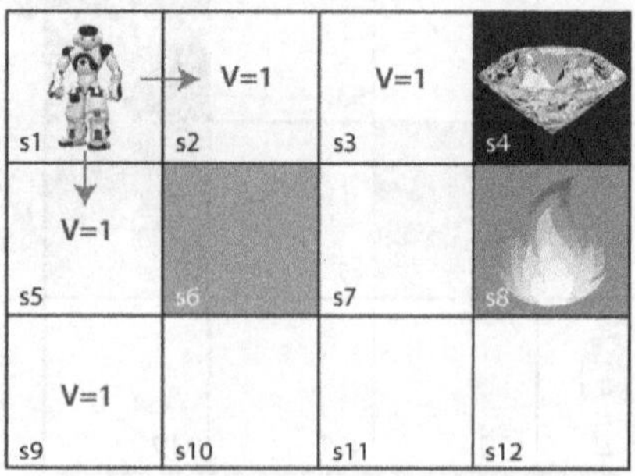

Fig. 12.3: Bellman Equation (RL)

It will be a difficult condition for the agent whether he should go up or down as each block has the same value. So, the above approach is not suitable for the agent to reach the destination. Hence to solve the problem, we will use the **Bellman equation**, which is the main concept behind reinforcement learning.

The Bellman Equation

The Bellman equation was introduced by the Mathematician **Richard Ernest Bellman in the year 1953**, and hence it is called as a Bellman equation. It is associated with dynamic programming and used to calculate the values of a decision problem at a certain point by including the values of previous states.

It is a way of calculating the value functions in dynamic programming or environment that leads to modern reinforcement learning.

The key-elements used in Bellman equations are:

- Action performed by the agent is referred to as "a".
- State occurred by performing the action is "s".
- The reward/feedback obtained for each good and bad action is "R".
- A discount factor is Gamma "γ".

The Bellman equation can be written as:

1. V(s) = max [R(s,a) + γV(s`)]

Where,

V(s)= value calculated at a particular point.

R(s,a) = Reward at a particular states by performing an action.

γ = Discount factor

V(s`) = The value at the previous state.

In the above equation, we are taking the max of the complete values because the agent tries to find the optimal solution always.

So now, using the Bellman equation, we will find value at each state of the given environment. We will start from the block, which is next to the target block.

For 1st Block:

V(s3) = max [R(s,a) + γV(s`)], here V(s')= 0 because there is no further state to move.

V(s3)= max[R(s,a)]=> V(s3)= max[1]=> **V(s3)= 1.**

For 2nd Block:

V(s2) = max [R(s,a) + γV(s`)], here γ= 0.9(lets), V(s')= 1, and R(s, a)= 0, because there is no reward at this state.

V(s2)= max[0.9(1)]=> V(s)= max[0.9]=> **V(s2) =0.9**

For 3rd Block:

V(s1) = max [R(s,a) + γV(s`)], here γ= 0.9(lets), V(s')= 0.9, and R(s, a)= 0, because there is no reward at this state also.

V(s1)= max[0.9(0.9)]=> V(s3)= max[0.81]=> **V(s1) =0.81**

For 4th Block:

V(s5) = max [R(s,a) + γV(s`)], here γ= 0.9(lets), V(s')= 0.81, and R(s, a)= 0, because there is no reward at this state also.

V(s5)= max[0.9(0.81)]=> V(s5)= max[0.81]=> **V(s5) =0.73**

For 5th Block

V(s9) = max [R(s,a) + γV(s`)], here γ= 0.9(lets), V(s')= 0.73, and R(s, a)= 0, because there is no reward at this state also.

V(s9)= max[0.9(0.73)]=> V(s4)= max[0.81]=> **V(s4) =0.66**

Consider the Below Image

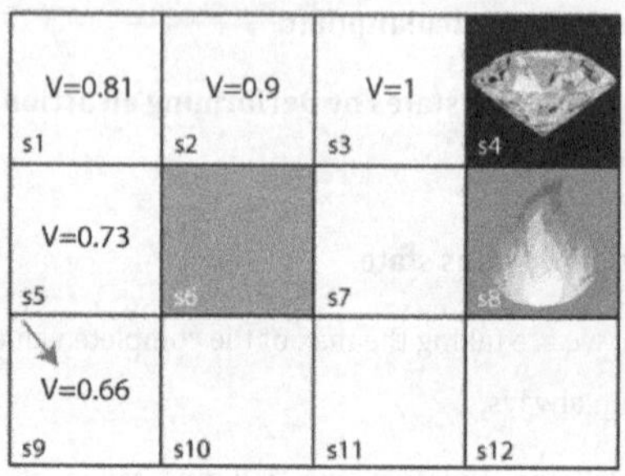

Fig. 12.4: Bellman Equation Steps

Now, we will move further to the 6th block, and here agent may change the route because it always tries to find the optimal path. So now, let's consider from the block next to the fire pit.

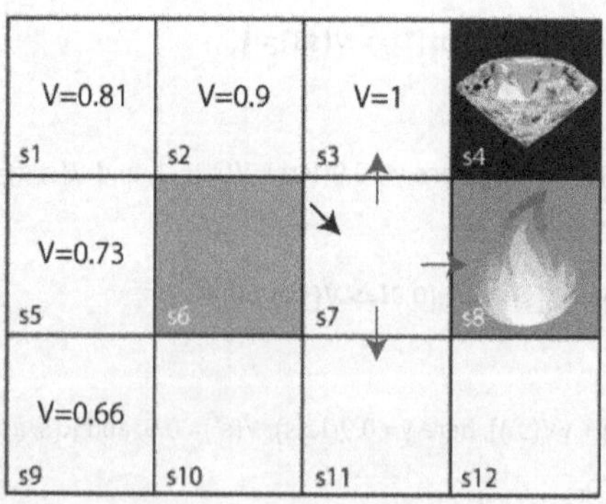

Fig. 12.5: Bellman Equation Steps

Now, the agent has three options to move; if he moves to the blue box, then he will feel a bump if he moves to the fire pit, then he will get the -1 reward. But here we are taking only positive rewards, so for this, he will move to upwards only. The complete block values will be calculated using this formula. Consider the below image.

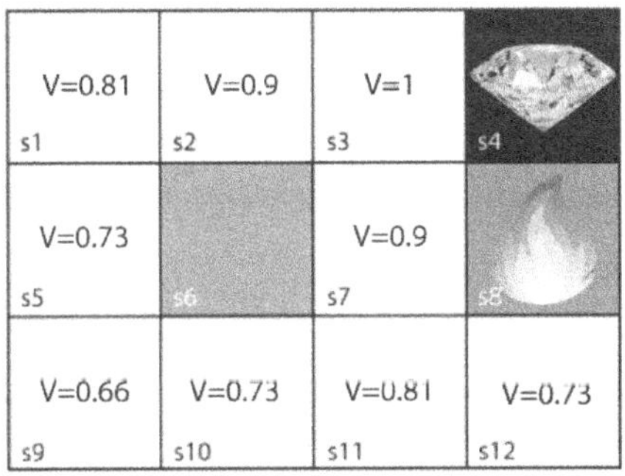

Fig. 12.6: Bellman Equation Steps

Types of Reinforcement Learning

There are mainly two types of reinforcement learning, which are.

- **Positive Reinforcement**
- **Negative Reinforcement**

Positive Reinforcement

The positive reinforcement learning means adding something to increase the tendency that expected behavior would occur again. It impacts positively on the behavior of the agent and increases the strength of the behavior.

This type of reinforcement can sustain the changes for a long time, but too much positive reinforcement may lead to an overload of states that can reduce the consequences.

Negative Reinforcement

The negative reinforcement learning is opposite to the positive reinforcement as it increases the tendency that the specific behavior will occur again by avoiding the negative condition.

It can be more effective than the positive reinforcement depending on situation and behavior, but it provides reinforcement only to meet minimum behavior.

How to Represent the Agent State?

We can represent the agent state using the **Markov State** that contains all the required information from the history. The State St is Markov state if it follows the given condition:

$$P[S_t+1 \mid S_t] = P[S_t+1 \mid S_1,......, S_t]$$

The Markov state follows the **Markov property**, which says that the future is independent of the past and can only be defined with the present. The RL works on fully observable environments, where the agent can observe the environment and act for the new state. The complete process is known as Markov Decision process, which is explained below.

Markov Decision Process

Markov Decision Process or MDP, is used to **formalize the reinforcement learning problems**. If the environment is completely observable, then its dynamic can be modeled as a **Markov Process**. In MDP, the agent constantly interacts with the environment and performs actions; at each action, the environment responds and generates a new state.

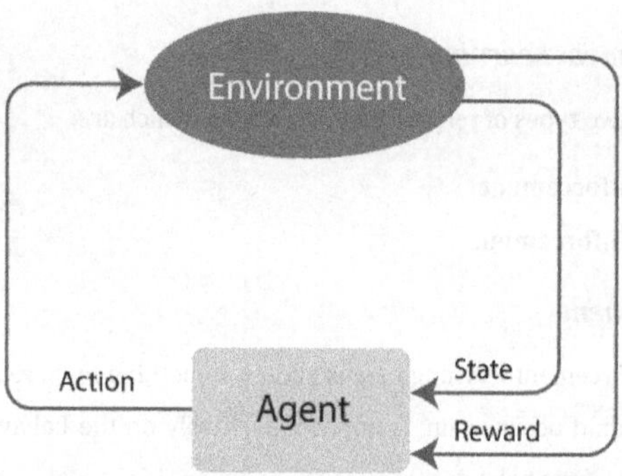

Fig. 12.7: RL Procedure

MDP is used to describe the environment for the RL, and almost all the RL problem can be formalized using MDP.

MDP contains a tuple of four elements (S, A, P_a, R_a):

- A set of finite States S.
- A set of finite Actions A.
- Rewards received after transitioning from state S to state S', due to action a.
- Probability P_a.

MDP uses **Markov property**, and to better understand the MDP, we need to learn about it.

Markov Property

It says that ***"If the agent is present in the current state S1, performs an action a1 and move to the state s2, then the state transition from s1 to s2 only depends on the current state and future action and states do not depend on past actions, rewards, or states."***

Or, in other words, as per Markov Property, the current state transition does not depend on any past action or state. Hence, MDP is an RL problem that satisfies the Markov property. Such as in a **Chess game, the players only focus on the current state and do not need to remember past actions or states**.

Finite MDP

A finite MDP is when there are finite states, finite rewards, and finite actions. In RL, we consider only the finite MDP.

Markov Process

Markov Process is a memoryless process with a sequence of random states $S_1, S_2, \ldots, S_t$ that uses the Markov Property. Markov process is also known as Markov chain, which is a tuple (S, P) on state S and transition function P. These two components (S and P) can define the dynamics of the system.

12.4. Reinforcement Learning Algorithms

Reinforcement learning algorithms are mainly used in AI applications and gaming applications. The main used algorithms are:

- ***Q-Learning***
  - Q-learning is an **Off policy RL algorithm**, which is used for the temporal difference Learning. The temporal difference learning methods are the way of comparing temporally successive predictions.
  - It learns the value function Q (S, a), which means how good to take action "**a**" at a particular state "**s.**"
  - The below flowchart explains the working of Q-learning.

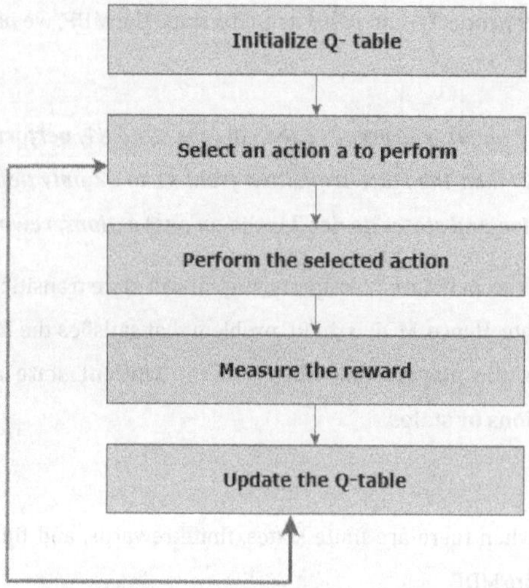

Fig. 12.8: RL Flow Chart

- ***State Action Reward State Action (SARSA)***
    - SARSA stands for **State Action Reward State action,** which is an **on-policy** temporal difference learning method. The on-policy control method selects the action for each state while learning using a specific policy.
    - The goal of SARSA is to calculate the **Q π (s, a) for the selected current policy π and all pairs of (s-a).**
    - The main difference between Q-learning and SARSA algorithms is that **unlike Q-learning, the maximum reward for the next state is not required for updating the Q-value in the table.**
    - In SARSA, new action and reward are selected using the same policy, which has determined the original action.
    - The SARSA is named because it uses the quintuple **Q(s, a, r, s', a')**. Where,

      s: original state.

      a: Original action.

      r: reward observed while following the states.

      s' and a': New state, action pair.
- ***Deep Q Neural Network (DQN)***
    - As the name suggests, DQN is a **Q-learning using Neural networks.**

- For a big state space environment, it will be a challenging and complex task to define and update a Q-table.
- To solve such an issue, we can use a DQN algorithm. Where, instead of defining a Q-table, neural network approximates the Q-values for each action and state.

Now, we will expand the Q-learning.

Q-Learning Explanation

- Q-learning is a popular model-free reinforcement learning algorithm based on the Bellman equation.
- **The main objective of Q-learning is to learn the policy which can inform the agent that what actions should be taken for maximizing the reward under what circumstances.**
- It is an **off-policy RL** that attempts to find the best action to take at a current state.
- The goal of the agent in Q-learning is to maximize the value of Q.
- The value of Q-learning can be derived from the Bellman equation. Consider the Bellman equation given below.

$$V(s) = \max [R(s,a) + \gamma \sum_{s'} P(s,a,s')V(s')]$$

In the equation, we have various components, including reward, discount factor (γ), probability, and end states s'. But there is no any Q-value is given so first consider the below image.

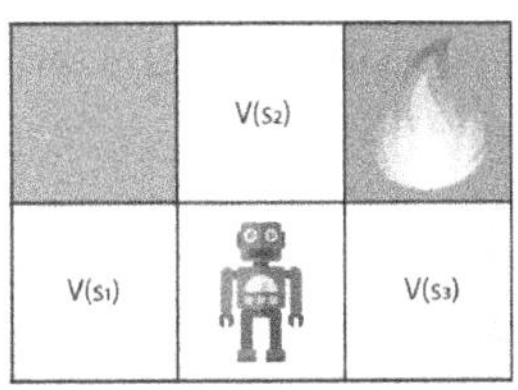

Fig. 12.9: Q Value Computation

In the above image, we can see there is an agent who has three values options, $V(s_1)$, $V(s_2)$, $V(s_3)$. As this is MDP, so agent only cares for the current state and the future state. The agent can go to any direction (Up, Left, or Right), so he needs to decide where to go for the optimal path. Here agent will take a move as per probability bases and changes the state. But if we want some exact moves, so for this, we need to make some changes in terms of Q-value. Consider the below image.

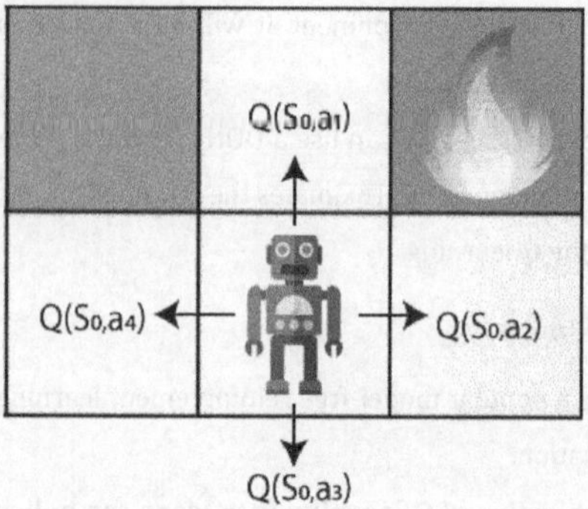

Fig. 12.10: Q Value Calculation

Q-represents the quality of the actions at each state. So instead of using a value at each state, we will use a pair of state and action, i.e., Q(s, a). Q-value specifies that which action is more lubricative than others, and according to the best Q-value, the agent takes his next move. The Bellman equation can be used for deriving the Q-value.

To perform any action, the agent will get a reward R(s, a), and also he will end up on a certain state, so the Q-value equation will be:

$$Q(S, a) = R(s, a) + \gamma \Sigma_{s'} P(s, a, s')V(s`)$$

Hence, we can say that, ***V(s) = max [Q(s, a)]***

$$Q(S, a) = R(s, a) + \gamma \sum_{s'} (P(s, a, s')\max Q(s', a'))$$

The above formula is used to estimate the Q-values in Q-Learning.

What is 'Q' in Q-learning?

The Q stands for **quality** in **Q-learning**, which means it specifies the quality of an action taken by the agent.

Q-table

A Q-table or matrix is created while performing the Q-learning. The table follows the state and action pair, i.e., [s, a], and initializes the values to zero. After each action, the table is updated, and the q-values are stored within the table.

The RL agent uses this Q-table as a reference table to select the best action based on the q-values.

Difference between Reinforcement Learning and Supervised Learning

The Reinforcement Learning and Supervised Learning both are the part of machine learning, but both types of learnings are far opposite to each other. The RL agents interact with the environment, explore it, take action, and get rewarded. Whereas supervised learning algorithms learn from the labeled dataset and, on the basis of the training, predict the output.

12.5. The difference Table between RL and Supervised Learning

Reinforcement Learning	Supervised Learning
RL works by interacting with the environment.	Supervised learning works on the existing dataset.
The RL algorithm works like the human brain works when making some decisions.	Supervised Learning works as when a human learns things in the supervision of a guide.
There is no labeled dataset is present	The labeled dataset is present.
No previous training is provided to the learning agent.	Training is provided to the algorithm so that it can predict the output.
RL helps to take decisions sequentially.	In Supervised learning, decisions are made when input is given.

Reinforcement Learning Applications

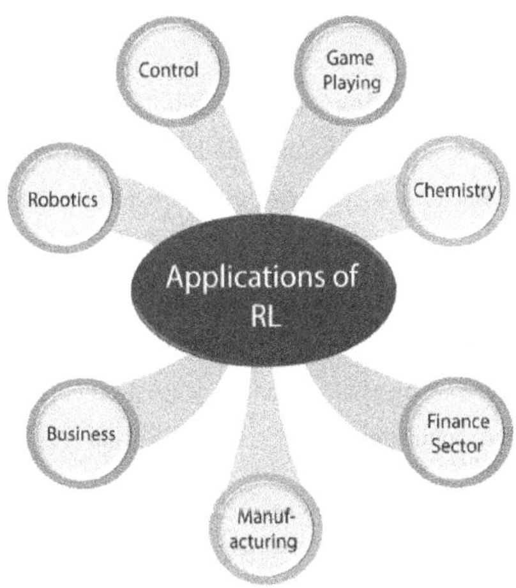

Fig. 12.11: Applications of RL

1. Robotics

a. RL is used in **Robot navigation, Robo-soccer, walking, juggling**, etc.

Control:

b. RL can be used for **adaptive control** such as Factory processes, admission control in telecommunication, and Helicopter pilot is an example of reinforcement learning.

Game Playing:

c. RL can be used in **Game playing** such as tic-tac-toe, chess, etc.

Chemistry:

d. RL can be used for optimizing the chemical reactions.

Business:

e. RL is now used for business strategy planning.

Manufacturing:

f. In various automobile manufacturing companies, the robots use deep reinforcement learning to pick goods and put them in some containers.

Finance Sector

g. The RL is currently used in the finance sector for evaluating trading strategies.

12.6. Temporal difference Learning

Temporal difference (TD) learning is an approach to learning how to predict a quantity that depends on future values of a given signal. The name TD derives from its use of changes, or differences, in predictions over successive time steps to drive the learning process. The prediction at any given time step is updated to bring it closer to the prediction of the same quantity at the next time step. It is a supervised learning process in which the training signal for a prediction is a future prediction. TD algorithms are often used in reinforcement learning to predict a measure of the total amount of reward expected over the future, but they can be used to predict other quantities as well. Continuous-time TD algorithms have also been developed.

Temporal Difference Learning (also known as TD Learning) is an unsupervised learning technique that is very commonly used in reinforcement learning for the purpose of predicting the total reward expected over the future. They can, however, be used to predict other quantities as well. It is essentially a way to learn how to predict a quantity that is dependent on the future values of a given signal. Temporal difference learning is a method that is used to compute the long-term utility of a pattern of behavior from a series of intermediate rewards.

There are also continuous-time temporal difference learning algorithms that have been developed.

Essentially, TD Learning focuses on predicting a variable's future value in a sequence of states. Temporal difference learning was a major break through in solving the problem of reward prediction. You could say that It employs a mathematical trick that allows it to replace complicated reasoning with a simple learning procedure that can be used to generate the very same results.

The trick is that rather than attempting to calculate the total future reward, temporal difference learning just attempts to predict the combination of immediate reward and its own reward prediction at the next moment in time. Now when the next moment comes and brings fresh information with it, the new prediction is compared with the expected prediction. If these two predictions are different from each other, the TD algorithm will calculate how different the predictions are from each other and make use of this temporal difference to adjust the old prediction toward the new prediction.

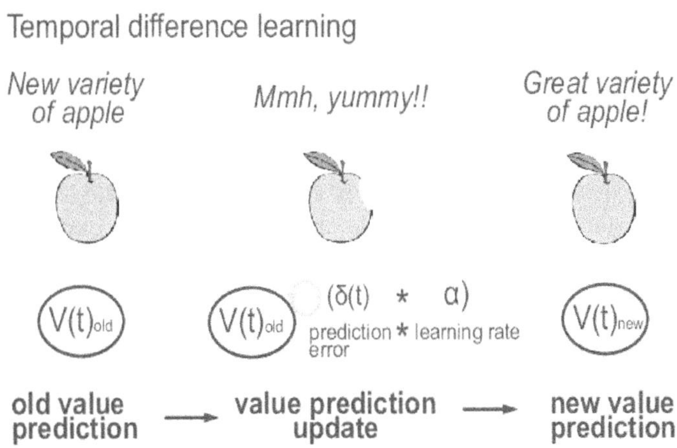

The temporal difference algorithm always aims to bring the expected prediction and the new prediction together, thus matching expectations with reality and gradually increasing the accuracy of the entire chain of prediction.

Temporal Difference Learning aims to predict a combination of the immediate reward and its own reward prediction at the next moment in time.

In TD Learning, the training signal for a prediction is a future prediction. This method is a combination of the Monte Carlo (MC) method and the Dynamic Programming (DP) method. Monte Carlo methods adjust their estimates only after the final outcome is known, but temporal difference methods tend to adjust predictions to match later, more accurate, predictions for the future, much before the final outcome is clear and know. This is essentially a type of bootstrapping.

Temporal difference learning got its name from the way it uses changes, or differences, in predictions over successive time steps for the purpose of driving the learning process.

The prediction at any particular time step gets updated to bring it nearer to the prediction of the same quantity at the next time step.

These TD methods bear relations to the temporal difference model of animal learning.

12.7. Parameters

- Alpha (α): learning rate. It shows how much our estimates should be adjusted, based on the error. This rate varies between 0 and 1.
- Gamma (γ): The discount rate. This indicates how much future rewards are valued. A larger discount rate signifies that future rewards are valued to a greater extent. The discount rate also varies between 0 and 1.
- *e*: The ratio reflective of exploration vs. exploitation.

  This involves exploring new options with probability e and staying at the current max with probability *1-e*. A larger *e* signifies that more exploration is carried out during training.

EX: How is temporal difference learning used in neuroscience?

Around the late 1980s and the early 1990s, neuroscientists were trying to understand the manner in which dopimine neurons behave. These dopimine neurons are clustered in the mid-brain, but they send projections to several areas of the brain, potentially even broadcasting some globally relevant messages. It was obvious that the firing of these neurons were related to rewards in some way, but their responses were also dependent on sensory input and they changed as the animals gained more experience in a particular task.

Luckily, some researchers had a good idea about the recent developments in neuroscience as well as artificial intelligence. They noticed that responses in some dopamine neurons represented reward prediction errors. Their firing signified the points when the animal received greater or lesser rewards than it was trained to expect.

The firing rate of the dopamine cells did not increase when the animal received the predicted reward, but the firing rate for the dopimine cells fell below the normal activation levels when the reward was less than that which was expected. This very closely mimics the way in which the error function in temporal difference is used for reinforcement learning.

These researchers saw that and then proposed that the brain makes use of a temporal difference algorithm - a reward prediction error gets calculated, it is then broadcast to the brain through the dopamine signal and employed to drive learning.

After that, the reward prediction error theory has been widely tested and validated in thousands of experiments, and has since turned into one of the most successful quantitative theories in neuroscience.

The relationship between the temporal difference model and potential neurological function has generated research that attempts to use temporal difference to explain several aspects of behavioral research. Temporal difference learning has also been utilized to study and understand conditions like schiophrenia or the consequencies of pharmacological manipulations of dopimine on learning.

12.8. Benefit of Temporal Difference Learning

The advantages of temporal difference learning are:

- TD methods are able to learn in each step, online or offline.
- These methods are capable of learning from incomplete sequences, which means that they can also be used in continuous problems.
- Temporal difference learning can function in non-terminating environments.
- TD Learning has less variance than the Monte Carlo method, because it depends on one random action, transition, reward.
- It tends to be more efficient than the Monte Carlo method.
- Temporal Difference Learning exploits the Markov property, which makes it more effective in Markov environments.

Disadvantages of Temporal Difference Learning

Temporal Difference Learning has two main disadvantages. They are:

- Temporal Difference Learning has greater sensitivity towards the initial value.
- Temporal difference learning. It is a biased estimation.

12.9. Dynamic Programming

Dynamic programming is a method for solving complex problems by breaking them down into sub-problems. The solutions to the sub-problems are combined to solve overall problem.

The two required properties of dynamic programming are:

- ***Optimal substructure***: optimal solution of the sub-problem can be used to solve the overall problem.
- ***Overlapping sub-problems***: sub-problems recur many times. Solutions of sub-problems can be cached and reused.

Markov Decision Processes (MDP) Satisfy Both of these Properties

- *The Bellman Equation gives recursive decomposition* which tells us how to break down the optimal value function into two pieces. i.e the optimal behaviour of one step and then the optimal value of the remaining steps.
- *The Value function stores and reuses solutions.* Cache with all the good information of the MDP which tells you the optimal reward you can get from that state onward.

Planning by Dynamic Programming

Dynamic programming can be used to solve reinforcement learning problems when someone tells us the structure of the MDP (i.e when we know the transition structure, reward structure etc.). Therefore dynamic programming is used for the ***planning*** in a MDP either to solve:

- ***Prediction Problem (Policy Evaluation)***

Given a MDP <S, A, P, R, γ> and a policy π. Find the value function v_π (which tells you how much reward you are going to get in each state). i.e the goal is to find out how good a policy π is.

- ***Control Problem (Find the Best Thing to do in the MDP)***

Given a MDP <S, A, P, R, γ>. Find the optimal value function *v_π and* the optimal policy π^*. i.e the goal is to find the policy which gives you the most reward you can receive with the best action to choose.

Policy Evaluation

Problem: Evaluate a given policy π and MDP. (Find out how good a policy π is).

Solution: Iterative application of Bellman Expectation backup.

Approach

Start with initial value function v_1 (a value of all states in the MDP). E.g. start with a value of 0. Therefore there is no reward. Then use the *Bellman Expectation Equation* to compute v_2 and repeat many times, which will eventually converge to *v_π.*

$$v_1 \rightarrow v_2 \rightarrow v_3 \rightarrow \cdots \rightarrow v_\pi$$

One method to achieve this convergence is to use *synchronous backups* where we consider all states at every step.

1. At each iteration k+1, for all states s ∈ S.
2. Update $v_{k+1}(s)$ from $v_k(s')$, where *s'* is a successor state of *s.*

   $v_k(s')$ is updated using the Bellman Expectation Equation discussed in Part 2.

$$\upsilon_{k+1}(S) = \sum_{\alpha \epsilon A} \pi(a/s)\,(R_S^a + \gamma \sum_{s' \epsilon S} P_{ss'}^a\ \upsilon_k(S'))$$

Bellman Expectation Equation

Example

Suppose we have a grid world with *14 states,* where each block represents a **state**. We also have 2 **terminal states,** one in the bottom right and the other in the top left of the grid world. We can take the **actions** of moving *up, down, left* and *right* with each transition we take gives us a **immediate reward** of *-1* until a terminal state is reached. With a **discount factor** of *γ=1* and our given policy π for our agent follows a uniform random policy:

$$\pi(up|.) = \pi(down|.) = \pi(left|.) = \pi(right|.) = 0.25$$

We need to compute the value of being in each state to determine how good our defined policy π is.

1. By following our approach described above we can start with an initial value function v_0 with all values being 0.

0.0	0.0	0.0	0.0
0.0	0.0	0.0	0.0
0.0	0.0	0.0	0.0
0.0	0.0	0.0	0.0

v_0

2. **Next we compute the new value function v_1 using the Bellman Expectation Equation by applying a one step look ahead.**

0.0	-1.0	-1.0	-1.0
-1.0	-1.0	-1.0	-1.0
-1.0	-1.0	-1.0	-1.0
-1.0	-1.0	-1.0	0.0

v_1: Blue block is calculated using the Bellman Expectation Equation such that 0.25(-1+1(0))+0.25(-1+1(0))+0.25(-1+1(0))+0.25(-1+1(0)) = -1

3. **Repeating the processing using v_1 to compute v_2.**

0.0	-1.75	-2.0	-2.0
-1.75	-2.0	-2.0	-2.0
-2.0	-2.0	-2.0	-1.75
-2.0	-2.0	-1.75	0.0

v_2: Blue block is calculated using the Bellman Expectation Equation such that 0.25(-1+1(-1))+0.25(-1+1(-1))+0.25(-1+1(-1))+0.25(-1+1(0))=-1.75

4. Repeating this process with $k=\infty$ will eventually converge our value function to v_π.

0.0	-14.	-20.	-22.
-14.	-18.	-20.	-20.
-20.	-20.	-18.	-14.
-22.	-20.	-14.	0.0

vπ

We have therefore computed the value associated to being in each state in our MDP for our policy π.

How to Improve a Policy?

In the above approach we have evaluated a given policy but not found the best policy (actions to take) in our environment. In order to improve a given policy we can *evaluate* a given policy π and improve the policy by *acting greedily* with respect to v_π. This can be done using ***Policy Iteration***.

Policy Iteration

Problem: Find the best policy π^* for a given MDP.

Solution: Bellman Expectation Equation Policy Iteration and Acting Greedy.

Approach

Start with a given policy π.

1. Evaluate the policy π with Policy Evaluation (described above).
2. Improve the policy π by ***acting greedily*** with respect to v_π with Policy Improvement to get a new policy π'.
3. Repeat until the new policy π' converges to the optimal policy π^*.

In order to act greedily we use a one step look ahead to determine the action which gives us the maximum ***action value function*** (described in Part 2):

$$\pi'(s) = argmin_{a \epsilon A q_\pi}(s, a)$$

Recall the action value function has the following equations:

$$q_\pi(s,a)=\mathbb{E}_\pi[R_{t+1} + \gamma q_\pi(S_{t+1,}A_{t+1,})|S_t = s, A_t = a]$$

$$R_s^a + \gamma \sum_{s' \epsilon S} P_{ss'}^a v_\pi(S')$$

$$R_s^a + \gamma \sum_{s' \epsilon S} P_{ss'}^a \sum_{a \epsilon A} \pi(a'|s') q_\pi(s', a')$$

Action-value Function

Value Iteration

An alternative approach to control problems is with value iteration using the *Bellman Optimality Equation*. First we need to define how we can divide an optimal policy into its components using the ***Principle of Optimality.***

12.10. Principle of Optimality

Any ***optimal policy*** can be subdivided into two components which make the overall behavior optimal:

- An optimal first action *A∗*.
- Followed by an optimal policy from successor state *S*.

Theorem (Principle of Optimality)

A policy π(a/s) achieves the optimal value from state s, v_π(s)=v∗(s), if and only if:

- *For any state s′ reachable from s.*
- *π achieves the optimal value from state s′, v_π(s′)=v∗(s′)*

Value Iteration (Applied)

Problem: Find the optimal policy π^* for a given MDP.

Solution: Iterative application of Bellman Optimality backup.

Approach

Using synchronous backups update the value function until the optimal value function is computed without computing the action value function.

$$v_1 \to v_2 \to v_3 \to \cdots \to v_*$$

1. At each iteration k+1, for all states s ∈ S.
2. Update $v_{k+1}(s)$ from $v_k(s')$, where *s′* is a successor state of *s*.

$v_k(s')$ is updated using the Bellman Optimality Equation discussed in the Part 2:

$$v_{k+1}(s) = max_{a\epsilon A}(R_a^s + \gamma \sum_{s'\epsilon S} P_{ss'}^a v_k(S'))$$

Bellman Optimality Equation

By repeating the above process, it will eventually converge to v^*. Note this process differs to policy iteration in that intermediate value functions may not correspond to any policy.

CHAPTER 13

ANALYTICAL LEARNING - 1

13.1. Analytical Learning

Analytic Learning is an analytical approach to learning that uses prior knowledge as a base from which concepts can be described, hypotheses can be developed, and concepts can be rationally generalized by analyzing the components and the structure of the concepts.

13.2. Learning with Perfect Domain Theories

- A perfect domain theory is correct and complete.
- A domain theory is ***correct*** if each of its assertions is a truthful statement about the world.
- A domain the is ***complete*** with respect to target concept and X, if it covers every positive example in the instance space.
- So, if we have a perfect domain theory, why do we need to learn?
- Chess. Often the theory leads to too many deductions (large breadth) making it impossible to find the optimal strategy. The examples help to focus search.
- Perfect domain theories are often unrealistic, but, learning in them is a first step before learning with imperfect theories (next chapter).
- Prolog-EBG is an EBL learner. It uses sequential covering.

13.3. Prolog-EBG

Prolog-EGB(Target Concept, TraningExamples, Domain Theory)

1. Learned Rules = {}
2. Pos = the positive examples from TraningExamples.
3. **for each** Positive Example in Pos that is not covered by Learned Rules **do**
    1. Explanation = an explanation in terms of Domain Theory that Pos satisfies the Target Concept.
    2. Sufficient Conditions = the most general set of features of Positive Example sufficient to satisfy the Target Concept according to the Explanation.
    3. Learned Rules = Learned Rules + {Target Concept ← Sufficient Conditions}.
4. **return** Learned Rules

Explaining the Example

- Give a proof, using the domain theory, that the (positive) training satisfies the target concept.
- In our ongoing example the positive example of SafeToStack(o1,o2) can be explained by using the domain theory, as such:
    1. *Volume(o1,2) ∧ Density(o1,0.3) ∧ Equal(0.6, 2*0.3) → Weight(o1,0.6)*
    2. *Type(o2,endtable) → Weight(o2,5)*
    3. *Weight(o1, 0.6) ∧ Less Than(0.6, 5) ∧ Weight(o2,5) → Lighter(o1,o2)*
    4. *Lighter(o1, o2) → SafeToStack(o1,o2)*
- In Prolog-EGB this explanation is generated using backward chaining search, as done by Prolog.
- Like Prolog, it halts when it finds a proof.

Analyze the Explanation

- Which of the many features of the objects are relevant to the target concept?
- Those that appear in the explanation we just built.
- We can collect these and substitute x,y for o1,o2 to get

  Volume(x,2) ∧ Density(x,0.3) ∧ Type(y,endtable) → SafeToStack(x,y).

  So, we now have the most general set of features, right?

Analyze the Explanation

- Which of the many features of the objects are relevant to the target concept?
- Those that appear in the explanation we just built.
- We can collect these and substitute x,y for o1,o2 to get

  Volume(x,2) ∧ Density(x,0.3) ∧ Type(y,endtable) → SafeToStack(x,y)

  So, we now have the most general set of features, right?
- **Wrong!** An even more general rule can be obtained using a more careful analysis of the explanation.

13.4. What is Prolog

- Prolog stands for programming in logic. In the logic programming paradigm, prolog language is most widely available. Prolog is a declarative language, which means that a program consists of data based on the facts and rules (Logical relationship) rather than computing how to find a solution. A logical relationship describes the relationships which hold for the given application.

- To obtain the solution, the user asks a question rather than running a program. When a user asks a question, then to determine the answer, the run time system searches through the database of facts and rules.
- The first Prolog was 'Marseille Prolog', which is based on work by Colmerauer. The major example of fourth-generation programming language was prolog. It supports the declarative programming paradigm.
- In 1981, a Japanese computer Project of 5th generation was announced. After that, it was adopted Prolog as a development language. In this tutorial, the program was written in the 'Standard' Edinburgh Prolog. Prologs of Prolog II family are the other kind of prologs which are descendants of Marseille Prolog.
- Prolog features are 'Logical variable', which means that they behave like uniform data structure, a backtracking strategy to search for proofs, a pattern-matching facility, mathematical variable, and input and out are interchangeable.
- To deduce the answer, there will be more than one way. In such case, the run time system will be asked to find another solution. To generate another solution, use the backtracking strategy. Prolog is a weakly typed language with static scope rules and dynamic type checking.
- Prolog is a declarative language that means we can specify what problem we want to solve rather than how to solve it.
- Prolog is used in some areas like database, natural language processing, artificial intelligence, but it is pretty useless in some areas like a numerical algorithm or instance graphics.
- In artificial intelligence applications, prolog is used. The artificial intelligence applications can be automated reasoning systems, natural language interfaces, and expert systems. The expert system consists of an interface engine and a database of facts. The prolog's run time system provides the service of an interface engine.
- A basic logic programming environment has no literal values. An identifier with upper case letters and other identifiers denote variables. Identifiers that start with lower-case letters denote data values. The basic Prolog elements are typeless. The most implementations of prolog have been enhanced to include integer value, characters, and operations. The Mechanism of prolog describes the tuples and lists.

- Functional programming language and prolog have some similarities like Hugs. A logic program is used to consist of relation definition. A functional programming language is used to consist of a sequence of function definitions. Both the logical programming and functional programming rely heavily on recursive definitions.

Applications of Prolog

The applications of prolog are as follows:

- Specification Language
- Robot Planning
- Natural language understanding
- Machine Learning
- Problem Solving
- Intelligent Database retrieval
- Expert System
- Automated Reasoning

Prolog - Additional

- Prolog is a logic programming language. It has important role in artificial intelligence. Unlike many other programming languages, Prolog is intended primarily as a declarative programming language. In prolog, logic is expressed as relations (called as Facts and Rules). Core heart of prolog lies at the **logic** being applied. Formulation or Computation is carried out by running a query over these relations.
- **Installation in Linux**

  Open a terminal **(Ctrl+Alt+T)** and type.

  sudo apt-get install swi-prolog.
- **Syntax and Basic Fields**

  In prolog, We declare some facts. These facts constitute the Knowledge Base of the system. We can query against the Knowledge Base. We get output as affirmative if our query is already in the knowledge Base or it is implied by Knowledge Base, otherwise we get output as negative. So, Knowledge Base can be considered similar to database, against which we can query. Prolog facts are expressed in definite pattern. Facts contain entities and their relation. Entities are written within the parenthesis separated by comma (,). Their relation is expressed at the start and outside the parenthesis. Every fact/rule ends with a dot (.).

So, a typical prolog fact goes as follows:

- Format: relation(entity1, entity2,....k'th entity).
- **Example:**
- friends(raju, mahesh).
- singer(sonu).
- odd_number(5).
- **Explanation:**
  - These facts can be interpreted as :
  - raju and mahesh are friends.
  - sonu is a singer.
  - 5 is an odd number.
- **Key Features**

  1. Unification: The basic idea is, can the given terms be made to represent the same structure.

  2. Backtracking: When a task fails, prolog traces backwards and tries to satisfy previous task.

  3. Recursion: Recursion is the basis for any search in program.
- **Running queries:**

  A typical prolog query can be asked as:
  - Query 1: ?- singer(sonu).
  - Output: Yes.
  - Explanation: As our knowledge base contains the above fact, so output was 'Yes', otherwise it would have been 'No'.
  - Query 2: ?- odd_number(7).
  - Output: No.
  - Explanation: As our knowledge base does not contain the above fact, so output was 'No'.
- **Advantages:**

1. Easy to build database. Doesn't need a lot of programming effort.
2. Pattern matching is easy. Search is recursion based.
3. It has built in list handling. Makes it easier to play with any algorithm involving lists.

- **Disadvantages:**

1. LISP (another logic programming language) dominates over prolog with respect to I/O features.

2. Sometimes input and output is not easy.

13.5. Explanation-Based Learning (EBL)

- In terms of Machine Learning, it is **an algorithm that aims to understand why an example is a part of a particular concept to make generalizations or form concepts from training examples**. For example, EBL uses a domain theory and creates a program that learns to play chess.

In simple terms, it is the ability to gain basic problem-solving techniques by observing and analyzing solutions to specific problems. In terms of Machine Learning, it is an algorithm that aims to understand why an example is a part of a particular concept to make generalizations or form concepts from training examples. For example, EBL uses a domain theory and creates a program that learns to play chess.

Intuition

The objective of EBL is to understand the essential properties of a particular concept. So, we need to find out what makes an example, part of a particular concept. Unlike FOIL algorithm, here we focus on the one example instead of collecting multiple examples.

The ability to explain single examples is known as **"Domain Theory".**

An EBL accepts 4 kinds of input:

1. **A training example:** what the learning model sees in the world.

2. **A goal concept:** a high level description of what the model is supposed to learn.

3. **A operational criterion:** states which other terms can appear in the generalized result.

4. **A domain theory:** set of rules that describe relationships between objects and actions in a domain.

From the above 4 parameters, EBL uses the domain theory to find that training example, that best describes the goal concept while abiding by the operational criterion and keeping our justification as general as possible.

EBL involves 2 steps:

1. **Explanation** — The domain theory is used to eliminate all the unimportant training example while retaining the important ones that best describe the goal concept.
2. **Generalization** — The explanation of the goal concept is made as general and widely applicable as possible. This ensures that all cases are covered, not just certain specific ones.

EBL Architecture

- ***EBL Model During Training***
    - During training, the model generalizes the training example in such a way that all scenarios lead to the Goal Concept, not just in specific cases. **(As shown in Fig.)**

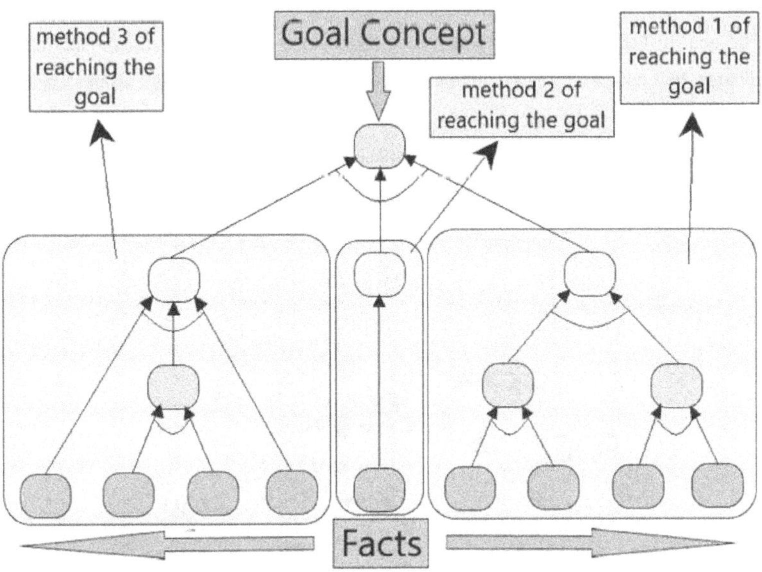

Fig. 13.1: Training EBL Model

- ***EBL Model After Training***
    - Post training, EBL model tends to directly reach the hypothesis space involving the goal concept. **(As shown in Fig.)**

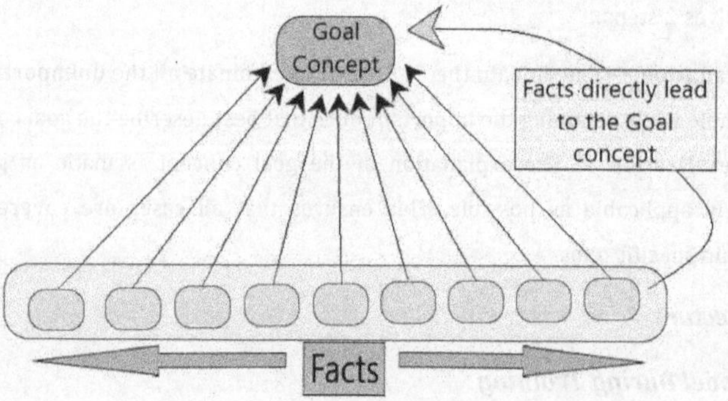

Fig. 13.2: Trained EBL Model

FOCL

The goal of FOCL, like FOIL, is to create a rule in terms of the extensionally defined predicates, that covers all the positive examples and none of the negative examples. Unlike FOIL, FOCL integrates background knowledge and EBL methods into it which leads to a much more efficient search of hypothesis space that fits the training data. **(As shown in Fig).**

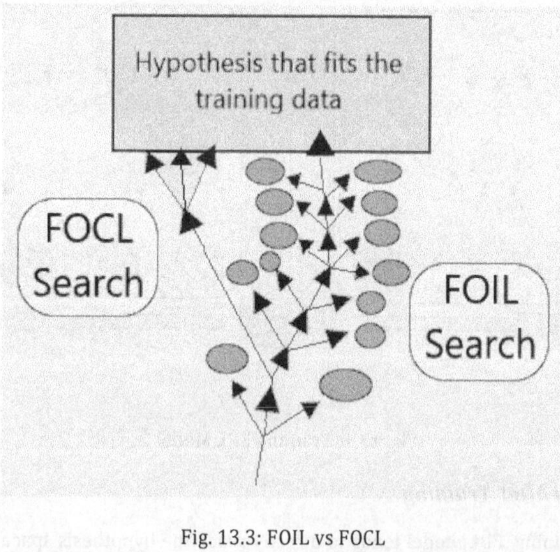

Fig. 13.3: FOIL vs FOCL

FOCL: Intuition

Like FOIL, FOCL also tends to perform an iterative process of learning a set of best-rules to cover the training examples and then remove all the training examples covered by that best rule. (Using a sequential covering algorithm).

However, what makes the FOCL algorithm more powerful is the approach that it adapts while searching for that best-rule.

A literal is called **operational** if it can describe the training example properly leading to the output hypothesis. In contrast, literals that occur only as intermediate features in the domain theory, but not as primitive attributes of the instances, are considered **non-operational**. Non-operational predicates are evaluated in the same manner as operational predicates in FOCL.

Algorithm Involved

//Inputs Literal --> operationalized

List of positive examples

List of negative examples

//Output Literal --> operational form

Operationalize (Literal, Positive examples, Negative examples)

If(Literal = operational):

Return Literal

Initialize Operational Literals to the empty set

For each clause in the definition of Literal

Compute information gain of the clause over Positive examples and Negative examples

For the clause with the maximum gain

For each literal L in the clause

Operational Literals<-- **Operationalize (L, Positive examples, Negative examples)**

Working of the Algorithm

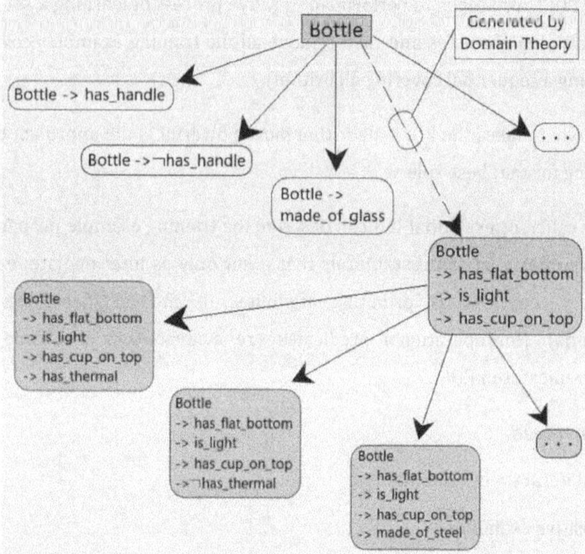

Fig. 13.4: FOCL Example

Step 1 – Use the same method as done in FOIL and add a single feature for each operational literal that is not part of the hypothesis space so as to create candidates for the best rule. **(Solid arrows in Fig denote specializations of bottle).**

Step 2 – Create an operational literal that is logically efficient to explain the goal concept according to the Domain Theory. **(Dashed arrows in Fig denote domain theory based specializations of bottle).**

Step 3 – Add this set of literals to the current preconditions of hypothesis.

Step 4 – Remove all those preconditions of hypothesis space that are unnecessary according to the training data.

Let us consider the example shown in Fig.

- First, FOCL creates all the candidate literals that have the possibility of becoming the best-rule (all denoted by solid arrows). Something we have already seen in the FOIL algorithm. In addition, it creates several logically relevant candidate literals of its own. (the domain theory).

- Then, it selects one of the literals from the domain theory whose precondition matches with the goal concept. If there are several such literals present, then it just selects one which gives the **most information** related to the goal concept.

For example, If the **bottle (goal concept)** is made of **steel** (while satisfying the other domain theory preconditions), then the algorithm will select that as it the **most relevant information related to the goal concept.**

i.e. the bottle.

- Now, all those literals that removed unless the affect the classification accuracy over the training examples. This is done so that the domain theory doesn't overspecialize the result by addition irrelevant literals. This set of literals is now added to the preconditions of the current hypothesis.
- Finally, one candidate literal which provides the maximum information gain is selected out two specialization methods. (FOIL and domain theory).

FOCL is a powerful machine learning algorithm that uses EBL and domain theory techniques, reaching the hypothesis space quickly and efficiently. It has shown more improved and accurate results than the Inductive FOIL Algorithm.

Additional

Learning

Learning is a fundamental component of intelligence, and a key consideration in designing cognitive architectures such as Soar [Laird *et al.*, 1986]. This chapter considers the question of what constitutes an appropriate general-purpose learning mechanism. We are interested in mechanisms that might explain and reproduce the rich variety of learning capabilities of humans, ranging from learning perceptual-motor skills such as how to ride a bicycle, to learning highly cognitive tasks such as how to play chess.

Research on learning in fields such as cognitive science, artificial intelligence, neurobiology, and statistics has led to the identification of two distinct classes of learning methods: inductive and analytic. Inductive methods, such as neural network Backpropagation, learn general laws by finding statistical correlations and regularities among a large set of training examples. In contrast, analytical methods, such as Explanation-Based Learning, acquire general laws from many fewer training examples. They rely instead on prior knowledge to analyze individual training examples in detail, then use this analysis to distinguish relevant example features from the irrelevant.

The question considered in this chapter is how to best combine inductive and analytical learning in an architecture that seeks to cover the range of learning exhibited by intelligent systems such as humans. We present a specific learning mechanism, Explanation Based Neural Network learning (EBNN), that blends these two types of learning, and present experimental results demonstrating its ability to learn control strategies for a mobile robot using vision, sonar, and laser range sensors. We then consider the analytical learning mechanism in Sofar, called chunking, and recent attempts to complement chunking by including inductive mechanisms in Soar. Finally, we suggest a way in which EBNN could be introduced as are placement for chunking in Soar, thereby incorporating inductive and analytical learning as architectural capabilities.

The following section provides an overview of inductive and analytic principles for learning, and argues that both are necessary for a general learning mechanism that scales up to handle a broad range of tasks. The subsequent section presents the EBNN learning mechanism, together with experimental results illustrating its capabilities. Finally, we consider the general learning mechanism for Soar, and the question of how to best incorporate both inductive and analytic learning within this architecture.

Why Combine Analysis and Induction?

At the heart of the learning problem is the question of how to successfully generalize from examples. For instance, when people learn to ride a bicycle or learn to play chess, they learn from specific experiences (e.g., riding a specific bicycle on a particular day in a particular place). Somehow they are able to generalize away from the myriad details of specific situations, to learn general strategies that they expect to apply in "similar" sub sequent situations. In doing this, they must differentiate between the many irrelevant details of the situation (e.g., the angle of the sun on that particular day, the color of the bicyclist's shirt), and the few essential features (e.g., the velocity and tilt angle of the bicycle). This section provides brief overviews of analytical and inductive methods for generalizing from examples, then considers the complementary benefits of these two learning paradigms.

Analytical Learning

Analytical learning uses the learner's prior knowledge to analyze individual training examples, in order to discriminate the relevant features from the irrelevant. The most common analytical learning method is explanation-based learning. To illustrate, consider the problem of learning to play chess. More specifically, consider the subtask of learning to recognize chess positions in which one's queen will be lost within the next few moves.

Fig. 13.5: Example Playing Chess

A positive example of the concept "chess positions in which black can be forced to lose its queen within 2 moves." Note the white knight is attacking both the black king and queen. Black must therefore move its king enabling white to capture the black queen.

A positive example of this class of chess positions is shown in Figure. As explained in the figure caption, this is a positive example of a chess position in which black can be forced to lose its queen. To learn a general rule from this example, it is Necessary to determine which board features are relevant to losing the queen, and which irrelevant details to be ignored are. Inductive learning methods generalize by collecting multiple training examples, then determining which features are common to the positive examples, but not to the negative examples. In the chess example above, there are many features that happen to be true (e.g., the feature "4 white pawns are still in their original positions"), but only a few that are relevant (e.g., "the black king and queen are simultaneously under attack"). In this chess example, inductive techniques will require hundreds or thousands of training example chessboards to statistically determine which features are relevant, and to generalize appropriately.

In analytical learning such as explanation-based learning, a justifiable generalization of the chess position can be derived from just this one training example. This is accomplished by the learner explaining how the training example satisfies the target concept, then identifying the features mentioned in the explanation as relevant. Given prior knowledge of the legal moves of chess, it is possible for the learner to construct an explanation of why the black queen is lost in the particular training example of Figure. The explanation is given in the figure caption. Notice this explanation mentions the feature that "the white knight is attacking both the black king and queen." This feature is thus determined to be relevant in general, and forms a condition under which black will in general lose its queen. In contrast, other irrelevant features that would be considered in inductive learning (e.g., "4 white pawns are still in their original positions") are not even considered, because they play no part in the explanation. Explanation-based learning generalizes through explaining and analyzing training instances in terms of prior knowledge. While our purpose here is to examine computer learning algorithms, it is interesting to note that research on human learning provides support for the conjecture that humans learn through such explanations.

Analytical learning methods have been used successfully in a number of applications – notably for learning rules to control search. For example, Prodigy is a domain-independent framework for means-ends planning that uses explanation-based learning to acquire search control knowledge. Prodigy learns general rules that characterize concepts such as "situations in which pursuing sub goal? X will lead to backtracking." Given a specific problem solving domain defined by a set of states, operators, and goals, Prodigy learns control rules that significantly reduce backtracking when solving problems in this domain. It has been demonstrated to learn search control rules comparable to hand-coded rules in a variety of task domains.

The chunking mechanism in Soar also provides an example of analytical learning, In Soar, problem solving corresponds to search in problem spaces (a problem space is defined by problem states and operators). Whenever Soar has no control knowledge to choose its next search step, it reflects on the current situation by using a higher-level problem space, resulting in a choice of an appropriate search step. The trace of reasoning performed in this higher level space forms an explanation of why the selected search step is appropriate in this specific instance. The architecture automatically records this explanation whenever it reflects in this fashion, and the chunking mechanism forms a new control rule (called a production) by collecting the features mentioned in the explanation into the preconditions of the new rule. Soar's analytical chunking mechanism has been shown to learn successfully to speed up problem solving across a broad range of domains. For example, presents results in which over 100,000 productions are learned from such explanations within one particular domain.

Inductive Learning

Whereas analytical learning can produce appropriate generalizations by analyzing single training examples, it requires strong prior knowledge about its domain in order to construct appropriate explanations. Its determination of which features are relevant will only be as correct and complete as the prior knowledge from which explanations are formed. In many domains, such complete and correct prior knowledge is unavailable. For example, consider learning the concept "stocks that double in value over the next year." In this case, an explanation of a training example would require explaining which features were responsible for the increase in value. Unlike the chess domain, in which the effects of each possible move are known perfectly in advance, the stock market domain cannot be modeled so correctly and completely. In such cases, inductive techniques that identify empirical regularities over many examples are useful.

To illustrate inductive learning, consider the task of learning to drive a motor vehicle. Describes the computer system ALVINN that learns to steer a vehicle driving at 55mph on public highways, based on input sensor data from a video camera. Notice this task involves learning control knowledge, much like the control knowledge learned by Prodigy and Soar. In this domain, however, a complete and correct model of the effects of different steering actions is not known a priori. Therefore, an inductive learning method, neural network Backpropagation is used to learn a mapping from the camera image to the appropriate steering direction. Thousands of training examples are collected by recording camera images and steering commands while a human drives the vehicle for approximately 10 minutes. These human-provided training examples of visual scenes and corresponding steering commands are generalized by the neural network to acquire a general mapping from scenes to steering commands. The resulting network has been demonstrated to drive unassisted for intervals up to 100 miles at speeds of 55 mph on public highways. The neural network learning technique is a method for fitting hundreds of numeric parameters in a predefined, but highly expressive non-linear functional form. These parameters are fit by performing a gradient descent search to minimize the error (i.e., difference) between the network output and the desired output for the training example set.

13.6. Learning with Perfect Domain Theories: PROLOG-EBG

A perfect domain theory is correct and complete. A domain theory is *correct* if each of its assertions is a truthful statement about the world. A domain the is *complete* with respect to the target concept and X, if it covers every positive example in the instance space. So, if we have a perfect domain theory, why do we need to learn? Chess Often the theory leads to too many deductions (large breadth) making it impossible to find the optimal strategy. The examples help to focus search.

Perfect domain theories are often unrealistic, but, learning in them is a first step before learning with imperfect theories. Prolog-EBG is an EBL learner. It uses sequential covering.

Prolog-EBG

Prolog-EGB(TargetConcept, Training Examples, DomainTheory)

1. LearnedRules = {}
2. Pos = the positive examples from Training Examples.
3. **for each** PositiveExample in Pos that is not covered by LearnedRules **do**
    1. Explanation = an explanation in terms of DomainTheory that Pos satisfies the TargetConcept.
    2. SufficientConditions = the most general set of features of PositiveExample sufficient to satisfy the TargetConcept according to the Explanation.
    3. LearnedRules = LearnedRules + {TargetConcept ← SufficientConditions}.
4. **return** LearnedRules

Explaining the Example

- Give a proof, using the domain theory, that the (positive) training satisfies the target concept. In our ongoing example the positive example of SafeToStack(o1,o2) can be explained by using the domain theory, as such:
    1. *Volume (o1, 2) ∧ Density(o1,0.3) ∧Equal(0.6, 2*0.3) → Weight(o1,0.6)*
    2. *Type (o2, endtable) → Weight(o2,5)*
    3. *Weight (o1, 0.6) ∧ Less Than(0.6, 5) ∧ Weight(o2,5) → Lighter(o1,o2)*
    4. *Lighter (o1, o2) → SafeToStack(o1,o2)*
- In Prolog-EGB this explanation is generated using backward chaining search, as done by Prolog. Like Prolog, it halts when it finds a proof.

13.7. Remarks on Explanation-based Learning

As we saw in the above example, PROLOG-EBG conducts a detailed analysis of individual training examples to determine how best to generalize from the specific example to a general Horn clause hypothesis. The following are the key properties of this algorithm.

- Unlike inductive methods, PROLOG-EBG produces ***justified*** general hypotheses by using prior knowledge to analyze individual examples.
- The explanation of how the example satisfies the target concept determines which example attributes are relevant: those mentioned by the explanation.
- The further analysis of the explanation, regressing the target concept to determine its weakest pre image with respect to the explanation, allows deriving more general constraints on the values of the relevant features.

- Each learned Horn clause corresponds to a sufficient condition for satisfying the target concept. The set of learned Horn clauses covers the positive training examples encountered by the learner, as well as other instances that share the same explanations.
- The generality of the learned Horn clauses will depend on the formulation of the domain theory and on the sequence in which training examples are considered.
- PROLOG-EBG implicitly assumes that the domain theory is correct and complete. If the domain theory is incorrect or incomplete, the resulting learned concept may also be incorrect.

13.8. Explanation-based Learning of Search Control Knowledge

As noted above, the practical applicability of the PROLOG-EBG algorithm is restricted by its requirement that the domain theory be correct and complete. One important class of learning problems where this requirement is easily satisfied is learning to speed up complex search programs.

For example, one target concept is "the set of states in which sub goal A should be solved before sub goal B." An example of a rule learned by PRODIGY for this target concept in a simple block-stacking problem domain is to understand this rule, consider again the simple.

IF	**One subgoal to be solved is $On(x, y)$, and**
	One subgoal to be solved is $On(y, z)$
THEN	**Solve the subgoal $On(y, z)$ before $On(x, y)$**

Block stacking problem illustrated in the problem illustrated by that figure, the goal is to stack the blocks so that they spell the word "universal."

CHAPTER 14

ANALYTICAL LEARNING - 2

14.1. Hypothesis Space Search

How can the domain theory and training data best be combined to constrain the search for an acceptable hypothesis? One way to understand the range of possible approaches is to return to our view of learning as a task of searching through the space of alternative hypotheses. We can characterize most learning methods as search algorithms by describing the hypothesis space H they search, the initial hypothesis ***ho*** at which they begin their search, the set of search operators ***0*** that define individual search steps, and the goal criterion G that specifies the search objective.

14.2. The KBANN Algorithm

The KBANN algorithm exemplifies the initialize-the-hypothesis approach to using domain theories. It assumes a domain theory represented by a set of propositional, on-recursive Horn clauses. **A** Horn clause is propositional if it contains no variables. The input and output of KBANN are as follows:

KBANN(*Domain_Theory, Training_Examples*)
Domain_Theory: Set of propositional, nonrecursive Horn clauses.
Training_Examples: Set of (input output) pairs of the target function.

Analytical step: Create an initial network equivalent to the domain theory.

1. For each instance attribute create a network input.
2. For each Horn clause in the *Domain_Theory*, create a network unit as follows:
   - Connect the inputs of this unit to the attributes tested by the clause antecedents.
   - For each non-negated antecedent of the clause, assign a weight of W to the corresponding sigmoid unit input.
   - For each negated antecedent of the clause, assign a weight of $-W$ to the corresponding sigmoid unit input.
   - Set the threshold weight w_0 for this unit to $-(n - .5)W$, where n is the number of non-negated antecedents of the clause.
3. Add additional connections among the network units, connecting each network unit at depth i from the input layer to all network units at depth $i+1$. Assign random near-zero weights to these additional connections.

Inductive step: Refine the initial network.

4. Apply the BACKPROPAGATION algorithm to adjust the initial network weights to fit the *Training_Examples*.

Given

- A set of training examples.
- A domain theory consisting of non-recursive, propositional Horn clauses.

Determine

- An artificial neural network that fits the training examples, biased by the domain theory the two stages of the KBANN algorithm are first to create an artificial neural network that perfectly fits the domain theory and second to use the BACKPROPACATION algorithm to refine this initial network to fit the training examples. The details of this algorithm, including the algorithm for creating the initial network.

14.3. Using Prior Knowledge to Alter the Search Objective

An alternative way of using prior knowledge is to incorporate it into the error criterion minimized by gradient descent, so that the network must fit a combined function of the training data and domain theory. In this section, we consider using prior knowledge in this fashion. In particular, we consider prior knowledge in the form of known derivatives of the target function. Certain types of prior knowledge can be expressed quite naturally in this form. For example, in training a neural network to recognize handwritten characters we can specify certain derivatives of the target function in order to express our prior knowledge that "the identity of the character is independent of small translations and rotations of the image."

14.4. The TANGENT PROP Algorithm

TANGENTPRO accommodates domain knowledge expressed as derivatives of the target function with respect to transformations of its inputs. Consider a learning task involving an instance space X and target function f. Up to now we have assumed that each training example consists of a pair that describes some instance ***xi*** and its training $(x_i, f(x_i))$ value f (x_i). The TANGENTPROP algorithm assumes various training derivatives of the target function are also $(x_i, f(x_i), \frac{\partial f(x)}{\partial x} |x_i)$ provided. For example, if each instance ***xi*** is described by a single real value, $\frac{\partial f(x)}{\partial x} |x_i$ then each training example may be of the form. Here denotes the derivative of the target function f with respect to ***x,*** evaluated at the point ***x = xi.***

To develop an intuition for the benefits of providing training derivatives as well as training values during learning, consider the simple learning task depicted in Figure. The task is to learn the target function f shown in the leftmost $(x_1,f(x_1)), (x_2,f(x_2))$ plot of the figure,

$\left(x_{3,}f(x_3)\right)$ based on the three training examples shown: and Given these three training examples, the BACKPROPAGATION algorithm can be expected to hypothesize a smooth function, such as the function ***g*** depicted in the middle plot of the figure. The rightmost plot shows the effect of providing training derivatives, or slopes, as (e.g., $(x_{1,}f(x_1),\frac{\partial f(x)}{\partial x}|x_1))$ additional information for each training example.

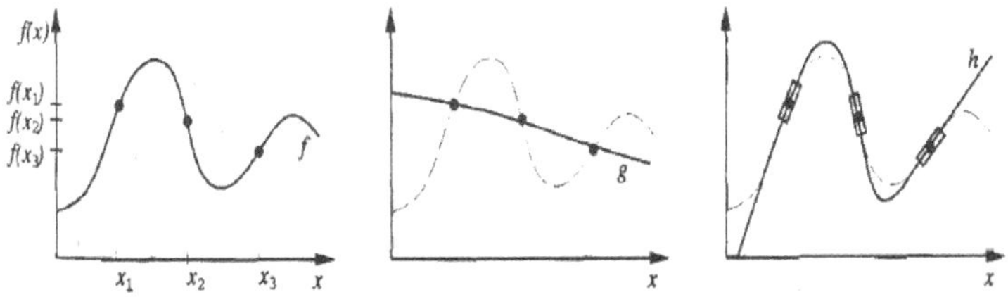

The derivative of the target function with respect to this transformation is zero (i.e., that rotating the input image does not alter the value of the target function). In other words, we can assert the following training derivative for $\frac{\partial f(s(\alpha, x_i))}{\partial \alpha} = 0$ every training instance xi.

Where f is the target function and ***s (α,*** xi) is the image resulting from applying the transformation s to the image xi.

The BACKPROPAGATION algorithm performs gradient descent to attempt to minimize the sum of squared errors where xi denotes the ith training instance, f denotes the true target function, and *f* denotes the function represented by the learned neural network.

$$E = \sum_i (f(x_i) - \hat{f}(x_i))^2$$

TANGENT-PROP considers the squared error between the specified training derivative and the actual derivative of the learned neural network. The modified error function is where ***p*** is a constant provided by the user to determine the relative importance of fitting training values versus fitting training derivatives.

$$E = \Sigma_i[(f(x_i) - \widehat{f}(x_i)^2 + \mu \Sigma_j(\frac{\partial f(s_j(\alpha,x_i))}{\partial \alpha} - \frac{\partial \widehat{f}(s_j(\alpha,x_i))}{\partial \alpha})^2_{\alpha=0}]$$

Where ***p*** is a constant provided by the user to determine the relative importance of fitting training values versus fitting training derivatives.

14.5. Using Prior Knowledge to Augment Search Operators

The two previous sections examined two different roles for prior knowledge in learning: initializing the learner's hypothesis and altering the objective function that guides search through the hypothesis space. In this section we consider a third way of using prior knowledge to alter the hypothesis space search: using it to alter the set of operators that define legal steps in the search through the hypothesis space.

14.6. The FOCL Algorithm

The First Order Combined Learner (FOCL) Algorithm is an extension of the purely inductive, FOIL Algorithm. It uses domain theory to further improve the search for the best-rule and greatly improves accuracy. It incorporates the methods of *Explanation-Based learning (EBL)* into the existing methods of FOIL. But before getting into the working of FOCL, let us first understand the following:

- Domain Theory
- Explanation-Based Learning

14.7. Tangents and Normal's

For a given curve tangent at a particular point is a straight line that just touches that curve at that point, and it goes in the same direction as the curve at that point, i.e if the curve stopped tracing the function at this point then it will go straight and that would be a tangent line.

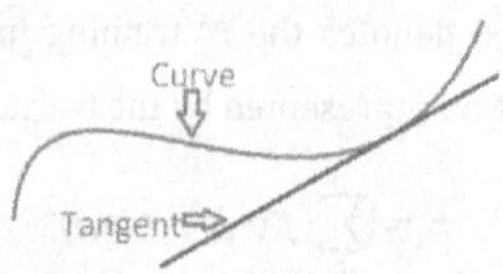

Let's understand this by an example:

Imagine that you are rotating a stone in a circle that is tied to a thread.

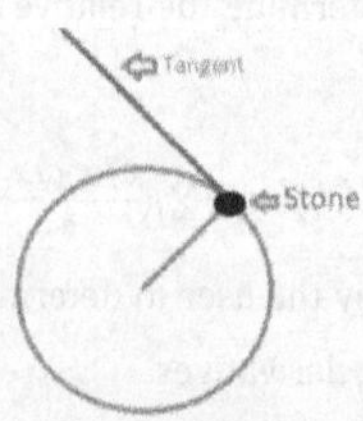

Fig. 14.1: Tangent

Now, if at any moment of time if you let go of the thread then the stone will follow a straight path, and that straight path is the tangent to the point of contact between the circular path and the stone when then stone is let go.

Properties of a Tangent

1. Tangents just touch the curve at the point of contact.
2. If any tangent to a curve y = f(x) make angle θ with the x-axis, then dy/dx = slope of the tangent = tan θ.
3. If the slope of the tangent is zero, then tan θ will be equal to 0 and so θ = 0 which implies that the tangent line is parallel to the x-axis.
4. If θ = π/2, then tan θ will approach ∞, i.e., the tangent line is perpendicular to the x-axis.

Applications of Tangents

1. If you are traveling by car around a corner and if you perform a drift then your car starts to skid, it will continue in a direction tangent to the curve.
2. If you hold a stone and swing it around in a circular motion and then let go, it will fly in a tangent to the circular motion.

Important Points

A normal line to a curve is a straight line that is perpendicular to the tangent of that curve at a given point.

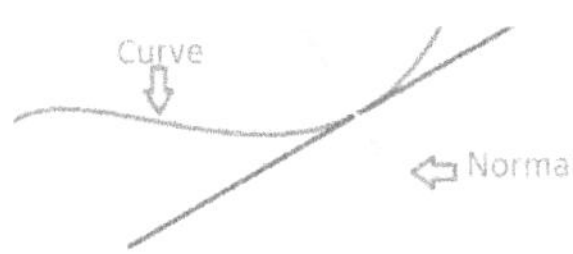

For Example: Let's take the curve y = x^2, if we want to draw the normal line at the point (1, 1), to the curve then we will draw the line tangent to the curve first at that point. Then we will draw a line perpendicular to the tangent. It will look like this.

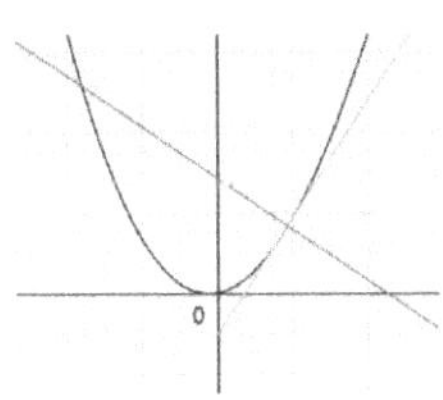

Properties of a Normal

1. A normal line at any point of a circle will always pass through the centre of the circle.
2. The normal to any curve is always perpendicular to the tangent at any point on the curve.

Applications of Normal

1. The centripetal force acting on a body that is moving in a circle is always normal to the point of contact at a given time.
2. The spokes in a wheel are normal to the rim of a wheel at each point where the spoke connects with the centre.

Equation of a Tangent and a Normal to a Curve

Equation of a Tangent and a Normal to a curve in the Cartesian Coordinates.

At a point on the curve, the gradient of the curve is equal to the gradient of the tangent to the curve at that point. So, the equation of a tangent can be found by the gradient at that point to the curve and the given point as follows:

As we know that the equation of the straight line passes through point P (x0, y0) is,

$$y - y0 = m(x - x0)$$

Here, m is the finite slope of the line. Now the slope of the tangent to a curve given is y = f(x) at point P (x0, y0) is f(x0)'. Then the equation of the tangent to the curve at point P(x0, y0) will be:

$$y - y0 = f(x0)'(x - x0)$$

For the normal, as we already know that the normal is always perpendicular to the tangent line. Then the slope of the normal to the curve will be:

$$-1/f(x0)'$$

So, the equation of the normal to the curve y = f(x) at the point (x0, y0) is :

$$y - y0 = [-1/f(x0)'](x - x0)$$

or

$$f(x0)'(y - y0) + (x - x0) = 0$$

Equation of a Tangent and a Normal to a curve in Parametric Form,

Let us assume the parametric form of the curve is,

$$x = x(t) \quad ....(i)$$

$$y = y(t) \quad ....(ii)$$

Now we find the slope of the tangent to a curve at the point (x0, y0), by using the differentiation rule:

$$m = \tan\alpha = yt'/xt'$$

Hence, the equation of the tangent is:

$$y - y0 = yt'/xt'(x - x0)$$

Accordingly, the equation of the normal is:

$$y - y0 = - xt'/yt'(x - x0)$$

or

$$y't(y - y0) + x't(x - x0) = 0$$

Equation of a Tangent and a Normal to a curve in Polar Coordinates.

Let us assume the polar equation of the curve is r = f(θ). It represents the dependence of the radius vector r on the polar angle θ. In the cartesian coordinates, this curve can be written in the following equations,

$$x = r = f(\theta)\cos\theta \quad ....(i)$$

$$y = r = f(\theta)\sin\theta \quad ....(ii)$$

So, we get the parametric equation of the curve. Now we find the slope of the tangent to a curve at the point (x0, y0).

$$m = \tan\theta = y'\theta/ x'\theta = r'\theta\sin\theta + r\cos\theta/r'\theta\cos\theta - r\sin\theta$$

Hence, the equation of the tangent is:

$$y - y0 = y'\theta/ x'\theta(x - x0)$$

Accordingly, the equation of the normal is:

$$y - y0 = - x'\theta/y'\theta(x - x0)$$

or

$$y'\theta(y - y0) + x'\theta(x - x0) = 0$$

Sample Problems

Question 1. Find the slope of the tangent and the normal to the curve y = 6x2 - 10x at x = 1.

Solution:

The given curve is y = 6x2 - 10x

Now the gradient, dy/dx = 12x - 10

So, the slope of the tangent to the given curve at x = 1 is,

$$[dy/dx]x{=}1 = 12 * 1 - 10 = 2$$

Slope of the normal will be:

$$= -1/2 = -0.5$$

Question 2. Find The slope of the tangent and normal to the curve y = 3x3 + 3sin(x) at x = 0.

Solution:

The given curve is y = 3x3 + 3sin(x)

Now the gradient, dy/dx = 9x2 + 3cos(x)

So, the slope of the tangent to the given curve at x = 0 is,

$$dy/dx]x=0 = 0 + 3 * 1 = 3$$

The slope of the normal will be:

$$= -1/3$$

Question 3. Find the equation of tangent to the curve y = 6x2 – 2x + 3 at P(1, 0).

Solution:

The given curve is y = 6x2 – 2x + 3

Now the gradient, dy/dx = 12x – 2

So, the slope of the tangent to the given curve at P(1,0) is,

$$dy/dx]1,0 = 12 - 2 = 10$$

The equation of the line will be:

$$y - 0 = 10(x - 1)$$

$$y = 10x - 10$$

Question 4. Determine the point on the curve y = 6x2 – 8x + 1 where the tangent is parallel to the line y = 4x – 5.

Solution:

The given curve is y = 6x2 – 8x + 1

Now the gradient, dy/dx = 12x – 8

Tangent is parallel to y = 4x – 5

so,

12x0 – 8 = 4

or x0 = 1

Putting x = 1 in equation of the curve

We get,

y0 = 6 – 8 + 1

y0 = -1

So the point is (1, -1)

CHAPTER 15

COMBINING INDUCTIVE AND ANALYTICAL LEARNING

15.1. Inductive-analytical Approaches to Learning

The Learning Problem

To summarize, the learning problem considered in this is,

Given

- A set of training examples D, possibly containing errors.
- A domain theory B, possibly containing errors.
- A space of candidate hypotheses H.

Determine

A hypothesis that best fits the training examples and domain theory What precisely shall we mean by "the hypothesis that best fits the training examples and domain theory? 'In particular, shall we prefer hypotheses that fit the data a little better at the expense of fitting the theory less well, or vice versa?. We can be more precise by defining measures of hypothesis error with respect to the data and with respect to the domain theory, then phrasing the question in terms of these errors.

That ***errorD(h)*** is defined to be the proportion of examples from ***D*** that are misclassified by ***h***. Let us define the error of ***h*** $error_D(h)$ with respect to a domain theory B to be the probability that ***h*** will disagree with B on the classification of a randomly drawn instance. We can attempt to characterize the desired output hypothesis in terms of these errors. For example, we could require the hypothesis that minimizes some combined measure of these errors, such as,

$$\underset{h \in H}{\operatorname{argmin}} \; k_D error_D(h) + k_B error_B(h)$$

15.2. Hypothesis Space Search

How can the domain theory and training data best be combined to constrain the search for an acceptable hypothesis? One way to understand the range of possible approaches is to return to our view of learning as a task of searching through the space of alternative hypotheses. We can characterize most learning methods as search algorithms by describing the hypothesis space H they search, the initial hypothesis ***ho*** at which they begin their search, the set of search operators ***O*** that define individual search steps, and the goal criterion G that specifies the search objective.

15.3. Inductive Learning Algorithm

Inductive Learning Algorithm (ILA) is an iterative and inductive machine learning algorithm which is used for generating a set of a classification rule, which produces rules of the form "IF-THEN", for a set of examples, producing rules at each iteration and appending to the set of rules.

Basic Idea

There are basically two methods for knowledge extraction firstly from domain experts and then with machine learning.

For a very large amount of data, the domain experts are not very useful and reliable. So we move towards the machine learning approach for this work.

To use machine learning One method is to replicate the experts logic in the form of algorithms but this work is very tedious, time taking and expensive.

So we move towards the inductive algorithms which itself generate the strategy for performing a task and need not instruct separately at each step.

Need of ILA in Presence of Other Machine Learning Algorithms

The ILA is a new algorithm which was needed even when other reinforcement learning's like ID3 and AQ were available.

- The need was due to the pitfalls which were present in the previous algorithms, one of the major pitfalls was lack of generalization of rules.
- The ID3 and AQ used the decision tree production method which was too specific which were difficult to analyze and was very slow to perform for basic short classification problems.
- The decision tree-based algorithm was unable to work for a new problem if some attributes are missing.
- The ILA uses the method of production of a general set of rules instead of decision trees, which overcome the above problems.

The Ila Algorithm

General Requirements at Start of the Algorithm

1. List the examples in the form of a table 'T' where each row corresponds to an example and each column contains an attribute value.
2. Create a set of m training examples, each example composed of k attributes and a class attribute with n possible decisions.
3. Create a rule set, R, having the initial value false.
4. Initially all rows in the table are unmarked.

Steps in the Algorithm

Step 1:

Divide the table "T" containing m examples into n sub-tables (t1, t2,.....tn). One table for each possible value of the class attribute. (repeat steps 2-8 for each sub-table).

Step 2:

Initialize the attribute combination count 'j' = 1.

Step 3:

For the sub-table on which work is going on, divide the attribute list into distinct combinations, each combination with 'j' distinct attributes.

Step 4:

For each combination of attributes, count the number of occurrences of attribute values that appear under the same combination of attributes in unmarked rows of the sub-table under consideration, and at the same time, not appears under the same combination of attributes of other sub-tables. Call the first combination with the maximum number of occurrences the max-combination 'MAX'.

Step 5:

If 'MAX' = = null, increase 'j' by 1 and go to Step 3.

Step 6:

Mark all rows of the sub-table where working, in which the values of 'MAX' appear, as classified.

Step 7:

Add a rule (IF attribute = "XYZ" -> THEN decision is YES/ NO) to R whose left-hand side will have attribute names of the 'MAX' with their values separated by AND, and its right-hand side contains the decision attribute value associated with the sub-table.

Step 8:

If all rows are marked as classified, then move on to process another sub-table and go to Step 2. else, go to Step 4. If no sub-tables are available, exit with the set of rules obtained till then.

An Example Showing the Use of ILA

Suppose an example set having attributes Place type, weather, location, decision and seven examples, our task is to generate a set of rules that under what condition what is the decision.

Example No.	Place Type	Weather	Location	Decision
I)	hilly	winter	kullu	Yes
II)	mountain	windy	Mumbai	No
III)	mountain	windy	Shimla	Yes
IV)	beach	windy	Mumbai	No
V)	beach	warm	goa	Yes
VI)	beach	windy	goa	No
VII)	beach	warm	Shimla	Yes

Step 1

Subset 1

S. No	Place Type	Weather	Location	Decision
1	hilly	winter	kullu	Yes
2	mountain	windy	Shimla	Yes
3	beach	warm	goa	Yes
4	beach	warm	Shimla	Yes

Subset 2

S. No	Place Type	Weather	Location	Decision
5	mountain	windy	Mumbai	No
6	beach	windy	Mumbai	No
7	beach	windy	goa	No

Step (2-8)

At Iteration 1

Row 3 & 4 column weather is selected and row 3 & 4 are marked. The rule is added to R IF weather is warm then a decision is yes.

At Iteration 2

Row 1 column place type is selected and row 1 is marked. The rule is added to R IF place type is hilly then the decision is yes.

At Iteration 3

Row 2 column location is selected and row 2 is marked. The rule is added to R IF location is Shimla then the decision is yes.

At Iteration 4

Row 5&6 column location is selected and row 5&6 are marked. The rule is added to R IF location is Mumbai then a decision is no.

At Iteration 5

Row 7 column place type & the weather is selected and row 7 is marked. Rule is added to R IF place type is beach AND weather is windy then the decision is no.

Finally We Get the Rule Set

Rule Set

- **Rule 1:** IF the weather is warm THEN the decision is yes.
- **Rule 2:** IF place type is hilly THEN the decision is yes.
- **Rule 3:** IF location is Shimla THEN the decision is yes.
- **Rule 4:** IF location is Mumbai THEN the decision is no.
- **Rule 5:** IF place type is beach AND the weather is windy THEN the decision is no.